THE LAST *REAL* WORLD CHAMPION

THE LAST REAL WORLD CHAMPION

THE LEGACY OF "NATURE BOY" RIC FLAIR

TIM HORNBAKER

Published by ECW Press
665 Gerrard Street East
Toronto, Ontario, Canada M4M 1Y2
416-694-3348 / info@ecwpress.com

Editor for the Press: Michael Holmes
Copy editor: Crissy Calhoun
Cover design: Jessica Albert
Cover photograph: © George Napolitano

LIBRARY AND ARCHIVES CANADA CATALOGUING
IN PUBLICATION

Title: The last real world champion : the legacy of "Nature Boy"
Ric Flair / Tim Hornbaker.

Names: Hornbaker, Tim, author.

Identifiers: Canadiana (print) 20230237053 | Canadiana (ebook)
2023023707X

ISBN 978-1-77041-626-0 (softcover)
ISBN 978-1-77852-180-5 (PDF)
ISBN 978-1-77852-181-2 (Kindle)
ISBN 978-1-77852-179-9 (ePub)

Subjects: LCSH: Flair, Ric, 1949- | LCSH: Wrestlers—United
States—Biography. | LCGFT: Biographies.

Classification: LCC GV1196.F59 H67 2023 | DDC 796.812092—dc23

PRINTED AND BOUND IN CANADA   PRINTING: FRIESENS 5 4 3 2 1

This book is dedicated to my wife, Jodi.
She is my best friend and the love of my life.

CONTENTS

CHAPTER 1
A NATURAL CHAMPION

I t was a decade that will forever live in infamy. From 1940 to 1949, the citizens of the United States experienced just about every emotional high and low. The incredible sadness and sorrow of World War II was overwhelming. When the war finally came to an end in September 1945, there was widespread relief. Families were reunited as servicemen and women returned from overseas, and there was an impetus to recover and rebuild after years of embattlement. But beneath the surface, the hardships of the war took a serious toll on the American family, and it was much worse than most people were willing to admit. Extramarital affairs were highly prevalent, with many occurring while military husbands were stationed on foreign battlefields. In 1944, it was estimated that 104,000 children were products of adulterous relations, and that number exemplified the breakdown of the American value system.[1]

At least, that's what many believed. In spite of the newfound postwar peace and prosperity, the number of children born to unwed mothers in the United States grew to record numbers. The U.S. Department of Health, Education, and Welfare reported that in 1950 there were 141,600 births by unmarried women.[2] With that, the national adoption rate went up. But the bureaucratic process for adoption was acknowledged as long and rigorous in most states. Prospective parents had to undergo extensive background checks, and with agencies bogged down by the sheer volume, the entire system moved at a snail's pace. As the years progressed, a new avenue for adoption was becoming more and more accepted amongst the social elite.[3]

Pundits dubbed it the "black market," but for wealthy couples looking to complete their families, it was the fastest route to bringing home a baby. Still, the "black market" had dreadfully negative aspects that involved sidestepping laws associated with adoption.[4] Instead of waiting a month following the birth of a child, underground operators were transporting babies across state lines after two weeks. No proper background checks into potential parents were done, and black market agents were profiting huge sums. The price for a baby ranged anywhere from $750 to $3,000, which equates at the high end to over $36,000 in 2022.[5] Typically, the adoptive parents attained the baby from the birth mother for little to no money, sometimes for just promising to pay the hospital bills.

There were other immoral facets to the black market, and Georgia Tann of Memphis, Tennessee, became the poster child for everything deplorable about the practice. In fact, she took things to a whole new level, skillfully exploiting the lax adoption laws in her state and taking advantage of every loophole. Originally from Mississippi, Tann was college educated and known for her iron-fist administration of the Shelby County branch of the Tennessee Children's Home Society.[6] For over two decades, she coordinated thousands of adoptions not only in Memphis but throughout America. Her reputation as a fierce advocate for adoptive couples grew substantially, and in 1948 she was named president of the Adopted Children's Association of America.[7] On the surface, Tann's humanitarian work appeared nothing but virtuous, but alarming rumors began circulating.

An investigator into her malfeasance later estimated that Tann made upward of $500,000 as a black market operator.[8] Using deceit, trickery, and threats directed at expectant or new mothers, she obtained babies with the express purpose of sending them out of state to affluent families, consistently sidestepping basic ethical principles to pull off these transactions in the quickest way possible. She'd arrange for overnight flights out of Memphis to limit attention and charge the adopting couple inflated transportation fees, increasing her profit. Her connections to politicians, judges, and influential figures ensured her crooked venture never missed a beat.[9] But cracks in the veneer became apparent by late 1948, and newly elected governor Gordon Browning pressed for a full inquiry into the Tennessee Children's Home Society.[10] Tann was suffering from cancer at the time and died the following September.[11]

Her damage was done. For mothers who had been lied to and lost their babies due to Tann's unscrupulous practices, it was a complete and utter nightmare. On the other side of the coin, childless couples across the United States received precious babies to raise as their own. They were thrilled by the opportunity to become parents and thanked Tann's agency for its otherworldly efforts. One such couple was Richard Reid and Kathleen Virginia Fliehr. The Fliehrs, both age 30, were graduates of the University of Minnesota and living in Detroit, Michigan, as Richard completed his medical residency at a local hospital. Kathleen, also known as Kay, had given birth to a daughter, Mary, in 1946, but due to complications, the child passed away the same day.[12] They were determined to have a child and pursued adoption routes, including reaching out to the Tennessee Children's Home Society in Memphis.[13]

It would have been standard procedure for the Fliehrs to be visited by a representative from Tann's organization, and more than likely, that's what happened. The couple was interviewed and filled out an application outlining their financial worth. Once everything proved to be in order, Tann signed off on the arrangement, and the Fliehrs were put on the list for a child. As fate would have it, a boy was born on February 25, 1949, and he was selected for Richard and Kay Fliehr.[14] The baby was probably shuffled off to the airport under the cover of night and flown to Detroit, where he met his new parents.[15] Undoubtedly, it was a life-altering and joyous moment for the Fliehrs. They now had a son to nurture and provide for — to give all of the opportunities in the world. It was the dream of all prospective parents, and the Tennessee Children's Home Society had come through as promised.

Richard and Kay named him Richard Morgan Fliehr and soon took him back to St. Louis Park, in the Minneapolis area, to reside at 3925 Colorado Avenue. Richard Sr. had served in the U.S. Navy during the war and earned his medical degree from the University of Minnesota in 1946.[16] He was an utterly determined man, and looking at his family's history going back to his German ancestors in the 1840s, resiliency and strength was in his blood. His great-grandfather, Charles B. Fliehr, was the first of his bloodline in America, and he served as a prominent evangelical minister in and around Lehigh County, Pennsylvania, for over 20 years.[17]

Charles had six children with wife, Katharina, and three of them became successful businessman in Pennsylvania and New Jersey during the last quarter of the 19th century. Daniel Fliehr became a tinsmith and later entered local politics.[18] Aaron Fliehr went into the meat industry, while Solomon operated a grocery across the Delaware River in Camden, New Jersey.[19] Economic prospects in the Upper Midwest were opening up, and after Solomon's son, of the same name, moved to the Minnesota North Country, Solomon decided to follow suit. In early 1909, he sold off his interests and settled in Virginia, Minnesota.[20] The area was in the midst of a financial boom due to its iron mining and lumber opportunities.

The elder Solomon was also joined by his son William Harvey Fliehr and his wife, Anna, and it wasn't long before William was an established purchasing agent for a reputable lumber firm.[21] A few years later, demonstrating the entrepreneurial spirit of the family, William and his father became officers in a newly incorporated business, the Central Auto Company in Virginia.[22] Their firm bought and sold cars, plus operated a garage to repair vehicles in the rapidly growing auto market. During the summers, the Fliehr family and friends enjoyed trips to Sand Lake, about 14 miles north of Virginia. For New Year's in 1913, William, Anna, and their two children, Harvey and Irma, made the jaunt up to Sand Lake with friends Alexander and Minnie Reid, along with their son, Alex Jr. The group made the news for being the first to traverse the wintery landscape in an automobile and did so "without mishap."[23]

The Scottish-born Reid was the owner of Alexander Reid & Co., a fashionable department store in Virginia. William and Alexander were a part of the same civic and social circles and became close friends. Their families spent a lot of time together, at the lake and hunting in the northern Minnesota woods. Education was important to William Fliehr, and he wanted his two children to live the American dream. Harvey, a half decade older than his sister, Irma, graduated from Virginia High School in three years and was a talented violinist.[24] He attended one year of college before enlisting in the U.S. Navy during World War I. Following his discharge, he entered business with his father in Virginia, and he became one of the youngest and most popular community leaders.[25] As for Irma, she was similarly successful and graduated from the University of Minnesota. She soon wed Arthur C. Regan, a Princeton graduate and employee of the Minneapolis Trust Company.[26]

Backtracking a little bit, it should be noted that Harvey and Irma were ages 19 and 14, respectfully, when their parents had their third child, Richard Reid Fliehr. The name Reid was presumably a tribute to the family's close friend Alexander Reid, who remained a confidant for many years.[27] Richard followed the path of his older siblings and attended local schools in Virginia. He enrolled in the University of Minnesota at Minneapolis and, around 1937, met the woman he was destined to marry, Kathleen Virginia "Kay" Kinsmiller. Miss Kinsmiller was originally from Brainerd, Minnesota, a town of 12,000 inhabitants, and a locale that was a good three hours' drive from Fliehr's hometown of Virginia. They were both thriving at the university, with Richard gaining esteem as a performer on the university theater stage and Kay as a journalism major.[28]

Kinsmiller's paternal grandparents, John and Crescentia Kinsmiller, relocated from Germany to Minnesota in the early 1890s and settled in Brainerd in 1914.[29] They had at least five children between 1887 and 1900 with their oldest being Frederick Edward. Fred, as he was known, became a copartner in the newly established Brainerd Foundry in 1923. He was an expert in the manufacture of brass castings, and the company held valuable contracts with the Northern Pacific Railroad and the Minnesota and Ontario Paper Company.[30] Married to Hattie Anna Frisk, Fred Kinsmiller had two daughters, Elizabeth and Kay, and both his daughters attended the University of Minnesota. Elizabeth was seven years older than her sister and graduated from college around 1938. She remained in Minneapolis and took a job at a coal company.[31]

As strong-minded as her future partner, Richard Reid Fliehr, Kay yearned for educational challenges while in school, and when other students were basking in their vacation time, she was helping publish a small-town newspaper in Willmar, Minnesota.[32] On June 15, 1940, she graduated from the University of Minnesota and was promptly hired by the Enterprise Publishing Corporation.[33] Nearly exactly a year later, Richard received his Bachelor of Arts degree from Minnesota, and the couple wed the following week in Brainerd's Congregational Church before family and friends.[34] Before the end of 1941, the U.S. was committed to fighting the Axis powers in World War II, and Richard was of prime age to serve in the military. He joined the U.S. Navy Reserves as a commissioned officer on October 29, 1942.[35] As a result, he was able to continue his education, and on January 21, 1946, he received his Doctor of Medicine degree at Minnesota.[36]

Following the arrival of their infant child Richard in 1949, the couple and their baby settled into a quiet lifestyle in St. Louis Park, the largest suburb of Minneapolis, and Richard was a practicing obstetrician-gynecologist.[37] St. Louis Park experienced rapid growth in the postwar years, both in terms of population and commercial development. Construction was rampant, and social and civic organizations, as well as churches, sprung up across the village.[38] It was a picturesque suburban environment in which to raise a family.

Dr. Fliehr was a busy man and worked extremely hard. He became a member of the medical staff at Abbott Hospital in Minneapolis and served as an advocate for improved nursing home conditions.[39] He made time to speak about medical issues at local community centers and tested his own intellect by participating in district Toastmasters International speech contests. In 1954, he placed second in such a competition, and his subject — to the horror of all Marvel and DC aficionados — was

"The Case against Comic Books."[40] By the late 1950s and early '60s, Fliehr was a prominent member of the Minneapolis Obstetrical and Gynecological Society and the American Medical Association's national speakers' bureau.[41] His eloquence and intellect were apparent under any circumstance.

Routinely on call, Fliehr was always at risk of being summoned away from a family function to deliver a baby. It even happened in the midst of a performance. An expectant mother at Abbott Hospital needed him right in the middle of a play, and he didn't hesitate to leave to be by her side. After delivering the baby, he rushed back to the theater "and didn't miss a cue."[42] Theater was a lifelong passion for Dr. Fliehr, and he acted on stage as often as he could. Regardless if he was performing at a church or high school before a limited audience, he loved it all the same. In the early 1960s, he joined the Golden Valley Community Theater, a decision that coincided with the Fliehr family's move from St. Louis Park to Golden Valley.[43] A few years earlier, Dr. Fliehr had objected to a newfangled report card system adopted by the St. Louis Park School Board, illustrating his concern for his son's education.[44] Now, young Richard was in the Golden Valley school district.[45]

Raised in an upper-middle-class home, Richard Morgan "Rick" Fliehr was doted upon by his parents as an only child.[46] He recognized his father's commitment to his profession and understood why he sometimes worked strange hours. When they had the chance, father and son enjoyed nature getaways and spent days camping, fishing, and swimming.[47] Those trips were great bonding experiences, providing memories that would last a lifetime. Dr. Fliehr taught his son the importance of being a gentleman, having respect for others, and a system of values that the young man embraced as his own. For many kids, being a Boy Scout was a traditional rite of passage, and for Rick it was no different, teaching him about responsibility and building friendships.[48] In his neighborhood, he'd ride his bike for hours, visiting his pals, and during the summers, he'd bask in the sun at local pools. Like his father, he became a strong swimmer and demonstrated his skills as a summer lifeguard.[49]

Although he respected his parents and their rules, Rick tested the limits of their patience at times and was a handful. In his early teenage years, he had a few minor scrapes with the law, transgressing the ideals his parents cherished.[50] After all, they were conservative through and through, and rather than being a studious, book smart child, he excelled in sports. As a seventh grader at Golden Valley High School in 1961–62, he attended daily hockey practices under Coach Gerald Peterson.[51] Basketball was his sport of choice the subsequent year. He was a member of the C squad under Coach Jerry Holewa, and after undergoing an impressive growth spurt, he became one of the tallest kids his age at school.[52] In Rick's sophomore year, he was an up-and-comer on the Vikings football team. That year, Tom Benepe led Golden Valley to a Minnesota Valley Conference championship with a 7–1 record.[53]

During a special banquet at the Golden Valley Golf Club, Fliehr was honored and named a letter winner for his performance on the football field.[54] Despite the accolades for Rick's athletic prowess, his parents were still concerned about his education and decided to pull their son out of Golden Valley and send him across state lines to a posh co-ed boarding school in Beaver Dam, Wisconsin.[55] The $6,000-a-year Wayland Academy was renowned for turning out first-class graduates prepped and ready to take on a high-pressure college environment.[56] The Fliehrs felt a school with no hometown distractions and an emphasis on academics was the best way to get their son on the right track. But Rick's grades continued to suffer at Wayland, and he had to repeat his junior year.[57] He was no longer part of the Class of 1967, and the following May, he'd see his fellow classmates graduate without him.[58]

In every other aspect of his life, Fliehr was flourishing. He was more than socially adept, extremely likeable, and handsome. "The thing about Rick was he was tough on the field," said Wayland Coach John Clay, "but off the field he was a gentleman. He never quit. He was very concerned about others."[59] Although he was a jock and a big one at that — standing around six feet and weighing 180 pounds — Fliehr wasn't a bully. In fact, he shied away from fighting but would stand up for his smaller friends and teammates. "Ric was a personality plus and the most popular guy on campus," Peter Radford recalled. "The ladies just loved him to say the least."[60] Without question, his tenure at Wayland was an interesting mix of scholastic challenges and social interaction. At any one time, there were less than 300 students spread across four grades, allowing for personal one-on-one attention between teachers and students. As for his peers, most students hailed from the Upper Midwest, but a few were from as far away as Germany and Taiwan.

Fliehr thrived in athletics and earned widespread acclaim. As part of Wayland's football team in 1966, he was a vital element on both offense and defense during a 5–2 season. His efforts gained him a berth on the second team All-Conference, voted on by coaches.[61] He put forth an extraordinary effort in what was his first major sports appearance on television in a game against Wisconsin Lutheran on November 4, 1966. Wayland annihilated its opponents, 40–13, and Fliehr rushed for 141 yards on 17 carries. His teammate Steve Bartell did him one better by rushing for 196 yards and scoring five touchdowns.[62] The game was broadcast on Milwaukee's WVTV (channel 18) and reached a wide regional audience. On the wrestling mat, he won his second consecutive Midwest Prep Conference championship in 1967 and went 13–0–0.[63] In an early match that season against the University School of Milwaukee, Fliehr displayed his tremendous grit by taking a decision victory over his opponent with only five seconds left on the clock.[64] It was a testament to his never-say-die attitude.

As a senior at Wayland in 1967–68, Fliehr suspended his wrestling career to concentrate on football and track. He gained further experience on the defensive side of the ball as a lineman, helping his school achieve a record of 5–2. Once again, Fliehr was selected All-Conference and was named the team's most valuable player.[65] On the track and field squad, Fliehr threw the shot put, and he used his size and strength to propel Wayland to a number of team victories. Faced off with St. Mary's Springs Academy in May 1968, he tossed the shot put 48 feet and three inches, and Wayland won the overall meet by capturing 12 of 14 events.[66]

All in all, Wayland had good success in track against small-to mid-sized schools but struggled against academies from larger cities, including those in Madison and Milwaukee. Fliehr was always progressing on a personal level, and it seemed assured that he'd continue to develop as an athlete in college. That is, if his grades improved.

Campus activities and social clubs were important to all Wayland students, and Fliehr's outgoing personality made him the center of attention in any group. He formed a friendship with Bruce MacArthur, and the two shared many memorable times.[67] MacArthur, who was nick-named "The General," was as gregarious as Fliehr.[68] The grandson of Arthur Wirtz, owner of the Chicago Black Hawks and Chicago Bulls, he graduated from Wayland in 1966. In addition to his sports commit-ments, Fliehr participated in the "W" and pep clubs and was a member of the choir.[69] With a lot of hard work, he graduated from high school in May 1968. His time in Beaver Dam left a lasting impression on many people, including classmates and the staff at Wayland. "Rick had the most amazing charisma," said Terrill Knaack, a former football team-mate.[70] Another alumni, George Davis, recalled Fliehr being "quiet and gentle, honest and kind," and George Cobb, Wayland's public relations representative, agreed. He remembered Fliehr's selfless act of helping friends in need by lending them money.[71]

"[Fliehr] was just one hell of a boy," said David W. Fierke, dean of senior boys at Wayland.[72] Fierke's comment, made in 1980, was complimentary, but twelve years earlier, he wasn't exactly Fliehr's biggest champion. He knew the young man's academic plight. After Fliehr had signed a letter of intent with the University of Michigan, Fierke refused to provide a formal letter in support of his admission, citing his academic troubles as justifica-tion.[73] It was a major blow to Fliehr. He had spent time in Ann Arbor and wanted to be a Wolverine.[74] But it was not going to happen, and during the summer of 1968, he found himself about an hour south of Beaver Dam in Whitewater for a summer football camp at Wisconsin State University. A local newspaper touted Fliehr as the "biggest man" on the incoming freshman squad, and he was one of 33 players vying for a position.[75]

"I remember recruiting Fliehr from Wayland Academy," Whitewater freshman coach Jack Dean later said. "We moved him to defense, and I recall him being a good player."[76] However, for reasons unknown, Fliehr's time at that institution was very brief, and he returned home to Minneapolis. By that time, Richard and Kay Fliehr had moved to the wealthy community of Edina, southwest of downtown Minneapolis.[77] His parents were as busy as ever, and 1968 was a noteworthy year. Right around the time of Rick's graduation from Wayland, Kay was awaiting the publication of her book, *In Search of an Audience: How an Audience Was Found for the Tyrone Guthrie Theatre*, co-written with Bradley Morison. The book was lauded by insiders and critics alike for its instructive guidance for developing a regional theater, and a Florida pundit stated that it was a must-read "textbook" for stage administrators.[78] Mrs. Fliehr was part of the publicity staff for the famed Guthrie Theatre when it opened in 1963.[79] After several years, she formed a consulting firm with her co-author, Morison, and together they were highly influential in assisting the growth of local and national arts organizations.

Dr. Fliehr balanced his work as an ob-gyn with his dedication to community theater, and he was prominently respected in both fields. He starred in plays, gave speeches, and appeared on television and radio programs to discuss various matters of health.[80] He became the president of the Theatre in the Round in Minneapolis and earned praise for his "reserved, patient direction" for the production of *Hay Fever*, which was called the "best-directed" play of the season.[81] A serious proponent of enhanced stage lighting, Dr. Fliehr returned to the University of Minnesota to improve his own knowledge base and received his Master of Arts degree in 1972.[82]

With the potential football opportunities at Michigan and Whitewater behind him, Rick considered attending his parents' alma mater. It helped that Mike McGee, an assistant coach and recruiter at Minnesota, already had him on his radar.[83] All things considered, Fliehr was a welcome addition to the freshman squad, a team coached by Wally Johnson. But because of a Big Ten Conference rule established in 1961, and the fact that

Fliehr was not predicted to meet the 1.7 grade point average minimum requirement, he was barred from participating in any organized practice.[84] Nevertheless, he enrolled in the University of Minnesota during the fall of 1968 and was briefly a member of the freshman team.[85] His teammate Doug Kingsriter, a 200-pound quarterback from the Minneapolis suburb of Richfield, later recalled Fliehr's tenure as lasting only "a few days."[86] In October 1968, a roster published in the school's *Sports News* listed 39 athletes on the freshman team. Notably, Fliehr was not among them.[87]

The entire situation was demoralizing. Fliehr wanted to play football, but he didn't have the grades, nor the motivation to do what needed to be done to meet the academic standards.[88] That included skipping out on summer school.[89] In terms of personality, Fliehr idolized famed New York Jets QB Joe Namath, and appreciated his grand flamboyance.[90] He could relate, on a much smaller scale, and he used his magnetic charm to bolster his popularity on Minnesota's social scene. From his time in the Frontier Hall dormitory to the Phi Delta Theta fraternity house, he was eternally charismatic and exceptionally good-natured.[91] "He had a great personality with that big smile, even back then," said Don Ewers, Phi Delta Theta chapter president at Minnesota from 1970 to '71. "Everyone liked Rick; he was infectious that way."[92] On fraternity row, Fliehr's fun-loving persona really came out, and in that kind of raucous atmosphere, it didn't matter what his GPA was — or if he really was enrolled in school at all.

According to the Office of the Registrar, Fliehr's active status as a student at Minnesota ended during the spring of 1969.[93] Despite that, he continued to live in the fraternity house at 1011 4th Street SE and enjoyed a unique college experience, majoring only in carousing and reveling.[94] The nightlife and social scene kept him thoroughly entertained, but responsibilities were calling, and as he approached his 22nd birthday in February 1971, he had to make a big decision about his future. As fate would have it, the Guardian Life Insurance Company in Edina was hiring, offering a starting salary of $880 a month for a salesman.[95]

They were seeking an "executive type man" aged 25 to 45, and in Fliehr, they found an enthusiastic and respectable young man with connections to the university as well as the medical profession through his father. Owned by Jerry Remole and George Klima, Guardian took a chance and hired Fliehr, and they weren't disappointed.[96]

Fliehr was successful almost from the start. His likeable nature was a vital tool as a salesperson, and he performed at the level of someone much more experienced.[97] He enjoyed it as a short-term occupation, and could've gone much further, but soon got bored.[98] Later he admitted that he took the straight job to "pacify" his parents, who had been uneasy about his decision to leave college.[99] He also took a temporary position as an orderly at Abbott Hospital, where his father had worked for many years.[100] But it was all unfulfilling. He had proven that he could earn a living wage, but it still wasn't what he was looking for. In his personal life, though, he had found fulfillment. On August 28, 1971, at the Plymouth Congregational Church in Minneapolis, he married Leslie Ann Goodman, his girlfriend of several years.[101] They were surrounded by family and friends, including William Light, a former teammate on the freshman football squad at Minnesota.[102]

Leslie Goodman was one of four daughters born to David and Leone June Goodman of St. Paul. She had graduated from Highland Park Senior High School and then the University of Minnesota on June 13, 1970, with a degree as a dental assistant.[103] Two years before that, she had suffered tragedy with the loss of her mother at the age of 46.[104] But Leslie persevered, displaying immense inner strength to complete her studies at Minnesota.

The newlyweds lived in the Edina Highland Villa Apartments at 5250 Villa Way, and it seemed as if everything was going their way. With 1972 approaching, they had everything to look forward to, and with their combined spirit and hard work, the sky was the limit. Neither of them knew at the time that Fliehr's childhood interest would soon change their lives forever.

CHAPTER 2

FROM FLIEHR TO FLAIR

For decades, sports in the Minneapolis–St. Paul market, and across the region, was dominated by the competitive ferocity of the University of Minnesota Golden Gophers. Football was always the driving force, and between 1904 and 1960, the Gophers won seven national championships. Attendance for games averaged between 40,000 and 60,000, and it wasn't until Minneapolis added professional teams in baseball and football, the Twins and Vikings respectively, that there was as successful a team in the state of Minnesota.[1] That was in 1961. Among the amateurs, there was always great interest in collegiate wrestling, and Minnesota had produced outstanding athletes on an annual basis. But no sport, outside of the Gophers, had the drawing power and overall popularity as professional wrestling. Dating back to the 1910s when Norwegian Henry Ordemann reigned supreme, local fans were enthralled by the intensity and gamesmanship of the pro mat sport.[2]

A Nebraskan named Tony Stecher came along in 1933 and revolutionized professional wrestling in Minneapolis. Knowledgeable from his years managing his brother Joe Stecher, the former world heavyweight champion, Tony streamlined the business in the Twin Cities, and by the mid-1930s, his organization was thriving.[3] He helped introduce football legend Bronko Nagurski to the sport and guided him to the world championship in 1937.[4] By making important connections in the media, including to sportswriters, who were typically jaded about pro wrestling, Stecher established himself as one of the most credible promoters in the profession, and the esteem for him was universal. During the summer of 1948, he joined a tight-knit group of Midwestern entrepreneurs to form the National Wrestling Alliance. The new organization's mission was to recognize a single world heavyweight champion, respect each other's territories, and to assist their fellow brethren with talent.

The following year, Stecher recruited another promising athlete into wrestling, Verne Gagne. A product of rural Hennepin County, Gagne grew up on a farm about 20 miles outside Minneapolis.[5] Following his mother's passing in 1938, the Gagnes relocated to Robbinsdale, a middle-class suburban area, where Verne attended high school.[6] He was a natural athlete and excelled in baseball, football, and wrestling. At age 17, he enrolled in the University of Minnesota, and he was a week shy of his 18th birthday when he captured his first Big Ten wrestling championship at 175 pounds.[7] Dutifully, Gagne joined the U.S. Marine Corps for the duration of World War II, and his time in service improved his strength, conditioning, and coordination. He was also much more mature when he returned to the University of Minnesota in 1946. Over the next three years, he went on a remarkable run, winning three Big Nine Conference titles, two NCAA championships, and a National AAU crown.[8]

On top of that, Gagne was a backup member of the 1948 U.S. Olympic team in London, England. Tony Stecher knew he had a premier athlete on his hands, and in May 1949, Gagne debuted at the Minneapolis Auditorium with a disqualification victory over Abe Kashey.[9] Despite an initial concern that perhaps he was too small to make a successful heavy-weight, Gagne lived up to all expectations as a professional and became, arguably, the most popular wrestler featured on television during the 1950s. His prized United States championship, which he held from 1953 to 1956, was second in status only to the NWA World Heavyweight title, and it seemed logical in the minds of many fans that he was the natural successor to NWA kingpin Lou Thesz. But due to wrestling's unfor-giving politics, Gagne was thwarted from reaching that goal.[10] In the late

1950s, he captured an offshoot "World" championship in Omaha and continued to sell tickets in an impressive fashion, but the NWA hierarchy refused to give him the nod.

Gagne was too smart to be completely encumbered by behind-the-scenes turmoil. He bought into the Minneapolis territory in 1960, six years after Stecher had passed away, and set up the American Wrestling Association (AWA), a new organization on par with the NWA.[11] Gagne was part owner of the AWA, as well as its leading wrestler, meaning that his role in the business had to be kept a secret from the public. It was later explained that he was in charge of negotiating with television stations to expand the reach of the extremely popular Saturday evening telecast, originating on WTCN-11 in Minneapolis. The AWA's weekly action — featuring the likes of Maurice "Mad Dog" Vachon, the Crusher and Dick the Bruiser, and Nick Bockwinkel — was mandatory viewing for wrestling fans throughout Minnesota. In terms of territorial size, the AWA was made up of five states in the Upper Midwest, plus parts of three others — extending westward to Colorado and a sliver of the Canadian province of Manitoba.[12]

Among those mesmerized by the dynamic personalities on AWA programming was young Rick Fliehr. By the age of six, he was hooked on the colorful athletes and wouldn't miss a second of the Saturday show.[13] Fliehr's zest for professional wrestling didn't fade as most childhood interests do, and every year for his birthday, his father took him to live arena matches to get an up close and personal look at the behemoths he'd seen on TV.[14] The dark and smoky atmosphere of a wrestling arena was also a revelation, but it didn't deter his enthusiasm in any way. The rowdiness only added to the excitement. Growing up, Fliehr had a few roundabout encounters with pro wrestling, directly or indirectly. One of his first jobs was as a paperboy in Edina, and the Vachon brothers, Maurice and Paul, were customers on his route.[15] The brothers from Montreal, two of the roughest in the business, were also regulars at the pool where Fliehr worked as a lifeguard.[16]

Interestingly Fliehr's family had a small connection to Verne Gagne. In 1966, the celebrated wrestler was hired as a technical consultant for a production at the Guthrie Theatre. Kay Fliehr's partner in the PR department and the co-author of her book, Bradley Morison, was the one who reached out to Gagne and brought him aboard.[17] This was mentioned in Fliehr and Morison's book as their "most spectacular accomplishment," particularly the fact that it received front-page coverage in the *Minneapolis Star*.[18] The arrangement undoubtedly provided positive publicity for all involved, and Gagne's standing as wrestling's number one local hero was affirmed once again. The entire experience was all in fun. But backstage at Gagne's home arena, the Minneapolis Auditorium, and among fellow wrestlers, it was purely business. There was absolutely no questioning Gagne's legitimate wrestling ability, toughness, or leadership. He ran a pretty tight ship and micromanaged the AWA's affairs.

Gagne was a nine-time AWA World Heavyweight champion, taking wins from the likes of Fritz Von Erich, Bill Miller, and Gene Kiniski. His feuds with monster heels and technical challengers were filled with drama and athleticism. The interview segments on his television programs were fueled by emotion, mixed with a perfect blend of intellect and hysteria, and flawlessly built up anticipation for house shows. Gagne respected and appreciated wrestlers with amateur backgrounds, while at the same time, giving a platform to wrestlers with a flair for showmanship. Brawlers like Dick the Bruiser were also welcome. Gagne knew by offering scientific wrestling, hardnosed battling, and a slice of flamboyance, he was increasing interest across the fan base. Like his predecessor and mentor, Tony Stecher, Gagne was constantly on the lookout for a possible star-in-the-making, and he closely monitored amateur events locally and nationally in search for a future prospect.

Gagne found a sizable one in 1971. Kenneth Wayne Patera of Portland, Oregon, was a 300-pound superheavyweight weightlifting champion. Over the two previous years, he had evolved from being an elite shot-putter into an American weightlifting record holder, a four-time Pan American champ, and was arguably the strongest man in the world. It was his surprise victory over world champion Joe Dube at the 1969 National AAU Senior tournament that elevated him from obscurity.[19] There was no turning back for Patera, and his dominance continued through the summer of 1971 at the Pan American games in Colombia.[20] By that time, he had moved from Portland to Minneapolis, and he gained the sponsorship of Gagne as he worked toward the 1972 Olympic Games in Munich, Germany.[21] Gagne would foot the bill for Patera's training, and after the Olympics, Patera would join the AWA as a pro wrestler.

That was exactly what Gagne wanted: a crossover star with name recognition, legit ability, and unlimited potential. Patera was a remarkable athlete, and he met all of Gagne's markers for a future wrestling standout. His reputation grew exponentially following his appearance at the San Francisco Invitational Weightlifting Contest on July 23, 1972. On that occasion, he became the first American to press 500 pounds, an astonishing achievement at the time.[22] Back in Minneapolis, his circle of friends was supportive and proud of his accomplishments. At the top of that list was 23-year-old Rick Fliehr. Fliehr and Patera had become friends around early 1971, just after Patera settled in Minneapolis. The two met at George's in the Park, a trendy dining and dancing establishment in St. Louis Park, where Fliehr was a bouncer.[23] Fliehr had seen Patera on ABC's *Wide World of Sports* and introduced himself to the weightlifting champ. Their friendship began almost instantly.[24]

It was a stroke of fate. That one meeting paved the way for a series of decisions that would shape Fliehr's entire life. Before Rick married Leslie, he was roommates with Patera in South Minneapolis, and they embodied the live-hard, play-hard mentality.[25] Fliehr called his time living with Patera his "endless summer," and there was never a dull moment.[26] Somewhere in between the partying and socializing, there was time for weight training, and Rick adopted many of the same disciplined habits as his friend.[27] They'd go to the gym together, but as Patera built muscle heading into the Olympics, Fliehr approached 300 pounds.[28] Although he was strong and a proven athlete, weightlifting at that level didn't come naturally to him, and his conditioning suffered as a result. Fliehr's options in the athletic world were limited. College football was in his rearview mirror, and pro football was out of the question.[29]

Patera's arrangement with Verne Gagne intrigued Fliehr, especially as it pertained to a special training camp to be held in the fall of 1972. Since he had Patera's inside track to Gagne, and also knew Verne's son Greg at the University of Minnesota, he felt there was potential for him to follow the same path. But first, Patera and Gagne went to Munich for the Summer Olympic Games, and there was great optimism surrounding Patera's medal hopes. But he surprisingly failed to place and left Germany empty-handed.[30] Gagne had returned to the United States early to make an important stadium booking at Chicago's Soldier Field on September 1, and defeated Ivan Koloff before 9,000 spectators.[31]

Final preparations were made for Gagne's initial training camp, which began on Monday, October 9, 1972. Five men were handpicked by Gagne to begin training to become pro wrestlers, and they included his son Greg, Jim Brunzell, Bob Bruggers, Khosrow Vaziri, and Patera. Gagne, Brunzell, and Bruggers were former football players at the University of Minnesota — and the latter had gone on to play five seasons in the NFL. Vaziri was an Iranian transplant and winner of the 1971 National AAU Greco-Roman championship at 180 pounds.[32] Of the five individuals, Patera was by far the largest physically, and his credentials were equally impressive.

Before the camp started, Rick Fliehr convinced Patera to introduce him to Verne Gagne. "We all finally piled in a car one day and I introduced him," Patera later explained. "Ric told Verne that he knew Greg and Jimmy [Brunzell]. Verne didn't want to train a sixth guy, but he eventually did."[33] Despite his nervousness, Fliehr had successfully sold himself and his merits to earn a place at the camp.[34]

With the support of his wife, Rick was encouraged to take this chance.[35] But he was still concerned about his father's reaction to the career choice. "Dad, if this is going to cause you any embarrassment, I won't do it," Rick told him. In response, Dr. Fliehr said, "Go ahead, do it. Just make sure you're the best."[36] It was advice that would resonate for years. When training officially commenced on Gagne's farm west of Minneapolis, each recruit quickly realized that Gagne's standards were extraordinarily and unusually tough, and he expected them to endure the rigorous workouts without hesitation or complaint. Cardiovascular exercises were Gagne's first priority, and the quintet was sent into the steep hills surrounding his property for a two mile run. As a result of his weightlifting, Fliehr weighed around 300 pounds, whereas Patera was up to about 330. Conditioning wasn't his forte, and Fliehr struggled to meet Gagne's demands.

The early physical training had nothing to do with wrestling holds or moves or even how to take a fall safely. It consisted of running, 500 free squats, 200 push-ups, and 200 sit-ups.[37] The better conditioned athletes in the group managed the challenge in a reasonable amount of time, but it took Fliehr and Patera upward of six hours to complete. After the second day, Fliehr was completely worn out and frustrated and quit the camp.[38] Gagne wasn't having it, went to Fliehr's house, and persuaded him to return with some loud talk, harsh words, and an aggressive move that sent Rick sprawling to the ground in his front yard. Needless to say, Fliehr followed orders without a rebuttal and resumed training.[39] These were crucial life lessons, and Gagne's intense discipline taught Fliehr how not to give up when faced with adversity. In addition to building up Fliehr's mental strength, Gagne instilled in him a deep enthusiasm for daily cardio training — and his remarkable stamina later became one of his most appreciated physical assets.

Over the course of five-to-six-hour days, Fliehr went through each and every painful step to become a professional wrestler.[40] That meant he was under the strict eye of Billy Robinson, a world-renowned wrestler from England, who was the camp's primary trainer. Robinson was a product of Billy Riley's Snake Pit, a legendary proving ground in Wigan, England, and knew all the tricks of legitimate professional wrestling. He was considered to be one of the most talented grapplers alive. As a wrestling educator, Robinson was fierce and unyielding, and his students were treated with an aggressiveness rarely seen on any level in the profession. Much like Gagne's approach, Robinson was grinding the men down and then rebuilding their confidence and strength with the basic skills needed to safely maneuver around the ring, protect their opponents, and defend themselves, if need be.[41]

While they might not have agreed on everything, Gagne was more than likely supportive of Robinson's often contentious training methods. He acutely understood the real-world challenges of being a pro wrestler. If someone was going to graduate from his camp, he would be thoroughly competent in the ring and on the mat. Not only did the recruits have to prove they wanted to be there, they had to excel, living up to Gagne's expectations day in and day out.[42] The bottom line was money. Each recruit had the capacity to be a future box office star, and Gagne's investment of time and resources illustrated his confidence in their growth. He wasn't charging them a training fee, but he required a commitment to his promotion following graduation. And the better trained they were, the bigger the asset they would be. Yet there was a line between being exhaustively trained and going completely overboard for the sake of discipline.

The conditions of Gagne's training center were far from ideal. The Barn, as it was known, was literally that — a horse barn on the rural property. A makeshift ring was setup next to bales of hay, and a single lightbulb hung overhead, barely illuminating the surrounding area. The ring was dirty and worn, the ropes saggy, and it looked anything but professional. There was considerable exposure as well, as the frail wooden structure wasn't insulated in any way from the outside elements. Harsh Minnesota weather hit the region hard in October and November 1972 with temperatures dipping into the teens and 20s, with occasional snow.[43] The recruits were pushed to tough it out, and the difficult environment was just another obstacle they had to conquer.

Fliehr was making great strides and his graduation was all but guaranteed. Robinson could see his potential and felt if Fliehr committed himself further, he would make a great catch-as-catch-can wrestler.[44] From his high school amateur work, Fliehr had the rudiments of freestyle wrestling under his belt, and he had been successful in competitive matches. That made learning the pro style a bit easier, compared to someone coming straight out of the football ranks with no previous grappling knowledge. Additionally, Fliehr had briefly trained under journeyman wrestler Rick Ferrara, who had been recommended by Maurice Vachon.[45]

With the end of training in sight, Fliehr was brimming with newfound confidence. The grueling workouts had helped him drop more than 30 pounds.[46] His stamina was vastly improved, and his skills were sharp enough for his impending in-ring debut. He'd been around seasoned wrestlers for nearly eight weeks and was picking up on pro wrestling's true nature, which was a highly guarded secret.[47] Gagne had taken a conservative stance on the matter, seemingly waiting for his students to finish training before breaking the news that pro wrestling was a prearranged sport. Maybe he wanted to ensure they were all the way committed before truly welcoming them into the fold. Nevertheless, that remained the final step in Fliehr's progression to the pro ranks, and in early December 1972, Gagne's recruits were physically and psychologically ready to take the plunge.[48] According to records, Bob Bruggers was the first wrestler from the camp to debut, on December 5, 1972, in Sioux Falls, South Dakota.[49] He beat George Gadaski, a 42-year-old hardworking veteran from Canada.

Gadaski was one of Gagne's most trusted employees, doing everything from driving the ring from town to town to setting it up on a nightly basis. He refereed matches and also got into the ring for preliminary contests. Since Gadaski was such a well-rounded and reliable performer, Gagne matched him up with his greenest of rookies, starting with Bruggers, then Ken Patera in Willmar, Minnesota, on December 9, and eventually Fliehr. Gadaski's task was to carry them through the motions, essentially allowing them to overcome their first-match jitters. It was a routine job for "Scrap Iron" Gadaski, and he helped Bruggers and Patera debut without issue.[50]

However, there was an issue in the way Patera's debut was reported in the press, which illustrates the haphazard way wrestling was treated by the media. At the same time, it might just have been by design. Willmar on December 9 was thought to have been Patera's first contest.[51] But the *Minneapolis Tribune* claimed the strongman was making his inaugural bow on December 10 in that city's auditorium against Quebecer Rene Goulet.[52] To make matters even more confusing, Patera was hyped as having made his debut for the third time in three days in Rice Lake, Wisconsin, on December 11, 1972. Perhaps it was Gagne's idea to build up his new star by touting his initial bout all over the territory, as a promotional tactic to stir up attention. Either that or it was indicative of the poor reporting that often surrounded wrestling. This confusion actually complicates the details of Fliehr's own pro debut, and as much as Patera's first match was glorified and misreported, it was the complete opposite for the former Wayland Academy athlete.

The complication stems from the fact that nearly every source, including his own personal autobiography, claims that Richard Fliehr made his first pro appearance on December 10, 1972, in Rice Lake, Wisconsin.[53] His opponent was Gadaski, as noted, and he went to a 10-minute draw. But Gagne didn't promote Rice Lake on that date, but Minneapolis, and Gadaski was the opponent of George Scott. At least that's what the *Minneapolis Tribune* reported.[54] The Rice Lake show was on December 11, and the local newspaper stated that Gadaski wrestled Patera. Not only that, but the *Rice Lake Chronotype* featured a photo of a wrestler, supposedly Patera, hoisting Gadaski up for a slam.[55] Although the grappler is turned away from the camera, his body shape and hair style matches Patera more than Fliehr, and seemed to further prove that the latter's first match didn't happen on that occasion.[56] If Fliehr didn't have his first match as reported, when did he really make his debut?

The entire situation is muddied by inaccurate real-time reporting and inconsistent "facts" that have lingered for decades. While there is no definitive answer, there are several possibilities. There is a small chance that Fliehr wrestled Gadaski in a brief contest in Rice Lake on December 11 that went unreported by the local newspaper. It would've been Gadaski's second match that night, and while unusual, it wasn't unheard of. Another possibility is that Fliehr wrestled Gadaski in a random small town in either Minnesota or Wisconsin, and an account of the match has gone undiscovered by historians for the past 50 years.[57] But it should be recognized that some rural towns didn't have daily or weekly newspapers, and if that was the case here, any search for contemporaneous proof of his debut will forever be in vain.

To further demonstrate the elusiveness of a definitive answer to this question, look at a 1982 article in *The Ring's Wrestling* magazine and a 1983 interview Fliehr did. The magazine feature, written by Kate Mast, stated that he had his first match in "January of 1972."[58] In the interview, done by Colleen Grimsey, he is quoted as saying, "I left [the] University of Minnesota in 1973 and started wrestling professionally after that."[59] It was pure storytelling.

Putting the date of his pro debut aside for a moment, it is believed that Fliehr wrestled his second match in Fargo, North Dakota, on December 13, 1972, against Rene Goulet.[60] It's notable that a lineup for the live event included "Rick Flair" — the new in-ring name for Richard Fliehr.[61] "Rick" would actually be shortened to "Ric," and since he adopted this life-altering moniker at this juncture, he'll be referred to by that name from this point forward.[62]

For the record, Flair and Gadaski were in one confirmed bout during Flair's first month in the business. It took place on December 30, 1972, at the Minneapolis Auditorium and was witnessed by the largest crowd of his short career, 7,091 fans. On a card filled with wrestling celebrities such as Verne Gagne, Billy Robinson, and Ray Stevens, they did draw in the opener, and Flair, despite any nerves, exhibited his early working knowledge of the pro mat business.[63] In a later interview, he recalled being "totally exhausted" after his draw with Gadaski and noted that his family and friends were in attendance on that memorable night.[64] But Flair's growing pains in the business were far from over.

When he wasn't in the ring learning the ropes, Flair was often called upon to handle errands for various AWA personalities. The jobs were part of his ongoing initiation, and depending on the circumstances, comprised of driving wrestlers to bookings or carrying luggage. In a lot of ways, the menial work was a test of his resolve. But Flair didn't see it that way. He respected the veteran wrestlers he drove and saw at the arena, calling them "sir" and "mister," and he absorbed every bit of advice they gave him. His bright and positive attitude made it difficult to not admire his youthful enthusiasm. He idolized the major players of the AWA. He had grown up watching Gagne, Dick the Bruiser and Crusher, and the vicious Mad Dog Vachon. They were legends, and to rub shoulders with them in the locker room, Flair was in seventh heaven.

Just as he was in high school and college, Flair was tremendously charming. He could adapt to his surroundings and was smart enough to sit back and listen to the more experienced grapplers rather than interject his own anecdotes. On long car rides, he'd pay attention to everything guys like Harley Race, Larry Hennig, and Ray Stevens had to say, and he trusted their guidance as he developed his in-ring persona. But no one in the AWA had as much influence on Flair as Virgil Riley Runnels of Austin, Texas. Under the wrestling tent, Runnels was known as Dusty Rhodes, and in 1972, he was in his fifth year as a professional. By that time, he was already one of the most recognizable names in the industry, and his partnership with Dick Murdoch as the Texas Outlaws created havoc across North America. At nearly 300 pounds, Rhodes didn't have the classic wrestler physique, but what he lacked in muscle definition, he made up in personality — in spades.

In pre-match interviews, Dusty delivered smooth and energetic promos, and captivated the TV viewing audience. Even as a heel, he was magnetic, and his off-the-cuff segments were big draws for the AWA. Outside the ring, Rhodes and Murdoch were hell-raisers wherever they traveled.[65] With a love of fast times, partying, and drinking, the cowboy-hat-wearing Outlaws were quick to throw a punch and enjoyed a good bar fight. They were featured in a riotous barroom brawl in Jim Westman's 1974 film, *The Wrestler*, which was produced by Verne Gagne. On the opposite side of the scuffle was Harold Sakata, better known as Oddjob from the 1964 James Bond movie, *Goldfinger*.[66] Near the end of the madcap scene, Dusty appears from behind the bar with a sizable smile on his face, holding two beers — which are promptly poured in the hat of a drunken bar patron and dumped on his head.

Flair also appeared in *The Wrestler* in a background role, befitting his greenness at the time. It was clear early on that Flair enjoyed hanging out with Rhodes and Murdoch and went out of his way to join them on road trips to outlying AWA towns. In a way, the atmosphere the Outlaws created was reminiscent of the nonstop good times and hilarity in college on fraternity row. With that came rookie teasing, and Flair was the butt of many childish pranks.[67] He didn't let it bother him and never complained. The boys in the locker room respected that, and Flair was welcome to travel with the top stars in the promotion. Rhodes and Murdoch even took him to Texas with them. In addition to matches in San Antonio and Corpus Christi, Flair spent time on Dusty's ranch near Austin, where he befriended the 6-foot-7 wrestling tough guy Blackjack Mulligan.[68]

The routine of a professional wrestler was the opposite of an insurance salesman, Flair's previous occupation, and his hours were scattershot and dependent on his booking schedule. Out-of-state trips were time-consuming and put distance between Flair and his wife, Leslie. She wasn't altogether thrilled by the wrestling lifestyle, and they had to adjust to the demands of his new career.[69]

Dusty Rhodes had probably the most striking influence on Flair's wrestling gimmick.[70] Flair saw himself as a cowboy-hat-wearing potential Outlaw of the squared circle. Carrying the weight that he was, north of 250, he appeared a physical equal of Rhodes and Murdoch, which may have been his goal. Mulligan, upon seeing him, thought he "looked like Curly" from the Three Stooges, and as funny as Curly was, that wasn't necessarily a compliment.[71] But Flair was portraying the image he desired, and his hope was to take it to the next level. He wanted to become an in-ring brother to Dusty and be dubbed "Rambling" Ricky Rhodes.[72]

Neither Dusty nor Verne Gagne liked the idea. As flattering as it might have been, Rhodes wanted Flair to find his own path in the wrestling business. He could already see his budding talent.[73] Although Rhodes was a mentor and role model for Flair, he was only three years and four months older than him. Their relationship was just beginning, and yet who could imagine in 1973 that they'd coexist as major players in the profession for the next four decades? Even wilder to contemplate, how would professional wrestling have been shaped if Dusty and Gagne had supported Flair's idea for the name change?

CHAPTER 3
ON THE RISE

Stardom and the vast financial rewards of being an internation-ally renowned professional wrestler were tremendous allures for many athletes. The money made the occupation worth it for those hoping for a better life. In the old days, newspaper articles touted the massive paydays for pioneers like Ed "Strangler" Lewis and Jim Londos, wrestlers who earned incredible fortunes during the Great Depression. The TV boom of the late 1940s and early '50s convinced a number of ex-football players and collegiate wrestlers that there was opportunity in the pro field with sound monetary prospects. Naturally, not every hopeful rose to the level of Londos and the Strangler — far from it. Prelim workers earned anywhere from $15,000 to $25,000 a year in the latter part of the 1960s, maybe a little more depending on how much they worked. This salary surpassed the median household income for families in the United States.[1]

It was enough money for a wrestler to support his wife and children, but without health insurance or a plan for retirement, it was a gamble to a certain extent. In fact, the entire business was a risk. Inside the ring, there was a constant danger of injury, and if a competitor couldn't perform, they'd have no check at the end of the week. It was that simple. There were no guaranteed contracts. The inflated monetary promises of promoters rarely came to fruition, especially if a wrestler failed to interest audiences as a box office draw. Instead of rising to the upper echelon of wrestling, they'd languish mid-card, or below, and settle into the respectable role of a journeyman. Those grapplers with the ability to light up a crowd and draw big houses were paid substantially greater sums, and it wasn't unusual for a star wrestler to earn close to $100,000 annually. A handful of wrestlers had earned a million or more over the course of their careers.[2]

Although money was the dominant prize in wrestling, egos always ran rampant. Power-hungry promoters sought their next conquest, and wrestlers clashed in and out of the ring while pursuing the top spot. The politics of the business was like a masterful game of chess, and everyone had a stake, whether they realized it or not. Industry leaders labored to coexist in harmony for the sake of the business, but it was the opposite of easy. Turmoil and backstabbing were commonplace. Wrestlers lobbied promoters for better positioning, and nepotism was rampant in nearly every territory. The steady competition for money and power made some individuals paranoid, and bitter conflict in the industry continued into the early 1970s.

Inside the ring, the competitive nature of wrestling took on a different form. Even though the business was prearranged, some wrestlers enjoyed sparring in a test of their legit skills. Seldom did two like-minded battlers lock horns in traditional shoot combat, but it did happen. For instance, in 1932, Ray Steele met Strangler Lewis in New York City in a dull and uneventful affair at Madison Square Garden. Their match had been prompted by politics and syndicate warfare, and it ended with Steele being disqualified.[3] The contest was an embarrassment, and to avoid another failure — and prevent irreparable damage to the sport — promoters pushed professional wrestling strictly as an athletic performance art. Striking personalities and awe-inspiring gimmicks set the profession ablaze, and when fans thought they had seen everything, someone new came along to blow their socks off.

Gorgeous George did exactly that in the late 1940s. His grandiose entrances to "Pomp and Circumstance," his perfume sprayers, and

"Georgiepins" were precisely — the kind of entertainment fans wanted to see at live events. Great superstars of varying ability and skill followed, "Nature Boy" Buddy Rogers, "Argentina" Antonino Rocca, and, of course, Verne Gagne among them. Gagne was as straitlaced as they came. He was a pure wrestling hero and routinely demonstrated his honorable character on AWA telecasts. But in the midst of a heated angle, he added traces of showmanship to spice things up. He kept his bottom line principles but conformed to the needs of the moment to sell tickets. At his training camp at the Barn, Gagne preached the basics to his pupils and believed they'd learn the necessary histrionics down the road. He was right, as Ric Flair and his mates received a crash course in wrestling's melodrama once they were on the active roster.

The performance side of professional wrestling came naturally to Flair. The in-ring emotion, exaggeration, and creativity played to his strengths. Growing up around the theater, the son of a gifted actor and director and a mother who literally wrote the book on how to draw an audience for stage shows, Flair gleaned many helpful points that would aid him in the world of wrestling. Whether it was his endearing self-confidence or the way he articulated himself, it was all part of his personal composition. Outsiders might have seen the sparkle and potential in the 24-year-old, yet it's unlikely they could have put a finger on what exactly was so special about the young wrestler at that time. The easiest explanation was to say that Flair just had "it."[4] With the right attitude and motivation to better himself, he was definitely on track for advancement.

Flair's size was still a hindrance. His strength was impressive, but his overall stout frame gave him the appearance of being out of shape. It was his attempt to mimic the roughneck images of Dusty Rhodes and Dick Murdoch, and Flair tried to make it work for him. Since his pro debut in December 1972, he had wrestled a diverse cross-section of the AWA's lower-card talent that included George Gadaski, Vic Rosettani, and "The Big K" Stan Kowalski. On January 6, 1973, in St. Paul, Flair took one of his earliest victories from John Heidman, a veteran wrestler who began his professional career the same year Flair was born (1949).[5]

Flair's early opposition tended to be far more experienced, for good reason, because Gagne wanted him to improve his dexterity against battle-tested grapplers. He essentially didn't have an assigned role as a "good guy" or "bad guy" yet, and wrestled foes of either persuasion in order to encourage his own development. "Verne Gagne's approach to his rookies' early matches in the business was to have them work with both heels and babyfaces," explained wrestling historian George Schire. "In the case of Gadaski, Heidman, and Rosettani, they were valued veterans that would put Flair over and make him look good doing it."[6] A review of Flair's opponents between April and June 1973 indicates a notable shift, as he began having contests with fellow graduates of Gagne's camp for the first time in public. Over a seven-week period, he wrestled 12 matches against his former training partners, and five of the bouts were with Greg Gagne in Wisconsin and Illinois.[7] Flair seemed to win as much as he lost, and time-limit draws tested his conditioning. Matches in Chicago at the International Amphitheatre were a major highlight for Flair and the other newcomers, and those trips created a lot of excitement.

Continuing his rookie initiation, Flair was tasked with driving 27-year-old French import André Roussimoff around the eastern part of the territory, including to Chicago and Milwaukee. André, who'd soon adopt the moniker André the Giant, stood nearly 6-foot-10 and weighed 400 pounds, and there were few wrestlers who attracted more attention than he did.[8] The scene as André and Flair enjoyed the night-life in Chicago together following cards at the Amphitheatre can only be imagined.[9] In June 1973, Flair traveled to Japan with Dusty Rhodes and Dick Murdoch for a tour with International Wrestling Enterprise (IWE), a promotion closely linked to the AWA.[10] It was a grueling campaign with 20 matches in 27 days, and on June 26, Flair wrestled his first ever cage bout in Odate against Rusher Kimura, a former sumo wrestler. Kimura, incidentally, had also been trained, in part, by Billy Robinson. In a contest that saw Flair bleed for the first time, Kimura beat him in nearly 18 minutes of action.

The tour was part of IWE's Big Summer Series, and it was physically and mentally taxing.[11] Upon returning home, Flair resumed his run of AWA cities and went to places like Denver, Green Bay, Fargo, and Winnipeg. On October 14, 1973, he wrestled 20 minutes to a draw with Tony Rocca in the opener at the Brown County Veterans Memorial Arena in Green Bay.[12] After the card, Flair traveled with Wahoo McDaniel to Texas for a five-day stretch beginning the next evening in Fort Worth.[13] McDaniel was Choctaw-Chickasaw from Oklahoma and played for four different professional football teams between 1960 and '68. Like the Outlaws, Wahoo was one of a kind, both in and out of the ring, and he was a top star everywhere he appeared. After Fort Worth, Flair engaged in matches in Dallas, San Antonio, Corpus Christi, and Houston, and the excursion proved memorable for the time he spent on the road with McDaniel and Blackjack Mulligan.[14]

Toward the end of 1973, pro wrestling welcomed Verne Gagne's newest prodigy: 23-year-old Chris Taylor of Iowa State University. Taylor was an extraordinary amateur grappler, having captured two NCAA championships and a bronze medal at the 1972 Olympic Games in Munich.[15] Weighing more than 400 pounds and standing just over 6-foot-5, he carried enormous presence, perhaps only comparable to André the Giant himself, and Gagne expected great things from him. That was confirmed by the six-figure contract Gagne offered Taylor in November 1973.[16] By the second week of December, Taylor was in the ring demonstrating his athletic prowess before AWA audiences.[17] In his fifth pro match, on December 14, 1973, Taylor entered the squared circle in Chicago against Ric Flair, and his sheer size advantage was stunning. Flair was no slouch in that department, but Taylor's dimensions were off the chart. Working as a heel, Flair was subdued by the Olympian's strength and defeated by submission to a backbreaker.[18]

In advance of the telecast of the Flair-Taylor bout in Chicago, sportswriter Tim Weigel hyped the contest and mentioned Taylor's impressive credentials and measurements, adding, "So say a prayer for Rick Flair."[19] The truth was that Taylor did dominate Flair for the most part, and outside a few moments against the ropes, where Flair landed an array of elbows and punches and raked the eyes, the offense was all Taylor. The way in which Flair lost was evidence of his own ring maturity. He made his opponent look like a future champion, taking bumps and pressing forward, effectively walking into Taylor's every move. Flair was far from being considered elite, but his understanding of routines and of his role was improving by the match. Chicago, interestingly, was the site of a couple of Flair's most notable early bouts, particularly against legends "Sailor" Art Thomas on August 11, 1973, and Pepper Gomez on October 31, 1973. Both matches ended up in the loss column for Flair, but he undoubtedly picked up some knowledge working with the two mat luminaries.

Flair's growth as a pro wrestler was visible to insiders, but his placement on AWA cards didn't change much between December 1972 and May 1974. Any natural ascension into better position was held back by Gagne, who filled the top spots with veterans. Among the younger class of wrestlers, Chris Taylor was working some semifinal events by his second month in the business, and Ken Patera was pushed into a high-profile feud with fellow strongman "Superstar" Billy Graham.[20] The preliminary ranks were an understandable place for a newcomer, but Flair, with 16 months of experience, needed some progression. But Gagne was in no hurry. His talent roster was full with a robust lineup of star performers, and he could run multiple events every night. Gagne had Flair penciled in for spots mid-card or below, and it didn't appear that things would change anytime soon.[21]

Money was a big concern for Flair. His household grew by one on January 6, 1974, when a baby girl named Megan Lee was born.[22] The family was living in the southern suburbs of the Twin Cities at 1965 Silver Bell Road in the town of Eagan.[23] Considering the financial needs of his family and his career prospects, Flair began to think about life outside the AWA.[24] In those days, it was quite common for wrestlers to jump between the AWA and the National Wrestling Alliance, an organization of unified booking agencies with a majority control in the United States. The NWA, with history dating back to 1948, was divided into territories, and local offices promoted shows within their designated areas. The AWA and the World Wide Wrestling Federation (WWWF), the third of the Big Three organizations, were outgrowths of the NWA, and there was a well-defined understanding between these groups.

The extended peace allowed wrestlers to move back and forth from territory to territory and organization to organization. Since they were considered independent contractors, wrestlers were free to give notice and depart for better prospects. But Flair's circumstances were a little different. He had committed himself to Gagne when he attended the training camp, and there was a heavy obligation to the Minneapolis promotion. However, there was precedent for a Gagne-trained rookie to move out of the territory, as Jim Brunzell, Bob Bruggers, and Khosrow Vaziri, all graduates of the 1972 camp, had each departed the AWA for bookings elsewhere. Brunzell went to Kansas City and was a regular in the Central States between July 1973 and May 1974, making sporadic appearances in AWA cities. Vaziri went to Tulsa, Dallas, Charlotte, and then Tampa by early 1974. Bruggers jumped to Charlotte where he found a territory on a major upward swing.[25]

During the spring of 1974, Flair received advice from a man he trusted, recommending that he, too, should venture to Charlotte. "I was offered an opportunity and Wahoo McDaniel, a man I had a lot of respect for, suggested that I go," Flair later said. "He said, 'You've got to get your feet wet sometime. I think you've got it.' I had confidence in myself. It was just a matter of getting the opportunity and then taking that step forward myself and walking out from under the umbrella."[26] The Charlotte wrestling market was in the midst of a metamorphosis, prompted by the sudden death of territorial boss James Allen Crockett Sr., who died of a heart attack on April 1, 1973, at age 64.[27] For over 35 years, Crockett had showcased the best and brightest in pro wrestling, and established an organization par excellence in the field. A man of great vision, "Big" Jim had branched out to other areas of entertainment as well, promoting concerts, musicals, and the Harlem Globetrotters.[28]

John Ringley, who was married to Crockett's daughter, Frances, was the heir to the throne, as designated by Crockett's last will and testament.[29]

But after it was discovered that he was having an extramarital affair, he was pushed out and replaced by James Allen Crockett Jr., the eldest of Crockett Senior's four children.[30] Jim, or Jimmy as he was known to his friends, was about 30 years of age in 1974, and he certainly had big shoes to fill with respect to carrying on the family business and the legacy of his father. Thanks to one of Ringley's wise decisions, the youthful president of Jim Crockett Promotions had an experienced right hand man, George Scott. Originally from a small village in Scotland, Scott entered the wrestling business in 1949 and had enjoyed 24 years as an active competitor.[31] He was an articulate and organized leader, and when he was hired to take over as booker for the mid-Atlantic promotion, a transformation began.[32]

To that juncture, the Crockett-run territory, which included the Carolinas, Virginia, and parts of West Virginia, Tennessee, and Georgia, was known as a haven for tag teams. It had been booked that way since the 1950s, and tandems such as Rip Hawk and Swede Hanson, George Becker and Johnny Weaver, and Aldo Bogni and Bronko Lubich engaged in legendary contests on regional mats. Crockett's style of booking was successful for its time and place, but it needed to be refreshed for the 1970s marketplace, and Scott was the imaginative mind behind the promotion's resurgence. Once he had the license to rebuild, he elevated the heavyweight singles division back to a main event spot and utilized an old friend, the 44-year-old Johnny Valentine, as his top heel. The move reverberated across the territory, and box office numbers increased as a result. Scott wanted to bring in additional fresh talent, and by May 1974, he actively sought to import Ric Flair from Minneapolis.

Having spent a greater part of 10 months in the AWA between 1972 and '73, Scott had seen a lot of Flair and was witness to his early evolution.[33] Wahoo McDaniel acted as a middleman for the two, giving Flair the option to head to Charlotte if he wanted to take the chance. It was a big decision. His parents and Leslie's family all lived in the Twin Cities area. There was no guarantee of financial success in Charlotte, and if he did fail, he'd have to return home defeated. Finally, Flair agreed to go, and unsurprisingly he had Verne Gagne's blessing.[34] Gagne wanted him to gain more experience out on the circuit, and he expected him to rejoin the AWA after completing his tour. A few years later, Flair shared his belief that they had been destined to go their own ways. "He could tell right from the start that he was losing hold of me," Flair admitted. "Gagne knows wrestling as well as anybody, but our personalities and styles [were] so different."[35]

In Flair's mind, his initiation process was over. Flair had carried bags, driven long hours between towns, and done whatever was asked of him. He was ready for new responsibilities and to test his athletic prowess under different circumstances. Flair's financial issues hadn't improved, and he boldly asked Gagne to borrow money. Gagne wished him well but refused, and Flair left for Charlotte with $50 in his pocket.[36] Notably, one of the final things he did before departing Minneapolis was dye his brown hair blond.[37] It was a new look for a new territory, and Flair was going to incorporate elements of "Superstar" Billy Graham's and Dusty Rhodes's wrestling personas into his own. As for his in-ring work, Rhodes was still a heavy influence, and Flair was already using a variation of the elbow smash Dusty so often used.[38]

But future Hall of Famer Ray Stevens may have been Flair's biggest inspiration in terms of the techniques he used in the ring. Stevens, by the early 1970s, had two decades of experience behind him. As a teenager, he got his first break in pro wrestling for Al Haft in Columbus, Ohio, and like Flair, he was incredibly enthusiastic about the business. He did all of the little things, from running errands and referring matches, all to get his foot in the door, and once he was given a spot on the roster, he never looked back. Regardless if he was wrestling singles or a tag team bout, Stevens became a master of his craft, and throughout it all, he never stopped learning. He picked up knowledge from guys like Buddy Rogers and Bill Miller, and was constantly improving. A match with Ray Stevens was a sprawling effort, and there was nothing he wouldn't do to sell the action. He'd brawl, wrestle technically, and bleed at the drop of a hat, and audiences were engrossed by the fluidity of his physical work. Scores of wrestlers from his generation were influenced by him one way or another.

At the top of the list of Stevens's positive ring attributes was the way he made his opponents look good. He wasn't all about putting himself over, but about increasing the importance of each match by elevating the work of his rival. If his foe wasn't skilled enough to pull off the type of bout he desired, Stevens made up for it by working twice as hard. He could make up for almost any deficiency, and for that reason, fellow wrestlers and promoters loved him. Flair admired Stevens, and if he was looking for someone to imitate, both physically and psychologically, he found the right man. Between 1972 and '74, Stevens teamed with Nick Bockwinkel to capture the AWA World Tag Team title a handful of times, and their appearances were must-see events for Midwestern audiences, even if most of the time fans wanted to see them beaten.[39] Flair treasured his time with Stevens and Bockwinkel, and as any eager student would have, he learned as much from them as he could.

With a fresh appearance and a yearning to apply his advanced knowledge, Flair arrived in unfamiliar territory and met with Jim Crockett.[40] They discussed the basic particulars of the promotion, and Flair mentioned his financial struggle. Without a second thought, Crockett agreed to lend him $2,000 in a demonstration of Southern hospitality.[41] Flair got a room at the Orvin Court, an establishment north of downtown, and made his first mid-Atlantic booking at the Charlotte Coliseum on May 13, 1974.[42] On that evening, Flair beat New Zealander Abe Jacobs in one fall.[43] Three nights later, he teamed with the hulking 6-foot-10 Chuck O'Connor (the future Big John Studd) to top Jacobs and Danny Miller before 3,500 fans.[44] Flair wrestled Les Thatcher of Cincinnati in his third bout for Jim Crockett Promotions (JCP). It took place on May 17 in Richmond, Virginia, and Flair was again victorious.[45]

George Scott's first plan for Flair was to team him with a veteran worker to aid in his development, a logical move that would pay off. Since Flair was already angled as one of the territory's top young heels, Scott needed someone with the background, the aptitude, and the reputation to help shape his in-ring character. Of the noted "bad guys" currently in the area, Scott chose Harvey Maurice Evers, a former Marine in his 24th year in the business. Evers went by the professional name Rip Hawk and was a legitimate tough guy with the scars to prove it. "Hurting other people never bothered me," Hawk said to a reporter in 1973. "I hurt them before they hurt me. In this sport, and in life, nobody ever just gives you anything. You have to go out and take it."[46] Fans hated the blond-haired Hawk for his arrogance, but those in the mid-Atlantic region had to respect his hard-hitting methods and longevity. He'd been in and out of the territory since his local debut in 1951 and was a multiple-time regional champion.[47]

The Flair-Hawk partnership began on May 27, 1974, in Greenville, and the dastardly pair defeated Danny Miller and Nelson Royal.[48] They fought a variety of fan favorites in subsequent weeks, including combinations of Johnny Weaver, Sandy Scott, and Bob Bruggers, while edging into a violent feud with Nelson Royal and Tiger Conway Jr. Before an audience of 7,400 at the Greensboro Coliseum on July 4, Flair and Hawk beat Bruggers and Paul Jones to capture the Mid-Atlantic Tag Team title, an event that marked Flair's first championship in pro wrestling.[49] In TV promos, Hawk was clearly the more mature of the two grapplers, and his steady confidence was reflected in his commentary against their baby face rivals. Hawk, who stood 5-foot-9 to Flair's 6-foot-1, was squat and husky, as he coolly smoked his cigar. Flair, with his multicolored shirts and oversized dark sunglasses reminiscent of "Superstar" Billy Graham, would often begin and end his comments with a quickly delivered "Wooooo!" and referred to himself as "Mr. Charisma."[50]

As a heel, Flair appeared right at home, and his aggressiveness toward opponents was successfully turning a lot of indifferent fans into virulent and loud detractors. He continued to add depth to his personality, thanks to help from Hawk, George Scott, and Johnny Valentine. A couple times, he teamed with Art Nelson, another blond-haired former Marine, and Nelson taught Flair the science to blading during matches.[51] In the right circumstances, a wrestler drawing blood from their forehead by use of a tiny razor blade was a remarkable way to add an element of realism to a heated battle. Fans responded to blood matches, and it was widely understood that "getting color" helped the box office draw. Flair was willing to test the waters in that regard, and if Scott wanted him to blade, he'd do it.

Altogether, life was improving for Flair. His financial situation was better by leaps and bounds, and not only was he able to bring his wife and daughter to Charlotte, but he bought a used Cadillac.[52]

The mid-Atlantic territory was brimming with life. Most of the time, two circuits ran simultaneously, and Scott expertly arranged talent to keep faithful crowds on the edge of their seats. On Monday nights, it was Greenville or Charlotte, and on Tuesdays, JCP wrestlers appeared in Columbia or Raleigh. Wednesdays were designated for television at WRAL Studios in Raleigh, and Thursdays were either Greensboro, Norfolk, or maybe Burlington. On Fridays, programs were booked for Winston-Salem and Charleston, and over the weekend, wrestling was staged in a number of different cities, including Roanoke, Spartanburg, Hampton, and Asheville. Comparing the schedule of Jim Crockett Promotions to that of the AWA was like night and day. A wrestler was constantly on the move, working matches in the mid-Atlantic region, and for an up-and-comer, the experience of wrestling nearly every night was invaluable.

Thanksgiving was a huge wrestling date for Crockett. Going back to 1961, the promotion had run an annual spectacular at the Greensboro Coliseum, which featured many of the biggest names in the industry. It was a tradition for local spectators, and on November 28, 1974, 11,268 people witnessed the exciting holiday card. Flair teamed up with former WWWF World Heavyweight champion Ivan Koloff to beat Johnny Weaver and Tiger Conway Jr., while his partner Rip Hawk lost a special cage match to Swede Hanson. In the main event, Wahoo McDaniel beat National Wrestling Alliance World titleholder Jack Brisco by disqualification when the latter threw his challenger over the top rope.[53] This particular DQ rule played a major role in JCP and allowed for inconclusive finishes. Although it was unpopular with fans, George Scott relied on it during extended feuds, giving him the rationale to offer multiple rematches, which ultimately led to cage bouts and/or no DQ stipulations.

Eight days after the triumphant Greensboro card, Flair and Hawk were scheduled to defend their championship against Tiger Conway Jr. and Paul Jones at the County Hall in Charleston. However, Hawk didn't show, and Flair was teamed with Brute Bernard in a losing affair. The title changed hands.[54] In January 1975, the Minnesota Wrecking Crew, comprised of Gene and Ole Anderson, made their return to JCP after an eight-month hiatus. The Andersons were old-school rough and tumble brawlers with mat knowledge and superior ring psychology. Both were from the Twin Cities, and because of that, Flair was given a fictitious familial relation. But Flair was not their cousin in real life, nor were Gene and Ole legitimate brothers. Ole wasn't even an Anderson. He was Alan Rogowski of Minneapolis, who had been a talented wrestler and football player at Alexander Ramsey High School. Gene, too, was a gifted amateur and, like Ole, was trained for the pro ranks by Verne Gagne.

On January 16, 1975, the Andersons and Flair teamed up for the first time, partnering in a six-man contest in Greensboro to defeat Conway Jr., Hanson, and Sandy Scott.[55] The match itself was relatively inconsequential, but symbolically, it established the foundation for the Flair-Anderson relationship — a connection that remained meaningful in and out of the ring for several decades. The Andersons became influential mentors to Flair, and he was smart to listen to their words of advice. A few weeks later, on February 8, 1975, in Winston-Salem, Flair beat Paul Jones to win the Mid-Atlantic TV championship. The victory marked the first step of his impending singles push, and greater things were expected.

Of all the various personalities in the territory, including the veteran performers who had offered him guidance, none were more personally important to Flair than Wahoo McDaniel. Flair had already traveled with Wahoo in the AWA and in Texas, and he knew what he was made of.[56] Wahoo was the real deal. Flair had gotten a taste of Wahoo's imposing wrestling style back on August 17, 1974, in Spartanburg, South Carolina, when he participated in a tag match with Rip Hawk against the "Chief" and Tiger Conway Jr. The "good guys" were victorious in that one.[57] George Scott was surveying the landscape, and as he made his booking plans for 1975, he believed a moneymaking feud between Flair and McDaniel could easily electrify the promotion. For Flair, working with a man he idolized was the perfect opportunity. With the TV championship belt strapped around his waist and a growing presence, Flair was becoming the sensation of the mid-Atlantic promotion. But Scott had a creative concept that would change everything for Ric Flair. It was a once-in-a-lifetime idea that was a natural fit for the performer in every way, and it would redefine Flair's image forever.

CHAPTER 4

A NEW DESTINY

During the late 1940s, a wrestling circuit operated in cities along Lake Erie in Ohio, and local promoters staged successful programs on a weekly basis. The operation was based out of Toledo, and Jack Pfefer, a diminutive entrepreneur originally from Poland, was the booking agent in charge. Called the "Little Napoleon of Wrestling," Pfefer was a cunning manipulator, and despite a laundry list of unusual quirks, he ascended to a position of power within the wrestling industry. Judging talent was perhaps his strongest asset, and in his career, he discovered the likes of Dave Levin, Paul Boesch, and the 600-pound Martin "The Blimp" Levy. In 1949, Pfefer hired 20-year-old George Scott for his Great Lakes circuit and renamed him Benny Becker. Scott was flanked by more experienced grapplers and an array of flamboyant performers, which was indicative of Pfefer's love of gimmicks and "freaks," as he called them.[1]

As a newcomer to the sport, Scott was probably somewhat overwhelmed by the colorful characters and the madcap scenarios Pfefer implemented, but there was one man in the troupe who really stood out.[2] He was Herman Karl Rohde, a Camden, New Jersey, native and one of the most dynamic and eccentric personalities in the business. Rohde was better known as "Nature Boy" Buddy Rogers, a blond-haired heel who spewed arrogance from every fiber of his being. He would saunter to the ring, roll his eyes at the crowd, and engage in bloody brawls that often left fans outraged. Rogers was full of energy, and his interviews were purposely condescending, provoking ticket-paying patrons to the brink of physical violence. Although he was still on the upswing of his career in 1949, Rogers's pioneering work was establishing a new trend, and everyone was taking notice. He made a lasting impression on George Scott.

After Ric Flair's rise in 1974–75, Scott wanted him to embrace the image of Buddy Rogers as a blond-haired, egotistical, "I'm better than you" heel. If anyone could pull off the "Nature Boy" gimmick, Scott felt, it was the young wrestler from Minnesota.[3] Flair had already developed into a fast-talking, rambunctious antagonist, and there was a noticeable reaction from audiences. But how far could Flair take it? Scott was confident in his protégé and gave Flair the opportunity to become more self-assured behind the microphone, and that element alone was increasing his notoriety. In his feud with Paul Jones over the Mid-Atlantic TV title, Flair displayed his bubbling charisma and spent a lot of time putting himself over, while disparaging Jones at every turn. "[I have] a body that looks like it was carved out of granite by Michelangelo," Flair bragged, his voice occasionally rising an octave in the fever of his rapid delivery.[4] His passions for money and women, alongside his willingness to hurt opponents in order to win matches, drove fans wild.

The Nature Boy gimmick only added a new dimension to Flair's overall wrestling persona, which was electrifying for the young performer. He talked about his impressive income and wardrobe — all in his conceited style — and his snobbish attitude disgusted the casual fan.[5] Hardcore enthusiasts may have appreciated his overbearing approach, realizing that he wasn't just another cookie-cutter professional wrestler. Flair may have been using the gimmick created by Buddy Rogers, but he was introducing his own take on the Nature Boy character. It was a stark contrast to many of his contemporaries, and his flashiness and perceived unpredictability were magnetic. George Scott was pleased, and he wasn't going to hold Flair back. The platform was his for the taking, and the future of Jim Crockett Promotions seemed secure with Flair on deck.

A young fan asked Flair about the Nature Boy nickname during a radio appearance on WESC Radio in Greenville, South Carolina, and he responded: "Young lady, I've waited for this question all night long. It just boils down to the fact that when Mother Nature constructed me, she broke the mold, only that she didn't miss one stroke. Therefore, I felt that I owed Mother Nature and everybody that was responsible for creating the one and only, some kind of a payback, so I gave myself the name 'Nature Boy' Ric Flair."[6] It was a creative response in keeping with Flair's narcissistic ring personality, and it differed greatly from the answer Buddy Rogers had provided a reporter more than a quarter century earlier about the nickname's origins. Interestingly, Rogers claimed that the moniker was given to him spontaneously by a rowdy Hollywood, California, crowd, shortly after a tune by the same name was released by the legendary jazz singer Nat King Cole.[7] In reality, it was just a product of Jack Pfefer's mind.

Flair was carrying the mantle now, and he was ready to inhabit every aspect of the Nature Boy image. In terms of timing, he was using the nickname as early as April 1975, months sooner than previously believed.[8] This stunning discovery was made by wrestling historians Dick Bourne and David Chappell when an audio promo for a show in Richmond, Virginia, on May 2, 1975, was unearthed.[9] In the interview segment, Flair calls himself the "Nature Boy" and delivers a "Wooooo!"[10]

Throughout the first part of 1975, the mid-Atlantic territory was a hot spot for wrestling, and Flair was joined by a number of familiar faces to include Ken Patera, Dusty Rhodes, Blackjack Mulligan, and "Superstar" Billy Graham. On February 20, Flair and Rhodes met for the first time in the ring and wrestled to a double disqualification in Greensboro.[11] In a bout that featured three of his mentors, Rhodes and Wahoo McDaniel beat Flair and Graham on March 9 in Charlotte.[12]

Flair often appeared in tag team main events, and as the year progressed, he received top billing as a singles competitor more and more. At first, his solo headliner roles were limited to smaller towns such as Lynchburg and Asheboro, but his feud with Paul Jones elevated him to top spots in

Roanoke, Charleston, and Richmond. George Scott's strategy to move Flair into a conflict with McDaniel sparked interest in June 1975, although many of their initial clashes were in tag team affairs. They graduated to singles matches in Spartanburg and Norfolk and then across the region. Away from the ring, Flair had a sincere appreciation for McDaniel and loved hanging out with him. They shared an affinity for the outdoors and went boar hunting together in North Carolina.[13] Their friendship didn't lessen the aggression in the ring, as Flair was up against one of the stiffest performers in wrestling. McDaniel was known for beating his opponents black and blue, and Flair didn't get any preferential treatment.

In fact, Flair was roughed up on a nightly basis. Part of McDaniel's brilliance was the way in which he made pro wrestling look real, and his brutality was the cornerstone of this illusion.[14] To Flair's immense credit, he never backed down. He took the chops and McDaniel's massive fists to his forehead, and he kept coming back for more. When the tables turned and it was Flair's chance to gain some revenge, McDaniel fully expected to be pummeled as hard as possible. It was part of the give and take of a match, and there were no hard feelings or debate. They were in the ring to portray extreme violence, and the loudness of the chops and the bloodshed were integral to their presentation. It was legitimate physical action within the scope of a predetermined, or "worked," match. Each time Flair stepped through the ropes against McDaniel, he became tougher.[15] His unflappable spirit earned McDaniel's respect and the respect of everyone in the locker room.

Johnny Valentine was very similar to Wahoo McDaniel in the squared circle. He, too, made every effort to legitimize pro wrestling as a vicious and cruel sport. Matches between Valentine and McDaniel are fondly remembered by fans to this day as an example of wrestling at its very best, pitting two intense fighters against each other in dire combat. Valentine was another of George Scott's old cronies, and his role at the top of the heel ranks was instrumental as the promotion switched its priority from tag team matches to singles competition.[16] Soon after his arrival in Charlotte from the AWA, Flair traveled with Valentine, and the two became friends. Flair was influenced by Valentine's work, and the face-forward plant that Flair later popularized was a variation of a trademark Valentine drop.[17] During the summer of 1975, Flair and Valentine teamed over a dozen times against baby face opponents, including a pair of bouts against Wahoo McDaniel and André the Giant.[18]

The towering and surprisingly agile André the Giant, who had been chauffeured by Flair a couple years earlier in the AWA, was now a national celebrity. Booked by Vincent James McMahon, head of the World Wide Wrestling Federation, André was sent to all territories and organizations and received incredible mainstream attention. His arrival in the Charlotte area was a boon to ticket sales, and Flair gained experience battling a much bigger man. In the midst of his ongoing feud with McDaniel, Flair dropped the Mid-Atlantic TV championship to Paul Jones on August 8, 1975, in Richmond.[19] The following month, he beat McDaniel for a more prestigious honor, the Mid-Atlantic Heavyweight title. The victory came in a special bout at the Hampton Roads Coliseum in Hampton, Virginia, on September 20. That night, Flair agreed to put his blond mane on the line in a hair vs. title contest, and after one fall, he was declared the new champion.[20]

It was the crowning achievement of Flair's wrestling tenure thus far, and his fame was certainly growing. His schedule was booked full, and things looked very bright going into the waning months of 1975. But an unexpected twist of fate was about to impact his life and alter the trajectory of his grappling career. At approximately 5:30 on the evening of October 4, 1975, a six-seat Cessna 310Q departed Douglas Municipal Airport in Charlotte en route to Wilmington, North Carolina. The twin-engine commercial plane was piloted by 28-year-old Michael Joseph Farkas of Wallingford, Connecticut. Farkas was a Vietnam veteran and a pilot of considerable experience, having logged 3,000 total air hours and 1,500 in that type of plane.[21] He taught flying lessons at Goose Creek Airport in Indian Trail, southeast of Charlotte, and was hired by Jim Crockett Promotions to shuttle wrestlers to various towns in the territory.[22]

Farkas was reportedly a "visual pilot," meaning that he relied on visibility and maps, not on cockpit instruments.[23] The hop between Charlotte and Wilmington was routine, and with daylight remaining and good conditions, it should have been just another flight.[24] The distance is approximately 180 miles, and the time in the air was about an hour versus more than three hours if the wrestlers had driven. Jim Crockett Jr., the president of the promotion, was initially slated to make the trip but was replaced by his brother David shortly before the flight.[25] David was an important figure on the TV end of things, not only behind the camera but as a commentator. He also held a valuable perspective from his brief wrestling career earlier in the 1970s. In addition to Crockett, the passengers included Tim Woods, a former amateur from Michigan State. Woods was a skilled tactician in the ring and had performed under a mask as Mr. Wrestling.

The popular Woods was positioned to feud with Johnny Valentine, and their rivalry was heightened after the latter put a bounty on Woods for anyone who could injure him. Ric Flair had taken on the challenge five nights earlier at Charlotte's Park Center, and the best he could muster was a double countout.[26] Woods and his two sworn enemies in the ring, Valentine and Flair, were flying together.[27] It made sense logistically and financially, but it could've shattered the illusion of "good guys" and "bad guys" hating each other in pro wrestling, had word gotten out. The loss of kayfabe, as it was called by insiders, was considered a death blow, and the business had to be safeguarded at all costs. But a private charter flight was something fans would never hear about. They were perfectly fine.

The final passenger on the Cessna was a fourth wrestler, Bob Bruggers. Bruggers, a hulking ex–football player, sat in the last row of the small plane, beside Crockett. Flair and Woods were in the middle, while Valentine was seated next to Farkas. The exact weight of the passengers is unknown, but it was probably somewhere between 1,400 and 1,500 pounds. Personal bags and wrestling gear added to that amount, and since the Cessna 310Q had a maximum payload of 1,749 pounds, they were approaching the weight limit.[28] In his 2008 shoot interview with Highspots, Flair said that Farkas carried less gas than normal to compensate for the excess mass.[29] That particular plane could carry 102 gallons of fuel and typically burned 25 gallons per hour. The flight to Wilmington was well within range, and even taking into consideration a reasonable reduction in fuel, they should have made it no problem.

But that's not what happened. One of the Cessna's two engines failed near Lumberton. Instead of landing there to inspect the malfunction, Farkas kept going, apparently confident he could make it to their destination safely.[30] A mile from the Wilmington airport, the fuel gauge dropped to zero and cockpit alarms sounded. Farkas lost both engines, and it became clear they were going to crash. They coasted downward quickly, slicing across treetops, and then hit a utility pole before violently crashing into a railroad embankment.[31] Despite the severity of the accident, there was no resulting fire (thanks to the empty fuel tanks) and all six men lived. Five were seriously hurt, and Farkas was in the worst shape, ending up in the hospital in critical condition with brain injuries. Valentine and Bruggers both suffered broken backs and never wrestled again.[32] Crockett had a concussion, fractured ankle, and cuts to his face.[33]

As for Flair, he suffered a broken rib and three compression fractures in his lower thoracic spine, and was initially told that his wrestling career was over.[34] "I don't remember if I thought I was going to be killed," Flair told a reporter a little over a week after the accident. "I just remember grabbing onto [a plane] seat."[35] He was released from the hospital on October 10, and the pessimism about his future pessimism about his future quickly dissipated. Jim Crockett told the *Charlotte News* on October 14 that he expected Flair to be "wrestling again in two or three months."[36] Wearing a back brace and using a cane, Flair faced a recovery that wouldn't be easy. He regained his ability to walk, and he told the press that he was going on the road to get some rest and relaxation: "I'm looking forward to getting back, but I'm really the restless type so I'll be traveling around during the next few months."[37] He was sensible about his back injury and didn't want to rush his recovery and risk further harm.

After an inquiry, the National Transportation Safety Board (NTSB) concluded that the "Pilot in Command," Farkas, was responsible for a "mismanagement of fuel" and a failure "to follow approved procedures." Weight was also a significant factor.[38] These glaring mistakes were acknowledged, but Farkas's experience as a pilot allowed him to put the plane down with the least amount of harm to its occupants. That being said, it was fortunate that no one was killed. The pilot would necessitate a high level of medical care for the rest of his life.[39] It's been said that Farkas died within a year or two of the accident, but that isn't true.[40] He lived for over 12 years, receiving the best care possible from the Veterans Administration and his family, and died on February 27, 1988, at age 41.[41] Two years after the crash, Johnny Valentine, in describing the accident, told a *Tampa Tribune* reporter that Farkas "seemed like a good pilot."[42]

Tim Woods was banged up in the accident, but he was the least injured of the six men on the plane. To conceal his identity in order to protect the business, he was described in press reports as a promoter and used his legal name, George Burrell Woodin.[43] Exactly a week after the crash, he returned to the ring in Greensboro and beat Spoiler II.[44] With Woods showing up as scheduled, there was no reason for fans to think he was on the doomed aircraft, and he was credited with saving Jim Crockett Promotions from a colossal embarrassment.[45] Ric Flair had been set to team with Gene Anderson against Woods and Paul Jones the afternoon following the crash in Asheville, but it was one of many bouts filled by substitutes in the wake of the fateful incident.[46] George Scott's entire booking plan had to be revised, and the promotion swiftly arranged to bring in Billy Graham and Blackjack Mulligan to fill crucial voids.[47]

In spite of his "bad guy" persona, the fans of the mid-Atlantic territory rallied around Flair, and within 10 days of the crash, he had received nearly 1,000 letters from well-wishers. News articles revealed his real name, and he was candid about everything that had happened during an interview with Jane Lisen of the *Charlotte News* in the October 15 edition of the newspaper.[48] His weight dropped dramatically while on the sidelines, from over 250 pounds to around 180, and he fought hard to regain his lost strength.[49] He was under the care of Dr. David Johnston at Charlotte's new Miller Clinic, which specialized in treating injured athletes.[50] It was determined that Flair didn't need surgery, and his recovery made tremendous strides by the end of 1975. George Scott, who had suffered a severe back injury himself in the ring during the 1950s, gave Flair important advice, and it seemed as if he was making significant progress in each passing week.[51]

As enthusiasts hoped, Flair's back healed enough for him to receive medical clearance for his wrestling comeback.[52] He returned to the road just before the end of the year, appearing in Columbia, South Carolina, for a December 30, 1975 program at the Township Auditorium. Instead of jumping straight into a match, Flair took it slow, acting as a second for Billy Graham and Blackjack Mulligan in their bout against Tim Woods and Rufus R. Jones.[53] The *Columbia State* newspaper noted that Flair had recovered "miraculously" from the near-fatal accident, and that was absolutely true.[54] He had defied the odds and demonstrated the resilience needed to once again perform at a high level. Exactly 119 days after the Wilmington crash, Flair resumed his wrestling career. On January 30, 1976, in Charleston's County Hall, he teamed with Mulligan and Angelo Mosca to defeat Woods, Wahoo McDaniel, and Tiger Conway Jr.[55]

The next night, Flair and McDaniel wrestled in the semifinal of a stacked card in Greensboro, and over 11,000 people saw the Nature Boy back in action. Flair beat his rival by countout, and although he had garnered sympathy during his time on the proverbial bench, he quickly reminded fans that he was indeed a vile rulebreaker.[56] He was a full-fledged heel. Understandably, Flair was a little hesitant about certain moves and wanted to protect his back from any sizable bumps.[57] Since his weight was down to the 230 range, he was more nimble on his feet, which gave him the chance to modify his ring work. He could move away from Dusty Rhodes's and Dick Murdoch's wild brawling style to fall closer in line with the top heavyweight technicians of the era, such as former National Wrestling Alliance World champions Jack Brisco and Dory Funk Jr.

The methods of Harley Race were perhaps more closely aligned with Flair's heel approach, but the point is that his weight loss allowed him to add to his skill set. Flair's feud with McDaniel demanded old-fashioned scrapping, and he was game. Blood and brutality were becoming second nature. But when he was booked against a more middle-of-the-road competitor, Flair had to alter his techniques to ensure a good match. These advanced ring skills were a work in progress, and Flair still had a lot to learn. Being around Blackjack Mulligan was always a benefit, and in February 1976, he teamed with Mulligan in tag matches seven times, including six-man affairs with Angelo Mosca.[58] Flair and Mulligan became close friends, and in March 1976, they bought homes on the same street in the Parkview East neighborhood of Charlotte.[59] At one point, they also invested in a van to make traveling easier between towns.

The plane crash was on Flair's mind, but it didn't dissuade him from further air travel. "You just can't let it stop you," he explained. "It was a one-in-a-million chance that this happened to me. If it happens again, then someone up there probably wanted it to."[60] Air travel was an essential part of the wrestling business, and Flair was back up in the air without much hesitation.[61] On March 1, 1976, he made a date at Madison Square Garden for the first time and beat Pete Sanchez in 10:21.[62] This was his first of two bookings for Vincent J. McMahon's WWWF in New York; the second was on April 26. On that occasion, he defeated Frank Williams in just under eight minutes before 17,493 spectators at the Garden. With him on the card were old friends Billy Graham, Ivan Koloff, and André the Giant.[63] Flair went to Florida and wrestled there for the first time at the Bayfront Center in St. Petersburg on April 17, 1976. He was initially booked against his trainer Billy Robinson, but faced Abe Jacobs instead, and was victorious.[64]

Flair's bookings in New York and Florida are indicative of the working relationships that existed between promoters. The brief jaunts were a great way to increase exposure, and athletes benefited from excursions outside their home territory. Performing at Madison Square Garden was a major addition to Flair's résumé, and the mainstream wrestling public was becoming acquainted with the blond heel from Charlotte. It helped that newsstand publications were taking an interest in his work. Months earlier, famed publisher Stanley Weston's *Wrestling 1975 Annual* magazine did a two-page spread on him: "Rick Flair Cries: 'I Love Bustin' My Opponents' Bones!'" It highlighted Flair's "human savagery" in the ring and put him over as a cruel and calculating villain.[65] For a wrestler, that was first-rate national publicity, and it gave him a huge boost.

Flair was constantly on the move and often wrestled more than 20 matches per month. His feud with Wahoo McDaniel dominated the majority of 1976, and over a 10-month span, they clashed at least seven dozen times in 20 different towns. Cities like Richmond, Columbia, Raleigh, and Greenville saw them fight between seven and 10 times each, and the Flair-McDaniel series were usually received with enthusiasm. But there were also bumps in the road. They drew a whopping 9,043 at the Memorial Coliseum in Winston-Salem on April 2, 1976, and then suffered a 77 percent decrease in attendance three weeks later, on April 23, when only 2,119 attended a program at the venue.[66] In Charlotte, the two battlers faced off 10 times between May and November 1976, beginning with a title change on May 3 at the Coliseum. The Mid-Atlantic championship flipped from Flair back to McDaniel in a bloody bout at a show that drew nearly 5,100 people.[67]

Fan support declined slightly in Charlotte too. Attendance for their rematch on May 24 dipped to 3,750, despite an enticing hair vs. title stipulation. Flair once again put his hair up against McDaniel's title, in an angle similar to the one from September 1975 in Hampton. The result was the same, as Flair won the Mid-Atlantic Heavyweight crown for a second time.[68] However, the finish didn't exactly go as planned. Referee Tommy Young, who was rapidly becoming one of the most respected officials in the business, took a bump from the ring late in the match. Flair and McDaniel went to the floor in a heap as well, brawling unmercifully. A wooden table was brought into the fracas, and Flair, in keeping with his extreme wickedness, pulled off a leg to use as a weapon. He struck McDaniel in the head and almost instantly recoiled from the "hard way" blood — Wahoo was genuinely hurt. The table leg had an exposed nail, which Flair hadn't seen, and it opened a gaping wound that needed prompt medical attention.

Not wasting any time, Flair pushed McDaniel back into the ring, revived the referee, and pinned McDaniel to end the bout. McDaniel was bleeding profusely and was taken by ambulance to Charlotte Memorial Hospital where he received 40 stitches.[69] The injury was accidental, but it played perfectly into Flair's persona as a bloodthirsty, bone-breaking terror. What was interesting was that in TV interviews, Flair came off as a passionate, arrogant blowhard, but he was annoyingly articulate for a "bad guy." He wasn't rambling incoherently or foaming at the mouth in promos. His interview segments helped sell the wrestlers' motivations in whatever angle he was in — and in a creative, interesting way. Since his weight loss, Flair looked more like a pretty boy, but in the ring he was the opposite of that, as his matches with McDaniel illustrated.

Flair was still honing the Nature Boy character. Between 1975 and '76, he contemplated changes to his appearance, curtailing his use of headbands, big sunglasses, and colorful shirts, which had been staples of his wrestling wardrobe.[70] George Scott introduced Flair to the wife of wrestler Johnny Walker, Olivia, who was a talented seamstress and fashion designer.[71] Olivia, a 33-year-old originally from Dublin, Ireland, was well-known for producing one-of-a-kind robes and jackets for personalities in the wrestling world and entertainment industry. Her creations, which took four to six weeks to make, were custom-made for each performer and sometimes used thousands of Austrian rhinestones. Flair was immediately hooked on "Olivia Original" fashion. "He wanted five robes right away," she later said.[72]

"I made him the first one, a very simple one — pink velvet, silver sequins and trim, and rhinestones — and he came absolutely unglued," she continued.[73] This was apparently the "pink crushed velour robe" he wore to the ring on May 24, 1976, against McDaniel in Charlotte.[74] These ring robes marked a turning point for Ric Flair as a wrestling personality. The glittering brilliance of Olivia Walker's rhinestones helped establish

Flair as a regal performer on the top tier of the wrestling ladder. Although he wasn't yet performing at the level of wrestling's greatest stars, he was making headway. The positive changes to his physical appearance, ring wear, and technical prowess marked his growth, and George Scott was touting his unlimited potential, even before the plane crash. "Over the next five years, Ric Flair will be the greatest draw around here," Scott said. "He excites people."[75]

While the accident temporarily put his career in peril, Flair fought back to not only regain his physical conditioning and health but his top role in Jim Crockett Promotions. He seemed destined to fulfill his promise. The near-death experience had strengthened his mind and body, and he was ready to live up to Scott's prediction. In fact, he had a prediction of his own. "I'll be world champion someday," he boasted in 1976.[76] Undoubtedly, George Scott believed him, as did a segment of fans in the mid-Atlantic territory. But to become the world heavyweight champion, an achievement of very few wrestlers, Flair needed to rise far above the average performer. He had to work harder, become better conditioned, and embody the unbreakable spirit of a champion. Considering everything he'd been through and his personal determination, Flair's goal seemed within reach. But in pro wrestling, anything was possible. Only time would tell.

CHAPTER 5

GREENBACKS, GOLD, AND GROUPIES

O ver the early 1970s, Ric Flair's life had changed in many substantial ways. He had gone from an aspiring powerlifter, living with his wife in a suburban Minneapolis villa, to a recognized regional champion pro wrestler, residing in a beautiful contemporary home on a quarter acre of land with a pool in Charlotte.[1] His annual income shot up from $30,000 in 1971 as an insurance salesman to $54,000 as a wrestler in 1974.[2] "I was going nowhere," Flair said of his pre-wrestling endeavors. "I was living the gimmick I portray right now without any money — international playboy, doing everything everybody wants to do, spending money I didn't have, taking loans from banks, late on payments. You know, just doing everything wrong."[3] Although the plane crash subtracted two months of wrestling work from 1975, Flair earned in the neighborhood of $75,000 that year.

Amazingly, the money was still getting better, and Flair couldn't have been more content with his career choice. The success of the mid-Atlantic promotion was a factor in the rapid improvement of his lifestyle, and he praised the territory, calling it a "hotbed of professional wrestling."[4] Jim Crockett and George Scott had supported his quick advancement in the company, and Flair was a dedicated team player for the local organization. "There is nowhere else that rivals the dollars and the fan participation here," he later said. "I try to stay in this area because

I've made the most money here. I like the climate, I like the people I work for, and I like having a home base."[5] A journalist estimated that there were 45 wrestlers on Crockett's circuit and, with the inside scoop from the promoter himself, revealed that seven of them were making $100,000 a year. Among them were Blackjack Mulligan, the Andersons, Paul Jones, and Wahoo McDaniel.[6]

"Last week I made $2,900, the week before $2,200, the week before $2,400, the week before $1,700, the week before $3,400," Flair said in May 1976.[7] His earnings grew and grew as the year went on, thanks to the strength of his feud with McDaniel. On September 5, 1976, Flair beat McDaniel at the Greensboro Coliseum, winning in only seven minutes after receiving outside assistance from Bolo Mongol.[8] Neither wrestler was safe from McDaniel's vengeance in subsequent weeks, and the Nature Boy was the first to incur his wrath. Six nights later in Greenville, the bruising former pro-footballer pounded Flair into defeat in a cage match and took the Mid-Atlantic championship from Flair.[9] On September 26, McDaniel polished off Bolo Mongol in Greensboro and sent him from the territory in a loser-leaves-town contest.[10] Interestingly, Mongol was repackaged as the Masked Superstar and returned the next day.[11]

Right in the midst of his eternal struggle with McDaniel, Flair formed a tag team partnership with 25-year-old John Anthony Wisniski.[12] Wisniski was a talented athlete, having trained under Stu Hart in Calgary, and had recently won regional titles in Southern California. His claim to fame was that he was a second-generation wrestler — the son of the legendary Johnny Valentine, whose career had been cut short in the Wilmington plane crash. Using the name Greg Valentine, he was positioned alongside the elite heels in the promotion, and George Scott believed there was gold in the pairing of Valentine and Flair.[13] One of the first things the new blond tandem did was set their sights on NWA World Tag Team champions, Gene and Ole Anderson, declaring war on Flair's alleged kin. The bad blood was apparent to fans as the four men got into the ring to settle their dispute, and JCP featured some of the most violent yet believable matches in the country.

Flair remained in a dual role, though, as he fought McDaniel night in and night out in singles contests. They had already traded the Mid-Atlantic belt three times since May, and before the end of the year, they passed the crown back and forth two more times. On October 16, 1976, at the Greensboro Coliseum, Flair dethroned McDaniel to begin his third reign in another hair vs. title bout.[14] That particular stipulation was in place for each of Flair's first three Mid-Atlantic title victories, going back to September 1975. It was reflective of the audience's deep desire to see Flair humbly relieved of his locks, but it was not to be. The October 16 show was a big success for Jim Crockett. By luring 8,233 fans to the Coliseum, their program outdrew a National Basketball Association exhibition between the Denver Nuggets and Buffalo Braves, held two nights earlier at the same venue. Wrestling attracted 102 more people, and while that was not an overwhelming triumph, it was a win nonetheless.[15]

The Flair-Valentine duo ascended to the NWA World Tag title on December 26 by defeating the Andersons in Greensboro.[16] Flair went to Richmond the next night and dropped his Mid-Atlantic championship to McDaniel in a no-DQ match.[17] The loss capped an incredible year for Flair, and he was finally a world champion, albeit in the tag team ranks. His earnings skyrocketed to $125,000, and his local notoriety was at an all-time high.[18] Over the course of the year, he was the subject of two in-depth articles in major North Carolinian publications. The first was published in the *Charlotte Observer* on May 30, 1976, and was penned by Robert Hodierne, who spent a good amount of time tagging along with the wrestler. Hodierne was in a privileged spot since his wife, Paula, had attended Wayland Academy with Flair and helped arrange an introduction.[19] In Hodierne's article, the observant writer not only described wrestling's environment, from the ring to the road, but he got Flair to open up, and it made for great copy.

On one occasion, Hodierne was a passenger in Flair's Cadillac Eldorado, as they departed Laurinburg, North Carolina, where a show had been held at the St. Andrews College gym.[20] Flair was worn out after a 60-minute draw against Paul Jones, and he casually tossed an empty beer bottle from the vehicle as they drove westward on US 74. "Do you believe that there's more than a handful of athletes making more money than me?" Flair asked. "There's nobody getting paid more than $200,000 a year. [Wilt] Chamberlain maybe was, but he's gone. Catfish Hunter is, but I don't know." The topic shifted to women, and Flair was exceedingly candid. "There are so many broads, it is unbelievable," he told the reporter. "Asheville, there will be 20 broads there. They just do what you say, you know what I mean? You go to Asheville or Greensboro or Richmond and there's broads that come along, their husbands are at home, it's unbelievable. If I wanted to, I could get [women] six times a week, three times a night."[21]

"You know, I have a really good relationship with my wife," Flair continued, "so I don't ---- around that much." Flair wasn't eager for Hodierne to write about his personal life.[22] In television promos, he portrayed himself as a suave lothario who could get any woman at any time, and his braggadocio knew no bounds. His private family life was the antithesis of his on-screen Nature Boy persona. In his article, Hodierne explained that the women at the various shows were "conspicuous by their total disinterest in the wrestling matches" and waited outside locker rooms to meet the performers. He referred to them as "groupies."[23] In wrestling, there was an insider term: they were known as "ring rats."[24] It should be noted that in the second major article on Flair in 1976, published on November 2 in the *Greensboro Daily News*, columnist Bob Heller revealed that the wrestler was "separated" from his wife, Leslie.[25]

The particulars of their separation are unknown, but the hardships of the wrestling lifestyle on a family were well understood within the business. The constant travel, upward of 50,000 miles in a year, with as many as six consecutive nights on the road, created an understandable burden on any family unit. For single wrestlers, going from town to town, meeting new people, and being able to party like a rock star was attractive and addicting. It was a dream scenario, especially when they were treated like VIPs wherever they went. But for married men, professional wrestling was a double-edged sword. The allure of companionship on the lonely roads was almost too much to pass up. With women literally waiting outside dressing rooms, ready to jump in the car with a wrestler, self-control was often tossed out the window like an empty beer bottle into the night.

"I wish I could tell you I live a quieter life, but I don't," Flair admitted. "I go 100 miles an hour at everything I do. I feel everyone in life is either an Indian or the chief, either the follower or a leader. And I'm a chief, which I feel you have to be in order to be successful, regardless of what you're doing." Heller discussed Flair's in-ring character, calling him the "rude one" who caused "havoc both inside and outside of the ring."[26] The chaos fostered by the blond heel was nothing to scoff at, and it was translating to real-world problems, plus an increased risk of injury. On the whole, the passion elicited from fans throughout the mid-Atlantic territory was remarkably hot, and that said a lot about the promotion's popularity at the time. However, the hatred for "bad guys" on the roster meant wrestlers faced serious threats from out-of-control spectators. On May 24 in Greenville, Ole Anderson was stabbed by a rabid fan.[27]

Fortunately, Anderson recovered from his injuries, and the situation could have been much worse. A Greensboro police captain, John Lewis, was well aware of the perilous journey "rule-breaking" wrestlers had to make from the locker room to the ring and back, and he assigned a half dozen police officers to safeguard them from knife-wielding patrons.[28] Flair was one of the ruffians in need of protection, and there were many times when he was on his own and faced unruly fans out for blood. He was most vulnerable in venue parking lots, before or after a show. Following an emotion-filled night of action, people waited outside venues to shout, throw things, and attempt to assault wrestlers leaving the building. On one hand, it was a compliment to the work of the heels, but on the other, their lives were potentially in danger.

Robert Hodierne of the *Charlotte Observer* witnessed the unrest first-hand outside the Memorial Coliseum in Winston-Salem. Flair was met by four dozen angry "kids" after an intense match with Wahoo McDaniel and was forced to dodge rocks en route to his car. There was no security.

Flair was pelted in the head by one of the rocks before reaching his car and driving off. "I've seen it a hundred times," Flair told the reporter. "We get hit with rocks all the time. I had to have my car repainted four times last year. It's a very dangerous business. People don't realize that."[29] Flair did what he could to avoid altercations with fans, trying to keep the violence contained to the squared circle.

His health and conditioning, generally, had been excellent since the plane crash, and Flair was entering 1977 in the prime of his life. But toward the end of January, he needed gallbladder surgery, which sidelined him for nearly five weeks.[30] Upon his return, he continued to divide his time between tag team contests with Greg Valentine and feuding with Wahoo McDaniel.[31] These two scenarios were mashed together on a number of occasions, and mid-Atlantic audiences were treated to at least seven instances when Flair and Valentine battled McDaniel and André the Giant. The latter pair won a nontitle affair from the World Tag champs on April 1, 1977, at the Richmond Coliseum before a crowd of 7,500.[32] McDaniel also teamed with the celebrated Bobo Brazil a couple times against the blond villains, making for another interesting matchup. In Greenville on April 4, Flair added to his laurels by downing Rufus R. Jones to capture the Mid-Atlantic TV championship. That same month, Flair had his first bout with a recent import to the territory from Georgia named Ricky Steamboat.[33] A successful amateur from the St. Petersburg, Florida, area, Steamboat trained under Verne Gagne in Minneapolis prior to his 1976 professional debut.

Still a little rough around the edges, Steamboat was blazing fast in the ring, and with good looks and a superior physique, he was a picture-perfect baby face. George Scott was impressed and ushered Steamboat into mid-card spots before green-lighting a feud between Steamboat and Flair. At the WRAL Studios in Raleigh, Steamboat beat the Nature Boy for the Mid-Atlantic TV title on June 15, 1977.[34] At that point, Flair was beltless, as he and Valentine had dropped the World Tag Team belts back to the Andersons the previous month in Charlotte.[35] But his championship void was short-lived. Flair and Valentine beat Dino Bravo and

Tiger Conway Jr. for the Mid-Atlantic Tag title on June 30, and then Ric was lined up for an important shot at the United States Heavyweight crown against Bobo Brazil on July 29 in Richmond. Brazil was a world-renowned superstar by 1977, having won the Detroit version of the U.S. title nine times, and in 1966, he had held the WWA World championship in Los Angeles.

Brazil was a pioneering Black American grappler at a time of racial segregation in the United States, and he earned tremendous popularity for his fearlessness in the ring. His veteran status in JCP was well respected and deserved, and he won the local U.S. strap from Blackjack Mulligan on July 7. On July 29, Brazil was defeated by Flair at the Richmond Coliseum, giving the Nature Boy the U.S. belt and one of the most significant victories of his career.[36] Previous champions in the territory included Harley Race and Terry Funk, and to put that into perspective, Race was the current National Wrestling Alliance World Heavyweight king, having won the prized belt from Funk in February 1977. Historically, the U.S. title was considered to be a single notch below the NWA World title, making Flair's new position a significant elevation. He was also honored that the great Bobo Brazil had been the man to put him over.[37]

Less than three weeks later, Flair ventured to Amarillo for his local debut at the Sports Arena on August 18, 1977. The West Texas territory was rich with wrestling history, and for the past several decades, the Funk family had not only dominated as top stars but were part owners of the business. Dory Funk Sr., the famous patriarch of the clan, had passed away unexpectedly on June 3, 1973, leaving his sons, Terry and Dory Funk Jr., to run the promotion.[38] The territory lost momentum over the 1970s, mainly because of the Funk brothers' arduous traveling schedule. Their absence from the Amarillo region hurt attendance, and attempts were made to save the business from a complete collapse. Flair's appearance was refreshing, and advertisements claimed he was in town "with hopes of landing a match for the world championship."[39] In a match against the massive Abdullah the Butcher, Flair was counted out after getting tied up with Abby's manager, J.J. Dillon, outside the ring.[40]

While in Amarillo, Flair made a special TV appearance on the region-ally broadcast *Championship Wrestling* program and defeated Gary Starr.[41] Flair was in tip-top shape and as boastful as ever, putting himself over to commentators Steve Stack and Terry Funk.[42] Footage of this bout was also televised in 27 states by the Atlanta "Superstation," WTCG-TV, which was owned by television mogul Ted Turner and part of a newfangled satellite-to-cable distribution arrangement.[43] Included in Turner's weekly programming was *Georgia Championship Wrestling*, booked out of the Atlanta office by longtime wrestling powerbroker Jim Barnett. The Saturday telecast was seen as far away as Montana and Texas, providing unbeatable exposure for the featured wrestlers. Through the cooperation of promoters, Flair made his Atlanta TV debut on July 23, 1977, and returned again on September 24. He was an immediate hit.

Although Bobo Brazil and Wahoo McDaniel remained in title contention, Ricky Steamboat was the primary challenger for Flair's United States belt in August and September 1977. During this time-frame, Flair was doing the full heel shtick, resorting to any and all tactics to win a match. He wasn't above using foreign objects, and crowds bemoaned his crooked ways each time he stepped into the ring.[44] Slow and methodical movements really stirred up the crowd, and Flair was getting better at controlling the emotions of the audience. Just standing in a corner, purposely avoiding his opponent, and looking out at the audience earned him a chorus of boos. He'd yell at the spectators, jaw with the referee, and mock his rival, all with the same result: the crowd ate it up. Fans may have wanted to see him lose, but they were entertained by his performance and got a good laugh from his zany gestures and wild actions.

In the midst of a monster push, Steamboat had already beaten Flair for the Mid-Atlantic TV title, and it seemed logical that he'd be the one to strip the Nature Boy of the U.S. championship as well. On October 21, 1977, at the County Hall in Charleston, Steamboat did just that and beat Flair for the belt.[45] Over on the tag team side of things, Flair and Valentine dropped the Mid-Atlantic Tag title to Steamboat (of course) and Paul

Jones on August 22, only to regain the World Tag Team championship from the Andersons on October 30.[46] The tag team picture in the mid-Atlantic territory was robust, and the new champions faced combinations of Steamboat, Jones, Wahoo McDaniel, Tiger Conway Jr., and Ole Anderson before the end of the year. Dusty Rhodes also got into the action, teaming with McDaniel to beat Flair and Valentine on November 27, 1977, at the Charlotte Coliseum. Their victory came on a disqualification after Blackjack Mulligan interfered.[47]

The Flair-Rhodes rivalry carried over into Atlanta, and they fought twice, on December 2 and December 9 at the City Auditorium. Flair earned himself a DQ in the first bout and outright lost the second one, which happened to be a Dusty specialty, a Texas bullrope match. Interestingly, Flair went back on the road the next week and returned to Texas for contests in Corpus Christi and Houston. The Corpus Christi event, on December 15, was a Parade of Champions, and Flair and Valentine successfully defended their tag straps against Tully Blanchard and Tiger Conway Jr.[48] Blanchard, who was the 23-year-old son of San Antonio promoter Joe Blanchard, had spent a good seven months honing his craft in the mid-Atlantic territory in 1977, and he was shaping up to be a future top star. Instead of flying straight back to Charlotte, Flair stopped in Miami Beach for a show at the convention center, where he was beaten by strongman Rocky Johnson. Rhodes, Steamboat, and Billy Graham were also on the card.[49]

As important as these brief visits were to increasing his stardom, Flair was scheduled to make an even bigger appearance in early January 1978. He was going to St. Louis, arguably the most important territory in the professional wrestling world. No, it didn't have the same sort of ambience as New York's Madison Square Garden, but it did have the same kind of history, with legendary matches going back over half a century. St. Louis, in many minds, was the capital of pro wrestling, not only in terms of heritage but for political reasons. It was essentially the lone seat of power, a position held by the great Sam Muchnick. Muchnick was the longtime president of the National Wrestling Alliance, and even though he ruled in a democratic environment, he was considered the legitimate boss of all things relating to the industry. Muchnick gave up the NWA presidency in 1975, but that didn't matter; he was still recognized for his extraordinary influence.[50]

To Flair, his appearance in St. Louis was all about impressing Sam Muchnick. If he successfully dazzled the veteran promoter, his name would be elevated to consideration for the NWA World Heavyweight title. And Muchnick wasn't swayed by any old wrestler. He came from the era of Ray Steele, Bill Longson, and Lou Thesz, and he appreciated no-nonsense competitors with extensive legitimate ability. He presented wrestling as a respectable sport, despite its antics and characters, and went out of his way to build credibility for his promotion. His administration of the NWA was nothing short of spectacular, and if anyone could be praised with keeping that organization afloat through thick or thin, it was Muchnick. When it came to talent, he was one of the harshest critics in the industry, especially as he evaluated potential NWA championship timber. He knew what the NWA belt meant to the profession and how much inherent value it possessed.

To determine who could hold the coveted championship, Muchnick assessed wrestlers' background, ring work and ability, and whether or not they could hold up under incredible pressure. The traveling schedule for the NWA champion was unlike anything in the business, and it took a rare individual to maintain that kind of continuous touring with no break in intensity. Guys like Harley Race, Jack Brisco, and Terry and Dory Funk Jr. had lived up to the high standard. Flair was among a new crop of wrestlers with championship aspirations, and the leaders of the NWA were also watching the development of Ted DiBiase, Ken Patera, and young David Von Erich. The NWA board of directors would have the final say, and the nine members would vote as they always did. But for Flair to be a contender, he needed to do well in St. Louis, and on January 6, 1978, at the Kiel Auditorium, he was ready to make his mark.

His opponent was slated to be Don Kernodle, a former protégé of Gene and Ole Anderson from North Carolina.[51] For whatever reason, he didn't show, and Muchnick rearranged his lineup to feature Flair against Venezuelan grappler Omar Atlas. In 8:42, Flair was victorious, and his tenure in St. Louis was off on the right foot.[52] Muchnick liked what he'd seen of the flashy Nature Boy. In fact, he didn't waste any time booking him for a return engagement, but this time he pushed Flair into a main event spot against former NWA World champion Dory Funk Jr. It was an incredible opportunity for Flair to showcase his talent, and he couldn't have been in a better position. Over the past four months, he'd headlined in two other NWA strongholds outside his home territory, Amarillo and Atlanta, and his match against Funk Jr. on January 27, 1978, in St. Louis was icing on the cake.[53] Flair pinned him with a back rolling cradle in 21:01 and cemented his place among the top heavyweights in the sport.

With two good appearances in the books to sizable crowds, Flair was headed for bigger things in St. Louis. Back in the mid-Atlantic region, his tag team with Greg Valentine continued to hold off threats by proficient teams, such as Jerry and Jack Brisco and Paul Jones and Ricky Steamboat. Wahoo McDaniel was also fighting for tag team gold, teaming with Ole Anderson and Dick Murdoch on occasion. Valentine had proven to be a valuable partner for Flair, and together they dominated opponents with technical prowess and brute force. Much of the time, they pounded foes into submission and enjoyed preying on one part of a foe's body, wearing them down before a final thrust to victory. In interviews, Flair was the boisterous one, always loud and flamboyant, while Valentine was cool and calculating. Both wore glitzy robes fashioned by Olivia Walker, and with the prestigious tag belts around their waists, they looked every bit like world champions.

Life was moving fast and furious. On April 5, Jim Crockett Jr. announced that Flair and Valentine had been stripped of the NWA World Tag Team championship for missing a defense.[54] Four nights later, Flair won the United States belt from Mr. Wrestling (Tim Woods) at the Charlotte Coliseum, in what was billed as a hair vs. title contest.[55] The arrogant Flair was very pleased with himself following his win, and he bloviated on *Mid-Atlantic Championship Wrestling* the following week.[56]

He was approached on set by his longtime friend Blackjack Mulligan, who congratulated him on his triumph. Flair was less than appreciative and nailed Mulligan with an assortment of backhanded compliments, and then flat-out disrespected him by saying he wasn't man enough to hold the U.S. belt. Mulligan lashed out in response, punching out Flair with a single blow. Fans were on the edge of their seats at the WRAL Studios in Raleigh as the scene continued to unfold.

Flair tore up Mulligan's prized cowboy hat, given to him by musicians Willie Nelson and Waylon Jennings. Mulligan then got his hands on Flair's famous peacock ring robe, a one-of-a-kind masterpiece with 1,000 real feathers. But Mulligan didn't think twice. He tore the robe into pieces in retribution, and the feud fans never expected, Flair versus Mulligan, began in a tempestuous manner.[57] Flair added to the simmering heat by placing a $10,000 bounty on his rival's head, a move that really riled up local fans.[58] This hot feud illustrated the depth of George Scott's booking in the mid-Atlantic territory. With so many skilled performers on the roster, and bad blood always at the point of erupting, Scott kept what could have been chaotic in complete organization. Every wrestler had a motivation, and feuds were devised for the long run — not for short gains. For example, Flair's hostilities with Wahoo McDaniel were still running strong an amazing three years after their feud began in 1975.

It was a solid match that could reliably draw box office returns. Flair's rivalry with Steamboat was fast becoming the same way. Their matches were intelligently crafted and called on the fly in the ring, meaning that the two athletes did not design their contests in the locker room before the match. They were wrestling so often that they instinctively knew what the other was going to do and what they were capable of. Flair and Steamboat were equally conditioned, and their matches were performed at an expert level rarely seen. The Flair-Mulligan feud would play out a little differently: instead of their bouts being lauded for scientific deftness, they were full of emotion, violence, and blood. They drew serious numbers for the promotion. In Greensboro, 11,267 people were in attendance on July 2, 1978, to see

Flair and Mulligan in a wild brawl before Flair was disqualified when the Masked Superstar interfered.[59]

Backtracking a little chronologically, just after Flair's feud with Mulligan began, Flair ventured overseas to work for All Japan Pro Wrestling. This was his second trip to Japan, nearly five years after wrestling for the IWE in 1973. The head of All Japan was 6-foot-10 Shohei "Giant" Baba, a celebrated former baseball player turned wrestler and one of the nicest guys in the business outside the ropes. Respect for Baba was universal, and that he brought in Flair for two matches in April 1978 was another key career moment for the Nature Boy. It was groundbreaking when Baba allowed himself to be pinned by Flair in a tag team match on April 21 in Tokyo.[60] Within an instant, Flair was propelled into the limelight in Japan. Getting that kind of "rub" from Baba was star-making, and seemed to deepen Flair's political support within the NWA.

Baba was a former National Wrestling Alliance World Heavyweight champion, having held the championship for a week in December 1974. Flair had beaten Dory Funk Jr., and he'd defeated Pat O'Connor on March 3, 1978, in St. Louis, which meant that the blond wrestler from Minneapolis had scored pinfalls over three former NWA titleholders.[61]

A few months later, Flair used what would become his trademark submission hold, the figure-four leglock, to subdue one of wrestling's top young challengers, Ted DiBiase. It took place in St. Louis on September 16, and cemented Flair's status as the number one local contender to the NWA World championship, held by Harley Race. On October 6, 1978, Flair walked to the ring in the biggest moment of his wrestling career to date, and he stood across from Race before a packed house at the Kiel Auditorium.[62] The two men fought gallantly for three falls, and at the end of the match, Race's arm was raised.[63] But everyone watching knew that the result could easily have been reversed. The era of Ric Flair had begun.

CHAPTER 6

THE RACE TO THE TOP

T he battle between heroes and villains was a time-honored element of professional wrestling and key to its enduring popularity. Promoters had learned decades ago that a clash of characters evoked raw emotion in the public, driving up ticket sales. Generally, fan favorites were portrayed as clean-cut sportsmen, who related to the everyman and celebrated the finer points of honest wrestling. They stopped to sign autographs, took pictures with their supporters, and received cheers every time they emerged from the back curtain. Heels, on the other hand, were dark and brooding or loudly flamboyant. They scowled at the audience, refused to shake hands, and were greeted with a chorus of boos. In the heat of an intense in-ring battle, anything was possible. Fists flew in every direction, and any semblance of actual wrestling was forgotten. The conflicting characters and the resulting mayhem were thoroughly entertaining.

Although the "good" and "bad" roles were assigned by the promoter, fans decided for themselves whom they rooted for. In the past, illustrious performers Gorgeous George, Fred Blassie, and "Nature Boy" Buddy Rogers transcended their designated roles, and went from being stereotypically hated to cheered for by a segment of the wrestling audience. The "Gorgeous One" was a spectacular showman, and his entire act was such an innovation for its time and place that people couldn't help but be overwhelmed.[1] He maintained a "rule-breaking" stance in the squared circle but did so with a grandiose, comedic style. Fred Blassie was a hardnosed "out for blood" villain, and it was obvious he went to the mat looking for bones to break. Over time, his cruel methods earned the respect and applause of a large subsection of the audience, and they enjoyed him and his calculating brutality much more than his vanilla baby faced opponents.

Then there was Buddy Rogers. Rogers was a Paul Newman or Steve McQueen of the wrestling world, known for his extreme coolness. He was a fierce combatant, who used his smarts to outwit rivals. Cheating was his second nature, and he'd use just about any tactic to undercut his foe, especially if it helped him win a match. In interviews, he sliced into his competition with an acid tongue, and he bragged about himself, his abilities, and the fact that no man measured up. Recognized for his fashion sense, Rogers wore expensive suits to and from arenas and was perpetually tanned, regardless of the time of year. He was the complete package, and because of his incredible talent and ability to draw at the box office, he became the first man to hold both the NWA and WWWF World Heavyweight titles. In the late 1970s, a number of wrestlers stood out for their impressive individuality, but only a few were on the level of George, Blassie, and Rogers.

Ric Flair was at the top of that short list. Since supplanting the likes of Johnny Weaver, Blackjack Mulligan, and other established stars to become the protagonist in the mid-Atlantic territory, Flair had catapulted into the upper echelon of wrestling stars, despite his relative inexperience. His athletic prowess and enthusiasm, combined with his ostentatious personality, had also earned him a love-hate relationship with fans. By 1978, Flair was despised up and down the East Coast. At the same time, he was adored by a growing legion of enthusiasts — some of whom liked him for his charisma and style, while others were drawn in by his good looks. After the Wilmington plane crash, Flair revealed that he had received nearly 1,000 letters from well-wishers, noting, "I'm not even supposed to be one of the popular wrestlers."[2] Greensboro

·columnist Bob Heller described them as a "cult following of sorts," and Flair wholeheartedly embraced the attention.[3]

"I like my appeal to the younger people," Flair said. "I can rap with them and I dig country and rock music, so I can identify with some of the same people they identify with, like Waylon Jennings, Willie Nelson, [and] Linda Ronstadt."[4] Flair's disciples were beyond loyal, and as time went on, they started following him around the mid-Atlantic circuit, turning up at his matches across the territory. Most of these admirers were women, and Gloria Fair, a Spartanburg journalist, later wrote that they ranged in age from grandmothers to "the very young."[5] They waited for him after matches, hoping for any sort of interaction, and Flair was gracious enough to say hello. "They don't hassle me," he said. "Most of the time, they just want an autograph. That's okay with me. I don't mind."[6] When it came time for business in the ring, he was back to his underhanded tricks, and his sneaky tactics didn't bother these ardent supporters one bit. They were committed to him.

During in-character interviews, Flair was amusing or disgusting, depending on the viewpoint of the observer. "Has there ever been anybody like me?" Flair shouted at TV announcer Bob Caudle. "Have you ever seen anybody in the whole world like me?"[7] Carol Hanner of the *Daily Tar Heel* wrote that Flair gave fans "one of the most flamboyant displays of emotion and braggadocio, in and out of the ring." She quoted Flair as saying, "To be honest, I don't like to put it like this, but I'm proud of it. There's nobody who has come out of the Carolinas — not David Thompson, Richard Petty, anybody, who has the notoriety of Ric Flair."[8] In advance of the mixed match between boxing champion Muhammad Ali and wrestling legend Antonio Inoki in June 1976, Flair acknowledged Ali as a "great athlete" but dismissed any chance he had against a good wrestler. "I wish I had the opportunity [to face Ali]," Flair said. "I'd bet all the money I have in the world that I'd beat him."[9]

Being a heel came naturally to Flair, and his unscripted promos were of his own design.[10] They roused viewers to no end, helping to propel his feud with Blackjack Mulligan into the record books. Between July and December 1978, Flair and Mulligan wrestled nearly 40 times, and their matches set a new standard for sheer intensity. The stipulations for bouts escalated over time, from lumberjack to Texas Death to cage matches, which was standard for booker George Scott.[11] The hostilities culminated in a finale at the Charlotte Coliseum, Christmas night, and 11,303 were in attendance to see Flair beat Mulligan in a frenzied battle. Jim Crockett told the press that it was the first sellout for wrestling in Charlotte in 15 years.[12] At the same time, Flair was continuing his crusade against Ricky Steamboat, and their matches left many in awe. The athleticism and creativeness of the two wrestlers remained unrivaled in the sport.

Steamboat's past performances in title matches against Flair were quite remarkable. Dating back to June 1977, he had won three championships from his adversary, and he wasn't yet done capturing gold from the Nature Boy. On November 5, 1978, Steamboat and Paul Jones regained the Mid-Atlantic Tag Team belts from Flair and the 6-foot-10 John Studd, who had beaten the popular tandem for the title six nights earlier in Greenville.[13] Then, on December 17, 1978, in Toronto, Steamboat came through again, toppling Flair for the United States championship in just under 31 minutes. Despite the authenticity of the title switch, the belt remained in Flair's possession in the mid-Atlantic territory, allowing for a big money match at the Greensboro Coliseum on December 30.[14] That night, before a deafening crowd of 10,327 people, Steamboat officially captured the U.S. crown in a hair vs. title cage bout, pinning Flair with a sunset flip.[15]

The response to their matches, both critically and commercially, was exceptional, and if attendance dipped, they came up with a new approach to spike interest. One such occurrence happened in October 1978 in Raleigh during a WRAL TV taping. Flair demonstrated his ruthlessness by relentlessly punishing Steamboat's face, and particularly one eye, rubbing it across the concrete floor of the studio and leaving a visible mark.[16] In subsequent contests, Flair targeted that spot on Steamboat's face, drawing the ire of audiences, and to loyal wrestling fans, Flair's actions spoke volumes about his diabolical cruelty. It strengthened his reputation and increased the hatred mainstream fans had for him. Appearing on the circuit nearly every night, Flair was a valuable workhorse, but occasionally he was forced to address a health issue. And after living through the rehabilitation following the plane crash, he wasn't about to take any chances.

Several months prior to his U.S. title loss to Steamboat in Greensboro, Flair began suffering from significant pain in his upper back. A lump had formed, and doctors were quick to recommend surgery. Flair agreed.[17] "It turned out to be a blood clot between the muscles, a rare condition that was eliminated by the operation," Flair later explained. He had been making a conscious effort to fall on one side of his back, instead of falling flat, concerned about reinjuring himself after the 1975 accident.[18] In trying to protect himself, he suffered a different trauma. The situation was very serious, but Flair was dedicated to his craft and returned to the mat prematurely.[19] "I wrestled too soon after surgery," he explained. "The stitches pulled, and the area became infected. It bothered me for a long time."[20]

As noted, Flair had adopted the figure-four leglock as his finishing hold.[21] All things considered, it was a major step up from his wind-up elbow drop, and use of a submission hold was on par with other leading heavyweights' choice of finisher, including those of the current and former NWA World champions. Jack Brisco was considered a master of the figure-four, while Dory Funk Jr. used the spinning toe-hold, and Harley Race, the Indian death lock. Buddy Rogers was the originator of the figure-four grapevine, and he made the move famous during his reign as NWA World titleholder in the early 1960s. Undoubtedly with advice from George Scott, Flair incorporated the figure-four into his repertoire to up his chances as a legitimate title contender. Incidentally, though, Flair applied his version of the figure-four differently than Rogers by crossing his opponent's left leg over right knee and adding a spin of his body when he employed the move. Rogers, as well as Brisco, crossed right over left, and neither used the spinning technique.[22]

Famed announcer Gordon Solie was quick to advise the television audience of Flair's "unusual application" of the hold to put over its effectiveness.[23] The maneuver was recognized by most fans, and it always garnered a loud response because it was considered a dangerous weapon. Audiences in St. Louis and Toronto were acutely familiar with the move, and Flair's version elicited great respect. Toronto was a new territory for Flair and the mid-Atlantic crew, thanks to an innovative booking agreement between Jim Crockett and veteran Maple Leaf Garden promoter Frank Tunney.[24] The deal provided Tunney with star talent from JCP, and in return, the monthly visits north of the border added a nice boost to the wallets of mid-Atlantic workers. It also raised Flair's international exposure and earned him political support from Tunney, who was one of the longest serving members of the National Wrestling Alliance. His membership card had been issued in 1949.[25]

Image enhancement was a responsibility Flair took seriously, and he went out of his way to ensure his ring wardrobe reflected the high falutin persona he portrayed. It was estimated in 1978 that he'd invested upward of $37,000 in "wrestling equipment," including robes from Olivia Walker, trunks by Karl and Hildegarde of Ohio, and stylish boots from Clifford Macias of Houston, Texas.[26] The robes were central to his character's attire and attracted the most attention. They also were the most expensive by far, costing "anywhere from $2,500 to $9,600 each," Flair later revealed.[27] He'd amassed a collection of 15 beautiful robes, and his ring entrances were a sight to behold, as arena lights flickered off the sequins of his flowing gowns. The captivating appearance of Flair from behind the curtain — in his expensive gear with his platinum hair perfectly coiffed and an air of superiority — left a lasting impression on spectators.

Flair projected his affluent image outside the ring as well. He did a promo for Mid-Atlantic TV, riding in the back of a white Rolls-Royce and pulling up to a waiting jet at a local airport. His chauffeur, a gentleman who was referred to as Sweet William, opened the door for him, and Flair launched into a classic diatribe, putting himself over as the best looking man alive. Accompanied by two women, Flair said he was going to Las Vegas that night, assuring the public that he actually lived the opulent lifestyle he claimed.[28]

Off camera, he was taking steps to make that a reality. Around 1976 or '77, Flair became a regular customer at a service station a short distance from his Pineborough Road home in Charlotte, and he got to know the proprietors, Odell and Ruth Brown.[29] With all of the driving he did, his automobiles needed regular work, and he trusted them for mechanical help and car advice.

Flair was thinking about buying a used 1969 Cadillac limousine, and he asked Odell to give it a look to see if it was worth purchasing. Around the same time, the Browns' son, Terry, offered to be his chauffeur. Flair went ahead and bought the Caddy and hired Terry to drive him around the territory.[30] They were met by rambunctious crowds wherever they traveled, and it was commonplace for bottles and bricks to be thrown at the vehicle. The limo was keyed on numerous occasions, and Brown had it repainted seven times in their first year together. Although the property damage was disconcerting, Flair liked the attention. To garner even more of a response, he had Brown affix a loud speaker on the front of the Cadillac, so he could shout at onlookers in various towns.[31] It was a dangerous way of drawing heat, but Flair thrived on the notoriety.

Flair's busy schedule occasionally put him in danger of being tardy for an out-of-town show, and Brown was responsible for making up the time on the road. During his tenure driving for the wrestling star, Brown racked up nine speeding tickets, including one for going 101 miles per hour.[32] Among insiders, Flair was known for having a heavy foot himself, and he reportedly received 82 moving violations over a four-year span.[33] The stress of the nonstop traveling wasn't lessening, and Flair was still working to balance a stable home life with the demands of pro wrestling. In 1977, his relationship with Leslie strengthened, and the two purchased a four-bedroom contemporary home in the upscale Charlotte neighborhood of Montibello.[34] With three fireplaces, a double car garage, and over 3,000 square feet, the home was befitting a sports figure at the top of his industry, and Flair's success continued to mount.

Throughout 1978, Flair's matches with Ricky Steamboat and Blackjack Mulligan invigorated the mid-Atlantic wrestling scene. The action was fast-paced and scientific, as well as vicious and bloody. Flair excelled either way. Headed into 1979, George Scott was priming new rivals to keep the region thriving. At the top of the list was the 5-foot-10 power-house Jimmy "Superfly" Snuka.[35] Snuka, a native of the Fiji Islands, had been a bodybuilder before turning to wrestling around 1970, and since his debut, he had made his mark in Hawaii, Texas, Japan, and the Pacific Northwest. In addition to his muscular frame, Snuka had incredible acrobatic abilities, and his intensity was practically unrivaled. As 1979 began, Flair reformed his tag team with Greg Valentine, and they were leading challengers to the NWA World Tag title held by Snuka and Paul Orndorff.[36] The feud was cut short, however, after Valentine jumped to the WWWF.

Flair and Valentine were reunited on March 4 in Toronto, which was a neutral city for the NWA and WWWF, and were disqualified against Ricky Steamboat and Dino Bravo when Flair threw the latter over the top rope. In the midst of the furious battle, a ringside fan instigated an altercation with the Nature Boy, and Flair routed the unruly patron in quick order.[37] Bravo was another prime opponent for Flair in mid-Atlantic cities, and the Italian-born Quebecer was as strong as he was popular. But despite the new blood in the territory, Flair's matches with Steamboat continued to outclass all others. On April 1, 1979, before 8,139 fans at the Greensboro Coliseum, Flair pinned Steamboat in a cage bout to regain the United States belt.[38] Less than two weeks later, he suffered a torn shoulder muscle, possibly in a bout against Jimmy Snuka, and missed a handful of shows.[39] He was back in the ring by April 21, when he defeated Randy Tyler in a rare appearance at the Superdome in New Orleans.

The next night in Greensboro, Flair tried one of his usual under-handed tricks, only to see it backfire on him and initiate an entirely new feud. The situation arose during Steamboat's Texas Death match with Paul Jones, and saw Flair, who had been sitting ringside, attempt to maim his foe with a steel chair. Rather than hit Steamboat, he nailed

Jones instead, causing him to lose the bout. Needless to say, Jones didn't let that miscue slide. He repaid the favor later in the evening, knocking Flair senseless with a chair shot and allowing Snuka to beat him by countout.[40] Flair and Jones locked horns in Greensboro on May 5, but their hectic brawl ended when Baron von Raschke jumped in to aid Jones, resulting in a DQ finish.[41] Jones and von Raschke, by this time, were the NWA World Tag Team champions, and to even the odds, Flair needed a partner by his side. After Flair and John Studd took a loss on May 20, Flair shifted gears and sought an ally from an unusual place: the baby face locker room.

In a shocking twist, Flair's arch enemy, the "American Dream" Dusty Rhodes, stepped forward and agreed to team with him.[42] It was a fantasy pairing, for sure, but the result on June 3 wasn't what Flair had hoped for. Jones and von Raschke got the better of them, and ultimately, Jones pinned Rhodes to retain their championship.[43] The bitterness between Flair and Rhodes never dissipated and built toward a U.S. title match on June 17, 1979.

George Scott had an ace up his sleeve: he would bring together the modern Nature Boy with the man who originated the gimmick, Buddy Rogers. Scott imported Rogers to referee the Flair-Rhodes title match, and 9,321 fans witnessed the contest at the Greensboro Coliseum. The struggle was fierce, and neither competitor wanted to give an inch. But obvious tension began building between Flair and Rogers, and at a crucial moment late in the match, Flair made a physical move directed at Rogers, and the original Nature Boy laid Flair out.

The single punch sent Flair to the canvas, and Rhodes covered for a successful pin. Dusty was crowned the new United States Heavyweight champion, and the audience went nuts in response.[44] Officials reportedly reviewed tape of the match in the days that followed, and Flair was returned the belt due to Rogers's illegal actions. This moment was essentially the dividing line between Flair, the longtime heel, and Flair, the redeemed fan favorite. He capitalized on the momentum of his feuds with Paul Jones and Buddy Rogers and transitioned to hero. In subsequent weeks, he teamed with Ricky Steamboat and Jim Brunzell, and he faced down the challenges of Jones, Baron von Raschke, and even Rogers. The 58-year-old Rogers had returned to wrestling earlier in 1979 after a 10-year layoff, wrestling more than two dozen matches in Florida. He looked great for his age but was limited by the physical handicaps that had sent him into early retirement in 1963. That included heart trouble, a fact he worked very hard to keep secret.

Rogers was capable enough to put on a good show in the ring, hiding his limitations well. Overall, it was about the storytelling, and the "Battle of the Nature Boys" was a dream match for old-school enthusiasts. On one side, there were fans who had grown up watching Rogers strut across the ring and obliterate opponents with his trademark wit. He was a true one-of-a-kind performer, and from his supporters' perspective, his comeback was long overdue. On the other side, a massive base of admirers rooted for Flair, and his history as a devious heel hadn't deterred them one bit. He was the only Nature Boy as far as they were concerned, and Flair would send Rogers right back into retirement. Behind the scenes, the two men were very cordial with each other. Rogers had been keen on Flair assuming the Nature Boy mantle and supported the imaginative ideas his old friend George Scott had implemented for the territory.

Even though he had the same bleached-blond hair, trademark name, and finisher as Rogers, Flair was not a clone. His Nature Boy persona had a new angle with fresh ideas and innovations, and Flair deserved all the credit for his ring accomplishments. Any misconceptions that Flair was completely recreating Rogers's Nature Boy were just that — misconceptions. That being said, there were fragments of Rogers in Flair's ring work, but that wasn't entirely unusual. Rogers had influenced scores of wrestlers through his impressive mat style and psychology, and one of those individuals had directly inspired Flair. That man was Ray Stevens.[45] Wrestlers adopted methods and moves from previous generations — it was a tradition in the business, and that was never going to change.

On July 8, 1979, Flair and Rogers met for the first time in the squared circle, and a loud Greensboro crowd responded positively to the historic affair.[46] According to the *Greensboro Record*, they wrestled for 23:30 before Flair achieved victory by submission, and the symbolic torch was passed.[47] They clashed again on July 21 in Spartanburg, and the result was the same.[48] With Flair's conversion to fan favorite complete, he teamed with several top stars looking for retribution on Paul Jones and Baron von Raschke to no avail. That month, his former friend, neighbor, and eventual enemy Blackjack Mulligan returned to the territory, and past problems were put aside for the common good. They partnered on August 12, 1979, in Greensboro and stripped Jones and von Raschke of the NWA World Tag Team title, winning in 24 minutes in front of 4,000 fans.[49] In turn, Flair hastily vacated the U.S. championship to better focus on his new prize, but his decision didn't pay off.

Only 10 days after winning the tag belts, Flair and Mulligan lost a televised rematch to Jones and von Raschke in Raleigh and dropped the title. They attempted to regain the championship but lost more than a half dozen rematches through late September. Buddy Rogers, in the meantime, took Jimmy Snuka under his wing, and the latter seized the United States belt in a tournament on September 1, 1979, in Charlotte.[50] Flair was committed to running Rogers out of the area, and he expressed his desire to regain the U.S. title. For months, he engaged in hard-fought battles against Snuka and members of Rogers's clique, which grew to include John Studd and Ken Patera.[51] Two other familiar faces joined the warfare late in the year: Ray Stevens in November, and Greg Valentine in December. Neither joined Flair's side. On December 9 in Toronto, Flair wrestled Stevens for the first time, and he beat his former mentor in 18:47.

Valentine was coming off a successful run in the northeast, where he participated in high-profile matches with Bruno Sammartino and WWF World champion Bob Backlund. During his time away from JCP, Valentine also adopted the figure-four leglock as a finisher, and his return to the mid-Atlantic region, as an adversary of Flair, raised a lot of questions of who was the better man. Flair won the first round of what would be a lengthy rivalry on December 30, 1979, at the Richmond Coliseum.[52] Long feuds were standard under George Scott's leadership, and, over the years, Flair had contended with Wahoo McDaniel, Blackjack Mulligan, and Ricky Steamboat, almost ad nauseam. Jimmy Snuka was next on the booking schedule, and between September 1979 and April 1980, Flair and Snuka wrestled nearly 50 times across the territory. There was great anticipation for a Flair title victory, and on April 6, 1980, a Greensboro audience went absolutely bananas when Flair pinned Snuka and apparently won the belt.[53]

But rules were rules, and since Johnny Weaver, and not the official referee, Stu Schwartz, counted the final pinfall, Snuka retained his championship. It was a disappointment, but Flair was determined to end Superfly Snuka's reign at any cost. Two weeks later at the same venue, Flair finally accomplished the feat when he dethroned Snuka to capture his fourth United States title.[54] The pressure was on, though, and Greg Valentine's emergence as a top challenger put his championship reign in jeopardy. Flair was able to withstand the pressure for several months, but Valentine was destined to be the next titleholder.[55] On July 26, 1980, at the Charlotte Coliseum, he beat Flair and won the United States belt.[56] Most fans weren't happy about the title switch but knew Flair wasn't out of contention. He was never without a title for too long, and it wouldn't be a surprise if he were to regain the strap from Valentine anywhere on the trail.

Flair's stock on the national stage was at an all-time peak. At the Kiel Auditorium in St. Louis on March 7, 1980, he won a grueling encounter with Jack Brisco, winning the first and third falls to take an important match.[57] The victory bumped him up to the number-one-contender spot for Harley Race's NWA World Heavyweight title, and it earned him a championship bout on March 28. In that contest, seen by over 10,000 fans, Flair beat Race with a figure-four to take the initial fall but lost the second. Both men were counted out during the third fall, and the match was declared a draw.[58] The show was an incredible success, and Flair earned $3,414.63 for the night's work, an astonishing amount.[59] A rematch was held on April 25, and another 10,000 packed the Kiel to see Flair and Race duel to a finish. Race started off strong, winning the first with a backslide, but again submitted to the figure-four to even the bout. In the third, Flair was caught in a rolling cradle and pinned, allowing Race to retain his crown.[60]

The Flair-Race series was drawing more interest and excitement than anything else Sam Muchnick could promote in St. Louis, and the athletes' compatibility made for great matches. Although he was a "good guy" in the mid-Atlantic region, Flair continued to ride the line between baby face and heel, and he never completely reformed his ring methods. "My personality hasn't changed at all," he told a reporter in 1980. "Eventually I guess wrestling people liked me more than the people I was wrestling."[61]

Away from the spotlight, it was a different story. He demonstrated his generosity by donating time to visit children at the Charlotte Rehabilitation Hospital. His kindness surprised people who expected him to be more like his character, and *Charlotte Observer* columnist Kays Gary wrote that wrestling "villains [were] sometimes actors."[62] Flair also delighted a throng of children with a special appearance at a Boy Scouts gathering.[63]

Back home, Flair's challenges seemed to ebb and flow as time went on. Being away from his family for long periods created an impossible strain, and there was little he could do to mend the problem. He was frank about it, too, clearly admitting that he wasn't the "home-loving type" of person.[64] "The Ric Flair you see on TV is me 24 hours a day," he explained. "I'm outgoing. I like parties, playing tennis, waterskiing. I have a hyperactive personality, and I like to be the center of attention."[65] The unremitting stress of Flair's day-to-day lifestyle caused great friction in his marriage, and he later admitted that Leslie left him "five times."[66] In November 1978, while pregnant with their second child, Leslie "deduced" that Flair was involved with another woman and asked him to move out of their home.[67]

A few months later, Leslie experienced some difficulty with her pregnancy and returned home to Minnesota to stay with a relative.[68] On March 7, 1979, she gave birth to David Richard Fliehr at a Minneapolis-area hospital.[69] Ric and Leslie officially separated "on or about" April 22 — only a few weeks later.[70] Leslie and the children remained in their Montibello home, while Flair rented a 1,300-square-foot apartment a short distance north, at the corner of Sardis and Providence Roads.[71] Custody was granted to Leslie, and Flair was to pay both child support and alimony.[72] The Fliehr family home was eventually sold on December 18, 1980, and Leslie moved back to Minnesota with the two children.

For Ric Flair, the changes in his personal life were significant and the only real constant was professional wrestling. Wrestling had given him the opportunity to earn the kind of living he had always dreamed of. It afforded him the chance to travel and meet people, and it furnished fame and notoriety on the level of other professional athletes across the spectrum. Being a wrestler seemed to come naturally to him, and his ring personality put him on a rare path, which few contemporaries shared. With multiple regional championships under his belt, a national reputation, and a proven record as a box office draw, he was one step away from the sport's ultimate prize. The breakup of his marriage was sobering, and yet Flair's commitment to wrestling never wavered. Ken Patera, his longtime friend, once told him, "This business was made for guys like you."[73] It was true, and Flair was in it until the very end.

CHAPTER 7

TEN POUNDS OF GOLD

A s the 1970s drew to a close, Jim Crockett Promotions stood among the top wrestling organizations in the world. The company's astonishing growth, in the face of many trials and tribulations, from the sudden death of "Big" Jim Crockett in 1973 to the horrifying 1975 plane crash in Wilmington, demonstrated the extraordinary perseverance of the Crockett family. James Allen Crockett Jr., who turned 35 in 1979, was the captain of the ship, and he had not only led the group to its current success but primed the promotion for further prosperity. The work of George Scott, as booker, was equally instrumental, and his expert command of talent had created a congruent system with multiple layers, a feat rarely seen in wrestling. His booking operations were consistent and realistic, and despite the longevity of some feuds, Scott's style of matchmaking kept the box office thriving. The popularity of the sport was indisputable, with more than a million fans watching wrestling every week on TV across the territory.[1]

Crockett's two television programs, *Mid-Atlantic Championship Wrestling* and *Wide World Wrestling*, were seen over two dozen TV markets in the region, which at its height extended to parts of Florida and New York.[2] Ratings were consistently high, and it wasn't unusual for the weekend showing of *Mid-Atlantic Championship Wrestling* to land a 25-plus share of the television audience in Charlotte. Always motivated to build his enterprise, Crockett understood the competitive nature of TV, and he upgraded production values to remain ahead of or at least on par with comparative programs. "TV is the maker and killer of us all," Crockett said in 1979. "[Wrestling is] just as entertaining and wholesome as anything on TV, including *Mork & Mindy*."[3] Weekly television production isn't an easy task, and it demanded a rigorous effort each Wednesday at WRAL Studios in Raleigh. In addition to the slate of matches, Crockett and Scott had promos recorded that were individually curated for each market on the circuit.

In that single day, they taped programming for both telecasts, as well as over 100 different interview segments to be edited into promotions for live events.[4] Altogether, the television production cost $250,000 a year, but the exposure was everything to their organization. "Our lifeblood turned out to be TV wrestling," Joe Murnick, a Crockett affiliate promoter in Virginia, told a reporter.[5] The crafty design of angles on TV, plus the madcap promos, were fantastic lures for audiences into arenas, and Murnick provided a great example of their recent success. He explained that they drew a $54,000 house in Norfolk one night, and then $45,000 in Richmond the next. "We were just $900 short of $100,000 for two successive nights," he said.[6] In Charlotte, they averaged between 6,000 to 8,000 fans per show at the Coliseum, and they ran the venue about 20 times annually.[7] The total gross in Greensboro in 1978 was in excess of $600,000.[8]

Bringing in and maintaining a roster of top talent was always a priority, and Scott helped Crockett develop a cast of characters that included veterans and up-and-comers. With a robust schedule, there was plenty of work to go around, and a motivated rookie had a nice opportunity to gain experience wrestling around the horn. In 1976, the territory purportedly had 45 regular grapplers on the circuit and grew to 135 only four years later.[9] Scott had the depth in his talent pool to book A, B, and C shows simultaneously, and could ensure that each program was filled with exciting and knowledgeable workers. It didn't matter if the show was at the Greensboro Coliseum or a spot show in Tappahannock,

Virginia. The traveling was constant, and to earn a six-figure income, it was mandatory. In 1978, Wahoo McDaniel revealed that he spent $22,000 on flights over the previous year, and he wrestled nine times a week on occasion. He estimated that he made $250,000 in revenue, which put him in the wealthiest class of wrestlers.[10]

As one of the top draws in the business, McDaniel earned 8 percent of the gate for his matches.[11] Ric Flair wasn't yet at that level. He received 5 to 8 percent, and it was reported he'd made $195,000 in his best year.[12] With regard to his own schedule, Flair told journalist Mike Mooneyham in 1978, "I wrestle four to five nights a week. I book myself and I'll wrestle seven nights a week if they pay me enough."[13] Over the course of 1979, Flair wrestled approximately 288 matches, according to current records, averaging about 24 contests per month.[14] However, this estimate is likely low because of incomplete television results from that year. In January 1979, for example, he wrestled 26 bouts and had nine days without a recorded match. Three of those nine days were Wednesdays, when they taped TV in Raleigh. Results for those televised cards are unknown, so it's possible Flair wrestled an additional match or matches on any of those dates.[15]

Even if Flair didn't have TV bouts on those dates, it's a good bet that George Scott had him in Raleigh to cut promos. It wasn't a day off. Add in travel time, and there really wasn't much room left for rest and recovery. His schedule was booked tight. On the bright side, not every month was as busy, and there were opportunities for brief sabbaticals. The summer of 1980 was not one of those times. After losing the U.S. belt to Greg Valentine in July, Flair continued his assault on his ex-partner in both singles and tag team affairs. Blackjack Mulligan was his ally of choice for a big contest against Valentine and Bobby Duncum on August 23, 1980, at the Charlotte Coliseum, and Flair's team was victorious.[16] The Nature Boy challenged Harley Race for the NWA World Heavyweight title on August 25, 1980, in Greenville, only to lose by countout, and then gained a draw with the champion the next night in Raleigh.[17]

Race was an indomitable spirit and had been the face of the NWA World championship since 1977. He was already a two-time champion entering 1979, and his total number of reigns doubled over the next eleven months after brief losses to Dusty Rhodes and Giant Baba.[18] Each time, the belt returned to the waist of Race, and his extended tenure as champion illustrated the continued support he had from the NWA's leadership. On September 4, 1980, he again lost a championship contest in Japan to Giant Baba, but he recaptured the belt before the tour was over. His September 9 win over Baba marked the beginning of his fifth reign. Less than two weeks later, Race, Baba, Flair, Crockett, and the members of the National Wrestling Alliance were in Reno, Nevada, for the organization's annual convention.[19] Wrestling luminaries from across the globe filled the Sahara Reno Hotel to greet old friends, brag about their accomplishments, and discuss key matters of the day.

The convention consisted of gatherings of different size, tenor, and responsibility. There was a main assembly of all official members, as well as an open meeting for members, affiliate promoters, and wrestlers. Committees of assigned officials handled an assortment of issues, from membership to rule changes. Families were welcome as well, and catered dining was provided at the hotel. Of all the distinct meetings during the convention, the one with the most consequence was the conference of the NWA's board of directors. Within an atmosphere of cigar smoke and high blood pressure were complex discussions about the future of the NWA and, particularly, who would wear the World Heavyweight title in the coming year. The nine members of the board brought their own preferences to that table every year, and they argued the merits of the top heavyweight wrestlers in contention.

The politics of wrestling was rife with the desire for supremacy. Generations of promoters, going back to the end of the 19th Century, fought tooth and nail for national authority, influence, and, of course, the all-mighty dollar. The World Heavyweight championship was always the ultimate symbol of power, and since the late 1940s and early '50s, the National Wrestling Alliance title was revered as the most prestigious in the sport. The hard work of the legendary Lou Thesz between 1949 and 1956 had set the standard for a nationally touring champion, which his successors attempted to follow.[20] That included "Whipper" Billy Watson, Dick Hutton, Pat O'Connor, and Buddy Rogers. Former footballer Gene Kiniski ended Thesz's final reign in 1966, and he carried the mantle until Dory Funk Jr. won the championship in 1969. Funk proudly wore the NWA strap until 1973 when he was dethroned by Harley Race. Race was soon beaten by Jack Brisco, and in 1975, Terry Funk won the belt.

These champions meant big money to promoters. They were idolized by fans for their distinctive traits, whether it was their outstanding sportsmanship or over-the-top villainy, and their positions as NWA titleholders put them in a rare class that everyone around the business knew was special. The allure of money and power drew out the base instincts of promoters within the NWA, and annual meetings were often a battle royal of ideas and agendas. The 1980 annual meeting was no different, and the convergence of big personalities set up a hot debate as members sought a replacement for Race. Of the nine directors, Race's biggest advocate was undoubtedly Bob Geigel, a hardnosed ex-amateur out of the University of Iowa. Geigel was a thirty-year pro and had been part owner of the Central States territory out of Kansas City since 1963.[21] Race was originally from northwestern Missouri, near the Iowa border, and was considered the territory's brightest star. In addition to his ownership role in the Central States area, Geigel had served two terms as NWA president in 1978 and '79 and was well respected among his associates.

Jack Adkisson was also a former NWA president, who had the distinction of succeeding Sam Muchnick when he bowed out of the position in August 1975. Known publicly as pro wrestler Fritz Von Erich, Adkisson was the head of the Dallas territory and was a highly influential leader within the industry. With three sons — Kevin, David, and Kerry Von Erich — in the infancy of their careers, Adkisson was playing a long game of political chess with his counterparts, and he expected the NWA championship belt to be passed to one of his kin sooner than later. His oldest, Kevin, was 23 and only had four years of experience in 1980. David, who'd soon be acknowledged as the better candidate, was 22.

Nevertheless, Adkisson's voice was important to other NWA promoters, and he'd have a say in picking the next champ.

Board member Jim Barnett was NWA royalty and had been affiliated with the organization in one way or another since the early 1950s. However, it wasn't until 1969 that he became an official member, first representing Australia and then his territorial ownership in Atlanta.[22] Barnett's role in the organization was substantial. He not only served as the secretary and treasurer of the NWA but also booked the World Heavyweight champion. That meant he was in charge of the champion's schedule, dictating where he went and when and resolving any conflicts between promoters. That position elevated Barnett's influence tremendously, and he embraced the role. Vincent James McMahon of the World Wrestling Federation was another member of the board, and his remarkable success in the northeast made him a powerbroker of great significance. His contemporaries respected his experience and knowledge immensely.

Ron Fuller of Alabama, Mike LeBell of Los Angeles, Victor Jovica of Puerto Rico, and Fred Ward of Georgia were members of the NWA board of directors as well, who each held a vote and offered their opinion on which wrestler was the best fit as the traveling champion in their territory. There was one promoter without a board vote, but his influence was as strong as any of his peers: Eddie Graham of Tampa, Florida. Graham had served as NWA president from August 1976 to March 1978 but abruptly resigned, relinquishing his seat on the board. The incessant politics, as well as stress and health problems, were rumored to have played a role in his decision, but despite his resignation, Graham's stature in the organization hadn't diminished one iota. Under his leadership, the Florida territory was thriving, and he had helped transform the "American Dream" Dusty Rhodes into a household name.

In fact, of all the wrestlers working the national circuit, few were situated better than Dusty Rhodes. He was a renowned star, a former world champion, and extraordinarily popular across North America. "When Dusty comes to town there is a little more excitement," wrote Bob

Quincy in the *Charlotte Observer* in 1977.[23] Rhodes was full of charisma and charm, and his connection to the audience was a bit different than Ric Flair's or other top-level heroes'. He appealed to the everyman, and his dynamic personality captivated audiences in Florida, the mid-Atlantic area, Texas, and wherever else he traveled. "The people clamor to see me," Rhodes said. "I've filled the biggest arenas in every major city in the country. I'm the biggest, toughest, strongest, prettiest wrestler in the history of the sport."[24] In another interview, he compared himself to football legend Joe Namath, saying, "I like fancy clothes, although I usually dress Texas style. I saw Namath wearing an expensive coat and I couldn't wait to get one. I had a $5,000 white mink made up for me."[25]

Graham sponsored Rhodes in his campaign for NWA recognition, resulting in the latter's five-day reign in August 1979. Other members of the board knew Rhodes's box office power but were unconvinced of his long-term viability as champion, especially against baby face opponents. Rhodes appeared to be out of shape in comparison to Harley Race and former champs, even though he was far better conditioned than most realized. Dusty Rhodes was Graham's man, and he wanted Rhodes to dethrone Race. Aside from a Von Erich, Rhodes, and Race himself, there were other names bandied about at the NWA meeting, mostly in a secondary fashion.

Notably, Crockett was the ninth member of the board of directors, and his position within the Alliance had increased greatly at the 1980 convention. His colleagues voted him the next NWA president, replacing Bob Geigel, and his success in the mid-Atlantic territory spoke volumes about his managerial ability. Crockett's father, "Big" Jim, had first joined the NWA in 1951 and served five terms as an officer in the organization, including three stints as the first vice president.[26] He was never elected president, though, and his son's rise to the top of the Alliance was a significant moment for Jim Crockett Promotions. It was also a defining moment, politically, for Flair. For the past few years, Crockett had worked Flair's name into the national conversation behind the scenes, and he wanted him considered for the NWA World title. The sport had seen the ascension of many talented up-and-comers, but in the opinion of Jim Crockett, none was more prepared to succeed Harley Race than Ric Flair. Flair's growth, both physically and as a personality, gave Crockett the leverage he needed to push Flair's candidacy.

Although the mid-Atlantic territory had never sponsored a home-grown talent for the top spot, Crockett was wise to the process. First and foremost, it was about making an impression in St. Louis, and after a series of carefully booked appearances, Flair had established himself as a box office attraction. In Texas, Florida, Atlanta, and Toronto, he demonstrated his ring skills and showmanship, which increased the confidence promoters had in him. That was essentially what it was all about. The members of the NWA needed to know that the next world champion could navigate all the challenges of the job, from drawing fans to conditioning to just being mentally mature enough for the intense responsibilities. If Flair had a weakness, it was that he wasn't a shooter in the old-school sense.[27] He didn't have the amateur background of a Dick Hutton or Jack Brisco, nor the pure toughness of a Harley Race.

But the demand for a shooter to protect the belt from a rogue challenger wasn't like it used to be. Such a situation would probably never arise, but if it did, Flair needed the wherewithal to guard the strap by other means — by getting out of the ring or getting disqualified. To some old-school promoters, this ability was still a factor in their decision-making.

There was another element at play at the time, which revealed the power struggle within the NWA. Since the mid-1970s and the void created by Sam Muchnick when he stepped away from the presidency, the hierarchy of the organization had centered on three individuals: Bob Geigel, Jack Adkisson, and Eddie Graham. They took the helm of the NWA and steered things in the direction they wanted. Crockett became the first non wrestler to take over as president since Muchnick, and the dominant rule of Geigel-Adkisson-Graham was brought to an end.

With that, though, there was concern, and borderline jealousy, that Crockett would also gain control of the NWA World Heavyweight title if they moved the belt to Flair. It was an additional reason to oppose Flair as a candidate. The battle lines were drawn in the sand, and the board of directors voted out of principle, self-interest, and what they considered best for the business. Flair, with his magnetism, resilience, and the rare "it" factor, earned the majority of votes, 5–4. It is believed that Flair was supported by Jim Crockett, Jim Barnett, Vince McMahon, Victor Jovica, and Ron Fuller. In what may have been a compromise to appease Eddie Graham, Dusty Rhodes was chosen as an interim champion between Race and Flair, and Bob Geigel's Kansas City was picked as the location for the Rhodes-Flair title switch. Olive branches were extended in all directions to keep the peace, and with the convention over, the members of the NWA went back to work, hustling for their next dollar.

The political gamesmanship was exhausting. Crockett and Flair returned to Charlotte to resume business, and the build to Flair's fateful day in Kansas City was going to last months. Flair made the first leg of that journey on November 20, 1980, when he made his Kansas City debut at the Memorial Hall. It was an introduction of sorts, and Flair humbly put over veteran "Bulldog" Bob Brown.[28] Four nights later, Flair beat Greg Valentine to regain the United States Heavyweight crown in Greenville, South Carolina. His feud with Valentine earned a spot in the lineup of Crockett's Thanksgiving Night Spectacular at the Greensboro Coliseum on November 27, and nearly 12,000 fans saw Flair win a brutal cage match.[29] In JCP's other special holiday program, Flair again beat Valentine on Christmas night at the Charlotte Coliseum.[30]

While all of these other things were happening, one of the biggest personalities in the history of professional wrestling arrived in the mid-Atlantic territory: 26-year-old Roddy Piper entered the region in October 1980 and immediately made his mark as an unpredictable, kilt-wearing, bagpipe-playing villain. His TV segments were full of life, and his charisma was off the charts. In the squared circle, he was an adept wrestler, and his previous tours in Southern California and the Pacific Northwest saw him win multiple regional titles, including the Americas Heavyweight championship in Los Angeles.[31] Brawling was his real specialty, and there was a genius to his volatility. He could assail opponents in the ring with a rapid-fire barrage of fists or through his sheer wit in an interview. Without question, he was innately humorous, and for fans who enjoyed the creative sharpness of an indifferent heel out to hurt the promotion's popular stars, Piper was number one.

Within weeks of his local debut, Piper captured the local television championship by winning a tournament final over Paul Jones in Richmond, Virginia, on November 1, 1980.[32] The prospect of bringing together two naturally gifted characters was too much for George Scott to pass up, and a Piper versus Flair feud began that same month. It wasn't the first time Flair had crossed paths with the Hot Scot from Canada, as they reportedly had at least one television match and one house show contest back in 1973 when Flair was 24 and Piper was 19.[33] Times were much different now, and both had since evolved into exceedingly confident performers. In fact, Piper was far above average as a trash talker, and his verbal torment of the blond U.S. champion was probably harsher than Flair had experienced before in wrestling. Piper called him "King Richard," made fun of his big nose, and, in one interview, called Flair the "Mae West of wrestling."[34]

Flair wasn't the kind of guy to take insults lying down. He dished it out equally, calling Piper's kilt a "skirt" and referring to him as a "punk." Their back-and-forth sparring was the epitome of entertaining, and they set the bar high for promos. The passion of their rivalry was present in their matches across the territory, and their hatred appeared very real. At the Dorton Arena in Raleigh on January 27, 1981, Piper displayed his wicked tricks by knocking out Flair with a foreign object. He scored a pin and captured the United States Heavyweight title.[35] Of course, the Flair-Piper feud didn't end there and lasted well into the summer. It's notable that outside the ring, Flair and Piper were instant friends and shared a zeal for life. When they weren't hindered by the rules of kayfabe and could be seen in public together, no nightspot in Charlotte was safe from their shenanigans, and the stories of their antics are legendary. The Nature Boy and the Rowdy One were in a class of their own.[36]

George Scott, the man behind the exponential growth of JCP and a key player in the rise of both Ric Flair and Jim Crockett himself, left the company late in the first quarter of 1981. His eight years as booker had transformed the territory and changed the lives of many people associated with mid-Atlantic wrestling. Just before his departure, he acted as a special referee for a handful of matches between Flair and Piper, including a few tag team bouts. On January 26, 1981, Scott returned to the ring to team with Flair in a loss to Piper and Valentine at the Greenville Auditorium.[37] With a job as booker for Georgia Championship Wrestling in Atlanta, Scott wasn't going far in terms of physical distance, but his exit marked the end of an era for Jim Crockett Promotions. Ole Anderson, one-half of the famed Minnesota Wrecking Crew, was hired to book JCP, and there was confidence that his fresh perspective would keep the promotion's success going.

Flair was getting closer to his date with destiny. In the mid-Atlantic territory, he continued to war with Piper and Valentine, while also engaging in a long, grueling battle with Ivan Koloff. He was a regular in tag team matches, working with Wahoo McDaniel, Blackjack Mulligan, and others against either Piper and Valentine, Piper and Koloff, or the Anderson brothers. But more important to his future as NWA World Heavyweight champion, Flair was back on the road to fulfill dates in Kansas City, St. Louis, Tampa, and Miami Beach. Between May and September 1981, he wrestled prospective future challengers for his championship and put each of them over — a time-honored tradition.[38] By losing matches to Jack Brisco, Mike Graham, Ted DiBiase, and others, he created future matchups that would drum up interest in various territories once he won the title.[39]

The momentum was building and Flair was perfectly positioned. His work was pristine, and his undying enthusiasm was respected by promoters. Between April 22 and May 5, 1981, he ran a streak of 13 straight days of bookings, which included 20 matches in five states and two countries. His tolerance for long trips on the road was tested and tested again. He made regular stops in Atlanta to work the Saturday telecast on WTBS (the station formerly known as WTCG) and received extensive nationwide exposure. Compliments from respected announcer Gordon Solie were invaluable. Finally, with the political wrangling over and the table set, Flair was headed for Kansas City to participate in the biggest match of his career.

The date was September 17, 1981, and the arena was the famed Memorial Hall, a landmark venue steeped in pro wrestling history.[40] Since it opened in the mid-1920s, the building had showcased luminaries of the sport, from Joe Stecher to John Pesek to Buddy Rogers. Orville Brown, the very first National Wrestling Alliance World Heavyweight champion, was an icon at the Memorial Hall in the 1940s, and it was fitting that forty years later such a consequential match returned to the same setting. To add luster to the affair, promoter Bob Geigel imported former NWA titleholder Lou Thesz to be the special referee, and it appeared that history and tradition were being acknowledged in the most appropriate way. Dusty Rhodes was the defending champion, as planned, having won the belt from Harley Race on June 21 in Atlanta.[41] As previously noted, Rhodes had been a personal mentor to Flair early in his career. The fact that Flair was in this position facing Rhodes seemed to speak to the manipulations of the wrestling gods — or it was fate, if that kind of thing is to be believed.

The match itself was exciting from beginning to end, lasting just under 24 minutes.[42] At a crucial moment, Flair locked in his dreaded figure-four and Rhodes was unable to break the hold. In the center of the ring, Rhodes writhed in pain and reached out for the ropes as Flair increased his leverage to secure a submission. Moments later, Dusty turned the move over and got his head under the ropes, causing Thesz to break the hold. Flair didn't waste a second. He rushed the corner post and went up to the top, but Rhodes was wise to this effort. He caught Flair and maneuvered his body for a big suplex out of the corner. After getting Flair up, Rhodes's knee buckled from the pain, and the two men dropped to the canvas. Flair landed on top in a pinning predicament, and Thesz counted to three.[43] The "Nature Boy" Ric Flair was the NWA

World Heavyweight champion and the new owner of the legendary "Ten Pounds of Gold."[44]

The friendship between Flair and Rhodes had been so important to Flair early in his career. They traveled the highways and byways together. They shared beers and laughs, wrestled in Japan, and formed a brotherhood that appeared unbreakable. Now, as they stood at the top of pro wrestling's proverbial ladder, they were being pulled apart by ego and the extremely competitive nature of both men. The respect between them remained, and the spirited rivalry between Flair and Rhodes was just beginning. Their greatest battles were yet to come.

CHAPTER 8
"DIAMONDS ARE FOREVER"

The championship victory of Ric Flair over Dusty Rhodes for the National Wrestling Alliance World Heavyweight title instantly elevated Flair into an exclusive club. His name was etched onto a list that included Lou Thesz, Buddy Rogers, Dory Funk Jr., Jack Brisco, and other exceptional legends. Flair was the 15th man to hold the NWA championship, which dated back to 1948.[1] The prestige of the NWA title was universal, and thanks to the hard work of previous champions, the belt was firmly established around the globe. The heavyweight champions of the American Wrestling Association and of the World Wrestling Federation, the other two major promotions in the United States, were each picked by one person, Verne Gagne and Vincent J. McMahon respectively, while the NWA title was decided by a majority vote of nine people. To insiders, that was a meaningful distinction, and it illustrated the significance of the NWA championship spot.

Flair's life changed in a big way after winning the strap on September 17, 1981. Instead of returning to the mid-Atlantic region the next night for a booking at the Richmond Coliseum, Flair traveled to Des Moines, Iowa, where he replaced the former champ, Dusty Rhodes, against Harley Race.[2] This was another NWA tradition: the incoming champion always assumed the scheduled bookings for the previous titleholder on the calendar maintained by Jim Barnett in Atlanta. This schedule was booked months in advance, and it was tailored to fit the needs of the NWA rather than the specific champion. Had Flair not won the belt that night, he would've traveled back to his home region and wrestled in a city he'd performed in hundreds of times before.[3] But Des Moines was uncharted territory for Flair, who was a relative unknown outside the exposure he received on WTBS cable television.[4] Diehard local fans would've also recognized him from articles in newsstand magazines.

The Des Moines audience, though, was expecting Rhodes, and the news of Flair's win might have been a disappointment to those wanting to see the charismatic fan favorite from Texas. Nevertheless, it was Flair's responsibility to enter each territory and demonstrate the traits of a champion, regardless of the opponent or situation. He had to deal with a lot of fan reaction as news spread about the title change, and there was a period of adaptation and acceptance. In many parts of the country, his notoriety was reliant on the WTBS national telecast, and it was vitally important to get him back in front of those TV cameras as quickly as possible to publicize his title victory. That's why he flew to Atlanta first thing the next morning for a studio appearance alongside host Gordon Solie. Solie, notably, revealed the title change as the *Georgia Championship Wrestling* program opened, and he began by saying he had "some rather, very disturbing news."

"We received a telegram yesterday regarding the World Heavyweight championship," Solie said. "We're very sorry to report that Dusty Rhodes, the American Dream, has lost the World Heavyweight championship. He was defeated by Ric Flair in Kansas City."[5] The announcement was unexpected and startling to most fans, as Rhodes's popularity was stronger than ever. When Flair arrived on set holding the NWA belt, disbelievers were convinced that it hadn't been some kind of mistake. Flair was in fine form, telling the large viewing audience,

> I came down here, just as I've appeared on every major wrestling program in the country, and I told the people that I was born with a golden spoon. That I wore the finest

clothes money could buy — the most expensive jewelry — driven in the biggest cars — flew in the nicest airplanes. Everything I've ever wanted in life has been mine. If I couldn't buy it, I went out and got it. Well, there was no buying the NWA championship!

It took a superb athlete, in superb condition, mentally and physically — one that is not going to be denied. I wanted this. I went out and got it. And now, this completes Ric Flair's attire. The biggest gold of them all — the most coveted trophy. It's mine, Gordon Solie. If there's a wrestler out there that wants to find out where he stands, where he ranks in professional wrestling, the greatest sport in the world today, then he better get in the ring with Ric Flair — because I am the illusion destroyer. There's a lot of men out there that think they ought to be where I am today, and I will destroy that illusion. Just sign the contract, get in the ring, and the great one, who is going to ride on forever, will show you why he is wearing the big gold now and for a long, long time.[6]

The overconfidence and cockiness of Flair was palpable, and it was quite unlike his predecessor, Dusty Rhodes. However, when Flair was back home in the mid-Atlantic area, his tone was much different.

In talking with Bob Caudle and David Crockett on Jim Crockett's *Mid-Atlantic Championship Wrestling* program, Flair was humble and respectful about winning the NWA title:

It's the greatest honor that I've ever achieved in any aspect of my life. Gentlemen, as anyone associated with wrestling knows, this is the key, this is the ultimate trophy. It's the most prestigious award in all professional wrestling. I feel I worked hard for a number of years to achieve this. I'm not saying it was because of my tremendous skill or my ability, or anything else that won it for me. It was one of those nights. It was my night. Things went my way, and now I'm the world champion. On behalf of the people out there, on behalf of myself, on behalf of the people who stood behind me, Crockett Promotions, etcetera, I will do my best to be a great world champion. I will do my best to be a great athlete. And I will do my best to show everyone out there that I deserve the recognition of being called the National Wrestling Alliance World Heavyweight wrestling champion. Thank you very much.[7]

The two appearances illustrated the dual role Flair was playing. On television shown across the country and in various NWA territories, he was an aggressive, take-no-prisoners heel. He was the type of wrestler who'd take shortcuts and cheat his way to an advantage. He'd poke a rival in the eyes and land a low blow, much to the chagrin of audiences, and if he was feeling particularly devious, he'd torture a prelim guy with his figure-four by holding it for a few moments after gaining a submission win. It was all part of his villainous act, and the champion was at the top of his game. "You think it's easy being the best looking man in the whole wide world, and be the world champion too?" Flair asked Gordon Solie, with his Nature Boy persona in full effect. "Well, brother, it is easy, especially when you're Ric Flair and you were born with a golden spoon and life has always been what you wanted it to be."[8]

In the mid-Atlantic region, before his home audience, Flair was a baby face, and his calm, courteous demeanor was that of a popular, sportsmanlike champion. The dichotomy was fascinating, and Flair continued to work his magic on both sides of the fence. Flair's first weekend as champion already exemplified his commitment to the NWA. After leaving the Central States in a rush to make it to Atlanta for a TV taping early on Saturday, September 19, Flair had to return to Kansas for an evening show in Junction City, about two hours west of Kansas City off Interstate 70. The event, with an 8:00 start time, was headlined by Flair and "Bulldog" Bob Brown at the Auditorium.[9] Junction City, with a population of less than 20,000, was a regular stop on the Central States circuit and saw most of the territory's top stars. It received the WTBS telecast as well, and Flair's title status would've been known by local fans who had watched the program earlier that day.[10]

One of the major adjustments Flair had to contend with was the range of his in-ring opposition. Wrestling for Jim Crockett the past seven years, he was never at a loss for top-quality rivals, and he usually engaged in long-running feuds with capable foes who only served to make him a better worker. As the traveling champion, he was booked against an endless stream of wrestlers of different sizes, shapes, and skill levels. Without question, he would face grapplers of much lesser ability, and it was his job to bring out the best in each adversary by working twice as hard. Going into the ring against a new opponent presented a lot of challenges, and Flair had to make the magic happen on the fly. On the other hand, he would be matched up with many of the finest wrestlers in the world, some for the very first time, and his aptitude would be sharpened tenfold.

Such a situation arose during Flair's first trip to Japan as NWA champion between October 6 and October 9, 1981. On the first night, he won a three falls match from a rising star in All Japan, Genichiro Tenryu, whom Flair had actually wrestled in 1980 when Tenryu toured JCP.[11] The next night, he measured up with former NWA titleholder Terry Funk in the opening stanza of what would be a years-long rivalry. Outside the ring, Flair and Funk were friends and had traveled together in the mid-Atlantic area in 1976–77.[12] Their exciting bout in Yokohama ended in a double countout, and a rematch was expected. Before returning to the United States, Flair participated in his second-ever singles contest with ex-Olympian Jumbo Tsuruta. Tsuruta was on the brink of international superstardom, and his wrestling knowledge set him apart from most of his contemporaries. Flair had lost his first bout against Jumbo in 1978, but he was victorious in Tokyo on October 9, 1981.[13]

Directly following his tour, Flair and several All Japan dignitaries traveled to Las Vegas to partake in the annual National Wrestling

Alliance convention.[14] Although being in Sin City presented every opportunity for revelry, the world champion had an exasperating legal issue hanging over his head. The matter stemmed from a fight at the posh 2001 VIP Club in Charlotte two months earlier. On August 2, 1981, Flair had been approached by a 29-year-old patron of the establishment, who said that wrestling was "fake."[15] The "loudmouth drunk," as Flair's attorney later called him, put his hand on the wrestler to spin him around, and changed the entire tone of the encounter.[16] Flair slapped the individual three times in response, and when it appeared that the man was going to hit Flair with a barstool, Wahoo McDaniel jumped in to defend his longtime friend.[17] The civilian never had a chance in a physical confrontation with two world-class pro wrestlers.

Assault charges were filed, and Flair was briefly placed under arrest.[18] The negative publicity surrounding the story, including coverage on the front page of the *Charlotte News*, was exactly what he didn't need, especially since he was in the final lead-up to his NWA title victory against Dusty Rhodes.[19] On October 14, 1981, two days after the NWA convention, Flair sat in a Mecklenburg County District courtroom, as Judge P.B. Beachum listened to arguments on both sides of the case. In the end, he found Flair and McDaniel guilty of simple assault, and McDaniel received a 30-day suspended sentence, plus a $50 fine. Flair was forced to pay only the court costs, which amounted to $31, but he wasn't happy about the decision.[20] An appeal was filed on his behalf, and the case was ultimately dismissed.[21] The ordeal was the perfect reminder to avoid hassles with fans. Nothing good could arise from that type of situation.

Flair ventured to the Dallas and Tulsa territories in October 1981, but otherwise he mainly worked the JCP territory and in Georgia prior to heading to Florida on October 26.[22] On that evening in West Palm Beach, he beat the state heavyweight champion, Charlie Cook, in 14 minutes.[23] Florida was long known as a hotbed for exciting performers and creative angles. The territory was centered in Eddie Graham's Tampa headquarters and extended to Orlando, Jacksonville, and Miami

Beach, with a dozen other regular spots on the map. The year-round good weather was an enticing lure for reputable wrestlers who wanted to evade cold conditions in the winter while steadily making good money. Over the course of his six-day run in the area, Ric Flair wrestled Charlie Cook and Mike Graham twice and also had successful title defenses with Harley Race and Dusty Rhodes.[24] When he returned to Florida for four days in November, he again wrestled Rhodes and Graham, and he had two bouts with Jack Brisco as well.[25]

Twice in November 1981, Flair ventured to Knoxville, Tennessee, where he had a personal interest in the local promotion. In fact, he had teamed with Blackjack Mulligan to purchase the territory from Ron Fuller for a reported $150,000.[26] With a Saturday television program, christened *NWA Championship Wrestling*, hosted by Les Thatcher, the Mulligan-Flair group imported a respectable lineup of wrestlers, from Big John Studd to Don Carson to the Iron Sheik.[27] In addition, they featured up-and-coming talent such as Terry Taylor, Tim Horner, and Jack Mulligan Jr., Blackjack's son. The 20-year-old Mulligan Jr. was one of the best newcomers in the business, and he had known Flair for years. "I grew up around Ric, from my high school days on," he later explained. "I trained with Ric. He is a close friend of mine and he helped me train in wrestling when I was in high school and in football. I have a lot of respect for him."[28] A few years earlier, Mulligan had attended East Mecklenburg High School in Charlotte.

The Knoxville promotion had all the potential in the world to be financially viable. Their operations at Chilhowee Park were strong, and it appeared they had the right elements in place for success. Blackjack was the lead heavyweight star, and despite the dire need for Flair to become a regular, his commitments to the NWA were more important. Between May and October 1981, he put in only two arena appearances, on May 29 and July 31. They compensated by inserting taped match segments and interviews with Flair into the weekend telecast, but the promotion struggled as the year went on. By the time November rolled around, the territory was flailing, and Mulligan was relying on talent from Jim

Crockett and Jim Barnett. Any hope for Knoxville to exist as an independent entity was gone. Both of Flair's matches there in November 1981 were against the "Russian Bear" Ivan Koloff, and their second contest occurred on the afternoon of Thanksgiving, November 26.[29]

As was customary, the focus of professional wrestling in the mid-Atlantic region shifted to the Greensboro Coliseum on the evening of Thanksgiving every year. Flair was the headliner in 1981, and he left Knoxville in a hurry to make the crucial booking, as did four others — Koloff, Johnny Weaver, and the Mulligans, Junior and Senior. Mulligan Jr. was in for a historic night in his young wrestling career. In the finals of a special 16-man elimination tournament, he pinned Koloff to win a brand-new 1982 Cadillac. Flair was victorious as well. He pinned Ole Anderson after a piledriver in a cage to retain his NWA championship. The card drew the largest attendance for wrestling at the Greensboro Coliseum, 15,136 people, and was another smashing achievement for JCP.[30] Before the year was up, Flair jumped around the horn for matches in St. Louis, Birmingham, Toronto, and San Juan, before spending Christmas night at the Omni Coliseum in Atlanta, where he defeated Dusty Rhodes.

Flair's feud with Dusty remained a hot ticket. In the opulent atmosphere of the Chase Park Plaza Hotel, St. Louis announcer Larry Matysik complimented Flair's wrestling ability during a December 1981 telecast of *Wrestling at the Chase*. Flair was having an easy time against preliminary worker David Price of Memphis and freely jawed with the audience. The close proximity of the television cameras to the ring caught the champion's every infuriating word. "This is Dusty Rhodes right here!" he shouted, before landing a suplex and then applying his figure-four for a quick submission. Matysik openly wondered about the status of the NWA World title after the New Year, because Flair was defending his belt against Rhodes at a major show in St. Louis on January 1, 1982. The important bout was the main attraction for promoter Sam Muchnick's retirement show, an event that was closing the books on a career that began five decades earlier in the 1930s.[31]

The excitement for the card and the public's desire to pay respects to Muchnick were massive, and the 11,000-seat Kiel Auditorium was deemed too small to accommodate the demand for tickets. The St. Louis Checkerdome was rented instead, and a sellout of 19,918 paying customers jammed the venue to see the wrestling spectacular live and in person.[32] In the main event, Flair beat Rhodes in two of three falls with Gene Kiniski serving as guest referee.[33] Muchnick, who had served as National Wrestling Alliance president 21 times, had committed his life to the organization, and his brilliant leadership and management of the World Heavyweight championship was responsible for the esteem of the NWA. Through thick and thin, he was always the voice of reason, and his retirement was a milestone moment for the Alliance. An ownership group led by Bob Geigel assumed control of St. Louis, but there was simply no replacing Sam Muchnick.[34]

The split personalities of Flair — an obnoxious heel in most NWA cities, and a popular hero in the mid-Atlantic territory — continued to play out.[35] National publications pandered to the wider audience and regularly named Flair the "Number One Most Hated." Readers in JCP areas disagreed with that rating, but the tides seemed to be turning in February 1982, and a TV match in Charlotte illustrated the slow metamorphosis of Flair's personality in the local ring.[36] Flair's opponent was Jay Youngblood, a popular 26-year-old, second-generation grappler from Texas, and he was full of the fighting spirit to win.[37] He was so energized against Flair that several times, it appeared he might stun the champion with a pinfall victory. Flair was overwhelmed and frustrated by Youngblood's aggressive assault, and after the bell rang to call an end to their bout, he continued to pummel the youthful star, which was a classic heel maneuver. He only stopped because Ricky Steamboat jumped in between the two athletes and pleaded with Flair to halt his attack.[38]

Flair later defended his actions by saying he didn't hear the bell. He reminded fans that he used to talk about being a "kiss stealing, wheeling dealing, Cadillac driving son of a gun," and that was before he won the world championship. "If you can imagine what kind of lifestyle I've got now," he said with a confident glare. "You're looking at the world champion, and remember one thing, diamonds are forever!"[39] It was another legendary promo by the best talker in the sport, and it was made even more unique by his willingness to face baby faces Youngblood, Steamboat, and Tommy Rich in defense of his title. On February 21, 1982, in Greensboro, Flair and Steamboat put on another technical clinic, and the champion won the bout.[40] As he rolled from the ring and collected his belt, Sgt. Slaughter and his Privates, Jim Nelson and Don Kernodle, attacked Steamboat. They were unmerciful in their assault, and Flair, demonstrating his true colors, jumped into the melee and attempted to save Steamboat.

At the time, the 6-foot-5, 300-pound Slaughter was one of Jim Crockett's top heels and the reigning United States Heavyweight champion. Billed as a former Marine from Parris Island, he was originally from the Minneapolis area, and, like Flair, he was a product of Verne Gagne's training camp. Flair's attempt to save Steamboat was unsuccessful, as Slaughter and his underlings turned their attention to him and beat the world titleholder bloody. Steamboat ended up running the trio off with a chair and carrying the wounded Flair back to the dressing room for medical attention.[41] The entire angle reaffirmed Flair's status as a fan favorite and set up a contest against Slaughter in Charlotte on April 4, which Flair won by disqualification.[42] But the national perception of Flair as a heel, and the fact that he was simply better in that role than as a baby face, made his full turn in mid-Atlantic inevitable. Throughout May and June 1982, he battled Wahoo McDaniel and Jack Brisco on house shows throughout the territory.

In Greensboro on August 7, 1982, Flair displayed the traits that had earned him the title of the "Dirtiest Player in the Game." In the midst of an arduous clash with McDaniel, the two wrestlers traded falls and were fighting for victory when Flair leapt from the ring and snatched the timekeeper's bell. In what was perceived to be a desperate attempt to not only maim McDaniel but save his belt, Flair smashed McDaniel and was disqualified.[43] The next week, Jim Crockett stepped up his on-camera presence to magnify the heat on Flair in the aftermath of the Greensboro bout. He announced that he had resigned as NWA president in protest of the board of directors' failure to punish the champion for his deliberate scheme to injure McDaniel. Flair proclaimed that he'd never wrestle McDaniel again.[44] During the August 21 telecast of *Mid-Atlantic Championship Wrestling*, Flair had strong words for Crockett and McDaniel and threatened to really hurt McDaniel the next time around. He then talked up Crockett's riches, adding, "I'm a big man too!"[45]

Outside the mid-Atlantic region, Flair made the rounds and continued to wrestle the best in the business. In Florida, "Hacksaw" Butch Reed of Kansas City was a perennially strong contender for his championship. Their feud kicked off with a special television engagement on February 17, 1982, that saw the two competitors wrestle to a 30-minute draw. Flair boldly called for the bout to continue, only to have Reed pin him in overtime. The nontitle loss fueled the interest in matches across the state, and attendance was impressive in places like Miami Beach, where they sold out the Convention Hall on April 7 with 5,724 fans in attendance.[46] Between February and October 1982, Flair and Reed had at least 20 contests in Florida, including a handful of 60-minute draws and cage matches. Jack Brisco scored a nontitle TV match pinfall victory over Flair on *Mid-Atlantic Championship Wrestling* in Charlotte in August 1982, which similarly increased the excitement for their matches in the area.[47]

Dallas was prime territory for professional wrestling, and Jack Adkisson was building momentum thanks to the popularity of his three sons, David, Kerry, and Kevin Von Erich. Flair had wrestled David, who stood 6-foot-7, three times to that point, each in St. Louis, and Flair was victorious twice. Their last bout, on November 20, 1981, saw Flair win the first and third falls to retain his NWA belt.[48] In Dallas, on January 25, 1982, he faced the youngest of the three brothers, Kerry, for the first time. Kerry was about five inches shorter than David, but what he lacked in size, he made up for in good looks and strength. He was a former football player and had set records as a discus thrower in school. Although Flair won their initial match by disqualification, it was clear that they were in the infancy of a long rivalry.[49] Twice in 1982, Flair visited the Portland territory and warded off the challenges of Buddy Rose, Brett Sawyer, and Rocky Johnson.[50] The local promoter, Don Owen, was as old-school as they came, and he was well-liked by the boys for his fair payoffs and congenial attitude.

An enthusiastic reporter for *The Ring's Wrestling* magazine, Kate Mast, lived in the Pacific Northwest and hoped to interview Flair when he came to town. There hadn't been a large feature article on the champion, and rumor was that he wouldn't do extensive interviews. Nevertheless, she made an inquiry to the promotion, and Flair agreed to sit down with her and photographer Linda Churchill for a lengthy discussion about his life. "Flair was very cooperative as he told us about his background," Mast later wrote. "We were impressed with his polite and gentlemanly manner."[51] He opened up about his upbringing, saying that he was born with the "proverbial silver spoon in his mouth," and his athletic accomplishments in high school. He discussed his training routine, including doing more than 500 Hindu squats every day, and his interests in music. On a personal note, he revealed that he was divorced with two children.[52]

Of course, the insightful four-page article illustrated Flair's bombastic personality and featured some of his over-the-top comments. But Mast was witness to Flair's personable side, and it was an eye-opener. He wasn't just the wild character he portrayed on WTBS. There was depth to Ric Flair, and anyone who had gotten close to him outside of the ring, quickly grasped that fact. From time to time, Flair let down his guard in public to give people a glimpse at the man behind the scenes. Before he won the world title, a television station in Charlotte did a favorable profile of him, perhaps presenting the most realistic depiction of Flair in the media to that juncture yet. On *Down Home with the Carolina Camera* with host C.J. Underwood in 1981, Flair revealed that he was adopted, discussed the difficulties of having a family as a wrestler, and mentioned his "new girlfriend," Beth.[53]

Elizabeth Ann "Beth" Harrell, the daughter of Robert and Mary Harrell, grew up in the suburbs of Tallahassee, Florida.[54] The oldest of six children, she graduated from Florida High School in 1973 and attended North Florida Junior College, in addition to Tallahassee Community College.[55] Her relationship with Flair wasn't exactly "new," as they had met around June 1978 and moved in together five months later.[56] There was no question that his breakup with Leslie was hard on family and friends, and after several years of separation, they were still legally married. Around this time, Flair was dealing with burdensome tax problems with both the Internal Revenue Service and the North Carolina Department of Revenue.[57] In a late 1982 legal document, Leslie named Charlotte lawyer Michael S. Shulimson as her power of attorney to negotiate with the IRS "in connection with any tax indebtedness already created or to be created."[58] She was living in New Hope, Minnesota, a suburb of Minneapolis, and raising Megan and David.

To assist with his tax issue, Flair appointed Thomas Rodney "Rod" Autrey and Dennis Lorenz Guthrie as his power of attorney, replacing John A. Mraz.[59] Autrey was a graduate of the University of North Carolina and a certified public accountant, whereas Guthrie was a Vietnam veteran and graduate of Mercer University School of Law.[60] Originally from St. Louis, Guthrie attended Myers Park High School in Charlotte as a classmate of Jim Crockett Jr. and had over a decade of experience, as an assistant district attorney and in private practice law, by the early 1980s.[61] He would not only represent Flair in legal matters, but Crockett and other wrestlers as well. It wasn't unusual for him to get a call in the middle of the night from a grappler in need of assistance, and Guthrie bailed a number of guys out of jail during the chaotic 1980s. In deference to his legal knowledge and ability to get them out of trouble, he was nicknamed Loophole, and Guthrie embraced the turbulent nature of the sport.[62]

Flair's tax problems were complex. According to a 1980 court filing, he owed in excess of $135,000.[63] The year before, in March 1979, his entire paycheck was garnished by the North Carolina Department of Revenue to pay back taxes for 1975 and 1976. To assist with the repayment of his debt, Flair hired Lillian Scott, the wife of booker George Scott, to be his bookkeeper. Through their tireless work, and the financial arrangements made by Scott, Flair's debt was reduced by over $40,000 during one 11-month period.[64] On top of that, Flair entered into a binding agreement with the Briarbend Investment Company, an outfit comprised of George Scott, Jim Crockett Jr., and David Crockett. The deal, which gave Flair a one-time lump sum payment of $30,000, granted Briarbend officials exclusive promotional rights for the blond athlete. In addition, Scott and the Crocketts would receive 10 percent of his gross earnings over the term of the agreement.[65]

The combined strain of his divorce and the pressure from tax authorities was undoubtedly difficult, and Flair kept his mind focused on his job, working harder than ever to satisfy NWA promoters and wrestling fans throughout the circuit. This wouldn't be the last time Flair found himself backed against the wall with respect to money. In fact, living the affluent lifestyle he established and enjoyed was going to cost a fortune to maintain. But since he prioritized "image enhancement," it was part of the role he'd adopted when he became the Nature Boy, and the rich playboy persona fit him like a glove. With his success and tremendous income, there were bound to be problems, and there was truth to the old saying: money *is* the root of all evil.

CHAPTER 9

THE MAGNIFICENT ONE

D uring his formative years in pro wrestling, Ric Flair was a devoted and dedicated student of the business. He was mindful of his position as a novice and keenly respectful of his elders, observing them with appreciation and awe. When Flair was breaking in, Verne Gagne was the AWA World Heavyweight champion, and Gagne's eye for detail, precision, and intellect were admirable qualities. Gagne was a dignified athlete who handled himself splendidly in the press and before audiences, and his reputation was well earned. After jumping to Jim Crockett Promotions, Flair saw the work of NWA World champions Jack Brisco, Terry Funk, and Harley Race. Each man was different in style, mannerisms, and personality, and their distinctive methods set them apart from others in the industry. There was no argument: they were the best of the best.

Flair witnessed these great world heavyweight champions at their peak and saw how they handled adversity, aggressive crowds, and the responsibilities of wearing the coveted title belts of their base organizations. The key word for Gagne, Brisco, Funk, and Race was *professionalism*, and Flair and other subsequent titleholders had to live up to their high standards. As a result of Flair's sensitivity to the sport's traditions and his love for wrestling, he understood the gravity of the position he was in as NWA World champion. He knew promoters depended on him, and he wanted to prove he was the best in the world. So he worked harder and harder, pushing himself to extremes of mental and physical conditioning. And since he was going to be the first NWA World champion since Harley Race in 1977–79 to hold the belt for longer than 10 months, he was in a terrific position to shine.

There was a basic formula to booking the NWA titleholder. Sam Muchnick, for years, maintained a sensible scheme to the champion's travels, and it wasn't an easy job. He appeased demanding promoters, while creating a schedule that didn't completely burn out the wrestler. He moved the champion in and out of a territory within five to six days and aimed to give him one or two days off a week. But it didn't always work out. Sometimes days off were hard to find, especially as the champion traversed the wrestling landscape. Jim Barnett, after taking over Muchnick's responsibilities, continued the same patterns and also struggled to make everyone happy. Often Barnett received last-minute phone calls from desperate promoters, and the champion was asked to take on additional dates. Previous champions had complained about this practice, but it didn't bother Ric Flair. He was receptive and agreeable.[1]

Most of the time, a weekend off was an impossibility. Flair not only worked Saturday and Sunday, but he typically had two matches on Sunday when in the mid-Atlantic region. He'd wrestle a matinee in Asheville and then travel to Charlotte for a program that night. This was on top of a full week of bookings, and altogether, it amounted to eight matches in seven days. Things would get a little dicey when in the middle of a week-long run in one territory, the champion had to fly out for a midweek appearance elsewhere and then return the next day. This kind of thing happened regularly. For example, on June 22, 1982, Flair wrestled Leroy Brown to a double countout in Saginaw, Michigan.[2] The next day, he flew to Miami Beach for a sellout event against Dusty Rhodes at the Convention Center — a match that Rhodes won under bunkhouse rules.[3] Flair traveled back to Michigan on June 24 to beat Brown in a rematch at Grand Rapids.

The Michigan bouts were booked by the Atlanta office as part of the expansion of Georgia Championship Wrestling. Based on the strength of its WTBS cable program, Jim Barnett and Ole Anderson decided to venture outside the Peach State to operate in an area previously run by the Sheik out of Detroit. They began promoting Columbus, Ohio, in September 1980, and followed up with events in Dayton, Canton, and Toledo, with further shows in Michigan in 1982.[4] The ambitious move drew an audience in a stale territory, and talent was the major reason for their success. All-star cards featuring Dusty Rhodes, Mr. Wrestling II, Tommy Rich, and Brad Armstrong electrified local audiences and recharged the wrestling scene. Flair's appearances were equally important, and fans were enthusiastic about seeing the flamboyant NWA champion in person.[5] His squash matches and interview segments on WTBS were must-see TV.

One of the highlights in 1982 was the special title vs. title match held on July 4 in Atlanta between Flair and WWF Heavyweight champion Bob Backlund. The latter, who was six months younger than Flair and also from Minnesota, had dethroned "Superstar" Billy Graham for his championship in 1978.[6] His lengthy title reign included four bouts with Harley Race when he was wearing the NWA belt and a contest with AWA titleholder Nick Bockwinkel.[7] Champion vs. champion matches were a rare occurrence in wrestling, facilitated by the working relationships between promoters. In this case, Vincent J. McMahon and Jim Barnett, two longtime allies, were the direct sponsors, and although there was the illusion of determining, once and for all, the undisputed heavyweight kingpin, there was never any real move to unify the NWA and WWF championships.[8]

Flair and Backlund were no strangers to each other. They had wrestled once before on July 15, 1979, in Toronto, and the WWF champion won by countout. The circumstances were different headed into their Independence Day contest at the Omni Coliseum, and during a pre-bout promotional interview on WTBS, Flair displayed his sly arrogance, casually referring to himself as "The Great One." Flair said, "Bobby Backlund, you're a hell of a man, but you're not Ric Flair, remember that!" Backlund, a traditional baby face, was poised and low-key throughout the segment, and attempted to shake Flair's hand at the end, but the Nature Boy turned his back and walked away.[9] Both historically and technically, the dream match at the Omni was memorable, but the finish left a lot to be desired, as the bout ended in an inconclusive double countout after 22 minutes.[10]

In St. Louis, Flair engaged in a heated feud with a distinctly different champion, Dick the Bruiser, a fierce brawler whom Flair had grown up watching on AWA TV in Minneapolis. The 52-year-old Bruiser was the exact opposite of Bob Backlund, and instead of scientific grappling, he prided himself on cigar smoking, street fighting, and ruthless aggression. Bruiser was in the midst of his third reign as the NWA Missouri Heavyweight titleholder and was considered the top local contender to Flair's belt. They wrestled twice, on March 26 and June 12, 1982, and attendance was 10,272 and 19,027 respectively. Flair nearly met defeat in their first bout, and Bruiser was later dubbed the "uncrowned champion" by Larry Matysik on St. Louis TV.[11] Their rematch at the Checkerdome was before a massive house, and Flair's resilience was his saving grace. With a back body drop, he scored a third fall pin and again beat Bruiser to remain champion.[12] Despite their box office success, this was the final time Flair and Bruiser wrestled in a singles match.[13]

As the NWA champion, Flair was called upon to satisfy bookings in towns of all sizes, and at various times, he fulfilled public relations chores as well. On August 9, 1982, he delighted a group of about 65 people at J.R. Mead's restaurant in downtown Wichita at a party arranged by KARD-TV marketing manager Bob Martinez and promoter Bob Geigel. In that kind of social scene, Flair was at his most charming, and he served as an excellent ambassador for the regional promotion and the NWA. "Ric really liked Wichita and the people here," Martinez told a reporter.[14] A few hours later, Flair and many of his new friends went down Douglas Avenue for a show at the Century II Convention Center, where he beat Mike George.[15] The Wichita date was the first of six straight nights of wrestling for the champion in the territory, and included stops in Joplin, Topeka, Kansas City, Hannibal, and Hutchinson.

Following his match in Hannibal, Missouri, on Friday, August 13, Flair made a rare trip to Memphis for a Saturday morning live broadcast of *Championship Wrestling* from the WMC television studio.[16] For several years, Memphis promoter Jerry Jarrett had maintained a loose affiliation to the NWA, and between 1979 and '81, he recognized a Continental Wrestling Association World Heavyweight champion in his territory. Jarrett was ready to roll the dice on a remarkably bankable angle between Flair and the top baby face in Memphis, Jerry Lawler, and Flair's TV appearance laid the foundation for a future high drawing affair at the Mid-South Coliseum. It also marked Flair's first wrestling showing in the city of his birth. With famed announcer Lance Russell holding the microphone, Flair was subdued in his comments at first, but his condescension toward Memphis and local fans was soon very apparent.

"Ladies and gentlemen, prepare yourself," Flair told the viewing audience, "because the Magnificent One is going to show you why he wears the Ten Pounds of Gold, [and] that makes him the greatest professional wrestler alive today."[17] Jerry Lawler spoke with Russell in a subsequent interview and expressed a desire to shake Flair's hand. Flair, who was en route to the ring for a planned squash match against Rick McCord, approached Lawler, and while extending his hand, asked, "What was the name?" Flair's dismissive response was expert-level psychology, and made fans burn in fury. Of course, Flair knew Lawler and had wrestled on the same shows as him multiple times in Florida over the previous year. Lawler convinced Flair to give up his easy match with McCord to wrestle him in a 10-minute contest with the NWA championship on the line. "You really want 10 minutes with the world champion?" Flair asked. "You want 10 minutes with Ric Flair? Daddy, you got it!"[18]

Early on in their bout, Flair and Lawler were evenly matched, and Lawler made some crafty reversals that raised the excitement of the small studio audience. As the match proceeded, Flair took the advantage and landed his routine vertical suplex. He applied a figure-four, and soon thereafter, the bell rang, signifying a time-limit draw. Flair's blood was boiling, and he asked if Lawler had given up, and after learning that he had not, he demanded another five minutes. However, Lawler quickly turned the tides, landing a series of punches and then his trademark second rope fist drop, only to see Flair rush from the ring back to the dressing room. Lawler told Russell, "I'm the champion," based on his apparent countout victory, but Flair refuted that claim. "Produce the contract," he demanded. Flair was livid and handed an unsigned $10,000 check to manager Jimmy Hart as a bounty on Lawler's scalp, a fee he'd pay upon delivery of "the blood, and the sweat, and the guts" of the Memphis hero.[19]

Russell called it "a rather unchampionship-like gesture." Nevertheless, it was clear the Flair-Lawler rivalry was headed for a spectacular payday, but due to wrestling politics, the expected rematch didn't happen in 1982. Instead, Jerry Jarrett strengthened his ties to Verne Gagne's American Wrestling Association, and he brought Nick Bockwinkel and his version of the world title to Memphis. On December 27, 1982, Lawler beat Bockwinkel for a claim to the championship before 10,086 fans at the Coliseum.[20] The victory gave Lawler great credibility, and in the eyes of fans, he was finally able to achieve the goal he'd been after for nearly a decade. Bockwinkel disputed the loss, and the title was reportedly held up pending a rematch — a contest in which Bockwinkel would prevail. But that didn't matter. Lawler was the big winner, and conceivably, this was the type of scenario Jarrett had originally wanted with Lawler and Flair, but when that was no longer an option, he shifted from the NWA and to the AWA champion.[21]

Immediately after the Memphis studio appearance, Flair was back on the road, headed to Kansas to fulfill his final date of his Central States tour. His exceptional showing in Memphis was matched by a unique card in Hutchinson, a town about 50 miles northwest of Wichita. The circumstances couldn't have been more extraordinary. For one, that Saturday was the hottest day of the year in Hutchinson, with temperatures reaching 105 degrees. Just before the program was set to start, the town was hit by a dramatic thunderstorm with gusty winds and dangerous lightning.[22] For a typical indoor arena show, the weather conditions might have hindered attendance but otherwise been of no concern. But Flair was heading for a special wrestling engagement in a makeshift ring outside the O'Mara Pontiac-Toyota car dealership.[23] Flair had actually met the owner of the dealership, Michael O'Mara, earlier in the week at the cocktail party in Wichita.[24]

O'Mara, a mid-30s businessman with an entrepreneurial spirit, had turned the monotony of car sales into a fun experience, with gimmicks to boost customer turnout at his dealership. One of his more popular strategies was a "What would you do to drive a Toyota" contest, and his marketing tactics were highly successful.[25] Wrestling was a natural extension for him, and through promoter Bob Geigel, talent was coordinated for a program on August 14, 1982. In the headline act, Ric Flair would defend his championship against the brother of mid-Atlantic favorite Jay Youngblood, Mark Romero.[26] In effort to make the event more comfortable for the performers, O'Mara rented a nearby gym for the wrestlers to change and shower, and he arranged for transportation to and from the dealership. "[The wrestlers] were all first-class guys," O'Mara later said. "Gracious, appreciative, engaging. Just nice guys."[27]

Regardless of the crowd size or venue, Flair had a job to do, and first and foremost, he was a professional. He easily could have railed against the small-town outdoor exhibition, claiming it was beneath his status as world champion. But he didn't, and O'Mara remembered him for his congenial, easygoing personality. The way Flair handled it was the mark of a real champion, on par with his predecessors. While he might have been the first NWA champion to appear at a dealership, Lou Thesz and other Alliance titleholders had wrestled before small audiences during their reigns, always upholding the dignity of the sport, the organization, and its championship belt. If Bob Geigel was testing Flair's commitment to the position, the Nature Boy passed with flying colors. His appearance in Hutchinson wasn't exactly financially rewarding, as attendance to the show was free, but in terms of connecting to people and local businesses, as well as establishing social ties in the territory, it was a victory on all fronts.[28]

Puerto Rico was becoming a frequent stop for Flair. Capital Sports Promotions was operated by Victor Jovica and Carlos Colón, and local crowds were hot for professional wrestling in 1982. Jim Crockett had built a good relationship with Jovica and Colón, and the goodwill extended to Flair. Toward the end of August 1982, the NWA champion headed to Puerto Rico for an 11-day stint. The trip was timed with a mass influx of NWA members to San Juan for the organization's annual convention, held on August 29 and 30. The day before the meetings were to begin, Flair wrestled the Invader (José González) in front of 15,000 spectators at Hiram Bithorn Stadium in San Juan, and he was pinned in an apparent title change. Officials reversed the decision and disqualified the challenger when it was determined that he had thrown Flair over the top rope.[29]

Only 10 members attended the NWA convention, while eight others designated proxies to represent them in San Juan.[30] Surprisingly, Jim Crockett not only stepped down as the president, but also as a member of the board of directors.[31] There was a long discussion about the booking of the World Heavyweight champion, and several clarifications were made. There was seemingly an expectation by certain members to receive visits by Flair whenever they requested him. According to the meeting minutes, it was confirmed to the membership that "every effort [was] made to accommodate the members consistent with circumstances." Furthermore, "the champion [remained] an independent contractor and, even though booked by the NWA, cannot be required to meet any engagement simply because a member [desired] that he do so and that nonmembers are entitled to use him if sufficient notice is given his booker."[32] As a unified body, the NWA was very pleased with Flair's hard work as champion over the past 10 months. The attending membership congratulated him for his "outstanding performance to date" in an affirmation of his performance.[33]

Before the end of the year, Flair returned to the Caribbean two additional times, and both trips were significant for Capital Sports.[34] First, on October 16, 1982, he put over 34-year-old Puerto Rican hero and co-owner of the promotion, Carlos Colón, in front of a crowd in excess of 20,000 people in San Juan. The bout was for Colón's WWC World championship, and Flair's title was not on the line. Two months later, on December 14, 1982, Flair faced Victor Jovica at the National Stadium in Port of Spain, Trinidad and Tobago, in a rematch from a bout they had during the summer. Flair had defeated Jovica by disqualification in an unpopular decision, and fans hoped for a better result in their follow-up battle.[35]

On top of his political influence in the NWA and part ownership of the territory, the Yugoslavian-born Jovica was beloved by fans across the Caribbean. The *Port of Spain Gazette* called him "one of the most entertaining and successful matmen to appear" in the area.[36] Jovica acknowledged Flair's elite skill in the local press, but he was confident he could beat the champion and take the belt.[37] December 14 was not his night. For 60 minutes, Flair fended off his fiery challenger and retained his championship in a draw. The following Sunday, December 19, the NWA champion wrestled Jack Veneno, a 40-year-old strongman, in the latter's native Dominican Republic. Their bout took place at the Palacio de los Deportes in Santo Domingo, and an enthusiastic crowd of 12,000 turned out to support Veneno in his effort to become the top heavyweight. It was a bloody match, inciting the passion of the audience, and after 17 minutes, Veneno pinned Flair and won the world title.[38] Fans swarmed in celebration of their idol's victory, and Flair, in desperate need to protect himself, escaped riotous conditions.[39]

It's been said that Flair allowed Veneno to pin him to avoid an even more dangerous situation, as a matter of self-preservation. That is likely true, and Flair's split-second decision prevented a full-scale outbreak of violence. Needless to say, the National Wrestling Alliance World Heavyweight championship didn't change hands in split-second decisions, and Veneno's victory was not authorized by the board of directors. That being said, Flair's actions were completely understandable and, with the belief that news of his defeat was unlikely to widely circulate due to the location of the match, the NWA wasn't overly concerned by the result. Flair was still the rightfully acknowledged champion everywhere but Santo Domingo.

Looking back at professional wrestling in December 1982 and Flair's bookings, it's hard not to be awestruck by the level of his opposition, the big-time angles, and the historical events happening on a weekly basis. Almost every territory was brimming with first-class challengers for Flair, and so many stars were either in or near their prime. Following his trip to the Caribbean, Flair went to Dallas for one of the most memorable matches of the decade. The setup match for the Flair versus Kerry Von Erich cage bout on Christmas night at the Reunion Arena was a masterclass in booking. It hit all of the right nerves heading into an emotionally charged holiday spectacular. The fireworks had kicked off four months earlier at the August Star Wars card in Dallas, and Flair and Kerry wrestled a classic that ended in a chaotic brawl.[40] From there, Flair implemented the old bounty gimmick to put Kerry out of contention, and he paid manager Gary Hart $10,000 to get the job done. Hart's charge, the Great Kabuki, injured Kerry's knee, as Flair wanted, but once Fritz Von Erich got wind of the controversial plan, tensions flared to a new level.

Kerry being called the "uncrowned champion" got Flair's blood going, and the NWA champ participated in a frenzied interview confrontation with Fritz via satellite on Dallas TV. The dialogue was anything but civil, with both men yelling at each other. Flair, as he always did, relished in putting himself over, and Fritz responded by calling him a "moron." By the end of the segment, the only thing settled was that the Christmas contest between Flair and Kerry Von Erich would be explosive.[41] The bookers were setting up a one-of-a-kind scenario that would shock, invigorate, and mark the dawn of a new era for wrestling in the Lone Star State.[42] From the fans' perspective, the bout seemed to lean in Von Erich's favor, as fan favorite Michael Hayes was assigned as a troubleshooting referee, while fellow Freebird Terry Gordy manned the cage door to prevent Flair from escaping.

But during the match, Hayes slowly and subtly demonstrated hostility toward Von Erich, surprising the audience. His objections to a move, such as to Von Erich's claw hold, impacted Kerry's ability to win the match. Later, Hayes physically interjected by punching Flair, allowing Von Erich to take advantage of the situation, but instead an argument ensued. Finally, Gordy had seen enough and slammed the door of the cage onto Von Erich's head, knocking him senseless. Von Erich tried to continue, but the match was stopped by referee David Manning, and Flair kept his championship.[43] The turn of the Freebirds against the Von Erichs launched an extraordinary feud, which changed the face of wrestling in the South. Although Flair was still a major opponent for the Von Erich brothers, fans wanted to see their heroes exact revenge on Hayes, Gordy, and Buddy Roberts, the third member of the Freebirds. Dallas was soon the hottest territory in the nation.

Back in his home region, Flair continued to feud with Roddy Piper. At the annual Thanksgiving night program in Greensboro on November 25, 1982, he defeated the Rowdy Scot by disqualification before a crowd of over 15,000.[44] On television, two days later, Piper embarrassed the champion by outdueling him in an amateur exhibition in Charlotte. He then landed his swinging neck breaker and pinned Flair. The humiliation was too much to bear, and Flair immediately attacked Piper. With the help of his former tag team partner Greg Valentine, he proceeded to rub Piper's face across the studio floor, similar to what he did to Ricky Steamboat a few years earlier in Raleigh. Bob Orton Jr., a gifted second-generation grappler, made the save for Piper, and tag team matches between the four competitors were booked for cities around the territory.[45]

This arrangement didn't last long. By March 1983, Flair returned to the baby face locker room in the mid-Atlantic territory and went to war with Valentine, the reigning U.S. champion. Piper became a public ally, even though their friendship was on firm ground behind the scenes. In fact, Flair had had Piper join him for what had been expected to be a difficult run in the Caribbean two months earlier, particularly the rematch with Jack Veneno in Santo Domingo on January 9. Flair expected to regain the championship claim he lost to Veneno in December, but once again, things turned out a bit differently than anticipated. Rather than a pinfall victory for Flair, he was disqualified, and Veneno retained his off-shoot version of the NWA World championship. This Caribbean tour also included an important contest against Carlos Colón in San Juan on January 6, and Flair was disqualified in that bout as well.[46]

In Florida, up-and-comers Barry Windham (formerly known as Blackjack Mulligan Jr.), Jake Roberts, and Terry Allen were gaining critical experience, while the "Prince of Darkness" Kevin Sullivan was terrorizing everyone he could. Sullivan, notably, had Dusty Rhodes's number on December 25, 1982, at the Bayfront Center in St. Petersburg when he beat the popular Texan in a loser-leaves-town match. The loss prohibited Dusty from wrestling anywhere in Florida for 60 days.[47] A new masked performer with the same build as Rhodes appeared on the circuit during the first week of January. Known as the Midnight Rider, this masked cowboy went to work against area heels, focusing on the likes of Jake Roberts and Kevin Sullivan. As soon as Flair entered the territory, the masked Rider received a shot at the NWA championship, and he beat Flair by disqualification on January 14, 1983, at the Sports Stadium in Orlando.[48]

Everyone knew that the Midnight Rider was Dusty Rhodes. It was more than obvious. But the storyline necessitated his identity be kept hidden to prevent a lengthy suspension across the NWA.[49] Flair was given the opportunity to reveal his archenemy and earn $50,000 in the process at the special Night of the Mask event in Miami Beach on February 9, 1983. The Miami Beach Convention Center was sold out, and 6,196 people saw the masked man pin Flair and capture the NWA World Heavyweight title.[50] The lid was blown off the building at the finish, and history was made. Bob Geigel, who had replaced Jim Crockett as the NWA president at the last convention, was the guest referee, and after the bout, he requested that Rider unmask, as he needed to know the real name of all reigning champions.[51] When the Rider refused, Geigel stripped him of the championship and returned the belt to Flair. The title change was permanently invalidated.[52]

Two nights later in St. Louis, without much buildup or a definitive angle in place, Flair and the 6-foot-8 Bruiser Brody drew a 16,000-person house at the Checkerdome and wrestled a 60-minute draw.[53] Brody was as unorthodox as they came, a wild brawler with the size and strength to outmatch nearly anyone in the business. His out-of-the-ring exploits and free thinking earned him a reputation as a troublemaker in some circles, but no one could deny his incredible drawing power. In St. Louis, he was a megastar, and his match with Flair created a lot of excitement. Adding to the importance of the bout was the fact that it was broadcast by All Japan Pro Wrestling on Nippon TV in Japan, and seen by millions of fans. With that kind of exposure, there was a lot on the line for both wrestlers, and it was critical they each remained credible for future moneymaking engagements in Japan. Flair and Brody went all out, delivering a ring masterpiece for the ages.

By that time, Flair was in his 17th month as NWA World champion, and there were internal rumblings about who his successor would be. His tenure had been successful from every point of view, and he had done everything in his power to strengthen the individual territories of Alliance members. It is estimated he had wrestled over 350 matches in that stretch of time, and his conditioning was more akin to a machine than a living, breathing human. His traveling schedule was borderline sadistic, and only the rarest of individuals could've endured his responsibilities. Dave Meltzer of the *Wrestling Observer Newsletter* wrote, "Being world champion in pro wrestling, through the schedule alone, is one of the toughest jobs in sports. You can see it on Flair's face, not only in the scars, but how he's aged five years [since winning the belt]. But during that period, there hasn't even been one night that he hasn't given the fans their monies worth."[54]

It should be noted that respected journalists, fans around the world, and discriminating promoters were all saying the same thing: Ric Flair was the preeminent world heavyweight champion of the early 1980s. Despite accolades and honors, Flair was hard on himself, and he later admitted that when he first got the belt, he just wasn't ready for the challenge.[55] But he worked through the difficulties and growing pains, and he established his own standards for the touring titleholder. By doing so, a new benchmark was also created for the NWA champion. Instead of looking back at the records of Lou Thesz or Buddy Rogers to gauge success, it was now measured against the "Nature Boy" Ric Flair. The time was approaching for him to step off the throne, but there was little doubt in anyone's mind that Flair would be a major superstar for the National Wrestling Alliance for years to come.

CHAPTER 10
A FLARE FOR THE GOLD

R ic Flair was proving to be a true wrestling enigma. Whether in the United States or on a distant continent, he was putting forth an extraordinary effort on the road, and his unremitting dedication to the backbreaking championship schedule was second to none. In the ring, his physicality never ceased to amaze — he'd work 60-minute matches like they were nothing — and when called upon to raise the proficiency of his opponent, and "carry" a match, Flair was the best in the business. As the NWA World champion, all eyes were constantly on him, and he continued to raise the bar. At the center of his personal evolution as titleholder was Flair's perseverance. He had gained a genuine working knowledge of being champion, which could only be attained by actually being the traveling NWA king. Nothing he was told beforehand could've prepared him for the responsibilities of being the top wrestler in the world. It was something he had to live to understand. By 1983, he was an expert.

"The pressure is unbelievable," Flair confessed to Paul Haskins of the *Winston-Salem Sentinel*. "You have to be ready every night. It takes a tremendous amount of wrestling skill and knowledge. To be the best, you have to put a lot of time into your trade."[1] Haskins had a similar experience interviewing Flair to that of Kate Mast of *The Ring's Wrestling* magazine. Flair's tone was again perceptibly different from that of the character he portrayed on television. He was laid-back and candid, and as Haskins wrote, he exhibited a "soft, articulate voice" that was the opposite of his excitable TV persona. This side of Flair was endearing to members of the press and fans he met behind the scenes. Many loyal enthusiasts, particularly in the mid-Atlantic area, had gotten to know Flair over the years and appreciated the kind nature he displayed, whether it was an autograph, handshake, or simply a smile and nice word.

An ardent wrestling supporter named Donna Kay Crawford from Pleasant Valley, Virginia, was one of those fortunate people. In 1981, the 30-year-old turned her interest in the sport into a part-time hobby, organizing the official "Ric Flair Fan Club" with the wrestler's blessing. Joined by her husband, Steve, she formed a personal friendship with Flair and saw his sweet-tempered qualities during visits when shows were held in her area.[2] Membership in the exclusive club was $8 per year, and Crawford sent out quarterly newsletters with updates, match results, and articles.[3] In addition, she went out of her way to coordinate gifts for Flair on behalf of the group, and in December 1982, Crawford hand-delivered an engraved gold pocket watch to the NWA champion. Photos of Flair opening the present appeared in a subsequent newsletter.[4] "To all my sensational fans," Flair wrote in special note to the membership. "Thank you so very much for all the support and vote of confidence! Your friend always, Ric."[5]

Toward the end of February 1983, Flair ventured to the South Pacific for an extended tour of New Zealand and expressed how much he was enjoying the country to Colleen Grimsey. "It's been a tremendous opportunity for me to come over here," he said. "I find the people have been tremendous. I find the country to be beautiful just as I heard it was. I'm really enjoying myself. I've been able to look around quite a bit in the four days I've been here and, of course, I'm looking forward to the next six days."[6] Flair talked up Mark Lewin, a veteran battler from Buffalo, New York, whom he faced at least five times during that run, as well as promoter Steve Rickard, his opponent on two nights. It was said at the time that Flair was going to take a much-needed vacation in Honolulu following the grueling series in New Zealand, which ended on March 4, but it's likely he was forced to cancel those plans at the last minute.[7]

While it's impossible to know the exact travel times and route taken, flights from Auckland, New Zealand, to Los Angeles with a stopover in Honolulu took in the neighborhood of 14 hours. Adding another five hours to fly to the East Coast, it's conceivable that Flair wrestled in Hamilton, New Zealand, on the evening of Friday, March 4, then traveled 19 hours to make a Saturday morning appearance in Atlanta on March 5. This is taking into consideration that New Zealand is 18 hours ahead of Atlanta in terms of time. Give or take other factors, such as any potential delays, and it's possible that Flair was at the WTBS studio filming a match against Denny Brown on the morning of March 5 on just a few hours of sleep.[8] Interestingly, if this is true, it's the perfect illustration of how the champion's schedule frequently changed to fit the needs of promoters. According to the original booking calendar for the champion, Flair was supposed finish up for Rickard on March 5, return stateside the next day, and resume matches in the Charlotte territory between March 8 and 12.[9]

In the mid-Atlantic region, Flair continued his feud with former tag team partner Greg Valentine. On March 12 in Greensboro, they were the co-feature for a huge show at the Coliseum and wrestled for an hour to a draw.[10] The other half of the main event saw Ricky Steamboat and Jay Youngblood dethrone Sgt. Slaughter and Don Kernodle for the NWA World Tag Team title.[11] On top of the more than 15,000 people in attendance, thousands were turned away in what Coliseum assistant manager John Bryson said was the venue's first wrestling sellout outside the annual Thanksgiving program.[12] Talent from the local promotion still went up to Toronto for regular cards at Maple Leaf Gardens, and although Flair's warfare with Roddy Piper had ceased in the Carolinas, they remained enemies in Canada. More than 18,000 people packed the Gardens on March 27 to see Flair prevail over Piper in 19:26. Their rematch — a matinee card on April 10 — drew another 12,000, and Flair won by disqualification.[13]

In interview segments, Flair often spoke about Toronto with reverence, and he recognized the exceptional tradition of Maple Leaf Wrestling. His admiration for beloved promoter Frank Tunney was evident, and his respectful comments further ingratiated him with fans in the region.[14] Crowds in Toronto cheered Flair, despite his reputation as a rule-bending brute, and his magnetism directed the booking scheme designed by the powers-that-be. Flair's popularity in Toronto was unrivaled for the time period, and his gate numbers were comparable with the biggest wrestling stars in the history of the territory. Tunney's sudden death on May 10, 1983, at the age of 70, rocked the wrestling industry, and his successor, nephew Jack Tunney, arranged two outdoor spectaculars at Exhibition Stadium that July. But before either of those two shows occurred, Flair was expected by the NWA's leadership to lose his championship.

The decision to switch the title was more about politics than any aspect related to Flair's performance. By mid-1983, NWA president Bob Geigel was in an unusual predicament in St. Louis, where he was a partial owner.[15] Larry Matysik had quit his job as general manager for the St. Louis Wrestling Club after a series of promotional disagreements with Geigel, and he was in the process of organizing a legitimate resistance to the NWA in a city that had always been known as the heart of the Alliance.[16] There was much more than money on the line in what was projected to be a bloody promotional war, and Geigel was prepared to do whatever it took to ensure his company survived. He had reason to be concerned. Matysik had a great mind for the business and had learned the inside tricks directly from Sam Muchnick. He knew what made St. Louis a thriving wrestling metropolis, and with connections to talent across the U.S., he was in a unique position to challenge Geigel and the NWA for territorial rights.

To strengthen his opposition to Matysik, Geigel wanted his partner in the St. Louis promotion, Harley Race, to regain the NWA World title. They felt that featuring the championship throughout the summer would give them the edge they needed to silence Matysik's effort and regain sole possession of the city.[17] The title change would happen at the

Kiel Auditorium in St. Louis as well, and that in itself was a significant event in the NWA's favor. Putting the belt back on Race created another landmark element to the overall story, which magnified the importance of the moment. For years, the record-holder for most NWA World Heavyweight title victories was Lou Thesz, the legendary wrestler whose career spanned six decades. Promoters and journalists attributed six championship reigns to Thesz, ignoring the fact that three of his victories were actually for the National Wrestling Association (not Alliance) crown, won between 1939 and 1948. Thesz had long been celebrated as the six-time champion — a feat that seemed insurmountable.

On May 1, 1981, in Gainesville, Georgia, Harley Race had tied Thesz's record when he beat Tommy Rich for his sixth NWA World Heavyweight championship. Geigel's push to give Race a seventh title would eclipse Thesz once and for all, displacing him from one of wrestling's greatest achievements. It could be argued that part of Geigel's motivation was spurred by Thesz's decision to join Matysik's side in the wrestling war. Thesz had agreed to referee the main event of Matysik's first show on June 18, 1983, at the Checkerdome.[18] Even though Matysik had a strong connection to Muchnick, the NWA's longtime leader and its greatest proponent, his promotion was considered an outlaw group and an enemy of the Alliance. For that reason, Geigel was going with a nuclear option: a world title change to give Race a record seventh championship victory. St. Louis was Thesz's hometown, and the symbolism of purposely diminishing his standing in that city, of all places, was not lost on astute observers.

With unlimited respect for Race, Flair was onboard with the plan to help the NWA, and he did an angle with Race on St. Louis TV to build excitement for the historic bout. During an interview segment in the ring with television host Mark Matthews, Race confidently spoke about winning his seventh NWA title, only to be confronted by Flair, who angrily denied it was ever going to happen.[19] Feigning like he was going to walk away, Flair sucker punched Race, but the latter quickly got the advantage and busted Flair open with a series of headbutts. The crowd cheered Race as he briefly held up the NWA belt after the fight, and fans were eager to see their championship match on June 10, 1983, at the Kiel. Flair spent June 4–8 touring Japan, including a 60-minute clash with Jumbo Tsuruta on the last night of the trip in Tokyo, before he made the long journey back to the States to engage Race in St. Louis.[20]

Race was dominant from the outset, and the audience enjoyed watching him batter Flair with his deep repertoire of maneuvers and holds. Utilizing a suplex, he pinned the champion to take a 1–0 lead in their best-of-three contest. Flair was more aggressive in the second and attacked Race's legs, leading to a win with his figure-four leglock. In the third, the momentum shifted back and forth, and each wrestler attempted a succession of moves to capture the fall. Flair applied a sleeperhold and an abdominal stretch, in addition to a figure-four, while Race went for his famed Indian death lock.[21] The challenger attempted a vertical suplex, but Flair dropped down behind him, lifting Race up for a belly-to-back suplex instead. Referee Sonny Myers began counting as the shoulders of both men were on the mat. Just before he got to three, Race lifted up his left shoulder, and he won his seventh NWA World title. For Race and his supporters, it was a clearly defined victory, but back in Charlotte, on the local telecast of *Mid-Atlantic Championship Wrestling*, the finish was called into question.[22]

In fact, it was stated that Flair's opposite shoulder, away from the camera, might have gotten up in time and that Race had received a favorable decision because he was in a friendly city. Despite any objections, the title change stood, and Flair sought retribution in a rematch.[23] He didn't have to wait long. Over the next 11 weeks, Flair wrestled Race at least 17 times. A dozen of those matches took place in the mid-Atlantic region, and most of those contests ended in disqualifications. Back in St. Louis, Flair regained standing on July 15, 1983, by going through four men to capture the vacant Missouri State Heavyweight title. The silver belt had been vacated by Race following his NWA title win, and in the tournament final, Flair beat David Von Erich.[24] The triumph also secured Flair a world title shot at the Kiel on August 5. Now, as the challenger, Ric was gaining popularity in St. Louis, while Race took on the win-at-any-cost role that a heel champion normally portrayed.

Flair was determined in their August 5 match and "looked fantastic," according to one eyewitness, but he was defeated in three falls.[25] He was already thriving in the position as a motivated challenger, and there were obvious similarities between the Flair of 1981 and the Flair of 1983. But the Nature Boy in the summer of '83 was much more technically proficient and self-assured. With that said, though, he had proven to be an even better champion. He was successful from Portland to Puerto Rico, and he had established feuds in every territory ready to draw at the box office. It was rumored that Race was only going to reign for about a month before losing the strap back to Flair, but Dave Meltzer of the *Wrestling Observer Newsletter* revealed that those plans changed due to political reasons inside the NWA.[26] Smart fans disliked the idea of a long run for Race and criticized his out-of-shape appearance and lack of charisma as compared to Flair.[27]

The debate over the world's heavyweight championship continued to dominate conversations within the National Wrestling Alliance. Every member had an opinion, and Bob Geigel's motivation to support Race was just as important as Jim Crockett's rationale for Flair. Essentially, it was all in the eye of the beholder. In terms of business, Flair's recent success in aid of the entire NWA couldn't be ignored, and there was enough enthusiasm to support a second reign. However, the *Wrestling Observer Newsletter* noted that Race's future as champion was "not" going to be discussed during the NWA's annual convention in Las Vegas, held August 22–23, 1983. Dave Meltzer added that Race was likely to be "king for a while."[28] That narrative was soon complicated by stories surrounding the push of David Von Erich toward the NWA title, and it appeared the young wrestler from Dallas was in the best position to dethrone Race for the championship.

But the fate of the NWA World title wasn't yet known to the public. Behind the scenes, Jim Crockett had moved back into a position of formal leadership after taking a year off. At the 1983 convention in Vegas, he was voted first vice president of the NWA and returned to its board of directors. In addition, he was arranging what was expected to be the biggest show in National Wrestling Alliance history with an expansion to JCP's annual Thanksgiving program in Greensboro. Moving Flair back into the top spot on that particular evening was his ultimate goal, and Crockett had the influence to get board approval.[29] In the meantime, a gripping angle developed on the weekly *Mid-Atlantic Championship Wrestling* telecast. It started with a promo by Harley Race standing with an open briefcase of cash, offering $25,000 to anyone who could knock Flair out of action.[30] Among the first attempting to seize the money was Dick Slater, a roughneck from Florida.

A bounty for injuring a wrestler was nauseating to the general wrestling public, but it made for good TV. The drama unfolded during a televised match between Flair and Race from the Civic Center in Greenwood, South Carolina, on September 10, 1983. Late in the bout, Flair was in control of the fight, but Slater rushed ringside to help the NWA champion. The odds were evened up when Bob Orton Jr., a baby face loyal to Flair, ran out to stop Slater's interference.[31] Then in a shocker, Orton suddenly attacked Flair, leaving fans in utter disbelief. Orton and Slater assaulted Flair with intent to maim and earned the $25,000 bounty by putting the blond grappler out of action with a neck injury.[32] The footage of Flair stretchered out was gut-wrenching for his supporters, and hearing Race's diabolical laughter, they wanted Flair to return for vengeance.

The memorable Greenwood match was taped on Wednesday, August 31. The weekend before that, Flair experienced a major moment in his personal life, as he wed Beth Harrell at the St. Stephen Methodist Church in Charlotte.[33] The wedding service, held on August 27, was presided by Minister Bill E. Bass, and Jim Crockett served as Flair's best man.[34] Roddy Piper and Ricky Steamboat were also part of the wedding party. Throughout September, Mid-Atlantic TV sold the graveness of Flair's injury at the hands of Orton and Slater, teasing the idea of his retirement.[35] An article in the *Charlotte Observer* on September 16 reported that he had suffered "damaged vertebrae and nerves," as well as a strained muscle in his neck. Flair was recovering in Minneapolis at the home of his parents, and it was going to be "at least two weeks" or longer before his return to the mat.[36]

Little did most fans in the mid-Atlantic area know, but Flair wasn't injured at all. He left the territory following his bout with Race to spend time in the Caribbean and Florida, balancing ring engagements and his honeymoon with Beth. On September 16, he appeared in St. Louis and lost the Missouri State title to David Von Erich. Without the internet to spoil the storyline, passionate enthusiasts in the Carolinas waited with bated breath for any kind of update on Flair's physical condition. Finally, the Nature Boy commented during the October 1 broadcast of *Mid-Atlantic Championship Wrestling*, and his words were the antithesis of what his faithful fans wanted to hear.[37] Wearing a neck brace, he expressed thanks to his followers and stunned everyone watching by announcing his retirement from professional wrestling. The news was shocking on every level, but fortunately the retirement didn't last long.

Later in the show, Flair rushed to the ring during a tag team match featuring Bob Orton and Dick Slater, and despite the brace protecting his neck, he was ready to engage both men with every fiber of his being.[38] And to equalize the two-on-one scenario, he had a trusty baseball bat. The crowd exploded as Flair chased Orton and Slater with unbridled fury, and then told Bob Caudle that he was not going to hang up his boots anytime soon. "It'll be a cold day in hell when someone can walk out here and make fun of me, put me in the hospital, try to break my neck, try to end my career, and most of all, try and take the greatest sport in the world from me," Flair exclaimed, ripping off his neck brace. "Orton, you and Slater will go to your grave because of me!" He also had words for Harley Race, and made it clear he wanted the gold NWA belt back.[39] The fiery performance was everything the promotion needed in the leadup to its 23rd annual Thanksgiving spectacular in Greensboro.

Dubbed "Starrcade '83," the special program on November 24 was a much more elaborate production than in years past, and it featured closed-circuit television outlets in several states.[40] Flair coined his own name for the event, calling it "A Flare for the Gold," which characterized his charge toward the NWA belt, and fans were firmly behind him.[41] The show was essentially built around Flair and his incredible resurgence after what was believed to be a career-ending injury. He was fit and fully prepared for the ultimate championship contest against Race on pro wrestling's biggest stage to date. On that extraordinary occasion, a sold-out audience of over 15,000 people hushed as the lights to the Coliseum went out prior to the main event.[42] The darkened venue was illuminated by laser lights and a huge disco ball hanging from the ceiling. The classic tone poem *Also sprach Zarathustra* played through the house speakers, creating a powerful sensory experience for those in attendance.[43]

Flair emerged from the dressing room area in an iconic blue Olivia Walker robe, extending his arms out to display the elegance of his flowing, bedazzled garment.[44] He was mobbed by excited fans en route to the ring, and the atmosphere was unlike anything Flair had yet experienced. To ensure a winner, a cage surrounded the ring, and a no-disqualification stipulation prevented the champion from saving his title on a technicality.[45] During their contest, Flair and Race stood toe to toe and gave an exhaustive performance that included psychology, violence, and, of course, blood. The hero of the evening, Flair took a great deal of abuse from Race, only to rise up at the end and deliver the result enthusiasts hoped to see. A cross body off the top rope and a chaotic landing on Race gave the Nature Boy his second NWA World Heavyweight title.[46] Afterwards, an emotional Flair told the crowd, "This is the greatest night of my life."[47]

Since 1948, only five wrestlers had regained the National Wrestling Alliance World Heavyweight championship: Lou Thesz, Jack Brisco, Harley Race, Giant Baba, and Dusty Rhodes. Flair had discussed his title loss to Race the June before, as well as his overall mindset, in a kayfabe interview with a small-town reporter in North Carolina. "I was disappointed but not discouraged or down about losing," he said. "My personality doesn't work like that. I just made up my mind [that] I was going to get back what Race had taken from me."[48] The reality was that Flair was positioned politically with support from both Jim Crockett and Race himself to get a second reign with the belt. Without Race's endorsement, it never would have happened, and Race could've remained champion well into 1984. But Race was happy to pass the torch to Flair and did the job with the utmost dignity.[49] Crockett, too, manipulated the NWA chessboard to ensure his man got the strap, and everything worked out.[50]

One of the first things Flair did as champion was venture to Atlanta for a TV taping at WTBS, similar to in his first reign. He told Gordon Solie that it was a "tremendous honor" to be the NWA titleholder again. "A lot of people said that Ric Flair disappeared from the wrestling scene, from the center of professional wrestling, which, let's face it, is right here [in Atlanta]," he said. "But I'm back, no brag, just fact, bigger and better than ever."[51] Appearing polite and respectful to Solie, Flair finished the interview by saying, "This time, Gordon, unlike before, the world heavyweight champion is going to defend this title when he wants to, and only when he wants to. Thank you, I'm sure it's been a pleasure for everyone."[52] After months of being a likeable and courageous idol, Flair was adjusting his ring personality to meet the demands of being the traveling champion. Within the first few weeks on the road, he was almost exclusively wrestling babyfaces, including the Von Erich Brothers and Tommy Rich.

On December 18, 1983, he appeared at Juan Ramón Loubriel Stadium in Bayamon, Puerto Rico, for a showdown with local world titleholder Carlos Colón. This wasn't the typical title vs. title affair with the expected inconclusive finish but a contest to determine the first Universal Heavyweight champion. Flair suffered a loss to Colón that night in a cage match, establishing the Universal title as the main championship for Colón's World Wrestling Council. A week later, he wrestled David Von Erich at the Christmas Star Wars program in Dallas in front of 20,000 spectators at the Reunion Arena. In a desperate act of an immoral champ, Flair nailed Von Erich with a microphone and earned a disqualification, saving his belt. Referee David Manning told Flair, "Everyone in the building knows you don't deserve to be the world champion."[53] The local crowd agreed wholeheartedly. As a matter of perspective, it wasn't but a month earlier that Flair was being lauded for his miraculous victory over Race.

Flair was back on top of the world — doing his job as champion at the highest possible level.[54] As for Von Erich, he was on a very short list of exceptional challengers, and his popularity, along with brothers Kerry and Kevin, had propelled him into a rarified category of wrestling superstars. With drawing power in Texas, plus experience in Florida, St. Louis, and Japan, David Von Erich was being positioned as a potential successor to Flair.[55] Standing 6-foot-7, he had imposing size, but he was also agile and versatile enough to wrestle to the strengths of his opponents, a necessary trait for a touring champion. He was already the Texas State titleholder when, on February 3, 1984, he beat Michael Hayes to win the NWA United National Heavyweight crown. Von Erich was booked for an important tour of Japan soon thereafter. But before his first match in that country, the 25-year-old was found dead in his Tokyo hotel room.[56]

The heartbreaking news stunned the wrestling industry, and insiders, as well as fans, wanted to pay their respects. Flair was in the midst of a swing through Florida, and following a grueling 60-minute Broadway with Barry Windham on the evening of February 14 in Fort Myers, he raced to Dallas to attend the funeral ceremony the next morning.[57] A reporter caught up with Flair, asking about his in-ring rivalry with Von Erich. "The fact that we were enemies in the ring didn't have anything to do with the tremendous amount of respect I had for him," Flair replied. "He had unlimited guts."[58] Immediately after the service, Flair flew to Miami Beach, where he wrestled Windham again.[59] His Herculean effort demonstrated his respect for a fallen wrestling contemporary, while remaining committed to his schedule as NWA champion.

Flair had a clear track record of being reliable, but things didn't always go according to plan. In March 1984, he was booked by promoter Steve Rickard for a seven-day tour of New Zealand and Southeast Asia. A problem with his itinerary caused him to miss a plane connection on Air New Zealand from Los Angeles, and he ended up no-showing the first date of the trip in Christchurch.[60] Rickard was upset by his absence and spent hours on the phone trying to find out what happened. He had a packed house, and some fans had traveled great distances to see Flair defend his championship against Harley Race. "We arranged all the international flights, but you have to leave it to the wrestler to see to the internal connections," Rickard told a local newspaper.[61] Race was sympathetic to Flair's situation. "I can understand it because I've been in his shoes for years," he said.[62]

The next day in Wellington, Flair was approached by Race with an idea.[63] In effort to help Rickard, and possibly as a way to soften the blow from the no-show in Christchurch, Race wanted to personally authorize a title switch of the NWA championship. He thought that if they flipped the belt, it would garner widespread attention for Rickard's promotion — without the NWA leadership back home being any wiser. Flair trusted Race and agreed to the unsanctioned title change.[64] On March 20, 1984, at the Town Hall in Wellington, Race pinned Flair to win his eighth NWA World Heavyweight title before a crowd of 7,000.[65] The plan was for Flair to regain the belt a few days later in Singapore, but this arrangement unraveled when Paul Boesch, the famed Houston promoter, who was unexpectedly at the event, notified NWA members back in the States as to what had transpired.[66] Naturally, NWA executives were upset by the news and wanted the title confusion quickly cleared up.

The story given to reporters and the public was that referee Chris Miller counted Race's pin too fast in the Wellington match, making the finish illegitimate.[67] Boesch's presence was also incorporated into the explanation behind keeping the belt on Flair. "Steve Rickard proved wise as he had invited Paul Boesch as an observer," Flair told Wally Yamaguchi for an article in Gong Magazine. "If he had not been present there, Harley would have insisted on his victory more loudly."[68] The tour continued in Singapore, and on the third night of the World Championship Series at Gay World Stadium in Kallang, on March 25, Flair beat Race to retain his NWA title.[69] Although reports of Race's victory in Wellington were spread by New Zealand wrestling historians Dave Cameron and Vern Ross, as well as *Gong Magazine*, a deep cloud of mystery surrounded this event for well over two decades. To this day, fans who appreciate the details of wrestling history find this footnote in the lineage of the NWA World Heavyweight title utterly fascinating.

CHAPTER 11

THE WRESTLING WAR

O ver the final weeks of 1983, as Jim Crockett Promotions and the National Wrestling Alliance celebrated the success of Starrcade, an innovative entrepreneur from Connecticut was laying the groundwork for systematic and cultural change in professional wrestling. Vincent Kennedy McMahon, the 38-year-old son of longtime promoter Vincent James McMahon, had quietly assumed control of the World Wrestling Federation, having purchased the promotion from his father and his partners in June 1982.[1] Known for his on-air role as a television commentator, the younger McMahon quickly demonstrated his astute understanding of the wrestling scene beyond the limits of the WWF's northeastern territorial boundaries. He sought expansion into Ohio and Southern California, including a complete takeover of the Los Angeles market. With shrewd financial offers to both veteran promoter Mike LeBell and executives at KHJ-TV, channel 9, McMahon attained a strong foothold in Los Angeles.[2]

The news sent shockwaves through the business, and rumors of further expansion spread like wildfire. At the annual NWA convention in August 1983, a wave of sudden resignations revealed the brewing political turmoil, and Alliance officials were anything but pleased. LeBell, the organization's first vice president, was first to depart the NWA. He was joined by two other influential figures, Vincent James McMahon and

Jim Barnett. All three were members of the Alliance's board of directors and had provided critical expertise and experience to the NWA for the better part of two decades. Barnett's resignation was the most surprising. He was the longest reigning officer in the promotional union, serving 13 consecutive terms as secretary dating back to 1970. He was also the NWA's treasurer, and he booked the world heavyweight champion.[3] His importance to the Alliance couldn't be overstated, and the loss of his leadership was immeasurable.

It was apparent that the exodus of LeBell, McMahon, and Barnett was tied to the expansion plans of the junior McMahon and his WWF, in one way or another. In addition to the agreement with LeBell in Los Angeles, McMahon was working with Barnett in parts of Ohio, and his father, who was in semiretirement, was his greatest advisor.[4] Although there were initial gestures of goodwill extended to the members of the NWA, the new WWF owner boldly rejected the old handshake agreements and territorial assignments that had bonded his father to the Alliance.[5] One of McMahon's first moves was into the time-honored capital city of the NWA, St. Louis. On December 27, 1983, the WWF held a TV taping at the Chase-Park Plaza Hotel, where Sam Muchnick's *Wrestling at the Chase* had been filmed for years. The symbolism of the event, plus the fact that St. Louis was run by NWA president Bob Geigel, erased any doubt that Vincent K. McMahon was declaring war on the establishment.

The massive increase of McMahon's promotional reach was only one part of the equation. The other key element was talent, and between late 1983 and early '84, the WWF improved its roster tenfold by signing some of the premier names in the industry. That included Roddy Piper, Greg Valentine, and Bob Orton Jr. from Jim Crockett Promotions.[6] But the biggest superstar McMahon lured to the WWF was actually expected to be the next world heavyweight champion of Verne Gagne's American Wrestling Association. Hulk Hogan, a 6-foot-7 former musician from Tampa, and a former student of Hiro Matsuda, was undeniably the most popular man in pro wrestling.[7] In St. Paul on April 24, 1983, before a crowd of 28,000 people, Hogan received thunderous applause after pinning Nick Bockwinkel for the AWA World title, only to see the belt returned to the former champ on a disqualification technicality.[8] Less than two months later, in Tokyo, he beat Antonio Inoki by knockout to capture the IWGP World Heavyweight championship.

Outside the wrestling ring, Hogan was a mainstream success. He appeared in a memorable role in Sylvester Stallone's *Rocky III*, as "Thunderlips, the Ultimate Male," and his magnetic charisma earned high praise. Hogan was on Vince McMahon's initial card in St. Louis on December 27, 1983, and nearly a month to the day, on January 23, 1984, he pinned the Iron Sheik to become the WWF World titleholder at Madison Square Garden. The push of Hogan to the top of the World Wrestling Federation was a no-brainer, and in terms of a larger-than-life popular persona, he was an attraction like no other. "Hogan is the #1 box office star in the business," declared journalist Dave Meltzer.[9] However, the "Nature Boy" Ric Flair was considered the better ring technician and was named "Wrestler of the Year" by the *Wrestling Observer Newsletter* for 1983. Hogan placed second.[10]

The new direction of the WWF, with Hogan on top and an energized platform for expansion, did threaten the balance of professional wrestling. Jim Crockett was already reeling from the unexpected loss of Roddy Piper, and with Ricky Steamboat sidelined by a self-imposed retirement, the mid-Atlantic promotion was dramatically weakened.[11] As per his responsibilities to the NWA, Flair was busy on the international circuit, which left JCP more vulnerable than it had been in years. Crockett needed a strong baby face, and during an episode of *Worldwide* on February 18, 1984, he offered Steamboat $10,000 to return to the ring to face Flair on March 17 in Greensboro. Steamboat agreed. Notably, Flair was still a hero in the mid-Atlantic region, and his contest with Steamboat was sportsmanlike and respectable — at least as much as Flair could muster. He drew cheers from his faithful, and against Steamboat in Greensboro, he wrestled a 60-minute time-limit draw.

Flair and Steamboat wrestled hour-long Broadways three additional times in April 1984, and fans certainly weren't complaining about the lack of a finish in Charlotte on April 22, Greenville on April 23, and Richmond on April 27. They were bowled over by the finesse, timing, and execution of two of wrestling's finest athletes. Flair's conditioning was nearly peerless, and his constant traveling as NWA champion was extraordinary. In April, he appeared in eight different Alliance territories and wrestled at least 27 matches.[12] There was no slowing Flair down, and the Alliance had no championship candidate in the wings with the same sophisticated set of qualities ready to replace him. There was no such individual. But the leaders of the NWA did plan to honor the memory of David Von Erich and bolster the Dallas promotion of Jack Adkisson (Fritz Von Erich). And in the process, Flair would lose the NWA World title.

The political intrigue was nuanced. For a period of months, there was clear evidence that Vince McMahon was strengthening the relationship between his company and Adkisson's World Class promotion. Kerry and Kevin Von Erich were highlighted on the WWF's cable program, *All-American Wrestling*, and a special "Update" segment on McMahon's syndicated *All-Star Wrestling* further extolled the virtues of the famous family from Texas.[13] Additionally, in the spring of 1984, an article on the Von Erichs ran in the inaugural edition of *WWF Magazine*.[14] There was also reason to believe Adkisson was exploring his options beyond the NWA cabal, particularly when he actively considered supporting Larry Matysik against Bob Geigel and the Alliance in the St. Louis wrestling war.[15] The NWA couldn't afford to lose the Von Erichs and Adkisson's influence to the WWF. Geigel knew how much was at stake.

To convince Adkisson to remain loyal to the NWA, Geigel and his allies authorized a World title switch to Kerry Von Erich at the Parade of Champions program at Texas Stadium on May 6, 1984.[16] The maneuvering and backstage politics meant nothing to the legions of diehard fans in Dallas. They wanted to pay tribute to the legacy of David Von Erich and to celebrate the crowning of a new champion. Ric Flair's role as defending titleholder was unique in that situation, and he played his part to perfection. The moment was about Kerry and the Von Erich family, and the buildup to the final pinfall was historic and exciting to the 32,132 spectators in attendance.[17] Flair did have brief moments of offense against Von Erich during their bout, but it was essentially Von Erich working at a brisk pace, running the champion through a gamut of holds, from a sleeper to an abdominal stretch to his famed clawhold. In the end, he caught Flair in a backslide and scored the three count, capturing the NWA gold.[18]

"I'll be back," Flair told Von Erich in a post-match showdown in the ring. As unfortunate as it was, the real-life tragedy of David Von Erich created this one-of-a-kind moment for pro wrestling in Dallas and boosted the spirits of thousands of emotionally pained fans. But with Kerry taking the NWA belt, there was an immediate conflict that had to be addressed. Even before the Texas Stadium match, promotions for a big program at the Meadowlands Arena, outside of New York City, had begun in the NWA's first attempt to grab headlines in the backyard of Vince McMahon's WWF.[19] The financial investment was significant, and Flair was advertised as the defending NWA champion against U.S. titleholder and "top contender" Ricky Steamboat. The show, billed as "A Night of Champions," was going to be held on May 29, and unless there was a plan in place to swap the belt again, Flair would be without the championship at the noteworthy event.[20]

The NWA took that into consideration, and officials felt it was prudent to pass the belt back to Flair before the Meadowlands card. The main event couldn't be watered down in the midst of a wrestling war. As a result, Kerry Von Erich was informed that his reign would last only 18 days, and he'd drop the NWA strap to Flair in a return match on May 24 in Yokosuka, Japan.[21] The schedule was set, and Flair was accompanied to Japan by his wife, Beth, who sat ringside for his contest at the General Gymnasium. Booked to wrestle three falls, both wrestlers were amped for another compelling, fast-paced battle. During the first fall, Von Erich caught Flair coming off the top rope with his clawhold and pinned his foe, but he succumbed to a figure-four in the second. The back-and-forth action culminated in a roll up attempt by Kerry, and the momentum carried over into an advantageous position for Flair, giving Ric the pin.[22]

Flair was now a three-time NWA World Heavyweight champion. Upon return to North America, he beat Dick Slater in Toronto on May 27 and then traveled to New York City for a round of publicity prior to the "Night of Champions" extravaganza. In Staten Island, he greeted upward of 400 fans at the Twilight Zone Family Amusement Center, a local arcade, and was "class personified," according to wrestling historian Charles Warburton.[23] Flair signed autographs and smiled for photographs, easily winning over wrestling fans with his charm.[24] In addition, he appeared for a high-profile interview with Spencer Christian of WABC-TV, and the 20-minute segment gave Flair and the NWA tremendous exposure.[25] The engaging, personable side of the world champion was on full display, and it was exactly the kind of favorable impression Jim Crockett and other Alliance leaders wanted to make in the valuable New York market. No one in wrestling could've done it better than Flair.

In an interview in the program for "A Night of Champions," Flair expressed his eagerness to wrestle before the northeastern fan base. "I'm ready, I'm willing, I'm able, and I can guarantee that the New York area wrestling fans will be seeing something that they've never seen in their lives, and that's me!" Flair said. "I'm gonna take a bite out of that Big Apple and give them a taste of the Nature Boy that they're not going to soon forget. New York is the big time, Ric Flair is the big time, the NWA is the big time, and all of it taken together spells excitement-plus for the New York area wrestling fans. Watch out, New York, because Ric Flair's on his way!"[26]

On the whole, running the Meadowlands on May 29, 1984, was a major gamble for the NWA, and it paid off. Crowd estimates ranged from just under 14,000 to 15,000 in attendance, and the thrill-a-minute Flair-Steamboat affair was a mat tour de force.[27] Flair eked out a winning pinfall with the help of Steamboat's tights in 41:49.

Wrestlers from Jim Crockett Promotions, Georgia Championship Wrestling, and the World Wrestling Council worked the Meadowlands card, and the NWA put its best foot forward in a practically alien territory.[28] At the same time, the organization was preparing to take a big hit in Atlanta, where Vince McMahon had purchased the Georgia promotion in a deal that included rights to the coveted cable TV weekend slot on WTBS. The loss of its invaluable national outlet was nearly crippling to the NWA, and GCW booker Ole Anderson tried to fight the sale in the courts, without success. Just a few months earlier, Flair had proclaimed that the "wrestling world [revolved] around *World Championship Wrestling*" during an episode of the Atlanta telecast.[29] As demonstrated prior to the Meadowlands program, WTBS was slated to promote Alliance events in new territories, but McMahon's clever negotiation skills and the almighty dollar stomped out those plans.[30]

Flair continued to reign supreme across the NWA circuit. A hot angle was cooked up in the mid-Atlantic region to bring Flair back together with his mentor and friend Wahoo McDaniel. The twist to the rekindled feud was that McDaniel was now the heel, who'd turned his back on the fans.[31] Between July 1984 and April 1985, they wrestled over 30 singles matches in the territory, and crowds were enlivened by the brutality of their old-school rivalry. They drew 7,421 in Greensboro on August 18, 1984, and improved on that figure seven months later on March 16, 1985, at a show dubbed "Silver Star '85."[32] Flair beat McDaniel in an Indian strap match in front of 9,947 spectators at the Coliseum.[33] In Charlotte on February 24, 1985, Flair pinned McDaniel before nearly 12,000 fans after 21 minutes of hard-hitting action.[34] Because of how well the Nature Boy and "Chief" knew each other, their bouts were always well received, and McDaniel was probably the MVP of the mid-Atlantic territory for his impressive run.

Outside JCP, Flair was still a typical "bad guy," and his war with Dusty Rhodes in Florida resumed just about every time he visited the Sunshine State. The sustained popularity of Rhodes and his unrelenting ability to draw at the box office illustrated his incredible star power. For the most of the last decade, he had outshined his contemporaries as *the* charismatic baby face in the southeast, and his ventures elsewhere were met with similar success. Behind the curtain, Rhodes was exceptionally intelligent and equally ambitious when it came to booking and promoting. He was

Eddie Graham's right-hand man in Florida, and his creative ideas kept gate numbers perpetually thriving. But Rhodes was starting to branch out, and in 1983, he helped Jim Crockett come up with the concept for Starrcade, the super card of all super cards.[35] Rhodes saw the writing on the wall and knew Crockett's grand ambition for national prominence matched his own. For that reason, he was ready to leave Florida.

Before his departure, Rhodes met Flair in Miami for a special "Lord of the Ring" contest at the Orange Bowl, home of the NFL's Miami Dolphins. The spectacle on June 30, 1984, drew 10,000 people, and at the climax of a two-of-three-falls bout, Rhodes beat the NWA champion by disqualification to win the match. According to the reported stipulations, the victory gave Rhodes a $100,000 prize, plus a $15,000 "diamond Super Bowl–type ring."[36] Later in the summer, Rhodes finished up his steady commitments for the Tampa office before assuming a full-time position in Charlotte for Crockett, replacing Dory Funk Jr. as booker.[37] It was a landmark moment for the promotion, and the combination of Rhodes's boundless innovations with Crockett's newfangled business strategies gave the NWA a true powerhouse in its fight with Vince McMahon's WWF. Local fans in the mid-Atlantic area knew Dusty Rhodes well and remembered the subtle challenge he had made to Flair at the end of Starrcade '83.

On October 6, 1984, at a "Starrcade Rally" in Greensboro, a formal announcement was made designating the main event for the annual Thanksgiving show as Flair versus Rhodes for the NWA title.[38] To heighten the bout's importance, Jim Crockett offered what was called the "largest single purse" in grappling history: $1 million to the winner. The "Million Dollar Challenge" was a first for pro wrestling, and the excitement for the contest was compounded when iconic former boxing champion Smokin' Joe Frazier was named the guest referee.[39] Both Flair and Rhodes were fan favorites as well, and that dynamic alone fashioned an uncharacteristic tone for their upcoming battle. At the Starrcade Rally, Flair told the crowd, "No one has to tell you, and no one has to tell me, that the pride and the prestige of representing not only the National

Wrestling Alliance, but representing Jim Crockett, and representing the greatest sport in the world today — I'm talking about professional wrestling — is an honor that I will cherish to my dying day. I'm proud to be here, and I'm proud to be the world champion."[40]

For some educated fans, the Flair-Rhodes matchup was already overdone, and an inexperienced referee, regardless of who it was, wasn't enticing at all. But the two combatants were experienced pros and knew how to entertain the masses. Flair's ring work against Rhodes was different than in his bouts with Ricky Steamboat or Kerry Von Erich. They were slower paced, less acrobatic, and maybe even less wildly physical at times. Their matches were more emotional and psychological, carrying the audience through every chop, punch, and elbow. At Starrcade on November 22, 1984, at the Greensboro Coliseum, they wrestled that way for 12 minutes and 9 seconds, and the 15,821 in attendance saw a heated athletic struggle to the very end.[41] The scene began to unfold as Flair locked a sleeperhold on Rhodes, but the latter had the wherewithal to drop to the mat, sending the champion from the ring. A moment later, Flair pulled Rhodes to the arena floor and sent him face-first into the steel ringpost.

Rhodes bladed heavy over his right eye, and although he tried to continue, referee Frazier stopped the match and awarded it to Flair. Angry that the contest was called, Rhodes had to be restrained from attacking Frazier, while Flair collected his $1 million check from Jim Crockett outside the ring. In a post-match interview with Tony Schiavone, Flair said he thought it was "unfortunate" that the bout ended the way it did but was thankful to be the world champion. "I'll be back here next year," he declared. "Count on it!" In contrast, Rhodes was furious and delivered an emotional message to Flair: "Ric Flair, if you call this a victory, you need to go home and get your momma. This ain't no victory. This ain't over. Leave you with this: spend your money well. Don't throw it away, cause the American Dream lives and will continue to live!" Another chapter in the Flair-Rhodes saga had been written, but their story was far from over.

The finish of Starrcade '84 left a lot to be desired and didn't live up to its predecessor's, despite the hard work of the wrestlers and JCP. Flair's positioning wasn't hurt in the slightest, and he recommenced his busy schedule through the remainder of the holiday season. In early 1985, he met a lot of familiar faces in their usual haunts, and that included Kerry Von Erich in Dallas and Fort Worth, Wahoo McDaniel in Charlotte and Greensboro, and Bruiser Brody in Kansas City and St. Louis. On February 5, 1985, Flair debuted in Philadelphia at the civic center in a further effort to advance on Vince McMahon's northeastern stronghold. Interestingly, the *Philadelphia Inquirer* pointed out that Flair was ranked number one in the nation by *Pro Wrestling Illustrated*, and listed Hulk Hogan, the WWF champion, at number four.[42] Philadelphia was a top-notch wrestling city, and its fans were extremely smart to the intricacies of the business. And for years, it had been a WWF-only locale.

But Crockett and the NWA wanted to change that. Flair wrestled Ricky Steamboat in his Philly debut and pinned him in 44 minutes before 3,770 fans.[43] JCP's subsequent program at the Philadelphia Civic Center on February 28 drew 4,000, and the Nature Boy beat Sgt. Slaughter by DQ.[44] Slaughter, a former employee of Vince McMahon, and former WWF champions "Superstar" Billy Graham and Bob Backlund were used as part of Crockett's invasion of the territory, and it was the same tactic McMahon was using against both the NWA and AWA. Talent raids were normalized in the current market and were incredibly damaging. In recent months, McMahon had made a number of serious moves, picking up young talent such as Mike Rotundo and Barry Windham, box-office superstars such as the Junkyard Dog, and legends like Jack and Jerry Brisco. In March 1985, the WWF added Ricky Steamboat to its roster, and the NWA lost one of its premier performers.[45]

Crockett and his NWA brethren were taking some painful hits but also scoring victories where they could. A merger of interests between JCP and Ole Anderson's upstart operation, Championship Wrestling from Georgia, took place, and Crockett snagged control of its WTBS timeslot on Saturday mornings. Then JCP became the exclusive host to all pro wrestling on the Superstation after a $1 million deal with Vince McMahon, of all people. Beginning on April 6, 1985, Crockett and the NWA became the sole provider of mat content on WTBS, and Ric Flair was back on the prized *World Championship Wrestling* telecast. Referencing his local hiatus and displaying a heelish persona once again, Flair told the audience, "Atlanta has been starved for the sight of a real man!" He put himself over in his customary fashion and concluded by saying, "Remember one thing. To be the man, you've got to beat the man."[46] It was one of Flair's legendary catchphrases, and if, by chance, any of the WTBS viewership had forgotten his stylish commentary, they were quickly reminded.

The political situation in Dallas never improved, and the complexities of the relationship between Jack Adkisson (Fritz Von Erich) and the NWA kept the rumor mill steadily churning. Approaching the second annual Parade of Champions on May 5, 1985, there was gossip about another temporary title switch to a Von Erich, and with Kevin booked to face Flair, he could be the next NWA champion. Kevin was scheduled to wrestle Flair again on May 12 in St. Louis, giving the NWA the opportunity to flip the title back to Flair in Missouri a week later.[47] A contemporaneous report in *Eastern Wrestling News* stated that a title change was "doubtful" and mentioned that Flair had blocked the idea. "I'm told Ric has 'outlawed' the short-term title change," Steve Helwagen wrote. "He's holding the fact that he could jump to the WWF any day over the heads of NWA promoters. [The] NWA can't afford to lose Ric."[48]

There is little question that Adkisson wanted the belt for his son Kevin, and he may have inquired about a potential repeat at his big stadium program. But it's not clear how far along the conversation got and if there was any real thought by NWA executives approving the title change. Furthermore, it can be said that Flair's personal political power was substantial, but he wasn't known for throwing his weight around, especially when asked to perform a duty for the benefit of the NWA. It also would have been unusual for him to use the threat of leaving for the WWF as leverage to keep hold of the championship in 1985. That's not to say there wasn't possible scuttlebutt about a Flair defection, and what the ramifications would be, among wrestling insiders and journalists. Obviously there was, and it only increased after George Scott, the man who sponsored Flair's rise in Jim Crockett Promotions and to the forefront of wrestling, became Vince McMahon's booker in the WWF.[49]

At the Parade of Champions show in suburban Dallas on May 5, Flair and Kevin Von Erich wrestled to a grueling double countout. The finish saw both men outside the ring, and Flair prevented the challenger from climbing back through the ropes. After the bell, the popular barefoot grappler snapped, locked in his Iron Clawhold, and refused to break it. His brothers, Kerry and Mike, tried to get him to halt his attack, but Kevin continued to put pressure on the head of the world champion. Finally his father, Fritz, entered the ring and convinced him to release the hold. The scenario strengthened Kevin's momentum against Flair, and Flair heavily sold the post-match assault to give the Von Erichs a boost on their biggest card of the year. But shockingly this was the final time Flair would wrestle one of the legitimate Von Erich brothers in the Dallas–Fort Worth area. Later in 1985, he'd meet Kevin and Kerry in St. Louis, but after his June 21 match with Kerry, the successful feud between Flair and the Von Erichs was over.[50]

Sure enough, this also marked the end of Jack Adkisson's working relationship with the NWA. Instead of recognizing Flair as the world champion, he elevated the American Heavyweight championship held by Rick Rude to World title status, and World Class ventured forward as an independent promotion. Adkisson's move illustrated the cracks in the armor of the Alliance, and the weaknesses in the NWA were exposed. At one time, the Alliance had been known as a worldwide organization of promotional offices and was 30-plus members strong. By 1985, the NWA was lucky to have half that number, and its influence was waning, particularly as the WWF continued its expansion. Jim Crockett was stuck in a difficult spot. As the NWA's strongest member and in the best position to fight the WWF on a national level, he had to balance his cooperation with the Alliance with the needs of running a rapidly growing enterprise.

The bottom line was that Crockett needed Flair available much more, as JCP went into new markets, and he could not set aside the number of dates he'd previously allotted to the NWA membership. To safeguard his relationship with Flair, Crockett signed him to an exclusive contract on May 1, 1985. The six-year deal granted Jim Crockett Promotions sole rights to book and promote Flair around the world and guaranteed that he'd make no less than $170,000 a year.[51] The contract explicitly referred to Crockett's extensive cable television reach and stated that it would "give [Crockett Promotions] the ability to expand into additional television market areas with live events," thus providing Flair with "more opportunities to wrestle and gain additional professional exposure." Included in the deal were merchandising rights and exclusive use of Flair's service marks and trademarks. Once a year, Crockett would provide Flair with a seven-day vacation and round-trip airfare.[52]

Historically, the NWA World Heavyweight champion was exclusive to the membership. In principle, it was the job of the traveling titleholder to appear in all NWA territories on an equal basis and to represent the entire organization over the course of a calendar year. In the early 1960s, there was much controversy over the way the original Nature Boy, Buddy Rogers, was booked as champion. His schedule had an overabundance of dates in the northeastern region, and members were critical about the lack of dates elsewhere on the NWA circuit. Subsequent champions corrected that mistake and defended their title in a balanced and fair manner. Now Jim Crockett had set in stone an exclusive agreement with the reigning NWA World Champion to book him as he saw fit — outside any dictum set by the Alliance. The old system of the NWA controlling the schedule of its champion, as least as it pertained to Flair, was over.

Crockett signed Dusty Rhodes to a similar exclusive contract, also on May 1, 1985. In one day, he signed his two biggest stars and guaranteed that neither man would jump to the WWF. For Flair, as the reigning champion with a new contract in his back pocket, he was in the best spot imaginable for a professional wrestler. There was already universal respect for his in-ring ability and dedication to the sport, and the potential for further growth was on the horizon. With Crockett and Rhodes laying out a detailed path for national expansion, Flair was headed to new cities in North America from Chicago to Los Angeles. Fans who had only read about Flair in magazines or maybe caught him on the Superstation would have the chance to see him live and in person. From incredible super cards to innovative matches and angles, Jim Crockett Promotions was entering a boom period, and Ric Flair was about to enjoy some of the greatest success of his career.

CHAPTER 12
A CUSTOM-MADE CHAMPION

T he die was cast. Professional wrestling was in the dawn of a new era, and the promoters of the NWA, WWF, and AWA were striving to achieve financial goals once thought impossible. Territorial boundaries that had separated wrestling organizations for decades were fading, and with the rapid growth of Vince McMahon's World Wrestling Federation, many NWA and AWA promoters were on the defensive. There was a dire need to protect their home operations while also cooperating against McMahon in key locations. Jim Crockett had shown the wrestling world the possibilities of an annual top-tier spectacle with Starrcade, and McMahon was going to take it to an entirely new level. On March 31, 1985, at Madison Square Garden, the WWF staged WrestleMania, a massive exhibition of athletic matches, celebrity appearances, and pomp and circumstance, all held under the banner of "sports entertainment." McMahon's multimillion-dollar success had everyone in the business talking.[1]

Hulk Hogan, the 302-pound muscleman billed as from Venice Beach, was the biggest star in wrestling.[2] The night before WrestleMania, he cohosted *Saturday Night Live* on NBC with his tag team partner, the popular actor Mr. T, and amused the television audience with his natural charm. At the Garden, Hogan and Mr. T beat Paul Orndorff and Roddy Piper in the show's main event, and the 19,121 fans in attendance roared in satisfaction at the conclusion of an exciting extravaganza. The intense media blitz that accompanied WrestleMania propelled Hogan further into the mainstream consciousness, and in the weeks and months following, he appeared on the cover of *Sports Illustrated*, as a guest veejay on MTV, and on *The Tonight Show*.[3] He was also the central figure in a new cartoon on CBS beginning late in the summer of 1985.[4] The WWF's impressive marketing, a sweeping merchandising campaign, and its national platform elevated Hogan to an unprecedented position for a pro wrestler.

Although every promoter in wrestling had taken note of the WWF's triumph, the anti-McMahon elements in the NWA and AWA were not ready to concede in any way. The competition was just heating up, and the mindset festering behind the scenes was all about gamesmanship and ultimate superiority. If McMahon's WrestleMania had superseded Starrcade, Jim Crockett and the NWA were prepared to try something even grander. But could Crockett create the same kind of exposure for Ric Flair that McMahon had for Hogan? That remained to be seen. Since Hogan was already the face of wrestling, with his fan-friendly persona and status as a role model, it would be difficult for anyone to touch him. Truth be told, Flair wasn't in the running for wrestling's top hero, despite his popularity in certain locales. Whereas Hogan and the WWF coveted the greenbacks generated by their wholesome approach, Flair and the NWA were sticking to their true nature — and it certainly wasn't always PG in tone.

Flair was famous for his slickly worded interviews laced with mature commentary and sexual innuendo, and his tailor-made phraseology was the exact opposite of the "take your vitamins, say your prayers" ideals of Hogan. Following a hard-fought battle with up-and-comer Magnum T.A., Flair told the WTBS viewing audience, "Magnum T.A. tells everybody that he took me to the limit. I've been to the limit one time in my life. It took Lynda Carter and Bo Derek back to back to make Ric Flair even flinch. I'm the greatest world champion of all time!"[5] In a different segment, he said, "All you young ladies that are headed for Florida — you don't have to go to Disney World to find Space Mountain. It's right here."[6] There was no limit to what he might say in a television interview, and his arrogance was endearing in a way. He owned his flamboyance. "It's just me," he told a Spartanburg reporter in 1980.[7]

The sheer cockiness of his promos was remarkable, and in the ring, he backed up every word. As the "heavyweight wrestling champion of the world," Flair performed at the highest level possible and was known as a wrestler, not a rebranded "sports entertainer." While the attention Hogan was receiving was impressive, no fan was interested in seeing Flair water down his shtick to appeal to the mainstream. It was quite the opposite. The priority was allowing Flair to be Flair and excel at what he did best — both in and out of the ring. For years, he had demonstrated his finely tuned ability to wrestle opponents of varying styles and skill around the globe, and his skills were still improving each year. His physical aptitude, conditioning, and gift of the gab made him the total package. Diehard fans appreciated those traits, and Flair garnered immense respect from old-school supporters of the NWA. These same people typically disliked the WWF product and Hogan's style of wrestling.

NWA wrestling was considered more athletic, more violent, and more emotionally charged than the content on WWF TV. The storylines were edgier and thus appealed to the older fan base. Vince McMahon courted a younger demographic with his colorful characters and gimmicks. Nevertheless, Flair and Hogan shared a connection to the people, and their magnetism translated to box office gold wherever they appeared. Since getting back on WTBS to once again reach a national audience, Flair was riding the line between baby face and heel. Against popular opponents in cities on the road, he was a full bore ruffian. But he was a "good guy" in areas run by Jim Crockett Promotions, a tradition going back a number of years. By April 1985, his longtime feud against Wahoo McDaniel began to fade in the mid-Atlantic territory, and booker Dusty Rhodes wanted to capitalize on the ambiguity of Flair's personality to put him in feuds with both heroes and villains.

At the top of the list was Rhodes's protégé, Magnum T.A., a handsome and well-liked rising star from Virginia. At 25 years of age, Magnum

T.A. was already recognized as the future of the industry and pegged as a coming world champion. On March 23, 1985, in Charlotte, he beat Wahoo McDaniel for the coveted U.S. championship, and he was vocal in TV interviews about wanting a shot at Flair's belt. He got his match on May 26 before a relatively small Greensboro crowd of 3,961, and wrestled Flair to a 60-minute draw.[8] Despite the result, Flair downplayed Magnum's status as a challenger to his title. During the June 15 WTBS telecast, he redirected the conversation to his own good looks, the fact that he was "custom-made from head to toe" and wore alligator shoes made in Hong Kong. Unfazed by Flair's deflection, Magnum confronted the Nature Boy and offered $1,000 cash if Flair could beat him right then and there in the studio. Flair confidently agreed, only to be held to a 10-minute draw.[9]

Pulling Magnum's hair and illegally using the ropes for leverage was evidence Flair wasn't about to play by the rules. "Slick Ric" used any means necessary to teach his rival a lesson. After the bell sounded, Flair tried to get the last word on Magnum, but the latter turned the tables. That's when Ole and Arn Anderson, the reigning National Tag Team champions, who had been talking with commentator Tony Schiavone, rushed the ring and attacked Magnum with a flurry of punches and kicks. The Andersons held the popular star as Flair dove off the ropes with a knee to Magnum's upper back and neck. Buzz Sawyer and Dick Slater ran out to halt the three-on-one assault, and Flair yelled furiously at Schiavone as the show went off the air. The shocking scene was made even more dramatic by Ole Anderson's comments moments prior to the finish. He told the TV audience, "If people don't know it by now, I guess it's time they find out. You're looking at family. When you see Arn Anderson, Ole Anderson, Ric Flair, there's blood. That's family. Ric Flair is our cousin."[10]

It was a throwback to Flair's early days in the mid-Atlantic territory in the mid-1970s, when his purported familial relation to Gene and Ole Anderson was a big part of the storyline. Now with the no-nonsense 26-year-old Arn Anderson in a pivotal spot, the Andersons were again a leading heel tandem for Jim Crockett Promotions.[11] The spiteful attack on Magnum T.A. was enough to declare Flair a bonafide villain, but booker Dusty Rhodes wasn't yet ready to completely commit Flair to that role. In fact, he wanted Flair to ride the line headed into the summer and the very first Great American Bash super card. Flair was booked to headline at Memorial Stadium in Charlotte on July 6 as a fan favorite against the dastardly Russian Nikita Koloff.[12] In the meantime, fans were meant to temporarily forget his behavior against Magnum and chalk it up to "Slick Ric" just being "Slick Ric." After all, in the Carolinas, Flair could do no wrong, and he would be cheered anyway.[13]

The buildup for the Bash created a swell of interest, and the pro-U.S.A. crowd was out in full force against Nikita and his uncle, Ivan. The Russians were highly unpopular and, at the time, held the NWA World Tag Team title. Originally from Minneapolis, Nikita Koloff possessed impressive size and an intimidating look, and was a natural heel. His only drawback was his inexperience. With just over a year of mat work, he was pushed into a main event position that typically went to wrestlers with far greater skill. But Koloff was capable. He relied on Flair's instincts and ability to lead a match, and the two delivered a hard-fought battle for the 25,721 fans in attendance. Of note, Flair made a historic entrance for his Bash contest with Koloff. He arrived via helicopter and walked a red carpet to the ring.[14] It was a majestic showing, fit for the world titleholder. In the end, special referee David Crockett counted Koloff's shoulders down and Flair retained.[15] After the match ended, though, the Koloffs pummeled Flair unmercifully, and he looked like anything but a triumphant champion.[16]

On the road, Flair made dates on his normal circuit, while adding a number of appearances in the territory of "Cowboy" Bill Watts in Louisiana and Oklahoma, as well as stops in Houston for Paul Boesch. The cooperation between Watts and Crockett had strengthened, and it was significant because Watts was not a dues-paying member of the NWA, nor had he ever been. Watts and Crockett had a similar enemy: the World Wrestling Federation. In an era of consolidation and hostility, the support of influential, friendly allies provided a timely boost when needed. Flair's four trips to New Orleans between June and August 1985, in defense of his NWA championship, helped Watts, and the Cowboy gave Flair top-notch talent to work with, Terry Taylor and Butch Reed. Over in Houston, Flair wrestled those two competitors, plus Kerry Von Erich, Magnum T.A., and Wahoo McDaniel between April and October 1985.[17]

Boesch provided Flair with some good publicity in his house arena program: "Ric Flair is a fighting champion who will defend his title wherever, whenever and against whoever the championship committee feels is the top challenger."[18] Magnum T.A. agreed with that sentiment and said something similar during an episode of *World Wide Wrestling* in early July 1985.[19] Interestingly, about a week earlier, Magnum and Flair ventured far outside the customary sphere of JCP and headlined at the Olympic Auditorium in Los Angeles on June 29. Flair was victorious by disqualification after Magnum threw him over the top rope. The show drew only 1,900 spectators, but it marked Crockett's willingness to expand his operations and was a milestone occasion for the promotion.[20] Flair and Magnum also took their feud to Chicago as part of Verne Gagne's SuperClash event at Comiskey Park on September 28, and Flair beat his foe in 25 minutes. The crowd in the Windy City was over 20,000.

Twice in September 1985, Flair faced Jerry Lawler, a man he'd only wrestled once before, and that was three years earlier in 1982 for a televised match in Memphis. Flair and Lawler battled on September 5 in Lexington and again on September 30 in Memphis, and in both encounters, Flair won by disqualification.[21] Throughout this period, Flair was wrestling a who's who lineup of star challengers, and Lawler joined the likes of Sgt. Slaughter, Billy Robinson, Wahoo McDaniel, and Harley Race as opponents for the NWA champ.[22] Dusty Rhodes was another name on that list, and to that point, he had jockeyed for position with Flair over the top baby face spot in the promotion. Flair was untouchable in his home territory, and his popularity outshined any negativity on cable TV or in national publications. But Rhodes, with the decision-making responsibilities as booker, was now ready to make a formal change, and wrestling history was going to be made.

On the evening of September 29, 1985, at the Omni in Atlanta, Flair pinned Nikita Koloff to retain his championship in a cage match. Seconds after the bell, Flair was victimized by Nikita and his uncle Ivan, as the third member of their triad, Krusher Khruschev, guarded the cage door. Of all people, Dusty Rhodes fought his way past Khruschev and cleared the ring of the Russians before facing Flair, who was still on the mat from the previous assault. At that moment, the Andersons appeared and assailed Rhodes. Not wasting any time, Flair locked the cage door, pummeled the American Dream, and then ascended the ropes. Ole and Arn held Rhodes down, and Flair delivered a knee drop onto his ankle, causing what was later called a "third degree sprain."[23] The incident kicked off a near riot at the Omni, as fans rushed the ring and prevented Flair and the Andersons from leaving the cage. Flair's unprovoked attack on Rhodes after the latter had saved him from the Russians turned him into public enemy number one. It was the first time he had been a "bad guy" in JCP since 1983.

Bob Caudle, the legendary voice of *Mid-Atlantic Championship Wrestling*, told Flair his faith in the champion was shaken. Flair responded in his casually cocky manner, saying, "You don't lose faith in winners, and Ric Flair, day in and day out, every day of his life, just keeps winning and winning and winning. I've got the most ability, I've got the greatest physical attributes, and I just happen to be the best athlete alive today — your world heavyweight champion!"[24] Rhodes approached the angle from his classic working man point of view and delivered one of his most iconic promos, telling Caudle that Flair had put "hard times" on him and his family. He told the audience, "The one way to hurt Ric Flair is to take what he cherishes more than anything in the world, that's the world heavyweight title. I'm gonna take it. I've been there twice. This time, when I take it, Daddy, I'm gonna take it for you."[25] Rhodes directed the statement at his legion of fans, and they were all for seeing Flair's reign end.

With the Flair-Rhodes feud on the minds of wrestling fans across the territory, Jim Crockett Promotions was successfully building toward its biggest show of the year, Starrcade '85. As for Flair, he continued to work harder than anyone in the business. The rigors of the road and his altogether demanding lifestyle didn't inhibit his conditioning or ability in the ring, and that in itself was thanks to his extraordinary constitution. His schedule was unrelenting, and his sustained determination was a credit to not only the NWA but wrestling as a whole. Between October 10 and October 19, Flair's endurance was put to the test, as he navigated a strenuous itinerary with eight matches in 10 days in five states and two countries. He started in Norfolk and visited Houston, Jacksonville, Asheville, and Charlotte, and then Saginaw and Lansing in Michigan. On the final day, he was in Tokyo, Japan, where he wrestled Jumbo Tsuruta to a draw. The estimated distance was over 9,940 miles.[26]

Facing Tsuruta was always a difficult chore, and Flair had his hands full with the former Olympian and All Japan mainstay. Although he was in front of an audience with different expectations than crowds in the United States, Flair didn't make huge adjustments to his physical style while wrestling in Japan. Fans in America were used to the entire Flair repertoire: a combination of sound wrestling skill mixed with his trademark villainy and boisterous showmanship. In Japan, enthusiasts had long enjoyed the traditional, competitive nature of pro wrestling, as well as its hard-hitting combat. There was less of an emphasis on personalities or performances outside the ring. Against Tsuruta, Flair was on the receiving end of an aggressive offensive attack, and he expertly sold the chops, kicks, and suplexes right down to the last minute.[27] At the end of their 15-minute bout, he was locked in Jumbo's figure-four and appeared close to submission before the match was called a draw.

Tsuruta had held the AWA World Heavyweight championship the year prior for two and a half months, having dethroned Nick Bockwinkel.[28] He ultimately lost the belt to the man Flair wrestled in a one-of-a-kind title unification match on October 21, 1985, in Tokyo — Rick Martel. The special contest was booked for the main event of All Japan's 13th anniversary card at the Sumo Hall, and it captured the attention of fans around the globe because of its significance. Martel was a well-respected and popular athlete from Quebec City, Quebec, and in the ring, he was known for his technical prowess and power, as well as his nimbleness in the air. Flair and Martel shook hands to start their encounter, and as the contest went on, the NWA champion refrained from breaking the rules in an apparent effort to keep their match clean. But that only lasted so long. Flair pulled Martel's hair several times, and the fiery tempers of both men exploded, giving fans their money's worth.

The spirited match exhibited the strengths of the two champions and lived up to expectations set by all the advance hype and publicity. As they approached the 34-minute mark, Flair attempted a cross body, but Martel caught him, and both flipped over the top rope and were counted out.[29] On that same tour, Flair and Martel teamed up three times, and their initial contest, on October 20, was a double countout against two former NWA champions, Terry and Dory Funk Jr.[30] Considering the recent angle with Dusty Rhodes and then this remarkable run in Japan, it seemed as if Flair was making history on a consistent basis. On November 6, 1985, the Nature Boy did it again, this time at Irish McNeil's Sports Club in Shreveport, Louisiana, during a TV taping for Bill Watts's Mid-South Wrestling. For some time, Mid-South had been producing among the most riveting wrestling content on television and garnering startling ratings. Watts himself was an exceptional commentator, adding sensible background and rationale for the important feuds they were engineering. It resulted in first-class programming.

Flair's emergence in Mid-South gave Watts a major cornerstone figure to build around, and on November 6, he was the central element in one of wrestling's best angles. There were layers to the storyline, starting with the $50,000 cash bounty placed on Butch Reed that Flair gave Dick Slater. Slater purportedly gave the money back, and Flair was asked about the situation by Watts in Shreveport. Flair mentioned that he didn't like Reed and claimed he didn't have the cash Slater was said to have returned. Later in the show, Flair entered the ring for what he believed would be a match against Al Perez, only to be confronted by Reed, who challenged the champion. Flair initially balked but tried to attack Reed when his back was turned. As Flair and Reed engaged each other, Watts mentioned that Flair had broken the ankle of Dusty Rhodes, and said that the NWA championship had consumed him, adding that it had taken "all moral aspect" out of Flair. "He sold himself out for the gold!" It was a perfectly reasonable kayfabe explanation for Flair's heel turn.

Reed landed his shoulder block off the ropes and pinned the NWA champion, much to the delight of the audience. The nontitle loss enraged Flair, and he aided Slater in a post-match assault on Reed, landing a spike piledriver. The attack moved Reed out of a championship contest, scheduled for the following week's TV broadcast, and Ted DiBiase, a renowned heel in the territory, was to get the shot instead. But before the bell rang for that bout, fan favorite Dick Murdoch told DiBiase to step aside and allow him to wrestle Flair. He claimed he was more deserving. DiBiase disagreed and told Murdoch so, but he was punched square in the face in response. Murdoch was knocked from the ring, and Flair interjected himself, sending DiBiase from the squared circle in tow. On the floor, Murdoch launched DiBiase into the metal ringpost, opening up a serious wound on his forehead.

With his match seemingly cancelled due to DiBiase's injury, Flair took the house mic and called it a "terrible tragedy" and said he was going home. But his night wasn't over yet. DiBiase wanted his title shot, and commentators put over his tremendous courage to fight through the blood loss to face the champion. They even warned viewers that the match could get "very gory." It was true: DiBiase's bleeding was a focal point of the bout, and Flair was covered in blood, which, on this rare occasion, wasn't his own. At the finish, DiBiase attempted a figure-four, and Flair kicked him off in reaction, sending DiBiase over the top rope and into the guardrail. He was then counted out. Dick Murdoch returned and delivered a brainbuster on the concrete, culminating an angle that turned him heel and put DiBiase over as a baby face.[31] The doubleturn was incredibly effective, and Flair's role was instrumental.

Flair's heel turn in JCP created another momentous opportunity, which, sure enough, impacted the course of wrestling history. Shortly after the injury to Dusty Rhodes, Flair told Bob Caudle on *Mid-Atlantic*

Championship Wrestling, "All of a sudden, I'm starting to like Tully Blanchard because he's a winner too. I like the Andersons, do you know why, because the Andersons are winners. The bottom line in this sport is, you walk down that aisle and you get in that ring, and you win!"[32] There was a growing bond between Flair, U.S. champion Blanchard, and the Andersons, who held the National Tag Team championship, and although it wasn't by design, a new powerful stable of villains materialized. The chemistry between the four men was instant, and during interviews, they delivered articulate and commanding performances, while complimenting each other in the ring. Arn Anderson causally referenced the "Four Horsemen of the Apocalypse" in a TV promo, and without even realizing it at the time, he had named their clique. The Four Horsemen were born.[33]

As Starrcade on November 28, 1985, neared, JCP worked to outshine previous years with "The Gathering." Rather than being limited to one venue, Crockett upped it a notch and arranged two cards — one for the Greensboro Coliseum and the other for the Omni Coliseum in Atlanta. The Flair-Rhodes rivalry was center stage that evening, live from Atlanta, and fans were decisively behind the American Dream in his quest to become a three-time NWA champion. Flair's strategy was to target Rhodes's injured ankle, and Rhodes reciprocated, focusing on Flair's leg in attempt to weaken him. After referee Tommy Young was injured in the melee, Rhodes locked in a figure-four but released the hold to fight off Arn Anderson. Ole Anderson nailed him from behind, and with a substitute official, it appeared Flair was going to retain his title. But Dusty kicked out. He suddenly maneuvered Flair in a small package and won the match — and the NWA championship.[34]

All told, this was an emotional ride for fans. The pro-Rhodes audience watched as he was nearly put out of wrestling before working his way back to defeat Flair for the gold belt. But any prolonged run at the top for Rhodes was not to be. NWA president Bob Geigel spoke with referee Young and decided to give the championship back to Flair, while at the same time, disqualifying him for the interference of the Andersons. Rhodes won the match but not the NWA crown. As expected, the feud between Flair and Rhodes would continue through the end of 1985, and it remained an exciting draw well into the new year. They actually head-lined a program at Hiram Bithorn Stadium in San Juan, Puerto Rico, on December 21, 1985, and drew an estimated 20,000 people. Flair successfully defended his belt against Rhodes, as he did four nights later in Atlanta on Christmas. In other matches, Flair teamed with Tully Blanchard and the Andersons against combinations of Rhodes, Magnum T.A., and the Road Warriors.

Looking back at 1985, Flair briefly engaged a rival Nature Boy in what was an unusual but intriguing storyline. The 25-year-old Tennessean Buddy Landel, an up-and-comer with bleached platinum hair and a swagger comparable to Flair and Buddy Rogers, was making waves in JCP with the great J.J. Dillon as his manager. During interviews, Landel accused Flair of avoiding him, and he wanted to prove that he was the official Nature Boy. Flair minimized Landel's challenge, yet still acknowl-edged him as an opponent during the summer. They wrestled a little more than a half dozen times, including bouts in Charlotte, Greensboro, and Raleigh, and Flair retained his belt. In an interview years later, Landel said that Flair had "given" him the Nature Boy gimmick to use and respected his abilities in the ring. He also claimed that Flair was going to take some time off for personal reasons and that Crockett was going to give him a temporary run with the NWA title. However, Landel missed an important TV taping in Atlanta and was subsequently fired.[35]

Flair never did take much time off from his busy calendar. On January 16, 1986, he went up to Winnipeg for a dream match against one of his former mentors, Nick Bockwinkel, the former three-time AWA champion. The well-respected Bockwinkel was a key figure in Flair's early development in the Minneapolis territory back in the 1970s. Before 8,000 fans at the Winnipeg Arena, the two stars wrestled their one and only singles encounter and battled to a double countout.[36] The following month, in the continuing cooperation between the NWA and AWA under the Pro Wrestling USA banner, a big card was held at the Meadowlands Arena in East Rutherford, New Jersey, on February 24,

1986. Flair met Magnum T.A. in a memorable defense of his champion-ship before 6,000 fans, and after 28:23, he pinned his challenger.[37] Following the card, Flair celebrated his birthday, which was the next day, with Chuck Berry at the Lone Star Café in New York City.[38]

On February 25, 1986, Flair turned 37. A decade earlier, he had predicted that he'd be retired by 35.[39] But it was an impossible thought, as he was considered by most to be professional wrestling's greatest active wrestler, and he was thriving on the success. It didn't matter the opponent, the scenario, whether he was a "good" or "bad" guy, it was all the same to Flair — and he was flourishing. In his personal life, he and his wife, Beth, had moved into a new home at 4267 Tottenham Road, just north of Jim Crockett's office on Carmel Road.[40] By September 1985, they were ready to move again, this time to a spacious four-bedroom property in the Coachman Ridge section of Matthews in suburban Charlotte.[41] Being at home was the perfect rest and relaxation for a normal man in a normal profession, but Flair was anything but that. He told a reporter in 1984 that he was "fortunate" if he was able to spend two or three days in a row at home.[42]

In a New Zealand publication, he said he spent 35 weeks a year on the road, but the hard truth was it was much more than that.[43] His traveling schedule as NWA champion was ceaseless, and even though the terri-tories were disappearing, and Jim Crockett had lessened his availability to other promoters, he was still working at an incredible pace. The long hours traveling by car and plane were often lonely, unlike his time wres-tling in JCP in his younger years. In those days, he'd travel within a pack of wrestlers, sharing the road and splitting the drive time. The difference between that kind of lifestyle and the world champion's was stark, but in all, a person would have to love what they were doing to embrace this life. And Flair did. He loved being the world champion, and he expressed that love in almost every TV promo he delivered. Although it was kayfabe, it was also the truth.[44] Flair was who he was — both the world champion and the living, breathing Nature Boy rolled into one. Fans could sense it. People who met Flair on the road knew it. And insiders were well aware that he really was the same man people saw on

TV every week. With that, there was a major trade-off: to be a successful National Wrestling Alliance World Heavyweight champion, there was little room for a home life. It was all about the calendar and the watch — and the watch never stopped ticking.

CHAPTER 13

THE HORSEMEN RIDE

T here was no doubt about it, the ongoing warfare in professional wrestling created a new normal for fans, wrestlers, and promoters. Super cards and closed-circuit TV broadcasts were capturing the imaginations of spectators, while cable had given the Big Three (WWF, NWA, and AWA) consequential national platforms.[1] Even network television outlets, like NBC and CBS, were capitalizing on the wrestling boom, and fans were never at a loss for new content in any given week.[2] As a result of the steady increase in ticket sales and TV income, wrestlers were well positioned to negotiate the best possible financial deal for themselves. Promoters were balancing the desperate need for critical talent with trying to hold on to as much cash as possible. This vacillating environment created a tug-of-war for key performers, and some athletes bounced around in search of the right opportunity and job security.

Late in the summer of 1984, Barry Windham left Florida to work for his mentor Dusty Rhodes in JCP. Windham immediately received a push, and it appeared he was being established for a run with the United States Heavyweight championship — a title recently declared vacant.[3] A tournament for the belt was scheduled for October 7 in Charlotte, but Windham didn't show. In fact, he walked away from JCP entirely and took his promising skills to Vince McMahon's WWF. Teamed with another gifted wrestler, Mike Rotundo, Windham captured the WWF

World Tag Team title twice in 1985 and built upon his credibility as a potential world heavyweight champion.[4] But the WWF had a ceiling for growth, particularly for a baby face, next to the success of Hulk Hogan, and Windham left the organization and returned to Florida in October 1985.

A short time later, on February 14, 1986, Windham received his first singles match for the NWA World title in more than 19 months.[5] His bout with Ric Flair was the main event of the syndicated Battle of the Belts II show from the Eddie Graham Sports Complex in Orlando, Florida. It was a career moment for Windham: back in the NWA spotlight and reunited with Flair, an old friend of the family. In a compelling pre-match interview, Flair acknowledged Windham as a "great wrestler" and mentioned his father, Blackjack Mulligan, as well as his younger brother, Kendall, the Florida State champion. "Barry Windham's a great one," Flair declared, "but he's going to have to be the greatest to beat Ric Flair!"

There were two things of note when the Nature Boy emerged from the dressing room that special evening in Orlando. For one, he didn't appear to his customary theme song, *Also sprach Zarathustra*, which had been routine for his big matches since 1983. *Easy Lover* by Phil Collins and Philip Bailey played instead. The other outstanding detail was the belt around Flair's waist.[6] It wasn't the recognizable Ten Pounds of Gold, emblematic of the National Wrestling Alliance World Heavyweight title, dating back to 1973, but an incredibly eye-catching new gold belt. Purchased by Jim Crockett Promotions and crafted by a jeweler in Reno, Nevada, the "Big Gold," as it would become known, was an ornament befitting the heavyweight king and the glitz and glamour of JCP's new era of national prominence.[7] It also corresponded well with Flair's on-camera gimmick, as he prized his fancy suits and Rolex watches. The gold complimented him perfectly.[8] Flair looked like wrestling's preeminent champion in advance of his bout with Barry Windham at Battle of the Belts, and as their match opened, fans quickly realized they were witnessing history.

Both wrestlers were in prime condition and exhibited the best qualities of an evenly competitive battle, complete with sound technical take-downs, reversals, and a variety of punishing holds. As in his match with Rick Martel in Japan, Flair was willing to shake hands at the outset as a gesture of sportsmanship, but he sneakily began to cheat, as hostilities flared.[9] That didn't interfere with the unmitigated classic the two grapplers put on, as Windham brought out the best in Flair and vice versa.[10] The seesaw action was intense and logical, and between the trade-off of chops and punches, each wrestler used a range of maneuvers. As frustrating as it was for viewers in the arena and those watching on television, Flair's expert timing in draping his foot across the bottom rope just before the referee counted three in a pin attempt was extraordinary. Each time he did it against Windham, the resounding disappointment was heard from all reaches of the venue.

After a hard-fought clash, which went over 41 minutes, Flair and Windham were counted out by referee Bill Alfonso, and Flair retained his new gold belt.[11] The match earned tremendous praise, including a five-star rating in *Wrestling Observer Newsletter*. "If anyone, even for a second, doubted that Flair is the best wrestler in the world, this match will change their mind," Dave Meltzer wrote.[12] Voters from that same publication named Flair "Wrestler of the Year" for the fifth year in a row following his 1985 campaign, and he was widely commended for his all-around abilities.[13] *Pro Wrestling Illustrated* also recognized him as "Wrestler of the Year" for 1985, his third honor from that magazine since 1981.[14] Going into the Battle of the Belts program, Flair had been the NWA World champion for nearly 21 months straight, and although his in-ring performances, work ethic, and overall wrestling aptitude were peerless, he did draw some critical opinions along the way.

One of the main gripes was a repetitiveness that seemed to surface when Flair wrestled less-skilled opponents.[15] On the nights he faced a below average rival, he was typically forced to carry the workload, and a prevailing routine ran its course. For instance, there would be a limited number of moves, a general slugfest with punches and chops, leading into a figure-four — or even two (by Flair and his opponent), a referee bump, and ultimately a disqualification. The entertainment value remained, but this type of standardized match, with sometimes only subtle changes, became obvious to fans who witnessed these bouts on more than one occasion. Conversely, when Flair wrestled a top-tier competitor, such as Barry Windham, Harley Race, or Ricky Steamboat, the dimensional physical entanglement tugged on the emotional heart-strings of the audience. Flair incorporated more moves in a wider demonstration of his technical prowess and added deeper psychology to the affair, providing a full sampling of his versatile skillset.

At times, Flair was too giving to his opponent. Pro wrestling was full of egos, and many top performers only agreed to sell a small amount of the time, whereas Flair was taking tons of punishment in the ring. He'd bleed nearly every night, and after the final bell rang, he looked as if he'd been to hell and back. In the WWF, Hulk Hogan was wrestling short matches, probably a quarter or less of the time Flair did nightly, and his dominant streak roused fans to no end. He'd crush his opponents, guys who were monstrous in size, and many fans felt Hogan was simply unbeatable as the world champion. But Hogan was an athlete in the pro wrestling sense, very different from Flair. The selling, the hour-long matches, and the physical toll on Flair put him in a different category of performer than the Hulkster.[16] By giving his opponent so much offense, Flair made his eventual victory more impressive since he had beaten a great man. Even when he squeezed out a win, Flair proved that he was too cunning for his rival and was unbeatable in his own way. But Flair's work also intentionally gave the impression of weakness. The way he sold for foes made every opponent appear to have at least a fighting chance to win the world championship. That kept the box office strong through months and months of Flair's continuous run at the top during the mid-1980s.

The other main criticism of Flair related to his adult-themed comments and humor during interview segments. For teenagers and older fans, Flair's risqué comments were side-splitting and expected from the Nature Boy. He was true to form and perpetuated the belief that he lived that way. To younger enthusiasts, his statements were more than likely confusing and illustrated the difference between a JCP program and a kid-friendly WWF show.[17] Dave Meltzer, in February 1986, mentioned the viewership of younger children and wrote that Flair's running Space Mountain joke was "getting out of hand."[18]

Meltzer, like most fans of JCP programming, respected Flair's interview ability a great deal and regularly credited him as one of the best in the industry. Putting any constructive criticism into context, Flair was constantly breaking new ground as an edgy, ultra-confident superstar, and he didn't have to work hard to differentiate his promo style from that of Hulk Hogan or anyone else. All he had to do was step in front of the camera, and the magic happened. In early 1986, Flair delivered a succession of notable verbal tirades at Ron Garvin, a 41-year-old veteran originally from Montreal, Quebec.[19] In many ways, Garvin was the opposite of Flair, as he prioritized physicality over showmanship in what was regarded as an old-school wrestling philosophy. Their rivalry took off following a heated TV contest during the December 28, 1985, edition of *World Championship Wrestling*, and Garvin's aggressiveness took a number of spectators by surprise.

Garvin was a maximum-intensity type of wrestler, and he stood toe to toe with Flair in a brutal exchange of blows, particularly the chest chops that were not only seen and heard, but also seemingly felt by viewers as well. Flair mocked him as a "tough guy," but the Canadian actually was, and his ruggedness created a lot of excitement as he came close to pinning the champion for the NWA belt several times. Their WTBS battle ended after Dusty Rhodes, the Andersons, and others entered the ring and a disqualification was called.[20] JCP commentators hyped Garvin as a credible challenger to Flair in the weeks that followed and promoted a "Dream Match" vote by fans to determine the matches for a special Superstars on the Superstation program, broadcast on WTBS on February 7. Flair and Garvin seemed destined to be the feature bout, and their interaction at the Atlanta television studio on January 18, 1986, might have clinched the deal. There, "Hands of Stone"

Garvin knocked out Flair with one punch to solidify his position as a top contender to the NWA championship.[21]

The Superstars on the Superstation event was taped a few days prior to broadcast from the Omni Coliseum in Atlanta.[22] As expected, Flair and Garvin was the final match of a four-bout televised card, and their encounter was more of a straight-up war than a wrestling match. They echoed their previous TV skirmish with vicious body chops, but their visible hatred for one another bubbled over, adding chokes, slaps, and painful strikes that elevated the believability of the contest. The commentators, Tony Schiavone and David Crockett, acknowledged Flair's uncanny ability to kick out of precarious pinfall situations, and essentially affirmed, "That's why he was the world heavyweight champion." Flair survived Garvin's knockout punch in Atlanta and pinned his foe, even though Garvin's foot was on the bottom rope.[23] The Flair-Garvin feud carried over to the house show circuit, and they wrestled more than a dozen times into the early summer.

Fans were undoubtedly interested. An estimated 9,000 people jammed the Philadelphia Civic Center to see their bloody struggle on March 22, 1986, and another 12,339 were on hand at the Greensboro Coliseum a week later.[24] Flair was victorious in both contests. Flair and Dusty Rhodes returned to the squared circle at the first annual Crockett Cup on April 19 in New Orleans.[25] The spectacular, held at the enormous Louisiana Superdome, featured a tag team tournament in memory of Jim Crockett Sr. and purportedly offered a $1 million prize.[26] The show was split into two parts between the afternoon and evening. Despite intense promotion and an impressive lineup of stars, the show drew approximately 16,000 total fans and failed to live up to financial predictions at the gate.[27] As for Flair and Rhodes, they left it all in the ring, as they typically did, and entertained the crowd. Their bloody match ended when Rhodes used his boot on Flair and was disqualified.[28]

The continued strength of Jim Crockett Promotions was the depth of its talent pool, and Rhodes was brilliantly devising strategies to keep things on a roll. As Flair was working with Rhodes and Garvin across the circuit, Dusty set the wheels in motion for the world champion's next priority feud, and his opponent was half of the hugely popular Rock and Roll Express tag team. Ricky Morton was a 29-year-old, blond high-flyer with outstanding charisma. He was also a second-generation competitor. With his tag team partner, Robert Gibson, he had captured the NWA World Tag Team title twice since arriving in JCP the July before. Morton and Gibson appealed to younger fans in a major way and built up a sizable following of preteen and teenage girls. Flair, who never failed to mention his contingent of women admirers, went out of his way to criticize Morton and Gibson for their "teenybopper" supporters and specifically disparaged Morton.[29]

Morton and Gibson approached Flair and exchanged words during an interview segment at the WTBS Studio in March 1986. Casually, Morton took off Flair's sunglasses, dropped them on the ground, and stomped them. Flair slapped him in response, setting off a wild brawl, which ended up in the ring. With a blazing fury of offense, Morton got the better of the Nature Boy, as the studio audience shouted in approval.[30] On April 20, 1986, in Greensboro, Morton pinned Flair in the finals of a six-man tag team elimination bout at the Coliseum. Afterwards, the losers in the contest — Flair, Arn Anderson, and Tully Blanchard — jumped Morton and Gibson in the locker room, and Flair rubbed Morton's face across the concrete floor, as he'd done to Ricky Steamboat and Roddy Piper years earlier.[31] The Four Horsemen, sans Ole who was out of action at the time, proceeded to injure Morton a second time in late May, collaborating to break the popular grappler's nose.[32] The injury didn't stop Morton for a second, and he wore face protection in subsequent matches.

Over a three-month period, April to July 1986, Flair and Morton wrestled over 20 times. Although Flair was several inches taller and weighed about 25 to 30 pounds more, their matches were exceptionally competitive. Flair recalibrated his style to work at Morton's faster pace and never missed a beat. He could manipulate the tempo of the contest as well by slowing things down or speeding things up. And if the fans needed an excitement rush, he just bumped more. At the tail end of their feud, Flair entered a new phase of his championship run, as the central headliner for the all-important Great American Bash series.[33] JCP invested big money into a cross-country tour and rented out a host of football stadiums in the process, anticipating massive crowds. Part of their expenditures went to a live concert performance held in conjunction with their wrestling card. Featured singers included David Allan Coe and Waylon Jennings.[34]

The concert idea, in theory, seemed to make logical sense in effort to lure a wider spectrum of people, but it backfired and was a bust.[35] In fact, Crockett's stadium aspirations were almost unrealistic, especially in Memphis and Cincinnati, where they failed to attract respectable numbers at the box office.[36] But the promotion drew explosively in its home area, and once again, Flair was treated like royalty. On July 5, the awestruck patrons at the Bash event at Charlotte's Memorial Stadium watched as Flair entered via helicopter for the second year in a row, and he drew a chorus of cheers from the estimated 20,000 in attendance.[37] Even as a heel, he was mesmerizing, and the territory's faithful, who had seen him rise from an overweight upstart to the champion of the world, applauded him with reverence. His opponent, Ricky Morton, was the designated crowd favorite, but Flair held the heart and soul of Charlotte's fan base. There was simply no one more important to pro wrestling in Charlotte than Flair.[38]

Morton took Flair to the brink of defeat in their memorable cage match at the Bash, but Slick Ric was far too underhanded to be beaten. At the conclusion, he used the ropes for leverage as he pinned his challenger and retained the NWA championship. In the middle of a bout, Flair was always cooking up new ways to be entertaining, whether it was his trademark "Wooooo!" a flashy strut, or yelling at a ringsider who annoyed him. He often hollered at the referee and occasionally pushed an official in frustration. Some referees, Tommy Young, for instance, wouldn't stand for that kind of aggression and shoved Flair back. In those moments, Flair's face would display a mix of disgust and astonishment that the referee would get physical with him, and it never failed to give the audience a good laugh. In his bout with Morton in Charlotte, Morton's face guard came off, and Flair put it on, giving fans a hearty chuckle.

The Bash tour hit 14 cities from July 1 to August 2, 1986, and Flair was booked to defend his belt every night. In truth, he placed his championship on the line 18 times in 26 days and had matches with Dusty Rhodes, Nikita Koloff, and Magnum T.A., as well as both members of the Rock and Roll Express and the Road Warriors.[39] Rhodes was his opponent in a cage on July 26, 1986, in Greensboro, and the card drew 14,817 spectators.[40] It wasn't a typical night with the standard DQ finish. This time, Rhodes pinned Flair with a small package and captured the NWA title, ending Flair's spectacular reign at 793 days.[41] The following Saturday, on WTBS, Flair credited Rhodes with a clean victory and said he had no excuse for the loss. On the same program, Rhodes confidently told Tony Schiavone, "One of 'Space Mountain' Ric Flair's greatest sayings of all-time was 'To be the man, you got to beat the man.' Well, Nature Boy, if you ever want to be the man again, you have to beat the man, Dusty Rhodes, the American Dream, world's heavyweight champion."[42]

Flair had been NWA titleholder for so long that it was actually weird to see him without the belt. He made it known that he wouldn't stop until he regained the championship, and pundits were predicting a short stint at the top for Rhodes, mostly because of his behind-the-scenes responsibilities at JCP.[43] With Flair as the challenger, the duo met five times, including on August 2 at Fulton County Stadium in Atlanta, which was the final stop on the Great American Bash tour. Rhodes won each match, but he was seriously hobbled after their battle on August 7 in Kansas City. That was because Flair's Four Horsemen stablemate, Tully Blanchard, blasted Rhodes in his bad leg with a steel chair, and then Flair put the champion in his figure-four. Two days later in St. Louis, Flair received another shot at the belt and focused on Rhodes's leg again. He used a chair and applied his figure-four until Rhodes could handle no more. He was pinned while in the hold, and Flair regained the NWA title.[44]

Throughout the Great American Bash series and particularly in Kansas City and St. Louis, it was clear that the Four Horsemen were a unified and incomparable combination of wrestling figures. Flair, Blanchard, Ole and Arn Anderson, and manager J.J. Dillon were the coolest faction in mat history and were revolutionizing the concept.[45] Cocky, menacing, well-dressed, and sporting gold, the Horsemen were the complete package, and their enemies were always at risk of a gang-style beatdown. Naturally, Rhodes was their primary target, because of their years of combat. But in October 1986, a real-world incident sharpened the angle between Rhodes and the Horsemen, and Rhodes capitalized on the moment to trigger a tidal wave of box office success. The momentum, unfortunately, was generated by a car accident suffered on October 14, 1986, in Charlotte that ended Magnum T.A.'s career.[46]

Magnum was only 27 years old at the time of his crash. He was on a very short list of potential world heavyweight champions and considered a logical successor to Flair.[47] The sudden loss of Magnum forced JCP to immediately change its booking structure, and Rhodes quickly devised a new plan. Four days after the accident, Rhodes was jumped by the Horsemen outside Jim Crockett's headquarters in Charlotte in an infamous daytime attack. The Andersons and J.J. Dillon tied his arms and smashed his right hand with a baseball bat. That same night, Rhodes turned up for a show in Philadelphia wearing a cast, and he introduced his new ally against the Horsemen, Russian Nikita Koloff. Since his debut in 1984, Koloff had been one of the biggest heels in Jim Crockett Promotions, and his change of heart in the aftermath of Magnum's injury stunned the wrestling world.[48] Within weeks, Koloff, the reigning U.S. champion, was announced as Flair's challenger at Starrcade '86.[49]

Being able to elevate a fellow athlete and to craft a vibrant and exhilarating match were extraordinary talents in professional wrestling. Time and again, against grapplers of varying experience and ring knowledge, Ric Flair managed to raise the workmanship of his opponent to a far greater level than their skills alone could achieve. It was a talent, and it was a gift. Against Nikita Koloff at Starrcade '86, Flair demonstrated to the fullest of his capabilities that he was a master at his trade, and he heightened the aptitude of his counterpart while masterminding an absorbing battle suitable for the main event of JCP's most important show of the year.[50] Held on November 27 at the Omni Coliseum in Atlanta, the contest was preceded by a video package devoted to Magnum T.A., and with Koloff fighting on behalf of his fallen comrade in arms, the emotional leadup to the bout was intense.[51] Flair and Koloff, in 19 minutes of action, brawled and bled and concluded in a wild, confusing manner. Their match was reportedly a double disqualification, although an on-screen graphic declared Flair the winner.[52]

The inconclusive finish between Flair and Koloff was designed to retain interest in their matches going forward. Instead of blowing up their box office potential, JCP wanted to keep fans on the edge of their seats, wondering if Koloff could unseat Flair for the NWA belt. It was quite similar to Dusty Rhodes's endless series of bouts with Flair and maintained the general interest of fans in the ongoing championship title chase. Flair looked good atop the mountain, holding the gold, as the popular stars of JCP lined up in a perpetual pursuit of title honors. Within days of Starrcade, a familiar fan favorite returned to JCP and joined the procession — Barry Windham.[53] Windham's previous accomplishments in the ring, and personal connection to both Flair and Dusty Rhodes, made him the odds-on favorite to supplant the Nature Boy, if Koloff didn't get the nod first.

Going into 1987, Jim Crockett Promotions was pushing the envelope in an attempt to become a national organization and in a de facto war with the WWF, AWA, Bill Watts's UWF, and World Class out of Dallas. With expanded syndication, JCP was venturing further and further west, staging programs in Albuquerque, Los Angeles, and San Francisco. Two months before Starrcade, the promotion had booked a card in suburban Minneapolis at the Met Center, right in the heart of AWA territory.[54] For Flair, it was his first opportunity to wrestle before his hometown crowd since he was a prelim wrestler in 1974, 12 years earlier.[55] He had gotten his start in the Twin Cities, but he'd become internationally famous in the NWA, and his return presented a special occasion for him and his family. Minneapolis sportswriter Bob

Lundegaard splashed a favorable article about Flair on the front page of the *Minneapolis Star and Tribune*.[56]

Even better, the newspaper featured a photo of Flair with his parents, Richard and Kay. The Fliehrs, who still lived in Edina, attended the card in nearby Bloomington and were proud of their son. "This is what he chose to do, and he's very good at it and very honored," Kay told Lundegaard. "I can't think of any mother who wouldn't like that."[57] The important advice Flair's father had given him all those years ago — to "make sure you're the best" at whatever he endeavored — was a substantial part of Flair's mindset and drive.[58] Richard Fliehr elaborated on that guidance in this article, telling the journalist, "I've always told him, 'Do what you want. Just be good at what you do.' I've seen too many of my compatriots who wanted their sons to go into medicine. It became a sore point and the sons ended up hating their fathers."[59] Although Flair's professional life differed greatly from that of his parents, he had lived up to and exceeded any possible expectations in his chosen field — and was considered by many to be "the best."

The two-page article claimed Flair had an income of over $500,000, had traveled 353,000 miles by air over the prior year, and only lost four matches in "his last 1,700 or so." He was also said to be 34, shaving three years off his actual age. On a personal note, the writer mentioned that Flair lived in Charlotte with his wife, Beth, and infant daughter. It was true. Several months earlier, on April 5, 1986, his third child, Ashley Elizabeth Fliehr, was born at Presbyterian Hospital in Charlotte.[60] The article didn't mention that Flair's other two children, Megan and David, ages 12 and seven respectively, were living in the Twin Cities area.[61] The oversight was likely intentional, reflective of the complexities in Flair's family life. It was no secret that, due to his constant travel, he was away from his family for long periods of time.[62] The fact that Minneapolis was AWA territory made seeing his parents and children more difficult, as he was always elsewhere in the country in sanctioned NWA cities.[63]

"It wasn't [that] I wanted to be away from my family," Flair later explained. "Once you're the world champion, what else is there for you?

What are you going to do?"[64] The challenge of balancing the demands of the world heavyweight championship, international bookings, a gregarious lifestyle, and a family life was nearly impossible. Normalcy was out the window.

From a business standpoint, Jim Crockett Promotions needed Flair more than ever as it enlarged its sphere of interest, and millions of dollars were on the line. In fact, the company's revenue with Flair on top had increased fourfold in some months, and, overall, it spiked from about $5–6 million a year to nearly $17 million in 1985–86.[65] The Great American Bash tour alone, in July 1986, drew $2.4 million for 36 live shows.[66] The entire roster and crew were instrumental in the enormous growth of the promotion, and there was no denying Flair's influence. Jim Crockett and Dusty Rhodes had surrounded him with the perfect cast of characters, and JCP was setting records.

Alongside that astronomical upswing in income, notoriety, and achievement, weaknesses in Jim Crockett's enterprise were slowly becoming evident. A festering battle of egos was consuming JCP's leading personalities, which impacted the central decision-making of the promotion. Despite the tremendous money being made, JCP was overspending. Expensive syndication deals and the nonsensical use of two private airplanes, particularly for short jumps that used to be made by car, were sinking the company. Again, ego played a part. The upper echelon of performers no longer wanted to spend time traveling by car or commercial airline. They used and overused private planes, at a great cost to JCP. Rather than balancing the books to ensure the financial well-being of the company through good days and bad, Crockett executives failed to provide the necessary oversight. And instead of further growth and prosperity, JCP was faced with a fast approaching reckoning.

That being said, the corporate missteps behind the scenes were no fault of Flair or any of the on-camera performers. Jim Crockett Promotions, in 1986 and going into '87, was a haven of superstar talent, and in the ring, big things were planned. Complementing Flair on NWA shows were the Midnight Express and Jim Cornette, the Rock and Roll Express, the

Road Warriors, Tully Blanchard and Arn Anderson, J.J. Dillon, Barry Windham, Ron Garvin, and, of course, Nikita Koloff. Guys like Rick Rude, Tim Horner, and Brad Armstrong were coming into their own and exhibiting immense promise. Down in Florida, there was another up-and-comer, a former football player named Lex Luger, whom Dusty Rhodes was eyeing for a future role in the company. It was hard to see fault in the on-screen product, but the backstage drama would soon make a visible impact — and affect everyone in the company. Ric Flair would not be spared.

CHAPTER 14
FIVE-TIME CHAMPION

The benefits of being the acclaimed world heavyweight champion were innumerable. The attention from adoring fans was relentless, all around the world, and Ric Flair completely embraced his status as a public figure. He shook hands and signed autographs, socialized with fans in public settings, and constantly revealed himself to be a down-to-earth, approachable celebrity. At heart, he was a people person and always had been, dating back to his school years in Minnesota and Wisconsin. His magnetism was genuine, as was his ability to connect with others in any type of situation, and those who met him were likely never to forget it. Flair had tremendous exposure and recognition, without question, and he appreciated the position he was in. He reveled in it.[1] There was never a moment in which he didn't wholeheartedly live up to the expectations of his television personality or of the world heavyweight champion. That included his picture-perfect attire, impressive gold jewelry, and coiffed hair.

"The purpose for making a living in this country is to make money and be able to enjoy life," Flair told a reporter. "I do just that. I make money. I spend money. I enjoy wearing the finest clothes, entertaining the most beautiful women in the world. I'm custom-made from head to toe."[2] On another occasion, he said, "Do you see this Rolex watch? Do you see that $500 suit? Do you see these alligator shoes? I don't lay bricks for a living, although there is nothing wrong with that. I don't punch a clock or work on an assembly line. The reason I have spent 15 years in this business is I don't want to be poor — I refuse to be poor. Even if I weren't in this business, I would be a success doing something else. I look at life this way: if you have to ask how much it costs, you can't afford it. I don't want my family — or me — to want for anything."[3] The combination of the money, adulation, and limelight was addicting and enveloping, and Flair didn't rush from the dressing room back to the hotel each night to enjoy peace and tranquility. He went out to bars, nightclubs, and restaurants, befitting his exuberance for life.

The expenses for his luxurious suits and accessories were attributed to the vast sums Flair was paying for "image enhancement."[4] He shopped at high-end men's clothing stores in Kansas City, Charlotte, and Atlanta, and he was fitted with top-of-the-line garments that matched his self-confidence and pride. "I think it's part of my job as champion," he explained when asked about his clothes. "Looking good is part of it. I usually have a sport coat on and dress slacks."[5] Flair was definitely not a blue jeans type of guy. In fact, he said that he never wore jeans at all, and coming from the "born with a silver spoon" character he portrayed, that was completely believable.[6] Vital to his overall look was his "flowing mane of peroxide, blow dried hair," which he kept in immaculate condition.[7] Flair's hair was described as blond or platinum by journalists, and he maintained its bleached appearance by visiting a stylist for a few hours every 10 days.[8]

Fans who had followed Flair's career for any length of time were accustomed to seeing his blond hair turn a shade of red when it was saturated with his blood during intense ring matches. That was another trademark of his, and Flair sometimes bladed on consecutive nights, leaving his forehead raw and sore. During the 1986 Great American Bash tour, he went to extremes to put over his popular adversaries by drawing blood from himself with small blades hidden in athlete tape around his fingertips.[9] During his typical Saturday morning interview segments on WTBS, Flair was always dressed to the nines, but his forehead bandages would illustrate the savagery of a recent hard-fought battle. And this wasn't anything new. Flair had been "getting color" for over a decade, and it was unusual when he didn't don a crimson mask in an important contest. David Newton of the *Greensboro Daily News* noted in 1980 that the skin of Flair's forehead was "sandpaper rough" and "cross-hatched" with tiny scars.[10] A Miami writer likened it to something you'd find on a "burn victim."[11]

"If I quit for awhile, it would all heal up," Flair explained. "But one gash ran up into my scalp, took 42 stitches."[12] Blading was an important tool for a professional wrestler to heighten the urgency of a match and the illusion of violence. Flair used the blood to assist in the storytelling, and it was a major asset in his repertoire. Blood worked for him where it might not have for a different wrestler, and it was advantageous to use the gimmick on a routine basis. From both his on-camera and off-camera interviews, it was obvious that Flair was a man's man, and he wasn't one to complain about the day-to-day rigors of being a wrestler. The bumps and bruises were normal. The entire wrestling world already knew that he was workhorse in a class by himself. But things did go wrong on occasion, whether it was a bad bump, a travel mishap, or something else completely unexpected — and he was willing to deal with the consequences. "I'm not a superman," he once told a Japanese reporter.[13]

Flair's constitution was tested at times. Beginning on March 24, 1985, he made 22 appearances in 22 days, traveling approximately 13,000 miles across 11 states.[14] This tour included stops in Greensboro, Miami, Cincinnati, Houston, St. Louis, and Portland. Following a match in Atlanta on April 14, it is believed he went home to Charlotte before venturing to Tokyo, which propelled him up over 20,000 miles traveled in less than four weeks. By the time Flair arrived in Tokyo on April 19, he was mentally drained and later admitted to avoiding Motoko Baba, the wife of Shohei Baba, the owner of All Japan Pro Wrestling, at the airport.[15] Instead of heading to his hotel to prepare for his first match, he immediately boarded a plane headed back to the United States, planning to skip out on his Japanese bookings.[16] He was seriously considering a break from not only the championship but from wrestling altogether.

Since Flair's arrival in Japan was expected, the public was told that he had to return to the U.S. because his mother was sick.[17] But as soon as he arrived in Charlotte, he was met by Jim Crockett, who immediately changed his mind about any kind of hiatus. He hopped on another plane, back to Tokyo, for a third 6,800-mile trip.[18] In all, going back to March 24, Flair traveled upward of 33,000 miles, and then wrestled three times in Japan, fulfilling dates on April 23 in Sagamihara, April 24 in Yokohama, and April 25 in Kisarazu. The need for time off the road and a momentary rest for mental and physical recovery were understandable. Thirty years earlier, renowned world heavyweight champion Lou Thesz expressed a desire to work under "humane conditions," and boldly demanded to be booked only five days per week and to wrestle two weeks with one week off.[19] The NWA, led by Sam Muchnick, strived to give Thesz the time off he requested, even though it was tricky business.

The state of professional wrestling between 1984 and '87, including the war with the WWF and Crockett's expansion plan, made it even more difficult to give Flair a reasonable break. "Humane conditions" for the NWA World Heavyweight champion were simply implausible in the modern environment, and Flair was the horse JCP was riding toward national acclaim. Flair understood his role and the importance of his job. When he was tired from jet lag, he pushed through and handled business to the best of his ability. Chuck Cavalaris of the *Knoxville News-Sentinel* interviewed Flair on an off night in late August 1986, and the champ admitted that he was "somewhat out of it." Having just come in from Los Angeles, he was tired and suffering from a torn muscle in his back, an injury that left a sizable purple bruise. In an attempt to hide the contusion, he applied makeup and went to the ring as normal, where he successfully defended his title against the Bullet — a masked Bob Armstrong.[20]

Despite his schedule, traumatic incidents, and his active social life, Flair never shirked his responsibilities. He respected the wrestling business too much for that. He didn't show up to matches inebriated, nor did he give any less of himself in the ring when he wasn't feeling 100 percent. In truth, he was known for getting up much earlier than his contemporaries and hitting the gym first thing in the morning, sweating off the night before.[21]

Cardiovascular exercise was his specialty, and his routine of 500 free squats a day — a habit he first adopted from Verne Gagne early in his career — was a voluntary task he enjoyed wherever he was in the world.[22] In 1986, as the StairMaster became the premier cardio machine in gyms around the United States, Flair gravitated to the "mechanical moving staircase" to improve his fitness.[23] His extreme conditioning and dedication to exercise contributed to his durability as the traveling world champion.[24]

For all of his hard work and perseverance, Flair earned great respect from the wrestlers around him. "I think I'm recognized by my peers as the best — if they answer in all honesty," Flair told a reporter in 1986. "I'm not into steroids. I'm not just a weight lifter. The guys who are most successful over the long run have a strong amateur background and a repertoire of wrestling holds."[25] Respect was a big thing with Flair. He wanted it from his colleagues, as well as fans. "I want the fans to see how hard I work and respect me for that," he explained. "I don't play around in the ring. It really doesn't matter whether they like me or hate me as long as they respect me. I know these people work hard for a living — just like I do — and I try to give them their money's worth. I usually don't get in there and pin a guy in five or six minutes. Because of the caliber of wrestlers I face day in and day out, I'm fighting for my life every night."[26]

Short matches, lacking science and psychological depth, were characteristic of main events under the World Wrestling Federation banner. But the WWF was acknowledged by the mainstream media as professional wrestling's most popular organization. WWF's network programming, massive merchandising machine, and entertainment that appealed to families had singlehandedly changed the image of the sport. Wrestling was a major element of 1980s pop culture. Vince McMahon wasn't really focused on siphoning traditional fans from the NWA or AWA. He was creating a legion of new enthusiasts, who appreciated the outlandish WWF style and its colorful gimmicks. And at the center of that world was the tanned behemoth in yellow, Hulk Hogan. "Hulkamania" was indeed "running wild," as Hogan liked to exclaim in promos, and his popularity was unrivaled. No other wrestler was even close.

"I like what he stands for," said wrestling fan Terry Spindle. "He's not a braggart. He doesn't talk about his sex life like Ric Flair does. Hulk takes his vitamins and says his prayers. He's a patriot. I just love him, that's all."[27] As much as fans, sportswriters, and publications wanted to compare and contrast Hogan and Flair, pitting them against one another in direct competition, Flair was laid-back about his WWF counterpart. "I don't begrudge Hulk Hogan one thing," he said. "But he's a movie star, and my job is different. The NWA sells wrestling. I'm not saying this in a derogatory sense, but I'd rather be Ric Flair than Hulk Hogan."[28] But Flair did defend his status as the world heavyweight champion. "There is only one champion and that is me. That is what makes the NWA special. The NWA is the oldest and most prestigious organization in this business. The WWF is more into marketing and Hogan makes most of his money out of the consumer part of the business. He makes his fortune selling dolls. I make mine in the ring."[29]

Although the WWF was outdrawing Jim Crockett Promotions at the box office, JCP was enjoying an impressive financial run. A lot of the credit was due to the imaginative booking of Dusty Rhodes. His innovative ideas and accomplishments earned him a "Best Booker" nod from the readers of the *Wrestling Observer Newsletter*, and his award was absolutely deserved.[30] But the positioning of Rhodes as Crockett's creative force *and* the central baby face generated criticism from smart fans, and there was a sense that Dusty was pushing himself too much and too hard. Since the middle of 1985, he had wrestled Ric Flair approximately 75 times in singles matches and in about two dozen tag team bouts. These contests were a headline act on the house show circuit, and while the two performers knew how to get the best from one another, and traditionally drew well, the repetition was deemed excessive and tiresome. Rhodes even won the NWA title during the Bash tour in 1986, and that, too, was knocked because it was seen as Rhodes manipulating himself into that top spot rather than doing what was good for business.

Rhodes employed what was dubbed the "Dusty Finish" in his booking strategy, and it was an overly prevalent feature on JCP cards, notably

Only four years into his career, in 1976, Ric Flair made his Madison Square Garden debut in New York City for the WWWF and was ready to make his mark on the wrestling business.

The physically imposing and intimidating Bruiser Brody was one of Flair's toughest opponents, and in the ring, they had a number of tremendous battles.

At Starrcade '83 in Greensboro, the proverbial torch was passed from Harley Race to Flair, and the Nature Boy won his second NWA World Heavyweight title.

Donning the infamous crimson mask, Flair was never afraid of getting "color" to sell the action, and he often bled every night while the defending NWA champion.

In the ring, few wrestlers were as technically sound as Flair, and he could punish his opponent with a variety of moves and holds.

Outside the ring, Flair was well-liked by fans throughout the mid-Atlantic area, and he was more than happy to pose for photos. Here he is with Donna Kay Crawford and her husband, Steve. Donna was the president of the Ric Flair Fan Club in the early 1980s.

Ricky Steamboat was Flair's equal when it came to scientific wrestling and overall conditioning, and their legendary matches are still talked about to this day.

On the international circuit, Flair made innumerable trips to Puerto Rico and battled local favorite Carlos Colon on many occasions. Their matches were always heralded by the public.

Saturday morning appearances on Superstation WTBS alongside host Gordon Solie helped turn Flair into a household name from coast to coast, and his interview segments were must-watch television.

Harley Race was rough and tough in the squared circle, and his matches were true slugfests from bell to bell. Race set the standard for a touring world champion, and Flair lived up to and exceeded all expectations as his successor.

Of all his opponents, no one could sell the heat and emotion of their rivalry like the "American Dream" Dusty Rhodes. Their competitiveness was as strong outside the ring as it was in.

Regardless of their personal feelings for each other, Flair and Rhodes were the ultimate professionals in the ring, and their matches packed arenas all over North America — and it was wrestling at its very best from beginning to end.

Flair brought the best out of his opponents and had the ability to make many relatively inexperienced wrestlers appear like coming champions, including the Russian powerhouse Nikita Koloff. Their feud was a top seller for Jim Crockett Promotions during the 1980s.

GEORGE NAPOLITANO

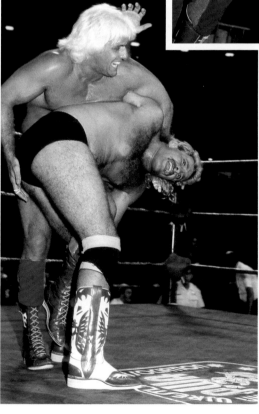

GEORGE NAPOLITANO

Up-and-comer Magnum T.A. was expected to ultimately beat Flair for the NWA World title and was being groomed for the top spot. His career was cut short due to a tragic car accident, altering wrestling history forever.

Ronnie Garvin's physical toughness was an equalizer for Flair's technical skill, and their battles were always a war in the ring. In 1987, Garvin upset Flair for the NWA World title, but the Nature Boy regained the belt at Starrcade.

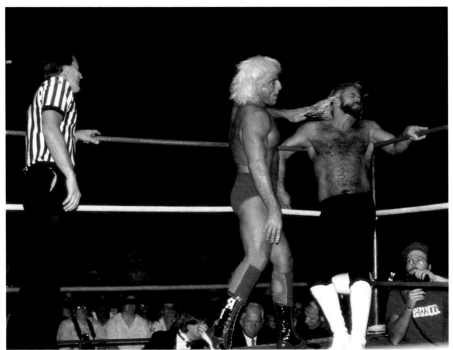

Flair's famous chest chop, accompanied by a chorus of "Wooooo" from the crowd, was a staple during his in-ring career. Freebird Michael Hayes was the recipient on this occasion, and it was as painful as it looked and sounded.

Embodying the class, showmanship, and demeanor of a world-class athlete, Flair went into big matches with a style all his own. In the ring, he'd wrestle rings around his opponent but was never afraid to cheat to gain a victory.

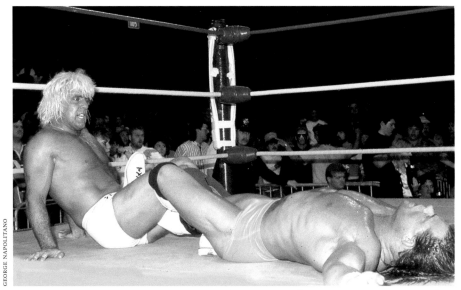

The figure-four leglock was Flair's dreaded submission finisher. During most matches, Flair would work on his opponent's leg, building tension, all leading up to the application of the hold. It was high drama, especially if his rival was able to flip the hold over and reverse the pressure.

As the touring World Heavyweight champion, Ric Flair was the premier athlete in all of professional wrestling. He toured cities big and small and performed before audiences of all sizes. At the core of things, he always gave his best in the ring, and the fans loved him for it.

Sting was a huge fan favorite and challenger for Flair's title during the late 1980s and early '90s. His off-the-charts charisma and energy gave fans many exciting moments.

Flair's craftiness against a youthful powerhouse like Sting was unrelenting, and he'd often rely on his "bag of tricks" to escape a dangerous predicament.

In 1989, Flair and Ricky Steamboat engaged in some of the most competitive and remarkable matches of the modern era. Their feud resumed again five years later.

Flair was commonly seen with a bevy of beauties, and while in WCW, he had the fortune of being surrounded by the legendary Woman (left) and Miss Elizabeth, as shown in this 1996 photo.

The legendary Four Horsemen, beginning in 1985, revolutionized the faction concept for pro wrestling, and with Flair at the center of the group, they terrorized fan favorites for years. Here, Flair delivers another passion-filled promo as interviewer Gene Okerlund, Arn Anderson, and Brian Pillman (from left to right) look on.

Recognizing the group's longtime influence, the Four Horsemen were later inducted into the WWE Hall of Fame. Flair stands at the podium in 2012 with Arn Anderson (left) and Barry Windham, two of his greatest allies and friends, by his side.

In WCW, Flair resumed his long-running feud with the Rowdy Scot, the great Roddy Piper. Their battles were as wild as ever, and behind the microphone, they provided great entertainment value for audiences.

Flair's run in World Championship Wrestling came to an end in 2001 when the company was sold to the WWE. It was the end of an era for the Nature Boy, and his name would forever be synonymous with Jim Crockett Promotions, the NWA, and WCW.

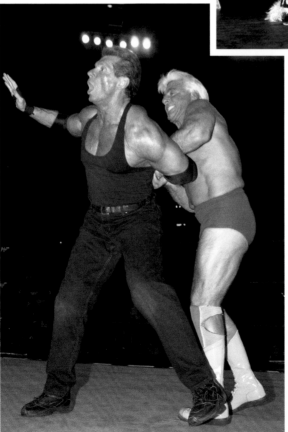

Joining the WWE later in 2001, Flair quickly became embroiled in a heated war with Vince McMahon, and their all-out battle at the 2002 Royal Rumble the following January ended with Flair winning by submission.

GEORGE NAPOLITANO

Triple H, a perennial world champion in the WWE, formed an alliance with Flair, and their friendship extended off camera as well. Triple H freely acknowledged Flair's influence on his career, and they had many memorable moments together.

GEORGE NAPOLITANO

In 2003, Flair, Triple H, and Batista (far right) formed the stable Evolution, along with Randy Orton. As a cohesive unit of superstars, the stable was dominant, and Flair continued to give all he had in the ring, despite his physical limitations.

Flair faced off with Shawn Michaels in his 2008 retirement match at WrestleMania 24, and their epic, emotional battle saw Michaels pin Flair after a superkick. It was one of the most powerful moments in wrestling history.

The WWE honored Flair by inducting him into the Hall of Fame in 2008, an honor that was very much deserved. Wrestling fans across the globe celebrated the Nature Boy, and paid respect for the decades he had given the business.

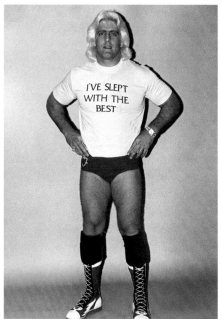

Outside the ring, Flair's personality, good looks, and superstar charisma made him a magnet for the opposite sex.

In retirement, Flair has remained in the public eye, and has appearing in commercials and at reunions, and finally wrestled his last match in 2022. Appearances by Flair always stir up attention, and fans will forever "Wooooo!" in unison whenever he's around.

Styling and profiling, Flair was the cockiest, most arrogant pro wrestler in the business, and in the ring, he could back it all up by delivering the most spectacular performance on the card. He did it night after night, and his legacy as the best of the best cannot be refuted. His mark on the business is cemented in stone.

Flair loved being the world champion. He worked hard to ensure he had the conditioning to endure the enormous stress the job of being the traveling champion required. As the business evolved, so did the Nature Boy, and in the end, he made his definite mark as the last "Real World Champion."

used at Starrcade 1985. A new champion would be declared, only to see the belt given back to the previous titleholder on a technicality, such as disqualification. This type of finish did pop the crowd in the moment, and depending on when the announcement changing the decision was made, spectators sometimes went home thinking they had just witnessed history. But it was ultimately a letdown, and the repeated use of such tricks degraded fan confidence. It was also regarded as a way to keep putting Rhodes over, time and again. Flair, on the other hand, appeared weak as a result, and smart fans blamed Rhodes's style of booking. Flair was further hurt by his reliance on the Four Horsemen, and outside interference plagued his matches. The constant inference that he needed his mates to retain his belt by DQ diminished the respect casual fans had for his wrestling ability.

"We sincerely hope none of you people out there think Ric Flair is a great wrestler or a great champion," wrestling writer Dr. Strange explained in the *Orangeburg Times and Democrat* in 1987. "He is not. He has become a mere shadow of what he used to be: a truly great athlete. All he is now is a sham, a crybaby, one who cannot win without resorting to cheating of one kind or another or without the help of the Four Horsemen."[31] In early 1987, the reemergence of Barry Windham arguably gave Flair his best legitimate mat opponent since Ricky Steamboat, and Rhodes smartly arranged for a Flair-Windham series around the country. Their matches were typically booked differently than Flair-Rhodes or Flair-Koloff, and saw the competitors exhibit excellent technical skill and conditioning. Between the varied strong and weak portrayals of Flair in this period, another dichotomy unique to the Nature Boy was born.

The public enthusiasm for Flair and Windham was hot from day one. After an impromptu encounter on *World Wide Wrestling*, broadcast in syndication on January 17, 1987, during which Windham nearly pinned the champ before the Horsemen attacked, the excitement went through the roof.[32] A week later, a Fayetteville crowd was on their feet as they wrestled again with the belt on the line. The television time limit expired just as Windham was executing a pin following a flying lariat, and the classic bout was declared a draw.[33] On the road, their feud was consistently more successful in established Crockett towns on the East Coast than it was in western cities. For instance, they drew 7,200 and 15,000 respectively on February 21 in Philadelphia and March 14 in Greensboro. But in Minneapolis on March 15, they attracted 2,500 people, and another 3,000 on March 19 in Los Angeles.[34] Although attendance fluctuated, the Herculean efforts of Flair and Windham didn't waver, and they delivered night after night.

Jim Crockett knew that attendance figures would be slow in new territories. It was common sense. The promotion needed time to establish itself, and with syndicated programming on local channels and its cable presence on the Superstation, the company had widespread exposure. In Chicago and Boston, fans couldn't wait to support JCP live. On December 14, 1986, JCP drew 12,500 to the Rosemont Horizon outside Chicago, and 11,000 for the promotion's debut at the Boston Garden on April 4, 1987. Conversely, JCP lured less than 2,000 for a program at the Civic Auditorium in San Francisco on April 23. The West Coast was a hard sell for JCP, but officials were determined to make it work. In the meantime, Crockett made arrangements to purchase the Universal Wrestling Federation (formerly Mid-South) and its expansive television network from Bill Watts. The *Charlotte Observer* noted that the deal made Crockett the "largest" wrestling promoter in the industry, able to present more shows on an annual basis than the WWF.[35]

The acquisition of Watts's syndication network, along with the addition of the UWF's talent roster into the NWA fold, provided a great opportunity for Crockett in his war with Vince McMahon. The deal opened up new parts of the country for expansion and gave JCP an advantage in valuable southern cities such as New Orleans and Houston. With so many new moneymaking possibilities, JCP was seemingly overwhelmed by the platform it now had, and instead of booking one roster of wrestlers, Dusty Rhodes was now overseeing two. And it was a complex situation in need of delicate management. For Ric Flair, he was juggling his feud against Barry Windham with regular matches versus Nikita Koloff, while also instigating Jimmy Garvin over the affections of the Garvins' valet, Precious.[36] Flair wanted her by his side and made no bones about it. Precious had a mind of her own, and during the April 4, 1987, telecast of *World Championship Wrestling*, she reached back and slapped Flair silly.[37]

The Flair-Garvin rivalry was a moderate sell at the box office, with pretty good houses in Baltimore, Philadelphia, and Norfolk. Their feud was assisted by an off-the-wall angle that transitioned from the mat to a hotel room, and it featured two controversial skits that are talked about to this day. The scenario began after Flair beat Garvin in a cage match in Greensboro on July 11, 1987.[38] With his victory, the world champion secured a "dream date" with Precious, and he had special plans for their time together. He demonstrated how hot to trot he was by kissing his "little private Precious" — a mannequin — the following Saturday on WTBS. A feverishly animated Flair cut an over-the-top promo discussing his plans for their evening together.[39] The setting for the dream date was a hotel suite, and Flair was prepared with champagne, ready to indulge in a night of fun and frivolity. But Precious was actually Ronnie Garvin in women's clothing, and "Hands of Stone" knocked out Flair with a single punch.[40]

As Flair's feud with the Garvin brothers played out, JCP was in the midst of the 1987 Great American Bash tour, and Dusty Rhodes had come up with another winner. "War Games" was his newest innovation: ten men were locked inside two cage-enclosed rings. It was the perfect battleground for Rhodes and the Horsemen. Twice during the month of July, Rhodes, Nikita Koloff, Paul Ellering, and the Road Warriors defeated a Flair-led Horsemen contingent, first in Atlanta on July 4 and then on July 31 at the Orange Bowl in Miami.[41] By this time, Ole Anderson had departed the Horsemen to become a baby face in opposition to his former allies. His replacement was the 6-foot-4, 250-pound Lex Luger, a former college and pro football player from upstate New York. Luger had started his wrestling career in Florida under the guidance of Hiro Matsuda, won several regional championships, and challenged Flair a half dozen times for the NWA belt in 1986.[42]

Though still very green, Luger was the most promising heavyweight wrestling prospect in several years, and he joined JCP in January 1987. The 28-year-old soon affiliated himself with the Horsemen, and he was propelled into main event tag team matches alongside Flair, Arn Anderson, and Tully Blanchard.[43] The excitement surrounding JCP and the NWA was at an all-time fever pitch in July 1987 for the Great American Bash, and JCP recorded its highest single month revenue in history.[44] Crowds were substantial in Atlanta, Greensboro, Baltimore, Chicago, and Miami, and soared over 20,000 at Memorial Stadium in Charlotte on July 18.[45] The Bash tour, which began on July 1 in Lakeland, Florida, was incredibly demanding on the performers, and Flair bled more times than not. It was reported that he suffered a pinched nerve in his neck, resulting in intermittent numbness in his fingers and arm.[46] Because of this injury, his match with Road Warrior Animal in Chicago on July 19 was cancelled.[47]

Flair, the unremitting trooper that he was, didn't let the irregular pain sideline him for any length of time. He soon entered a rough and tumble feud with Ron Garvin, and their history combined with the recent Precious angle energized fans at JCP arenas. But no one was ready for the news out of Detroit on September 25, 1987: Garvin was declared the new National Wrestling Alliance World Heavyweight champion. Using a sunset flip off the top rope, at the climax of a turbulent cage match, Garvin pinned the Nature Boy and captured the NWA crown.[48] The news was stunning, and to the common fan, it illustrated the unpredictability of pro wrestling. Garvin was undoubtedly a physically capable specimen and was merciless in his own way. He wasn't known for his charisma or color, and his interviews were straight to the point and intense. The elevation of Garvin to the world championship was an attention grabber, but the truth was JCP was using the title change to set up a rematch at Starrcade in November.

Flair's run in 1987, culminating in his loss to Garvin in Detroit, painted a bizarre picture that many smart enthusiasts were unenthused about. They saw the constant Horsemen interference, the lack of clean pinfall wins, the oversexed promos, and the entire Precious angle as a way of subtly humiliating Flair. Following the "dream date" incident, a pundit for the *Wrestling Forum* newsletter wrote, "That episode in itself did more to further Hulk Hogan as a champion than almost anything Hogan has done himself since winning the belt."[49] The segment was humorous to certain demographics, but others felt it strayed outside the lines of good taste. In all, though, these elements were hurting Flair more than they were helping him, and questions were being raised. Were any of these factors attributable to booker Dusty Rhodes more from an ego standpoint than from an unbiased and creative point of view? Was he deliberately trying to hurt Flair's popularity in order to stand alone as JCP's top baby face?

The relationship between Flair and Rhodes had been complex for years. Their rivalry extended outside the ring into a race for more money, better clothes and mink coats, and fancier cars. Over the years, their success was not equal, nor were they comparable in terms of their work rate or style. They did manage to leave their grievances behind before a big match, and Flair had proven agreeable to Rhodes's ideas, regardless of what they were. But their ongoing animosity was problematic, and J.J. Dillon and Jim Crockett carefully smoothed over an untold number of issues throughout this era, allowing business to continue unabated.[50] Rhodes usually got the best of Flair and the Horsemen in the ring during tag team matches, and fans loved it. Seeing Flair and his cohorts bloodied and battered was a welcomed sight, and many shows ended in just that manner, with Rhodes celebrating in the ring to the booming cheers of the audience.

The formula had been exploited in singles, tag team matches, and now War Games. Repeating it on a constant loop across the wrestling land-scape was not helping Flair in any way, and after years of similar brawls and beatdowns, there had to be an end point — something that allowed Flair and Rhodes to pivot away from each other for a much needed break. The push of Ron Garvin to the championship throne certainly raised eyebrows as JCP needed a thrilling headline matchup to carry the promotion through the end of the year. Garvin had not been established as the group's top star, nor were fans ready to embrace him as such now that he was carrying the Big Gold. That created a dilemma for Rhodes as a booker. The man he had chosen to wear the belt into Starrcade was less popular than the heel he was aligned against, and support for Flair seemed to grow even more without the title.

Crockett was in a bind. Serious booking problems, magnified by the failure of the UWF to achieve a modicum of success, turned the positive gains from the summer of 1987 into a potential calamity. He was positioned to lose a significant amount of money if TV ratings didn't live up to the numbers his company forecast to advertisers. By November, the JCP syndication package had dipped from a 7 share to 5.4, losing well over a million weekly viewers.[51] Adding to Crockett's problems, Vince McMahon decided to stage a pay-per-view event on Thanksgiving evening in direct opposition to Starrcade, and he used his past PPV success to lure the majority of cable companies to his corner.[52] It was a devastating blow to JCP in its first endeavor into the world of pay-per-view. Crockett then suffered a self-inflicted wound when he uprooted Starrcade from the southeast, particularly Greensboro, and staged the 1987 card at Chicago's UIC Pavilion.[53] By doing so, he alienated a dedicated fan base, which had been with him since day one.

The shift to Chicago was seen as a way for JCP to appear national in scope, and distancing itself from the southern territorial mindset. Like the country music concerts and purchase of the UWF, there was logic behind the move, but its risks had the potential to outweigh the rewards. Crockett had a lot riding on Starrcade, and Flair turned things up a notch during promos to attract attention. He talked passionately, taking off his coat mid-interview to demonstrate his seriousness, and hyped the importance of the event, which was named "Chi-Town Heat." He predicted victories for himself and the Four Horsemen and bragged about their planned post-show carousing in the big city. With respect to the options wrestling fans had between the NWA and WWF, Flair said, "Thanksgiving night, there's no choice to make. It's *the* choice. If you want to see the best, then buddy, you tune in to Chi-Town Heat because the best are going to be on display!"[54]

As anticipated, Flair and Garvin engaged in a bruising war on November 26, 1987, in Chicago. Between the vicious chops and use of the cage as a weapon, the bout was strictly about violence, and was not driven by story or technique. Toward the end of the bout, Garvin landed his knockout punch, but Flair surprisingly kicked out. The champion also landed a sunset flip off the top rope, the move that had beaten Flair in Detroit, but Flair again managed to save himself. Garvin attempted to down Flair coming off the ropes, but Flair caught him midair and slammed him headfirst into the cage. The momentum sent Garvin sprawling to the mat, and Flair scored a pinfall. The Nature Boy captured his fifth NWA World Heavyweight championship, and commentators lauded the match for its physicality. Despite the efforts of Vince McMahon, Starrcade achieved adequate numbers overall, once the live gate, CCTV, and pay-per-view figures were taken into consideration.[55] But it wasn't the success it could have been.

Jim Crockett's record financial achievements were lost in the chaos of mismanagement, bad accounting, and inconsistent booking. The wrestling war was doing them no favors either, but JCP wasn't giving up. The night before Starrcade, the company ran the Nassau Coliseum outside New York City, and planned a big return engagement at the same venue in January 1988 — right in McMahon's backyard. However, the heavy losses in TV ratings and the shuttering of the UWF as a standalone entity were painful reminders that Crockett was on the losing side in the war.[56] In early 1988, a cooperative agreement with Turner Home Entertainment, a subsidiary of the Turner Broadcasting System, would be reached to assist in marketing JCP's pay-per-view programs.[57] With the leverage of media mogul Ted Turner behind it, Jim Crockett Promotions was renewed in its fight for wrestling supremacy.

CHAPTER 15
A RETURN TO GLORY

The National Wrestling Alliance, as a unified organization of booking offices, was a shell of its former self by 1988. Despite being spearheaded by the success of Jim Crockett, the NWA failed to execute even the most basic functions to ensure its survival. The departure of big-time promotions like Dallas and All Japan were devastating, but at its core, Alliance leadership lost its grip on the one thing that was inherently valuable: the world heavyweight title. By allowing JCP to monopolize and control the bookings of the NWA championship, the Alliance squandered its ability to exploit the historic wrestling crown for monetary gain in its remaining territories. Of course, it was a trade-off, as officials hoped that by keeping the "NWA" designation in the news with JCP's nationwide platform, all Alliance members would benefit. That just wasn't the case. In fact, JCP became so synonymous with the NWA on TV and in publications, that many people believed it was the National Wrestling Alliance instead of just being a member of a larger promotional contingent.

On the creative end of things, Dusty Rhodes was in a tough position as booker for JCP. He was trying to boost television ratings after a dramatic dip in interest in late 1987. The promotion focused its efforts on the Bunkhouse Stampede concept, which was an anything-goes battle royal. The idea had been hatched two years earlier in the fertile mind of Rhodes, and the gimmick went hand in hand with his Texas roughneck style.[1] Participants were encouraged to wrestle in jeans and cowboy boots, and, again, that played right into Dusty's strengths as an everyman. Unsurprisingly, Rhodes was declared the ultimate winner of the Stampede in 1986 and 1987, and on January 24, 1988, he won a special event at the Nassau Coliseum in Long Island to once again take the Bunkhouse championship.[2] That show marked JCP's second foray into pay-per-view.

Ric Flair didn't participate in the Stampede match. He instead defended his world championship against Road Warrior Hawk and was disqualified for using a chair. Flair was in the midst of several different angles, including one with former Freebird Michael Hayes. But the Four Horsemen were dealing with a bigger threat, stemming from their ouster of Lex Luger from the group in December.[3] Luger, now a popular hero, was teaming with the likes of Rhodes, Ole Anderson, and Barry Windham against combinations of Flair, Arn Anderson, and Tully Blanchard, looking for retribution. In the meantime, another bright prospect appeared on the horizon, a carryover from the failed UWF project. The wrestler's name was Sting, a popular athlete from Santa Clarita, California, with just over two years in the pro ranks. Sting had come a long way in that short time, winning the UWF Tag Team title on three occasions with partners Eddie Gilbert and Rick Steiner.

With his colorful face paint and spiky blond hair, Sting was immensely charismatic, and Rhodes didn't waste any time elevating him into a feud with Flair. Beginning in December 1987, Flair wrestled the magnetic rising star at least 20 times in primary cities from Chicago to Los Angeles. These matches were fast-paced and dynamic, and whereas Sting brought his youthful vigor, Flair's experience carried both the tempo and action. Flair could play off Sting's energy and react to draw out an animated response from the audience. When they needed a boost, he'd work into one of Sting's big spots, from a gorilla press slam to a Stinger Splash in the corner. The intensity of their rivalry was perfectly crafted on TV, setting up an anticipated contest at the very first Clash of the Champions on March 27, 1988, in Greensboro. This spectacle was the first in a series of quarterly mega cards to be presented live on TBS, and it was specifically arranged to go head to head with the WWF's WrestleMania.[4]

In a match that lasted a hair over 39 minutes, Flair and Sting wrestled an incredible bout and went to the finish with the world champion caught in Sting's Scorpion Deathlock.[5] The crowd held its collective breath as Sting applied pressure to Flair's leg and, with the clock winding down, hoped for a submission. The excitement and precision timing was professional wrestling at its very best, and when the bell finally rang, fans were exhausted by the emotional rollercoaster. The match was a draw, and not only had Flair reaffirmed his status as the best performer in the United States, but he had catapulted Sting into the superstar class. Without question, Sting lived up to his end of the deal — his ring sophistication and conditioning were excellent for a grappler of his limited background. But Flair was the master artist, who directed each step of their encounter, turning it into a modern classic.[6]

"Besides being the best match of the year, the Flair-Sting match at Clash I gave fans a chance to view the champ as he once was, or more accurately, how he once was allowed to be and hopefully he'll be that way again," wrote Mark Madden in the 1988 yearbook of the *Wrestling Observer Newsletter.*[7] Madden, a sportswriter for the *Pittsburgh Post-Gazette*, was referencing the diminished role Flair had assumed over the past two years, which had depreciated his stature in the eyes of many smart enthusiasts. Flair rarely won clean anymore. His victories ended by some form of interference, use of a foreign object, or by holding the ropes for leverage. In other bouts, he'd be disqualified or win by disqualification, typically because of interference or the over-the-top-rope rule. Finally, there was the dreaded Dusty Finish — the reverse decision disqualification. None of these finishes strengthened the credibility of a world champion.

During his contest with Sting, Flair resorted to underhanded tricks, was cocky and yet feeble when his opponent suddenly appeared invincible, in a trademark performance of the old Flair. In facing a versatile young foe, the Nature Boy's star glimmered once again. Clash of the Champions was deemed a success, earning a 5.8 rating overall and a 7.8 rating for the final 15 minutes of Flair's battle with Sting. Dave Meltzer stated that it was the "most-watched match" in the history of the NWA with 3.4 million households tuning in.[8] On top of that, JCP's company-wide syndication numbers had increased to an 8.4 rating on 183 stations. Although JCP was still rated lower than the WWF (10.9 rating on 255 stations), it was a marked improvement, and from an outside perspective, Crockett seemed to be on the right track.

Behind the scenes, the story was quite the opposite. Wasteful spending, debt, and ballooning payments as part of exclusive contracts to top performers were crippling the company, and Crockett was slowly coming to terms with an option that was once considered preposterous: the outright sale of JCP's vital wrestling assets. The promotional business had been a way of life for the Crockett family for over five decades, and they had coordinated various brands of entertainment for millions of fans. The gravity of the situation was dire, and the widow of Jim Crockett Sr., Elizabeth, along with her four children discussed their options. By the summer of 1988, they were actively engaged in talks with Turner Broadcasting System to sell off their interests in professional wrestling.[9] Such a deal would solve their financial crisis — and alter the direction of the industry forever. As negotiations went into full swing, unbeknownst to the public, a number of significant events happened in the life of Ric Flair.

None was more important than the arrival of his fourth child, and second son, Richard Reid Fliehr, on February 26, 1988, at Presbyterian Hospital in Charlotte.[10] Flair's newborn, named after his grandfather, would go by his middle name, Reid, and his birth came after months of family anxieties as Ric and Beth tried to have another child.[11] Their prayers were answered with Reid's birth, and with his sister Ashley, they settled into the new family residence at 2722 Plantation Road in the Charlotte suburb of Matthews. The beautiful, recently built, two-story home included a pool and cost in the neighborhood of $385,000.[12] It was a palace fit for a world champion. Over the last three years, since Flair had signed a multiyear contract with Jim Crockett Promotions, he had worked perhaps harder than anyone in the business, helping the company achieve financial milestones, in spite of mismanagement. For every dollar he made, he really earned it the hard way, through blood and sweat in the ring.

Flair knew what Jim Crockett was doing. He understood that JCP needed to sign big contracts with key wrestlers to ensure they wouldn't jump to the WWF. That was the only way the promotion would be competitive. But things weren't exactly evenhanded in terms of salaries, especially as pertained to Flair, and there was a noticeable lack of recognition for his consistent effort as the heavyweight titleholder. As of May 1988, six wrestlers and two managers were making more annually than Flair, and four of those grapplers were part of tag teams. They were the Road Warriors Animal and Hawk, and Bobby Eaton and Stan Lane of the Midnight Express. Their managers, Paul Ellering and Jim Cornette, were receiving big bucks as well, and it was completely deserved. After all, Ellering was the glue behind the "Roadies," and Cornette was, with little disagreement, considered the best manager in the business. But was JCP compensating Flair adequately?

The competitive nature of professional wrestling was at an all-time high in 1988. Dusty Rhodes had the top singles contract at JCP, and to a degree, that made sense. He was not only a wrestler and a top draw, but he was the creative mastermind driving the company's success. The other in-ring talent to command a considerable salary was Lex Luger, the 29-year-old pro with less than three years' experience. Luger's value to JCP was sizable, and early on, he was slated to be an equalizing talent to the WWF's Hulk Hogan, which made him even more indispensable. Nevertheless, Flair's situation needed to be addressed, and he wasn't the only wrestler on the payroll with a grievance about money. Arn Anderson and Tully Blanchard, Flair's allies in the Horsemen and two of the hardest working athletes in the NWA, both saw their contracts run out between May and June 1988.[13] Like Flair, they were devoted workers and expected to sign new guarantees as part of the Turner takeover.

It only made sense that they would receive an ample raise, too, based on their track records and commitment to the organization. But negotiations fell off the rails. After Blanchard spoke candidly with Turner officials during their internal interviews with JCP wrestlers, he had a falling out with Jim Crockett. Crockett accused him of not being loyal, and Blanchard quit.[14] Anderson joined him, and the two ventured to the WWF, where they debuted on October 5, 1988.[15] Money hadn't been their only complaint. Late in the summer, they tried to leverage the threat of jumping to the WWF to force a creative change, which would have impacted Rhodes's job as booker. Rhodes, however, had political support from Crockett, which insulated him from any coup attempt. The interesting part of that incident was that Flair was in concert with them, in effect trying to push Rhodes aside.[16]

The continuously skewed finishes that put over Rhodes and other fan favorites had proven to be an unjust detriment to Flair and his cohorts, and Flair was at his limit. Strangely, Jim Crockett, who had been the best man at Flair's wedding to Beth, was seemingly closer to Rhodes than Flair at this juncture. As a result, Rhodes and Crockett held firm, and no changes were made. However, Crockett corrected the major financial discrepancy relating to Flair's salary after Flair asked for fair compensation.[17] It was no secret that Crockett and the NWA wanted to prevent Flair from leaving for the WWF, and it was believed that Anderson and Blanchard's defection could've been a tipping point. For Flair, the WWF was a farfetched possibility, only because of his loyalty to Crockett. But with that said, it was still an option. In fact, Vince McMahon wanted Flair to wrestle Randy Savage at the very first Summer Slam in August 1988.[18]

Flair was committed to Crockett Promotions and he wasn't going anywhere. His new contract, reportedly worth upward of $750,000 a year, satisfied his financial concerns.[19] But with the Turner deal on the horizon, he wasn't done negotiating. What he didn't know, though, was that Turner had already identified Flair and Rhodes as key players in the potential deal for JCP. They were instrumental to the revenue for live events and merchandising, and were considered to be crucial figures "both operationally and as stars."[20] The central negotiators behind the scenes soon understood that Flair, in particular, was vital to Turner, and the deal was unachievable without him. Blair Schmidt-Fellner, an industrious 30-year-old employee of Turner Broadcasting, was in charge of overseeing the purchase of Jim Crockett Promotions. He was tasked with signing over two dozen performers to exclusive TBS contracts, and he was quite successful, landing every major star they wanted but one: Ric Flair.[21]

Ted Turner heard about Flair's hesitation to sign and told Schmidt-Fellner, "If you don't have Ric Flair, you don't have shit." He then demanded to see Flair the following Tuesday for a private meeting in his Atlanta office. "Ric agreed to meet with Ted and showed up in an Armani suit," Schmidt-Fellner later explained. "He looked like a CEO. I walked ahead of Ric into Ted's huge office and Ted was standing on a folding chair behind the door waiting for Ric to walk in. When he did walk in, Ted dove on his shoulders and yelled in fun, 'I wrestled in high school and I can kick your ass!'" Flair was lighthearted about Turner's playful joke and listened intently as Turner explained the benefits of joining TBS. Plain and simple, Flair wanted more money and wasn't entirely convinced to sign at the conclusion of the meeting. As he reached the elevator, he turned to Schmidt-Fellner and said, "That man is crazy. I am not signing anything."[22]

"Within a couple of weeks, he did finally sign with TBS, without a change to his contract with the Crocketts, but with faith that TBS would be good to him and that he had a friend in Turner," explained Schmidt-Fellner. "It sealed the [Turner-JCP] deal, which was dead in its tracks until Flair capitulated. I am not sure why Ted assigned that kind of value to Flair himself, but Ted did watch pro wrestling and knew the roles of the key cast members. [Flair] has my total respect. He was always a gentleman and a team player."[23] Flair was unaware that the sale of JCP hinged on his signing, and it was Schmidt-Fellner who revealed that information to the Nature Boy more than a month after the deal was finalized.[24] Flair later expressed frustration with Jim Crockett because his longtime friend and ally didn't inform him about that valuable piece of leverage he could have used in negotiation.[25] It was the tipping point in a rapidly deteriorating relationship, and Flair's association with Crockett would never be the same. The sad truth is they soon stopped talking altogether.[26]

Over the course of 1988, Flair maintained a busy schedule, but his workload was far less than in previous years. According to records, he wrestled 207 matches that year, 70 less than in 1987 and his lowest total since his second full year in the business in 1974 (189).[27] In April, he missed at least four dates due to illness, proving that he was a human after all, but he bounced back with a vengeance.[28] "I watched [Flair] in Detroit go 20 minutes against Sting after being in a sick bed with a high fever for three days and he still pulled out all the stops," wrote Chris Zavisa in 1988. "The man is the consummate professional."[29] That same month, Barry Windham turned on Lex Luger and joined the Four Horsemen. Flair's feud with Sting lasted months, and despite their chemistry, enthusiasts were burned out by May. Dusty Rhodes tried to mix things up by elevating former All-American "Dr. Death" Steve Williams into a main event spot opposite Flair, but the conflict received an underwhelming response.

Fans wanted to see only one matchup, and that was the clash JCP specifically held back from the house show circuit: Flair versus Luger. The Nature Boy and Total Package wrestled a half dozen times in Florida in 1986, and once Luger joined JCP and became a Horseman, the two were often teammates. Following Luger's face turn, they lined up on different sides of tag bouts all over the country, but JCP protected the sanctity of their expected singles rivalry, building it up as the must-see battle of the year. On July 10, 1988, they wrestled in the main event of the Great American Bash, a highly anticipated program also offered on pay-per-view.[30] Although Flair's enduring popularity had many fans rooting for the blond champion to prevail, Luger was the crowd favorite, and many people predicted a title change. The atmosphere at the Baltimore Arena was electric, and Luger was in position to win with Flair in his Torture Rack backbreaker. The bell sounded, and while it appeared that Luger had won, it was really nothing more than another unsatisfactory finish.

The match was stopped by Maryland State Athletic Commission officials due to a cut on Luger's head, and Flair retained his championship. The illusion of Luger's near victory would carry over to live events, and Crockett hoped it would sustain the box office through the remainder of the summer. And it did. The disputed ending in Baltimore gave spectators reason to turn out and support Luger in rematches, and there was widespread enthusiasm for JCP cards into August 1988. Flair and Luger drew houses of 13,000 or greater in Richmond, Atlanta, and Charlotte, but again, the booking of match endings continued to be repetitive and disappointing. They teased a Luger title victory time and again, only to see the decision changed to a win for the challenger by disqualification due to outside interference. With occasional small changes, this routine made the rounds until the match no longer carried the same kind of excitement. Atlanta, on September 25, drew less than 7,000, whereas Greensboro had 2,500 on September 11 and then 4,000 on October 9.

The depressed attendance numbers, combined with less than stellar TV ratings, were glaring negatives at the end of the run for Jim Crockett Promotions. On November 2, 1988, a new era dawned with the formal announcement that Turner Broadcasting had obtained control of Crockett's wrestling talent and television empire.[31] The absorption of the "NWA" into the vast Turner media conglomerate created both a sense of exhilaration and concern. From the point of view of fans, the thought of wrestling growing by leaps and bounds because of Turner's influence was very stimulating. There was a lot of room to build upon what Crockett had started and foster a wrestling promotion with superior technology and production. Turner Broadcasting's television expertise and its ability to promote brands across its various platforms gave the outfit a new lease on life.

There were also concerns that the new corporate supervision would water down the product, as executives tried to transform the "NWA" into a family-friendly product. If Turner executives looked to mimic the WWF's brand of success, any sense of the old JCP promotion would certainly be lost. Turner didn't waste any time moving proficient businessmen into leadership positions, and Jim Crockett himself was still attached to the promotion to offer his expertise. But the unsettled dynamic between Flair and Dusty Rhodes remained a problem, and the tension between them needed to be resolved.[32] Rhodes was using his leverage to convince TBS officials, particularly the incoming executive vice president of wrestling operations, Jim Herd, to move Flair out of the title picture. His idea was to have 27-year-old Rick Steiner, a former amateur wrestler from the University of Michigan, dethrone Flair at Starrcade in Norfolk.[33]

Flair balked at that plan, and once again his future with the company was in doubt. Jack Petrik, president of Turner Home Entertainment and the man ultimately in charge of the wrestling division, understood Flair's importance to Turner. He quickly resolved the situation in Flair's favor, nixing the Starrcade title change and rebooking the main event to have Flair defend against Lex Luger.[34] This was a defining moment for Flair. As was previously mentioned, he had signed a contract with Turner without receiving the big raise he could have commanded. However, he did obtain a measure of creative control, meaning that he would have a say in any title change. Dave Meltzer, in the *Wrestling Observer Newsletter*, referred to Flair's new clout as an "unprecedented power for a world champion," and in the ego battle for influence, the Nature Boy had one-upped Rhodes to get the last word.[35] Rhodes, in turn, resigned as booker and soon left the promotion.[36]

The instability of the promotion's transitional phase was lessened with the hiring of George Scott as booker. Scott was an expert in dealing with talent, and he knew how to bring out the best in Flair. He also knew the guy they were bringing in to challenge Flair for the world championship in a renewal of one of wrestling's greatest all-time feuds, Flair versus Ricky Steamboat. During the January 21, 1989, broadcast of *World Championship Wrestling*, Steamboat appeared as a mystery partner for Eddie Gilbert against Flair and Barry Windham, in his first NWA showing since February 1985.[37] The Horsemen used their strengths to keep Gilbert in the ring as long as possible, but Steamboat got the hot tag and pinned Flair with a crossbody off the top rope. It was an auspicious return and immediately set the table for a championship match at the Chi-Town Rumble in Chicago on February 20.

Steamboat's arrival came at a critical time for the NWA and for Flair personally. With new management and discerning eyes watching from TBS, the promotion had to put its best foot forward. For Flair, in the aftermath of booking patterns that tarnished the reputation of the World Heavyweight title, he needed a top tier opponent who could raise the bar and reestablish the NWA to its former glory. Steamboat was the right man for the job, and on February 20 in Chicago, the two athletes, whose history dated back over a decade, wrestled a true classic. The local audience was spectacularly dialed in, reacting emotionally to each move performed, and Flair and Steamboat gave them a match of a lifetime. A small package by Steamboat secured a three count, and the Dragon captured the NWA World championship as the crowd screamed at the top of their lungs. The new Turner-owned "NWA" had needed a jolt of adrenaline to revive the promotion, and this single bout delivered just that.

For the fifth time in his career, Flair had lost his world title, but by no means was he being demoted. In fact, the Flair-Steamboat championship series would dominate headlines through May and provide fans with a stream of first class matches across the wrestling landscape. A big rematch was staged at Clash of the Champions IV on April 2, 1989, at the Superdome in New Orleans, and this time, Flair and Steamboat put on a masterful effort for over 55 minutes, in a special two of three falls contest. The bout was acknowledged as one of the finest pro matches of not only the current era but any era, and it was reminiscent of the legendary title matches of yore, particularly those between Dory Funk Jr. and Jack Brisco. Flair won the initial fall but lost the second by submission and the third when he was pinned, despite having his foot outside the ropes.[38] On the whole, the Clash event drew a lackluster rating and a poor live attendance (less than 5,500), and George Scott was relieved of his duties as booker.[39]

Replacing Scott was a booking committee made up of Jim Herd, Jim Ross, Eddie Gilbert, and Kevin Sullivan. Up until that point in his career, Flair had passively allowed others to dictate his matches, angles, and finishes, and he was ready to have more of a say, if only to protect his own interests more than anything else. He joined the booking committee as well, which added to his already rigorous schedule. On camera, Flair maneuvered into another rematch with Steamboat by having his lawyer Dennis Guthrie invoke some legalese, and the bout was arranged for May 7 at the Auditorium in Nashville. For the third time in a high profile setting, Flair and Steamboat left it all in the ring, delivering a stunning physical battle for the record books. Their WrestleWar encounter was a masterpiece on all fronts, and it concluded with Steamboat's leg buckling, a quick thinking move by Flair, and a three count. The Nature Boy captured his sixth NWA World championship.

"Not in character for Ric Flair, but Rick Steamboat is the greatest champion I've ever faced," Flair told the audience after the match. "And I'm proud to be here for a sixth time." Terry Funk, a former world title-holder, was on hand as part of a three-man panel of judges, and he entered the ring to offer his congratulations.[40] Funk surprised onlookers by issuing a challenge to the new champ, and Flair responded by saying that he was going to adhere to the promotion's top ten. He said that Funk had been in Hollywood, rubbing shoulders with Sylvester Stallone, and wasn't presently a contender. Funk protested briefly, then shook Flair's hand before landing a powerful punch to Flair's head. He proceeded to throw Flair from the ring, where the assault continued, and he managed to piledrive the champion onto the unforgiving surface of a ringside table. The scenario turned Flair into a fan favorite, propelled Funk into the title picture, and created a feud that would carry the promotion for months.

The impromptu attack, according to the storyline, knocked Flair out of action with a neck injury and threatened the future of his career.[41] Funk sparked tons of fan support for the champion through his relentless promos that targeted Flair in every which way, and it was difficult not to be entertained by his creative insults. Flair's increased popularity was notable as they headed for their eventual matchup. On July 1, Flair announced that he was going to resume wrestling and wanted a bout with Funk at the Great American Bash. The anticipated contest was booked, and on July 23 in Baltimore, Flair went to the ring looking for revenge. In the squared circle, Flair and Funk were just as compatible as Flair and Steamboat, but in a different way. Instead of a technically driven battle, Flair and Funk brawled to what appeared to be the human limitations in the worked wrestling environment. The violence was off the charts and exemplified the true NWA style.

Fans were heavily invested in the combat and collectively lost it when Flair pinned Funk to retain his championship. But the war was far from over, as Flair, Funk, the Great Muta, and Sting entered into an even more chaotic brawl after the match. In the weeks that followed, Flair remained steadfast in his efforts to be the organization's top performer, while contributing to the booking committee. He found it hard not to butt heads with Jim Herd, an executive with limited background in wrestling. Herd was in a difficult position himself, working to streamline the success of the NWA by making it more appealing to the masses. He also had to answer to Turner officials since corporate wanted tangible results from its wrestling investment. An argument arose in August 1989 between Flair and Eddie Gilbert, a fellow member of the booking committee.[42] Flair was vehement in his position against Gilbert, criticizing his Memphis booking style, and the latter was replaced by Jim Cornette.[43]

In turn, Flair was also promoted to chairman of the booking committee. Wade Keller of the *Pro Wrestling Torch* newsletter wrote, "Flair is a proven leader who fellow wrestlers respect, but with everything else he does, to also be lead-booker can't make life easy."[44] It was true that the demands of being booker were time-consuming and sometimes painful. Flair would soon learn that being booker would generate controversy in the locker room, and there was simply no way to please every wrestler who wanted a push. Even in situations that didn't directly involve Flair, he'd take the brunt of the blame because of his position. Being in such a role was completely opposite to his carefree days of years past, when he trusted promoters to have his best interests at heart. Now, as 1989 drew to a close, he had to fight to protect himself from madcap ideas that threatened his reputation and livelihood. If he had a real choice in the matter, he'd much rather have discarded the responsibilities and just been Slick Ric once again.

CHAPTER 16

THE ROAD TO TITAN

A s the dust settled in the wake of Turner Broadcasting's acquisition of Jim Crockett's wrestling interests, a few things were abundantly clear. For one, the tone and overall theme of Turner's new division was going to diverge from its predecessor in a number of important ways. At the top of the list was a focused effort to find a balance between appealing to the beer-drinking, old-school fans, who had been the core audience for Crockett and the NWA going back decades, and appealing to a broader demographic of potential supporters. The only way for Turner executives to grow its fan base and annual revenues was to follow the Vince McMahon playbook and cater to children and families. That meant a roster of colorful characters, light-hearted gimmicks, and wider merchandising operations. Jim Herd followed up with the debut of the skateboarding Dynamic Dudes, Ranger Ross, and the comical Norman the Lunatic — a recent release from a mental hospital.

The Ding Dongs, however, were probably a step too far in the wrong direction. The masked tag team, with their bright outfits and over-the-top enthusiasm, was considered hokey through and through, and older devotees were instantly turned off by their shenanigans. Herd's attempt to revamp part of the wrestling lineup was motivated by sound business sense, but the Ding Dongs weren't exactly a glowing example of inspired creativity.[1] The outrageous ideas didn't stop there either. "One thing we're going to do is add some wrestlers who are costumed radically differently — in high-tech outer space sort of machinery, for instance — to appeal to kids," Herd told the *New York Times* in 1989.[2] For the NWA's faithful, zany gimmicks weren't a sign of positive progress, and they had the potential to hurt the promotion more than help it. Another revelation made by Herd in that *New York Times* article was Ted Turner's ban on explicit violence and bloodshed in matches.[3]

Those had been major components of wrestling under Jim Crockett and across the NWA as a whole, and the ban required a restructuring of its entire philosophy. But despite Turner's proclamation, mayhem did ensue on WTBS, and one extreme situation on September 12, 1989, in Columbia, South Carolina, took violence to a new level. The show was Clash of the Champions VIII, otherwise known as Fall Brawl, and after a main event that saw Ric Flair and Sting defeat the Great Muta and Dick Slater by disqualification, Flair was attacked by Terry Funk. It was a continuation of their acclaimed and financially successful feud, but the post-match assault took a surprising turn when Funk tried to suffocate Flair with a plastic bag. The sheer savagery of the moment was captured on television before a nationwide audience and immediately sparked widespread blowback from Turner headquarters, as well as outraged viewers. Jim Herd himself was nearly fired over it.[4]

In response to the incident, Jeff Steele, a correspondent for the *Pro Wrestling Torch*, wrote, "Tonight we witnessed the most singly irresponsible action that I've ever witnessed in 25 years of being a fan. This show is the worst thing the NWA has done."[5] The controversial stunt didn't distract from the overall Flair-Funk feud, which was one of the most talked about rivalries in wrestling. Everything was building up for a climax of their war on November 15, 1989, at Clash IX in Troy, New York. That night, the two men battled in an epic I Quit bout — a fierce contest that is still discussed and heralded to this day. Flair was the fan favorite in his quest to finally eliminate Funk from title contention, and the Funker, with his unpredictability and natural skill, was ready to close out his run in the promotion with a one-of-a-kind performance. The result was an incomparable classic, which only served to enhance the legends of both men. Funk conceded at the finish, while locked in the figure-four, and graciously shook Flair's hand, signaling the end of their long conflict.

The succession of unforgettable matches Flair had first with Ricky Steamboat and then with Terry Funk made 1989, arguably, the best year of his career. Supporting that claim is the fact that five of his highest profile bouts were in contention for "Match of the Year," according to the *Wrestling Observer Newsletter*. The top four selections in that category involved Flair, with the Nature Boy against Steamboat on April 2 in New Orleans at number one. Flair's contests with Steamboat on May 7 and February 20 came in second and third respectively, and Flair's I Quit bout with Funk on November 15 was number four. An "Honorable Mention" on the list was Flair's battle with Funk on July 23 at the Great American Bash.[6] What makes 1989 even more notable for Flair is that he had scores of similar caliber matches with Steamboat and Funk on untelevised house shows. The intensity was very much the same across the board.

Several leading wrestling publications rightly acknowledged Flair as "Wrestler of the Year," including *Pro Wrestling Illustrated* and the *Wrestling Observer Newsletter* — his first such award since 1986.[7] The end of the 1980s triggered a lot of reflection, and fans had an opportunity to look back on the tremendous changes to professional wrestling in recent years. The territorial system was gone, and two organizations, Turner's "NWA" and the WWF, were vying for a national stranglehold. But in terms of individual success, pundits seemed to be unanimous. "If Ric Flair is not voted 'Wrestler of the Eighties,' there is something very, very wrong," wrote wrestling historian Evan Ginzburg.[8] In the *Observer*, Dave Meltzer didn't beat around the bush when declaring the "Wrestler of the Decade." He stated, "Okay, it's Ric Flair. Nobody even thought twice about it."[9]

Earlier in 1989, Flair had been proclaimed "Wrestler of the Decade" by the listeners of *Rasslin' Radio*, a popular Philadelphia grappling program.[10] Promoter Joel Goodhart arranged for a special banquet at Philly's Civic Center Plaza Ballroom on April 30, and Flair went out of his way to attend the event.[11] Flanked by Elliott Murnick, a longtime East Coast promoter, and by TV commentator Jim Ross, Flair was presented with an attractive, gold-plated Wrestler of the Decade World championship belt. During his thank-you speech, Flair appeared to let down his guard, and stepped away from his Nature Boy persona to show a real side of himself. "In moments like this . . . [it makes] me feel very, very good about the decisions that I made in my life," Flair told the audience. "And I'm glad that I'm where I'm at. It's a tremendous, tremendous honor — I'm saying this from the bottom of my heart — to know you all think so highly of me. Thank you."[12]

Elliott Murnick had been in the business a long time. As a second-generation promoter, he had seen all of the big names through the years, and he was a pretty good judge of talent. "For combining wrestling and showmanship, [Flair's] the best ever," Murnick said. "Gorgeous George, for example, may have been a better showman. Lou Thesz may have been a better wrestler. But if you take all items into consideration, there's never been better than Ric Flair."[13] Dave Meltzer added, "You could definitely say Flair is the best ever. For combining flamboyance, showmanship, athletic ability, and endurance, he's the best for sure."[14] From late 1989 into 1990, the accolades for Flair came from all directions. Industry experts and smart fans loved Flair's work, and his popularity remained strong. Of all people, Jim Herd, the executive vice president of what would become World Championship Wrestling, disagreed with their collective opinion. He saw Flair as a liability and wanted a change at the top.

This was the same Ric Flair who had just been crowned "Wrestler of the Year" and "Wrestler of the Decade." It was also the same Ric Flair who was so valuable to Ted Turner that his noninvolvement in the JCP-Turner sale would have been a deal-breaker. Flair had gotten an incredible one-of-a-kind contract with a measure of creative control, and in late 1988 into 1989, he had received unparalleled support from TBS leadership. At that time, Turner executives wanted to push Flair further and expressed interest in not only marketing a Flair home video tape, but a book as well.[15] Steve Chamberlain, the vice president and general manager of Turner Home Entertainment, even started working on the latter endeavor, spending time with Flair at his Charlotte-area home to collect anecdotes for what was surely going to be an amusing project.[16] Flair's appointment to head of the booking committee was another acknowledgment of his importance, and between his in-ring work and out-of-the-ring political standing, his position appeared to be stronger than ever.

But Jim Herd didn't care. He had seen a survey of fans and the reportedly negative feedback about Flair.[17] At the core of things, Herd believed young fans couldn't relate to him. As a result, he encouraged a change away from Flair as champion. It was an inconceivable thought, especially considering Flair's recent success, but Herd's ongoing anti-Flair stance was only one of the issues festering behind the scenes. A contemporaneous report in the *Pro Wrestling Torch* stated, "Ric Flair as a leader is getting over poorly with some people in the NWA. Some say his leadership qualities are lacking and the stress is leading to a lot of hard feelings."[18] On the heels of his quarrel with Eddie Gilbert, which led to Gilbert's ouster from the booking committee, Flair got into it with Paul E. Dangerously, an outstanding 24-year-old manager and personality. Their September 1989 argument during a TV taping at the Center Stage Theater in Atlanta led to Dangerously being fired on the spot by Flair.[19]

Claims circulated that Flair wasn't supporting the boys enough, and that the only people being pushed were those aligned in some way with the booking committee itself. Smart fans were conflicted by the reports. On one hand, they wanted to continue to show their appreciation for Flair's wrestling ability, but the backstage turmoil, blamed on Flair's work as booker, was earning plenty of criticism. "Ric Flair has become the Dusty Rhodes of 1989," Charles Joseph, a fan from St. Joseph, Missouri, wrote to *Matwatch* newsletter. "It makes me sick to say it. I have been one of Flair's biggest fans as a wrestler. Ric, stick to the ring and forget the book."[20] Steve Beverly, editor of that same publication, noted the mind-boggling hours Flair was putting into his dual roles and remarked that viewers could "see the strain" on his face during interview segments.[21] Nevertheless, Beverly credited Flair's tireless efforts with improving the TV ratings for weekly programs and Clash of the Champions events.[22]

If anyone needed proof of Flair's willingness to put over talent, they had to look no further than Starrcade '89, held on December 13 at the Omni Coliseum in Atlanta. On that evening, in the finals of a four-man round-robin, Sting used a small package to score a surprise pinfall over the world champion and, with 40 points, won the Iron Man tournament.[23] After the bout, Flair, who had recently been rejoined by Arn and Ole Anderson, celebrated with Sting in the ring.[24] Interestingly, the quartet had become a baby face version of the Four Horsemen, and they went right into a war with the J-Tex Corporation (Great Muta, Buzz Sawyer, and Dragon Master) led by manager Gary Hart. But the action centered on Flair and the top two contenders to his championship: Sting and Lex Luger. Jim Herd felt the time was right to replace Flair as title-holder, and Sting, with a title shot on February 25, 1990, at WrestleWar, seemed the logical choice.[25]

As part of the storyline, Flair demanded that Sting give up his title shot and kicked him out of the Horsemen at Clash of the Champions X in Corpus Christi on February 6. In a brawl later in the show, Sting suffered a legitimate knee injury and would be forced to miss the pay-per-view.[26] The situation turned Flair heel again, while Lex Luger, the man booked to replace Sting at WrestleWar, became a fan favorite. Herd still wanted his title change, but Flair refused. He later admitted that a promise had been made to Sting that he would be his successor, and despite the efforts of Herd to change his mind, Flair stuck to his word.[27] At the WrestleWar program in Greensboro, Flair and Luger delivered a well-contested bout with an emotional finish. Late in the match, Sting hobbled down to ringside on crutches to support Luger, but he was circled by Ole and Arn Anderson just as Luger was about to beat Flair with his backbreaker. Luger leapt from the ring to save Sting and was counted out.

Three days before the WrestleWar event, Flair had tendered his resignation from the booking committee, citing his problems with Herd.[28]

Publicly, it was said that he relinquished his position because of the strain of doing two jobs.[29] With regard to his mat work, an "insider" told *Matwatch*, "He just wasn't the same Ric Flair."[30] But on the whole, the promotion had benefited from Flair's extraordinary efforts both in front of the camera and behind the curtain. His feuds with Terry Funk, Sting, and Lex Luger garnered widespread interest and accolades. In TV matches, he worked as hard as ever, and his two contests with the ultra-talented Bobby Eaton, one-half of the legendary Midnight Express tag team, on December 3, 1989, and January 7, 1990, were phenomenal. Their matches, featured on *The Main Event* broadcast on TBS, drew impressive ratings, and on each occasion, had over 1.6 million homes tuned in.[31]

Also on television in early 1990, Flair had above-average matches with high-flyers Tom Zenk and Brian Pillman, elevating both men in the eyes of the public.[32] Although Jim Herd didn't get what he wanted at WrestleWar, he pushed for a Flair to Luger title switch on March 24, 1990, in St. Louis. Word got out that a title change was going to happen, so it was moved to the night before in Chicago. The situation was complex, with Flair apparently willing to drop the championship in exchange for a release from his contract so he could leave the company.[33] But Flair had an alternative for Herd. He'd agree to stay, but as a sign of good faith from the promotion, he wanted a contract extension — and he would keep his belt for the time being to boot. Herd was in a tight spot. He didn't want lose Flair altogether, and he needed him to play ball to ultimately transfer the championship. So he was the one to compromise, and within a matter of days, Flair's new contract was announced.[34]

Sticking to his original plan, Flair retained his World title against Luger at Capital Combat on May 19, 1990, and held out for Sting's return at the Great American Bash. In the meantime, the Four Horsemen expanded to include Barry Windham and Sid Vicious, and their feud with the Dudes with Attitudes, a baby face contingent consisting of the Junkyard Dog, Paul Orndorff, and the Steiner Brothers, intensified.[35] The Dudes were unified in their effort to neutralize the gang-style attacks of the Horsemen and to support their comrade Sting in his effort to dethrone Flair. On July 7, 1990, in Baltimore, ever-hopeful fans received their big payoff moment, as Sting pinned the champion for the NWA World Heavyweight title. Following his win, Sting graciously accepted the Big Gold belt and, stepping out of character, praised Flair. "Ric Flair is the greatest world champion of all-time," Sting told the live audience. "I've got some big shoes to fill."

In the aftermath of his Baltimore clash with Sting, Flair put things into perspective. He admitted to Alex Marvez of the *Miami Herald* that losing the belt was a "major letdown" for him. "For a week I went home and did nothing," he said. "Everybody kept telling me, 'That's it.' Why should I go out and work so hard every day? Then I finally woke up three days later and realized, 'You do that because you're Ric Flair. Whether you're the champion or not, you want to be recognized as the best.' As long as I know I'm one of the top five wrestlers in the world, I'll keep on wrestling."[36] Incidentally, less than a week after losing the belt, Flair was sidelined by a staph infection and missed at least five matches. Flair was adamant about returning as soon as possible, and Jim Herd told a reporter, "You know Flair, he won't stay out any longer than he has to."[37] Flair bounced back to resume bookings against Sting on the house show circuit. He also teamed with the Horsemen against various pairings of the Dudes.

Despite an influx of talent, from Big Van Vader to Stan Hansen, WCW (as it was now known) continued to struggle in the ratings department. Ole Anderson had assumed control as booker and was mixing things up in an attempt to stabilize their weekend numbers. Live-event attendance was another disappointment for Turner executives, and the promotion had significant ups and downs. Clash of the Champions XII, on September 5, 1990, proved to be a big winner with a surprising 5.0 rating from Asheville, North Carolina.[38] In the semifinal, Flair lost by disqualification to Lex Luger after Hansen interfered. With Anderson and Jim Herd pushing Sting's feud against the mysterious Black Scorpion, Flair was ushered out of the singles main event picture, and he became a fixture in tag team matches with Arn Anderson against Doom (Butch Reed and Ron Simmons). It was a jarring new role for Flair — one that fans weren't used to seeing.

The idea of moving Flair into a secondary position had been floating around for years. Herd had wanted to replace Flair as the heavyweight champion and considered giving him an entirely new gimmick to rebrand his character. At one juncture, Herd suggested Flair assume the name "Spartacus," the title movie character portrayed by Kirk Douglas in 1960, and recommended he get an earring.[39] Herd did convince Flair to cut his trademark blond hair in December 1990, which coincided with the decision to put Flair opposite Sting at Starrcade '90 in St. Louis.[40] Herd asked Flair to wrestle as the masked Black Scorpion in what was the closing stanza for the unpopular and unsuccessful angle. Flair went through with the cage match and was not only defeated but unmasked. Altogether, it wasn't a bright spot for World Championship Wrestling, and Flair was forced to make the most of an ugly situation.

Herd's perceived maneuvering, the attempts to change his look and persona, the negativity surrounding his time as booker, and the efforts to demote him from his usual top spots had all worn Flair thin. The promises from Turner, including a VHS release highlighting his best in-ring moments and a book, had disappeared from the agenda. When *Entertainment Tonight* had done a feature on the promotion in the summer of 1989, Flair hadn't even been mentioned, let alone hyped as the organization's top wrestler.[41] It was an embarrassing omission and displayed a disrespect rarely shown to franchise players in professional athletics. These factors spawned self-confidence issues in Flair, something that only added to his stress.[42] Through sheer professionalism, Flair plodded on, working through the difficulties as they arose, and allowing his natural in-ring ability to carry the day. As the Black Scorpion mess unfolded in December 1990, Ole Anderson was fired as WCW booker. In early 1991, his replacement was named, and it was none other than the "American Dream" Dusty Rhodes.

Ironically, though, instead of Herd continuing to diminish Flair's on-camera role, WCW went completely in the other direction. At the Meadowlands Arena, just outside New York City, on January 11, 1991, Flair pinned Sting and regained the World title. The finish was widely applauded by the local crowd, and the significance of the moment wasn't lost on longtime fans.[43] Flair's triumph marked his seventh NWA title win, which had him tied with Harley Race for most reigns in history. "Although I'd seen Flair in far better matches," wrote Evan Ginzburg, "his victory was a thrill I will not soon forget. For me, it was the Super Bowl and World Series all rolled up in one."[44] Substandard house show numbers were at the root of the shift back to Flair, and once again, the Nature Boy was called upon to spearhead a rebound at the box office. But, needless to say, change at WCW wasn't going to happen without a fair amount of controversy.

A little over two weeks after Flair regained the belt, a lengthy and revealing article about the champ appeared in the *Raleigh News and Observer*, written by Billy Warden and Jonathan Probber. The piece went far beyond the casual items found in kayfabe magazines to give readers a look at Flair's real life, family, and background. It included quotes from his father, Dr. Richard Fliehr, and a photo of Ric with his daughter, Ashley. Brad Muster, a fullback for the Chicago Bears, offered his insight into Flair from the viewpoint of a fellow professional athlete: "Ric Flair has been the quintessential wrestler over the past decade. They have to perform every day. He has a lot of athletic ability. People think they're just actors and performers, but it takes a great athlete to put in the years and take the bumps." The article also quoted a fan named Vicky Roberts, who bluntly said, "Flair is wrestling. When Flair quits, that's the end of wrestling."[45]

Even though the 41-year-old Flair was battling private self-confidence issues and a day-to-day rift with Jim Herd, it was obvious that wrestling fans, fellow wrestlers, and professional athletes across the spectrum respected him to no end. All they knew was the Flair they saw in the ring, performing at the highest level, and to them, nothing had changed. On January 30, 1991, at Clash of the Champions XIV in Gainesville, Georgia, Flair battled Scott Steiner, a ring innovator and one-half of the Steiner Brothers tag team. Steiner, with just over three years of experience, was seen as a potential successor to Flair, but their match failed to impress critics. Even worse, it was a ratings bomb, delivering the lowest ever rating for a Clash main event.[46] The following month, Flair, Barry Windham, Sid Vicious, and Larry Zbyszko went over Sting, Brian Pillman, and the Steiners in a War Games encounter when referee Nick Patrick stopped the bout following two devastating powerbombs by Vicious on Pillman.

As part of a promotional working agreement, WCW and New Japan Pro Wrestling, a group led by Antonio Inoki, staged a combined event on March 21, 1991, in Tokyo. In the main event, Flair was pinned by IWGP champion Tatsumi Fujinami and apparently lost his claim to the world championship. However, since Flair was technically recognized by both the NWA and Turner's WCW as titleholder, he had two distinct honors to potentially lose.[47] In this situation, WCW didn't recognize Flair's defeat, citing the fact that he had been thrown over the top rope, which amounted to an automatic disqualification. The NWA did acknowledge the title switch, and although Fujinami left the ring with the belt, Flair grabbed it back post-match. This led to a rematch on American soil, on May 19 at the Bayfront Center in St. Petersburg. That night, Flair beat Fujinami to regain the NWA championship — his eighth such victory — and broke the record he shared with Harley Race. The achievement for Flair was another notch in his belt in what everyone knew was a Hall of Fame career.

But WCW was strained more than ever. House show attendance was abysmal, demonstrated by the figures in Norfolk, Baltimore, and Philadelphia between June 6 and June 8, 1991. It was reported that crowd sizes amounted to 900, 1,400, and 1,000 respectively, in what used to be prime JCP-WCW cities.[48] TV ratings had not improved, either, and Jim Herd was scrambling to save what was perceived to be a sinking ship. Flair wasn't worried. After all, he was still champion, and he had gotten assurances from higher-ups that his job was secure.[49] But things were about to come to a head in the worst possible way for a wrestling promotion. The crisis actually began when the ratings for Clash of the Champions XV, held on June 12, were released. The program underperformed in key demographics, and the main event featuring Flair and Bobby Eaton didn't realize expected results.[50]

From Turner's perspective, the lackluster financials indicated a need for change. WCW was not flourishing, and the elements at play were cited as contributing factors. Flair was the number one guy, and considering his high work ethic, his own personal efforts were not to blame. But the various angles and matches were not holding the interest of fans, and the overall product was suffering. During this pressure-filled time, discussions between Flair and Turner over another contract extension came up. Turner was in retrenchment mode, whereas Flair wanted to be compensated fairly, based on his track record, experience, headliner status, and what was expected to be a pivotal role in WCW heading into the future. It was rumored that Dusty Rhodes, who was back as booker, was actively trying to curtail Flair's influence, perhaps even working to move him into a commentator position. Herd denied the gossip. "We have no plans for Ric Flair to come out of the ring," he said.[51]

Reports soon surfaced that WCW had offered Flair a contract extension at about half of what he was previously making, and the rift turned into a severe fracture. One informed account pegged the new offer at about $350,000 a year, way down from the $780,000 he was said to have been making.[52] The amount reflected the vision Herd and Rhodes had for Flair, and it was surely no longer in WCW's top spot.[53] "I don't know how they could possibly expect me to accept their offer," Flair told a reporter. "Imagine a baseball manager walking up to Jose Canseco and saying, 'Jose, tomorrow we're going to cut your check in half.' Would they expect him to say, 'Oh, fine'?"[54] The initial plan was for Flair to drop the title to Lex Luger at the Great American Bash on July 14. But once the situation started to fall apart, Flair agreed to pass the torch by losing the belt to Barry Windham at a TV taping in Macon, Georgia, on July 1.[55]

Turner officials didn't like that idea. They wanted a title change at the pay-per-view and felt a switch on TV would dilute sales for their important Bash card. Rather than continue negotiating to reach a mutually satisfactory deal, and citing the fact that Flair didn't agree to Turner's salary proposal, Herd abruptly fired him.[56] During the Saturday evening broadcast of *World Championship Wrestling*, on July 6, 1991, Herd told the viewing audience that the WCW championship had been declared vacant due to contractual problems with Flair, and a match between Lex Luger and Barry Windham for the belt would be staged at the Bash. As for Flair, he was still recognized as the world champion by the NWA and had physical possession of the Big Gold belt.[57] Within days of Flair's termination, Herd and the executives at Turner had second thoughts about their decision and arranged a meeting with the Nature Boy at the Ritz-Carlton in Atlanta.[58] They wanted Flair back and offered him $750,000 to return. This time, Flair held all the power, and he flatly turned them down.[59]

In the aftermath of Flair's firing, accusations and criticisms were launched in every direction. Herd took a great deal of heat, and he tried to explain how things went down to alleviate the fallout. "The stories that have been written about us wanting him to take a massive pay cut are exaggerated and completely erroneous," Herd said. "We even offered him his old contract at astronomical bucks through next May and his attorneys just started making outrageous demands. He wanted things written into the contract you just can't do, and all these assurances about how he was gonna be used."[60] But when the allegation was made that Flair had been offered the booking job, Herd's tone shifted. "The Ric Flair situation is over but as far as offering him the booking job — that is unequivocally not true," he stated. "It wouldn't surprise me if this is coming from him. You're talking about a guy that's never told the truth in his life. He wanted to go and we helped him."[61]

Herd's quote was controversial to say the least. Steve Beverly, editor of the *Matwatch* publication, which ran his comments, issued an apology for "any damage" to Flair's reputation the statement caused. Dennis Guthrie, Flair's attorney, told Beverly, "I know few people in or out of the wrestling industry that have the integrity Ric Flair does. He is one of the most honest people I know."[62] Since the sale of Jim Crockett Promotions in late 1988, Flair had endured the most tumultuous period of his professional wrestling career. The truth was that his problems with WCW management had caused incredible stress, well beyond reason, and by July 1991, he was more than ready to walk away from the organization. For fans, it was an extraordinary moment, as Flair's ties to WCW, JCP, and the NWA were always seen as thicker than blood. No one ever envisioned seeing Flair anywhere else. Flair, though, was indeed on a new path. In fact, it was a road to Titan Sports — the unthinkable — and he'd soon debut for the World Wrestling Federation.

CHAPTER 17

FROM WRESTLEMANIA TO STARRCADE

During the summer of 1991, professional wrestling was rocked by scandal, and negative national media reports threatened the very fabric of the industry. The situation stemmed from the February indictment of a Harrisburg, Pennsylvania, physician named Dr. George T. Zahorian. Zahorian was charged by a federal grand jury on multiple counts related to the distribution of anabolic steroids, and the case had a strong connection to pro wrestling.[1] The allegations soon revealed that he had prescribed steroids to several top World Wrestling Federation performers, including Hulk Hogan, and the news seriously jeopardized the Hulkster's squeaky-clean public image.[2] Hogan was still carrying the mantle as wrestling's top megastar and hero, and his ties to Zahorian and the allegations of steroid use endangered his reputation, as well as cast a huge shadow over the WWF and wrestling as a whole. Stories on network newscasts and in leading periodicals propelled the steroid controversy into the national consciousness, and great damage was done.[3]

Although Vince McMahon claimed the scandal didn't hurt the WWF at the box office, it did raise overall awareness of the problems festering inside the business.[4] McMahon addressed the critics head-on and promised a rigorous steroid testing program to clean up the sport. In the meantime, the WWF had endured its typical post-WrestleMania slump, and crowds were moderately sized between April and July 1991.

Hulk Hogan was the WWF World titleholder at the time, having captured the belt from Sgt. Slaughter at WrestleMania VII on March 24. The organization's roster was full of talented athletes and veterans, from Randy Savage to Ted DiBiase, while up-and-comers, like the Undertaker, were just starting to make a name for themselves.[5] Well-known stars Kerry Von Erich, the Legion of Doom (Hawk and Animal), and Sid Justice (formerly Sid Vicious in WCW) were key assets for McMahon, and it was known that he was always on the hunt for marketable new blood.

McMahon had wanted the Nature Boy in the WWF for a long time, and his inquiries about Flair dated back to the heart of the WWF-JCP wrestling war. During the heyday of expansion, McMahon had lured many of Flair's contemporaries to the WWF with the promise of better money. Roddy Piper, Greg Valentine, Ricky Steamboat, Dusty Rhodes, and even Harley Race, a man whose name was synonymous with the NWA, had made the jump years earlier. Every member of the Four Horsemen, with the exception of Ole Anderson, went to work for McMahon at one point or another. Arn Anderson, Tully Blanchard, Barry Windham, and manager J.J. Dillon each departed the NWA for New York and adjusted to the WWF style.[6] Flair held out, and as the backbone of JCP and WCW, he seemed to be permanently situated there. But the Rhodes-Herd regime had other ideas, and even though WCW did try to re-sign him at the last minute, Flair was through.[7]

The WWF offered Flair a new opportunity to shine, and he was optimistic about his future.[8] He went to New York to discuss a potential deal with McMahon, whom he'd never met in person, and agreed to terms with a handshake.[9] Though ready to get back in the saddle, Flair was temporarily constrained by a no compete clause until September 1. McMahon had a creative idea on how to build anticipation for his debut. Over the weekend of August 10–11, 1991, the WWF's syndicated programs, *Superstars of Wrestling* and *Wrestling Challenge*, featured brief segments with Bobby "The Brain" Heenan, one of the best on-camera performers in the business. Heenan had been a manager and commentator, and his wit was an enjoyable hallmark of WWF TV. He was known for his heelish tone and characteristics, but when he was behind the microphone, his humor prevailed. With his decades of wrestling experience, Heenan was a gem. That weekend, he appeared on camera brandishing the Big Gold belt and became the first man to mention Flair by name on a WWF telecast.[10]

The hype continued in subsequent weeks. Heenan proclaimed Flair the "real" world heavyweight champion and noted that he was still under contract by another organization. During *Superstars of Wrestling* on August 31, Heenan joined Paul Bearer for a special "Funeral Parlor" segment and talked up Flair, while putting down Hogan, Hogan's WWF belt, and "Rowdy" Roddy Piper. Handling commentary duties alongside Vince McMahon that week, Piper stepped away from the booth to confront Heenan, spit on Flair's belt, and threw it to the ground. Without uttering a single word, Flair had two ready-made feuds in the WWF, one against his longtime personal friend and ring rival Piper, and the other against Hogan. The latter was essentially a dream match, and pundits were already fantasy-booking the affair for the headline bout at WrestleMania VIII.

Shortly thereafter, "dirt sheets" announced that Flair had formally signed a two-year deal with the WWF, and with the no compete clause expired, the Nature Boy was ready for his debut.[11] On September 9, he appeared from behind the curtain before a studio audience on *Prime Time Wrestling*, wearing a trademark silver, white, and black robe, and confidently asserted himself into the WWF's main event picture.[12] He had a message for both Piper and Hogan, and his customary intensity was on full display. "Hogan, put up or shut up!" he declared, and those in the audience were anything but pleased — booing Flair throughout the interview.[13] The fact that Vince McMahon was promoting Flair as a claimant to the world championship, and pushed him with essentially zero change to his well-known persona, said a lot about the respect the WWF boss had for the former eight-time NWA champ. Nearly everyone who had jumped from the old territorial system to the WWF had been given a gimmick, including the "Texas Tornado" Kerry Von Erich and "King" Harley Race.

Very quickly, Flair was established as a skilled, calculating heel, and his altercation with Piper on September 28 was shocking to faithful WWF fans unaware of Flair's past villainy in the NWA. En route to the ring for a bout with Mark Thomas, Flair stopped at the broadcast booth to jaw with Piper and then proceeded to slap him in the back of the head. Piper wasn't one to be pushed around, but Flair proved to be slicker than ever, nailing the Rowdy Scot with his championship belt. This kick-started a wild melee, and Flair's aggressiveness was front and center. By the end, Piper had accidentally hit Vince McMahon with a chair, and Flair had smashed a chair over Piper's head. Flair walked away from the chaos triumphant, still wearing his robe and holding the gold belt.[14] In untelevised bouts, Flair and Piper had a series of encounters, and Flair's cunning tactics usually gave him the nod. He was adept at pulling on the tights or putting his feet on the ropes for leverage, much to the dismay of crowds.

The WWF went to Europe in early October, and Flair had his first contests with Kerry Von Erich in over six years.[15] Once the most successful box office match in the country, Flair and Von Erich were, of course, at different stages of their careers in 1991, but they still knew how to tell a story in the ring. Flair used the same tactics he was employing against Piper, and he was victorious in four matches against Von Erich in England and Spain. Upon Flair's return stateside, a surprising thing happened. Vince McMahon had placed Flair and Hulk Hogan on the house show calendar, and their highly anticipated first match up was set for October 25 in Oakland, California.[16] Finally, after years of endless comparisons, the two biggest names in the business were going to wrestle, and the excitement was extraordinary. The bout, while not a technical classic, didn't disappoint in terms of emotion. Flair, using a foreign object, pinned Hogan to win the WWF belt, stunning the 15,000 fans in attendance. That decision was reversed moments later, leaving Hogan with a DQ victory.

Flair, in his clashes against Hogan and Piper, adjusted his personal style to meet the strengths of his opponents. He wasn't turning out a scientific masterpiece every night, but instead he mixed elements of his customary routine with brawling and over-the-top cheating. He'd garner heat from the audience, give it back, regain it once more, and then play out the finish. If he pinned Piper, usually Piper would get a measure of revenge post-match. The encounters were not ego driven, and no one was trying to get over through backstage politics or power plays. "You've got to give Titan credit," wrestling historian Steve Yohe said after seeing the Flair-Hogan October 26 contest in Los Angeles. "They're giving Flair his respect and Hogan is doing his best in putting Flair over."[17] The WWF ran Flair versus Hogan and Flair versus Piper on a continuous loop through the rest of 1991. During those three months, the Nature Boy battled Piper at least 20 times and faced Hogan upward of 30.

Attendance fluctuated. The promotion had some really strong houses built on the interest in and curiosity about the Hogan-Flair rivalry, but at the same time, the WWF was burning the feud out. The longer those two were promoted on house shows, the smaller any hope for a huge WrestleMania moment became. Rather than withhold the anticipated contest for pay-per-view and the grandest stage of them all, McMahon gave Flair versus Hogan to fans in arenas from coast to coast, including twice at Madison Square Garden.[18] Flair was embroiled in two simultaneous feuds, as was Hogan. At the 1991 Survivor Series on November 27, Hogan was pinned by his other main ring opponent, the Undertaker, and lost his WWF championship. Flair had his hand involved in that one, too, placing a chair in the ring just as the Undertaker delivered his tombstone piledriver on Hogan. The move knocked Hogan out, and he was easy pickings for the 1-2-3.

Hogan losing by pinfall was a rare thing. Enthusiasts fully expected him to regain the title at the special Tuesday in Texas program on December 3, 1991, in San Antonio. With WWF president Jack Tunney ringside to ensure the contest went off without a hitch, Hogan was well on his way to recapturing the championship when Flair once again appeared, looking for trouble. Hogan slammed Flair in the back with a chair, and the momentum carried Flair into Tunney, knocking both to the ground. Flair rebounded in an attempt to help the Undertaker, but his efforts failed, and Hogan pinned the champion to regain the WWF title. Tunney wasn't pleased, and he proceeded to strip Hogan of the WWF championship, citing the "grievous circumstances" and the "flagrant and far-reaching oversight" on the part of the referee. He announced that the winner of the 30-man Royal Rumble, which was going to be held on January 19, 1992, in Albany, New York, would take the vacant World title.

The Royal Rumble was in its fifth year, and several wrestlers had already distinguished themselves by enduring more than a half hour of ring combat before being thrown over the top rope and eliminated. Even fewer had gone over 40 minutes. During the 1991 Rumble, former AWA World champion Rick Martel lasted a trifle over 52 minutes, setting a new record.[19] But his accomplishment would be overshadowed by the stamina and craftiness of Ric Flair, who went just over 60 minutes and emerged victorious. Flair entered the match at spot number three and, with the help of Hulk Hogan, eliminated Sid Justice to win the event and the WWF World title.[20] After the match, in a display of genuine emotion, Flair exclaimed, "I'm going to tell you all, with a tear in my eye, this is the greatest moment in my life. When you walk around this world and you tell everybody you're number one, the only way you get to stay number one is to be number one. And this is the only title in the wrestling world that makes you number one. When you are the king of the WWF, you rule the world!"

Historically, Flair became only the second wrestler to have captured both the NWA and WWF championships, following the original "Nature Boy" Buddy Rogers. He was also the first person to have held the NWA, WCW, and WWF titles. Right out of the gate, the situation seemed primed for a Flair-Hogan main event at WrestleMania VIII, but maybe that was just wishful thinking on the part of fans. Vince McMahon burst that bubble by going in a much different direction, sending Hogan into a feud with Sid Justice, and Flair against Randy

Savage. Flair had a long history with Savage and his family dating back to at least 1976. Savage's father, Angelo Poffo, was a grizzled veteran in the mid-Atlantic territory at that time, and he shared his knowledge and experience with up-and-comers. Poffo's two sons, Randy and Lanny, were in the infancy of their own careers and worked prelim bouts for JCP, while Flair was a headliner.

Incredibly, the paths of Flair and Savage had never intersected in the years that followed, and their first ever singles match occurred eight days after Flair's WWF title win, on January 27, 1992.[21] In that contest, held in Lubbock, Texas, Savage beat Flair by DQ. The build up for their WrestleMania bout centered on Flair's claim that he had a past relationship with Miss Elizabeth, Savage's wife, and to instigate matters further, Flair produced photos of himself and Elizabeth together.[22] Flair's ultra-confident personality and snide remarks ramped up the angle and the venom of WWF fans against him, selling the storyline perfectly. After winning the WWF belt, Flair continued to face Roddy Piper on the house show circuit, wrestling him nearly two dozen more times. He also teamed with Sid Justice against Piper and Hulk Hogan in a number of cities. But WWF fans were anxiously awaiting his contest with Savage at WrestleMania on April 5, and over 62,000 packed the Hoosier Dome in Indianapolis to see the affair live.

Savage was emotionally charged because of the Elizabeth angle and took the fight to Flair in the aisle, before being separated by Flair's second, Mr. Perfect. In the early going, Flair held the advantage, punishing Savage with a variety of moves. The Macho Man recovered, though, and scored several near falls. One particular axe handle, from the top rope to the floor, sent Flair into the ring barrier and busted him open. Moments later, Mr. Perfect handed Flair a foreign object, and Flair smashed Savage in the face. Elizabeth, in a move that brought the crowd to its feet, hustled from backstage to encourage Savage. In the meantime, Flair worked on Savage's leg and locked in his figure-four. Upon turning the maneuver and getting free, Savage was badly limping, and he appeared down and out. But he shocked Flair, and the audience, with a sudden roll up and pinfall for the WWF belt.[23] Afterwards, Flair kissed Elizabeth only to be slapped, and then beaten by Savage, setting off a chaotic brawl.[24]

In typical WWF fashion, Flair and Savage were headed for the live event circuit, and they anchored programs for the next six months. It is estimated they wrestled in singles bouts at least 60 times around the country, milking every possible dime from the box office. Attendance for the promotion wasn't overwhelming, and continued bad publicity stemming from steroid and sexual harassment allegations hurt the organization's public image.[25] But Flair and Savage, the professionals that they were, gave it their all every night regardless of the crowd size. Weirdly, Flair wasn't booked for a match at SummerSlam '92 in London on August 29, 1992, but he was at Wembley Stadium and made an impact anyway. In fact, his involvement in Savage's title contest with the Ultimate Warrior affected the decision. Along with Mr. Perfect, Flair interfered in the championship matchup, and his actions in hitting Savage in the knee with a chair, caused him to be counted out.

That knee injury carried over to September 1 in Hershey, Pennsylvania, where Flair was set to challenge Savage for the title at a TV taping. With help from Mr. Perfect and Razor Ramon, Flair disabled the defending champ and cinched in his figure-four leglock. For dramatic effect, Savage fought through the pain and held on as long as he could, but he ultimately succumbed to the hold, apparently passing out in the process. The referee counted his shoulders down, and Flair became a two-time WWF champion.[26] A return to the top spot was an admirable achievement, and while it was well-earned, Flair was already positioned to be a transitional titleholder. The WWF and Vince McMahon were searching for an inspirational baby face champion to improve turnout, one with more technical ability than huge physical form and superhuman strength. McMahon's choice was Bret "The Hitman" Hart, a second-generation grappler out of Calgary, Alberta.

Hart was one of the most skilled wrestlers of the era, and for years he had languished in the sphere of tag team competition as a member of the Hart Foundation. His standalone push resulted in two runs as WWF Intercontinental champion, and his more recent reign culminated in a legendary bout at SummerSlam '92 in London — a bout he lost to his brother-in-law Davey Boy Smith. With a clean image and unlimited proficiency, Hart was exactly the kind of athlete McMahon needed. But before a title switch could happen, Flair appeared in a series of title defenses against Hart, the Undertaker, and the Ultimate Warrior.[27] One such contest — a routine clash versus the Warrior on October 8, 1992, at the America West Arena in Phoenix — threatened his career. It wasn't that Flair suffered an obvious trauma, but rather a freak inner ear injury that caused immediate dizziness and nausea. He was unsteady on his feet, with his balance completely thrown off, and he fell to the mat twice in distress.[28]

Flair's condition was very serious, and he needed medical attention. However, he soldiered on despite his condition, fulfilling approximately five dates between October 9 and 16, including a television taping in Saskatoon, Saskatchewan, on October 12. It was there that he lost the WWF championship to Bret Hart.[29] But losing the title was secondary to his health. The issue persisted, and Flair went to the Mayo Clinic in Rochester, Minnesota, for an exhaustive examination. Doctors diagnosed Flair with benign paroxysmal positional vertigo, a condition brought upon through years of landing hard on the wrestling mat.[30] Unfortunately, during his encounter with the Ultimate Warrior, it is believed that a crystal in his right ear became loose and landed in one of his semicircular canals, disrupting his balance.[31] A precise recovery time was unknown, and one doctor estimated that Flair would be out of action for a year.[32]

Miraculously, the issue healed itself, and Flair was able to return to the mat in just under five weeks.[33] In December 1992 and January 1993, Flair wrestled Hart in more than two dozen matches from coast to coast, losing all of them by pinfall or submission. The fans enjoyed seeing the two tacticians battle, and their contests were praised. After seeing a marathon bout between Flair and Hart in Boston on January 9, 1993, Jerry Lane, a correspondent for the *Pro Wrestling Torch* newsletter, wrote, "Words can't do this match justice." The five-star "classic" went

60 minutes and saw Hart win with three falls to two.[34] It was apparent to Flair that Vince McMahon was making changes, and with a recalibration of his top tier lineup, Flair's role would be diminished in the weeks and months ahead. Based on an agreement he had made with McMahon when he first joined the organization, Flair had the option to leave the WWF if he was moved out of the main event picture.

At the same time, WCW executives were yearning to see the Nature Boy return to Atlanta. Interestingly, former Mid-South promoter Bill Watts was now in charge of wrestling operations at WCW, and he understood what Flair brought to the table. The promotion, in an effort to boost ratings on the weekend, had dipped into its film library and broadcast several of Flair's old matches, which was unusual since he still was an employee of the WWF. It was a unique way for Watts and the hierarchy at WCW to demonstrate its sincerity in offering Flair a leading spot. In early January 1993, Flair agreed to terms with WCW, and he met with officials on January 12 in Atlanta, reportedly signing a three-year deal worth $420,000 annually.[35] McMahon upheld his side of the bargain and released Flair from his WWF contract months before it was due to expire. Flair also did what was asked of him. He put over Mr. Perfect in a loser-leaves-WWF match on *Monday Night Raw* and appeared in nine matches in Europe, ending his run on February 10, 1993.[36]

When it was all said and done, Flair was leaving the WWF on a high note. There was no question that he had suffered losses at house shows and on television, but he was still a former two-time WWF champion. He delivered a record performance at the 1992 Royal Rumble and never missed a beat throughout his tenure, regardless of his role. Readers of the *Wrestling Observer Newsletter* acknowledged his success by voting him "Wrestler of the Year" for the ninth time — an unprecedented feat.[37] Headed back to WCW, a new opportunity presented itself: to redefine his legacy in what was considered his home promotion, especially after his unceremonious exit in 1991. Jim Herd, who had been at the root of so much controversy, was long gone, and new management was desperately trying to revitalize the organization.[38] But controversial matters and WCW were essentially synonymous, and Bill Watts, even before he had a chance to book Flair, abruptly resigned from the company on February 10, 1993, as a result of a firestorm over past comments.[39]

Although a former member of the Four Horsemen replaced Watts, he wasn't necessarily on good terms with Flair. Ole Anderson was given the job, and his bumpy past with Flair was pretty well-known. Anderson had been the force responsible for the lackluster Black Scorpion angle in late 1990, but his experience was respected among TBS officials. Nevertheless, Flair's return was anticipated with bated breath, and all eyes were fixed on the SuperBrawl III pay-per-view on February 21, 1993, in one of Flair's old stomping grounds, Asheville, North Carolina. Prior to the NWA World title match between champion the Great Muta and Barry Windham, Flair was introduced to the crowd, and he received a powerful ovation. He assisted with commentary for the bout, and he presented the belt to Windham after his victory. The Flair-Windham rivalry, which began in 1982, had always been a hot ticket and gave Flair a chance to regain the championship he never lost in the ring.[40]

At house shows, Flair debuted his "A Flair for the Gold" interview segment and then launched his TV version on May 1, 1993.[41] The skit was setup like a talk show, complete with a colorful set and music. Flair's charisma was on full display as he introduced his French maid, Fifi, and guests Big Van Vader and Harley Race. Appearing lighthearted, even when the intense Vader grabbed him in response to a question, Flair charmingly carried the interview and followed up the next week with more of the same.[42] The segment built on his popularity and kept him at the forefront of weekend telecasts. Flair's in-ring return came on June 9, 1993, in Lake Charles, Louisiana, and he teamed with Arn Anderson and Paul Roma to beat Barry Windham and the Hollywood Blonds, Steve Austin and Brian Pillman, by disqualification. The following week, at Clash of the Champions XXIII, Flair and Anderson again beat the Blonds, but this time, Windham interfered and caused a DQ.[43]

From a business standpoint, the attempts by Turner to revitalize WCW were failing. The June Clash on TBS drew the event's lowest rating in history — a 2.6 — and an immediate turnaround was not expected despite exhaustive efforts.[44] The Flair-Windham feud, if history was any measure, was going to please the smart audience thanks to their in-ring chemistry. WCW, at least, had that to look forward to. But when Windham suffered a devastating knee injury and needed surgery, those plans were forcibly changed. Windham was able to perform at Beach Blast on July 18 in Biloxi, Mississippi, and lost the NWA World title to Flair. It was Flair's ninth NWA championship win and 11th overall world title. The crowning of a new NWA king didn't have the same luster it had in the past, and WCW had watered down the achievement by acknowledging two "world" champions. Big Van Vader was the reigning WCW World champion, and his position was generally considered superior to that of his NWA counterpart.

Fans were indifferent for the most part, and their apathy toward the product was reflected in both ratings and attendance. WCW wasn't helping itself in some respects. A massive TV taping in Orlando in July revealed the outcome of future matches, including, in some cases, who the next champions would be, which destroyed the element of surprise weeks in advance. Journalists spread the news far and wide, including a report that Rick Rude was wearing the Big Gold NWA championship belt. If that was the case, it meant Rude would beat Flair for the title at Fall Brawl on September 19 in Houston.[45] The revelation of a big pay-per-view finish was a mistake, but Flair, Rude, and even Fifi made the most of the angle. During an edition of "Flair for the Gold," Rude forcibly kissed Fifi and attacked Flair from behind with the belt. He then delivered his Rude Awakening neckbreaker on the floor.[46]

With the Fall Brawl title match established, a behind-the-scenes political quarrel played out, which changed the parameters of the Flair-Rude bout. The Orlando TV taping that disclosed that Rude would be the next NWA World champion had irked the leadership of the National Wrestling Alliance. NWA officials had not approved a title switch to Rude, and once they pushed back against that decision, WCW withdrew its membership from the Alliance completely. WCW rechristened the title as the "International World Heavyweight championship" and followed through with its original booking for Fall Brawl, meaning that Rude pinned Flair to capture the Big Gold belt.[47] As for the NWA, it stripped Flair of title status and went without a heavyweight champion until the summer of 1994, when a special tournament was held in conjunction with Eastern Championship Wrestling (ECW). Shane Douglas would go on to win the title but surprised the world by throwing the NWA belt down and proclaiming himself the ECW World champion instead.

On October 3, 1993, for a card headlined by Flair and Rude, a mere 800 people were in attendance. This wasn't a spot show in the middle of nowhere, but in Atlanta, Georgia, the home of WCW, at the famed Omni Coliseum.[48] If there ever was an alarm bell for a promotion in dire need of a spark, this was certainly it. Turner executives and the creative powers-that-be looked to Flair once again, and of all the talent in the promotion, they figured he could carry the organization into 1994. With Starrcade on the not-so-distant horizon, officials began to push Flair and Big Van Vader for the WCW World championship. At the time of Flair's return, pundits had speculated about the value of a Flair-Vader feud and whether it could generate widespread interest. Flair was the group's most charismatic star, while Vader was a mammoth, bigger-than-life heel. Harley Race, as Vader's manager, added to the dynamic, and WCW went all out promoting the matchup as the main event for its biggest show of the year.

The run-up to Starrcade '93 was an incredibly busy period for WCW. At Halloween Havoc, on October 24 in New Orleans, Flair was disqualified in a rematch against Rude. A few days later, the Nature Boy joined a contingent of wrestlers for a tour of England and Germany.[49] On November 10 in St. Petersburg, Flair met Vader at the Clash, and although he won by DQ, he was on the receiving end of tremendous punishment from the powerful WCW champion. Vader, at 400-plus pounds, was astonishingly agile in the ring, and his bruising shots against Flair were unforgiving. Flair was clearly the underdog, and fans had a hard time believing that his customary bag of tricks would work against the invincible brute. But that made their matchup even more interesting. During the BattleBowl event on November 20, Flair and his lottery tag team partner, Steve Austin, advanced to the battle royal and were among the final four in the ring, joined by Vader and Sting.

Vader, in a demonstration of his viciousness, delivered a big splash to Flair on the ramp, knocking him out of the contest. Officials rushed to his aid and carted him off on a stretcher for medical assistance. Commentators wondered if Flair would even make it to Starrcade, and for loyal fans of the Nature Boy, that only served to intensify the angle. Enthusiasts knew that if Vader's attack at BattleBowl wasn't enough to permanently shelve Flair, the WCW champion had another opportunity at Starrcade. That was because Flair had agreed to put his career on the line and retire if defeated by Vader on December 27, 1993. And with the show being held in Charlotte, Flair's hometown, the blond wrestling icon had everything to lose and yet, everything to gain — all before his family and friends. Ric Flair was headed back to Starrcade, and the eyes of the wrestling world were watching intently.

CHAPTER 18
THE HEART AND SOUL OF WCW

In Charlotte, all sports fans knew the name Tom Sorensen. He was the ever-professional and multitalented journalist for the *Charlotte Observer*, and his insightful columns had kept readers informed since 1981. Displaying his vast knowledge, he wrote about everything under the sun, and his enjoyable commentary was appreciated by readers throughout the Queen City. In 1987, as pro wrestling enjoyed another year of robust popularity in the region, Sorensen presented a "Wrestling Profile" column to satisfy enthusiasts hoping to see the names of their favorite grapplers in print. He went right to the top of the list and featured the "Nature Boy" Ric Flair, whom Sorensen called "Charlotte's best-known wrestler." Sorensen wrote that he had attended the University of Minnesota around the same time as the blond athlete, and he revealed that although he was a traditional villain in the wrestling world, Flair was a "nice guy" out of the ring.[1] Sorensen's straitlaced but lighthearted tone in writing about wrestling differed from most disdainful sports-writers, which earned him esteem in mat circles.

More than six years later, Sorensen devoted his entire column of December 27, 1993, to Ric Flair and his challenge of Vader for the WCW World Heavyweight title. The special article was timed perfectly to promote Starrcade at Charlotte's Independence Arena that evening, and it emphasized the fact that Flair's career was in jeopardy if he was defeated. "If Vader wins, Charlotte loses, too," Sorensen wrote. "Flair is more than the world's greatest wrestler and only 11-time champion. He is an ambassador for our city. Flair knows everybody and everybody knows him."[2] Flair said that putting his career on the line was the only way he could secure the title bout, and he talked up the great skill of Vader. "He's an unbelievable athlete," Flair said. "He's the most talented athlete I've ever seen for a guy his size."[3] But Flair was confident in his own abilities and rightfully so. Even as he approached his 45th birthday, which was but two months away, he was in prime ring condition. "I'm in better shape than I was 10 years ago," he told Sorensen.[4]

Starrcade was billed as the 10th anniversary of the annual spectacle, and the show began with a slideshow of photos from Flair's childhood. Commentator Tony Schiavone confirmed that the program was going to be a "celebration" of Flair's career, as he headed into what could potentially be his final match. After a segment at Flair's home, where he received words of encouragement and hugs from his family, Gene Okerlund reiterated the same thing. Flair appeared emotional, and viewers could see that this wasn't the typical wrestling hype. Between the segments at Flair's home, in the limo ride to the arena, and then backstage, the sense of authenticity added a great deal of emotional weight to the main event matchup. Flair was the underdog in the fight of his life, and after reflecting on the situation in his conversation with Okerlund, Flair pronounced, "I'm ready." Fans were, too, and everyone in the crowd was excitedly waiting to "Wooooo!" in unison with their hero.

When Flair emerged wearing a stunning purple robe, the audience erupted.[5] He couldn't help but smile in reaction, but his overall demeanor was much more serious than normal. He was a man on a mission, and it was evident once the contest started that he had his hands full. Vader was brutally aggressive and used his strength to establish dominance during the early going. Punches, clotheslines, and powerful slams had Flair reeling, and multiple times, he escaped the ring to get his bearings. But Vader was relentless, and his hard blows seemed to be landing, shoot-style, square onto Flair's face and head, only adding to the realism.

Before long, Flair was bleeding from the mouth, and his groans of agony had loyal supporters worried. Even when Flair turned the tables to land a few chops, Vader appeared invincible and shrugged the wallops off. However, it was just a matter of time before Flair began fighting like a man possessed, and his own stiff shots took effect. He worked on Vader's knee, and spectators were verbalizing their emotions with every twist and turn of the action.

At a crucial juncture, Flair slyly moved out of the way of Vader's moonsault, and then Harley Race, who had interfered several times already on Vader's behalf, mistakenly landed his flying headbutt onto the prone champion. The crowd was on its feet as Flair grabbed one of Vader's legs and jumped on him for a quick pinfall. Physically and psychologically, the match was a winner, and fans in Charlotte were thoroughly elated by the result. "The pop Flair received after beating Vader was the most emotional one I've heard since Kerry Von Erich beat Flair in 1984," wrote Carlie Gill in the *Pro Wrestling Torch*. "The pop and Flair's tearful reaction to it was an incredible scene."[6] Dave Meltzer, in the *Wrestling Observer Newsletter*, acknowledged the buildup and production of Starrcade as being the greatest in WCW history. "Ric Flair's finest hour as a professional wrestler came many years after numerous people in management, and even many fans, had come to the conclusion his days as a key performer were over," he noted.[7]

Given his turbulent history in WCW, and the perception that he was well past his prime, Flair had once again proven wrong those who tried to diminish his stature in the business. His tremendous effort, both prior to the event in rousing interviews and then in the actual physical performance, was yet another reminder of his importance to the promotion. Flair appreciated the outpouring of affection from the audience, and his emotion was visible on his face following the bout. With his parents, wife, and four children all in attendance, Flair appeared humbled by the enormity of the moment, and his natural reaction endeared him more to those watching.[8] It was one of those glimpses of true life rarely seen in pro wrestling, and WCW handled it perfectly. Where WCW went wrong was in its haste to promote its next pay-per-view event, SuperBrawl IV in February 1994, by releasing an advertisement indicating that Flair was the defending world champion and that Vader was the challenger. This image was printed in the *New York Daily News* four days before Starrcade was held.[9] Revealing the result of Flair versus Vader was a needless blunder, but it didn't overshadow the importance of the occasion on any level. During the Starrcade telecast, it was said that Flair had won his 11th world championship, which was technically correct if you counted his nine NWA titles and his initial reign as WCW champion in 1991. But with his two WWF title victories, he was a 13-time champion at that point.

Away from the ring, Flair was busier than ever. The previous April, after a year of hard work, Ric Flair's Gold's Gym opened in the upscale SouthPark area of Charlotte.[10] The 15,000-square-foot facility featured a wide range of modern equipment, as well as aerobics and fitness classes for all ages.[11] Adjacent to the gym was the All Sports Cafe, a trendy bar and restaurant owned by George Shinn, the owner of the Charlotte Hornets basketball team. Flair was a major supporter of the Hornets and a season ticket holder.[12] He was also a big college football fan, and, along with Beth, he watched the Florida Gators beat West Virginia from the sidelines at the 1994 Sugar Bowl in New Orleans.[13]

Representative of his popularity in sports circles, Flair was approached by members of the Gators for autographs, and he was happy to oblige.[14] A similar thing happened at the Dapper Dan Charity Banquet on February 11, 1994, in Pittsburgh. Flair was recognized as "one of the more sought-after" guests in a room full of NFL, NHL, and MLB celebrities.[15] Flair was grateful for the outpouring of respect. He told a reporter, "I'm very honored to be held in the same esteem as so many quality athletes, athletes like Mario Lemieux and Jay Bell, and I feel very privileged to be associated with Dapper Dan, one of the most prestigious charities in the country."[16] The following week, Flair appeared on Larry King's radio show and spoke candidly about a wide array of topics, everything from sagging attendance to his opinion of Bret Hart.[17] The latter was notable because Hart had essentially referred to Flair as being "overrated" during a 1993 press conference.[18] On King's show, Flair took the high road and complimented Hart as a great wrestler and champion.[19]

The fourth installment of SuperBrawl occurred on February 20, 1994, from Albany, Georgia. Flair and Vader got their rematch, as anticipated, and the Nature Boy overcame a two-on-one double team by Vader and Harley Race inside a steel cage to retain his title. The Boss (formerly known as Big Bubba and the Big Bossman) was the special referee for the cage bout, and he abruptly stopped the action after Flair locked in his figure-four leglock. It was a rather flat end to the contest, and aside from a series of upcoming matches between Flair and Vader on house shows, their feud was quickly being overshadowed by two noteworthy rivalries for the champion. Ricky Steamboat reentered the main event picture and earned a shot at the world title by defeating Steve Austin by DQ on March 12 in Atlanta.[20] Moments after his victory, Steamboat was so caught up in fighting off both Austin and his manager, Col. Robert Parker, that he accidentally chopped Flair. Despite Steamboat's apologies, Flair was peeved about the incident, and thus began a slow and subtle heel turn, building up to Spring Stampede on April 17 in Chicago.

Meanwhile, a strange thing was happening with regard to the second potential Flair feud. It wasn't only strange for WCW but for all of professional wrestling. Beginning in February, an unsigned, inactive wrestler was mentioned on numerous WCW telecasts, and his prospective arrival in the promotion was the source of much speculation.[21] That man was Hulk Hogan. Hogan's employment in the WWF ended in August 1993, and he had been spending time on his Hollywood acting career. He made it known that he'd be open to a wrestling return and to resuming his conflict with Flair, this time in WCW.[22] Flair didn't waste any time firing back at Hogan, and in some interviews, he lashed out at both the Hulkster and Steamboat.

Politically, Flair's stock in WCW was at an all-time high. He was named head booker, and with Eric Bischoff, the enterprising 38-year-old vice president of WCW, the promotion was making headway in terms of growth.²³ The pitfalls that had hindered Flair during his first tenure as booker in 1989–90 were gone, and the organization was more willing to take the risks necessary to achieve financial success. Landing Hulk Hogan was seen as a momentous step in that direction, and Flair would play a pivotal role in negotiations with the popular former WWF champion.²⁴ Flair had Hogan's respect, and once Hogan understood Flair's steadfast willingness to concede the spotlight to feature him as WCW's top star, the foundation for a deal was laid. Of course, there was a lot more to it, but the bottom line from a business standpoint was money. Bischoff wanted to exploit the Flair-Hogan feud far beyond what the WWF had done and to highlight the matchup center stage on pay-per-view.

As discussions continued, Flair and Ricky Steamboat turned A-plus promos into another classic bout at Spring Stampede. The affair wasn't on the level of their legendary 1989 battles, but it was a fiercely competitive bout. Their personal drive was always at the heart of their encounters and they shared a natural enthusiasm to perform at the highest level. In this 32-minute clash, a double-pin situation ended the bout, and Flair was declared the winner.²⁵ The controversy stemming from the match persisted, and Flair relinquished his belt to WCW commissioner Nick Bockwinkel, pending a rematch. On April 21 in Atlanta, Flair pinned Steamboat and regained the championship, his third.²⁶ The following month, he pinned his former Horsemen stablemate Barry Windham in the main event of Slamboree on May 22 in Philadelphia. Windham was a mystery opponent managed by Col. Robert Parker, and he left the promotion immediately after the match.²⁷

Hogan officially joined WCW before the summer, and a widespread promotional campaign hyped his anticipated bout with Flair at the inaugural Bash at the Beach show on July 17, 1994, in Orlando. That included a rare press conference with Ted Turner, signing the two to a contract for the Bash. To elevate Flair's status and the importance of his championship, the Nature Boy was matched with WCW International World titleholder Sting at Clash of the Champions XXVII on June 23 in Charleston, South Carolina. Sherri Martel, a former AWA and WWF Women's champion and more recently the manager of Randy Savage, was hunting for a new client and appeared wearing face paint like Sting, seemingly displaying her loyalty to the International champion. But during the Clash match, her involvement cost Sting the bout, and afterwards she celebrated with Flair. As a result of the contest, Flair became the unified WCW title-holder, and as a full-fledged heel with "Sensuous" Sherri in his corner, he was prepared to meet Hogan in what was shaping up to be WCW's biggest moment to date.

The promotion pulled out all the stops. TV and radio spots flooded the Orlando market and sold the Hogan-Flair spectacle as a once-in-a-lifetime happening. Linda Shrieves, in the *Orlando Sentinel*, called it "pro wrestling's biggest match in years" and referenced Flair as the "big-mouthed bad boy."[28] All things considered, it was Hogan's popularity that propelled the excitement among media and fans, and the exposure WCW received was the greatest in company history. With that, a Hogan victory was all but guaranteed, and at the Bash, Flair ensured that Hogan's arrival lived up to the hype. Before 14,000 people at the Orlando Arena, and a substantial viewing audience on pay-per-view, he played to the Hulkster's strengths and gave casual enthusiasts a reason to yell and scream.[29] The pinfall that ended the bout, and stripped Flair of his championship, created the extraordinary moment WCW was hoping for, and with authority, the Hogan era in WCW had begun.[30]

The day following Hogan's triumph, the *Orlando Sentinel* featured a front-page story with the news and heralded the overall success of the event. At the conclusion of the article, it was noted that Hogan souvenirs sold quickly at arena merchandise booths, and a salesman was asked about it. His response was "Ric Flair doesn't sell."[31] From an outside point of view, it was obvious that the mass marketing push behind Hogan was enormous, and his ability to sell red and yellow T-shirts and bandanas was incredible. However, WCW executives and business insiders understood that Flair's intrinsic value to the promotion was not based on his merchandise sales. Ever since Turner purchased the company in 1988, and notwithstanding his time working for Vince McMahon, Flair had been the heart and soul of the organization. Whenever WCW needed a ratings boost or a reliable box office draw, officials looked to him, and time and again his ability to sell the storylines, good or bad, gave the promotion a fighting chance to compete nationally against the WWF.

The signing of Hogan, though, began a new phase in WCW's war against the WWF, and despite the loud anti-Hogan calls from loyalists, the promotion was firmly behind its new champion. The second of what would be three major battles between Flair and Hogan occurred on August 24, 1994, in Cedar Rapids, Iowa, at Clash of the Champions.[32] Early in the live TBS broadcast, as part of the developing angle, Hogan was attacked by a hooded individual, and his knee was smashed with a pipe. He was taken by ambulance to a nearby hospital, only to courageously return to the venue later in the program to face Flair. To keep the feud hot enough to stage a third high-profile match, Flair won from Hogan by countout after Sherri Martel targeted the latter's injured knee. Fan interest in the Flair versus Hogan bout at the Clash was immense. With over 4.1 million homes tuning in, their contest became the most watched wrestling match in cable television history.[33]

While the Clash numbers were impressive, WCW's syndication ratings remained mediocre, and there was internal pressure to heighten the importance of the Flair-Hogan rubber match at Halloween Havoc. The idea was to put the careers of both men on the line, with the loser forced to leave the business. It was a consequential stipulation, and with the tremendous resources being put behind Hogan as the organization's new franchise wrestler, Hulk wasn't going anywhere anytime soon. That meant Flair was going on sabbatical, regardless if he or the traditional fans of WCW liked it or not. In fact, the *Wrestling Observer Newsletter* reported that the retirement plan was "against his wishes."[34] "I don't want to retire," Flair told a reporter in a kayfabe interview a week before the Havoc match. "But if I have to lose it, [it] might as well be to someone as good as Hogan."[35]

Prior to the show, which was held on October 23 at the Joe Louis Arena in Detroit, Flair entered into talks for a two-year contract extension. The negotiations were time sensitive, as the dialogue coincided with the fast approaching Havoc event. Considering the circumstances, particularly the unique demand for Flair to step away from active wrestling, WCW was in no position to counteroffer or delay, and the deal was quickly done.[36] Once the ink was dry, Flair entered a steel cage to face Hogan in what was to be the final bout of his career.[37] From beginning to end, their contest was a chaotic brawl, and even with renowned tough guy Mr. T as guest referee, things were almost unmanageable. Flair once again received outside help from Sensuous Sherri, and another masked man attempted to level Hogan, but it was not enough. Hogan absorbed the punishment, "Hulked up," and laid out Flair with his leg drop for the three count.[38]

After the match, all focus centered on Hogan, although commentator Bobby Heenan sounded emotional about Flair's defeat. But there was no extended acknowledgment of Flair's importance to wrestling and what this moment actually meant in the grand scheme of things. For that reason, many longtime fans were confused and even angry at the perceived disrespect shown Flair.[39] A reader of the *Charlotte Observer* wrote, "As a life-long wrestling fan, I am very upset with the forced retirement of Ric Flair. WCW has decided to showcase Hulk Hogan and the silly transplants from the World Wrestling Federation. Wrestling as we've known it for years is gone."[40] In the *Pro Wrestling Torch*, Brian Friban wrote, "If that was Flair's last match, I feel awful for him and I don't understand how he could go out like that after such a distinguished career."[41] According to a report in that same publication, Flair wasn't downcast about the turn of events, stating that, "He was in good spirits, almost jovial" at a post-match dinner in Detroit.[42]

As the *Charlotte Observer* reader noted, WCW was placing heavy emphasis on former WWF performers in a glaring strategic shift. In addition to Hogan, Eric Bischoff brought aboard Ed Leslie, Jimmy Hart, the Honky Tonk Man, Jim Duggan, John Tenta, and ultimately Randy "Macho Man" Savage. These additions created an entirely new environment for wrestling under the WCW banner, earning the promotion more criticism for trying to mirror the WWF. The image of WCW was being revamped right before the eyes of supporters, and while some embraced the changes, others looked to independent promotions, such as Philadelphia-based ECW, to satisfy their wrestling needs. For Flair, he remained on the WCW payroll as booker, and he attended programs in his backstage role. But it was evident that there were philosophical differences among WCW's powerbrokers, and essentially there was one set of rules for Hogan and another for everyone else. Thus, Hogan and his allies in the company were untouchable.

Flair as an on-camera superstar was much more valuable to WCW than in a corporate position away from the limelight. Three months after his pronounced retirement, the Nature Boy returned for an appearance during Clash of the Champions on January 25, 1995, in Las Vegas. Fans were happy to see him, but without a full-time in-ring role, it was disappointing. By mid-February, Flair was angling for a return and discussed the possibility with WCW commissioner Nick Bockwinkel. On February 19, 1995, in Baltimore at SuperBrawl, Flair again appeared, but this time, he interfered in the main event match up between Hogan and Vader, causing the latter's disqualification. Several weeks later, during an episode of *WCW Saturday Night*, Flair and Vader attacked Dave Sullivan, a lower card grappler, and sent him to the hospital.[43] Bockwinkel indefinitely suspended Flair, but that didn't deter the former world champion from making an impact.

On March 19 in Tupelo, Mississippi, at WCW's Uncensored program, Flair shockingly jumped the railing dressed as a woman, and attacked Randy Savage. He also accompanied Vader against Hogan in the main event, but he was on the receiving end of a thorough beating, as he was fastened to the Hulkster and dragged to each of the four corners — as per the rules of a strap match. For whatever reason, Flair, as a substitute for Vader, caused Vader to lose the bout. As for Flair making a full comeback, the WCW International board of directors initially deadlocked in a vote on restoring him to active status.[44] The vote was 2–2 with one member abstaining. At a second meeting, Christine LeBlanc of France, who had previously withheld her vote, elected to support Flair's return, and with three backers, he was reinstated.[45] Before the end of April, Flair participated in the International Sports and Culture Festival for Peace in Pyongyang, North Korea, and wrestled the legendary Antonio Inoki for the first time.[46] Inoki pinned him in front of 190,000 spectators — the largest live audience in wrestling history.[47]

The Flair versus Randy Savage feud intensified in May 1995. During the Slamboree card in St. Petersburg, Florida, on May 21, Flair and Vader were defeated by Hogan and Savage in a tag team affair, but the heels gained the advantage after the bell. Savage's 70-year-old father, wrestling luminary Angelo Poffo, entered the ring in an attempt to stop the onslaught but was assailed by Flair and placed in the figure-four. That made it personal for Savage, and the heat between the two men was reminiscent of their WWF conflict when Miss Elizabeth became a pawn in their quarrel. On June 18 at the Great American Bash, Flair scored a main event pinfall victory over Savage in another acclaimed match. On the limited WCW house show circuit, which had been scaled down to almost nothing because of weak ticket sales, Flair and Savage fought approximately 10 times over a three-month period in the summer of 1995. Savage won nearly all of those contests.[48]

Early in July, Flair's term as WCW booker concluded, and he was replaced by Kevin Sullivan.[49] A well-experienced creative force behind the scenes, Sullivan helped facilitate an unexpected feud between Flair and his best friend and Horsemen stablemate Arn Anderson.[50] Their rivalry had great potential, and no one really knew what to expect. Once Flair and Anderson began delivering emotionally charged interviews, utilizing their extensive history as a sales point, it was golden. Both men could start a promo with a calm demeanor and walk viewers through a gamut of thoughts and feelings before ending on a loud, powerful note — reeling fans in the entire time. Anderson said that Flair always expected him to lend a hand, rather than being able to fight his own battles, and he was done. Flair took offense to that, and the bad blood grew from week to week from there.[51] They finally locked horns at Fall Brawl on

September 17 in Asheville, North Carolina, and Anderson pinned Flair with some outside help from Brian Pillman.

A few weeks earlier, WCW inaugurated a weekly telecast on Monday nights to go head to head with the WWF's *Monday Night Raw*. Flair wrestled Sting on the very first episode of *Monday Nitro* on September 4, 1995, from the Mall of America in suburban Minneapolis, and he was disqualified. Right from the start, *Nitro* was fashioned as a high energy and unpredictable program, and the grudge between Flair and Anderson was given plenty of air time. They traded wins on October 2 and October 9, and the following week, Flair teamed with Sting to beat Anderson and Pillman by countout.[52] Flair had previously tried to convince Sting to join him in his war, and to that point, Sting had refused. Now convinced that he could trust Flair, Sting agreed to partner with him once more against Anderson and Pillman, at Halloween Havoc on October 29. Unfortunately for him, Slick Ric was about to reemerge. Flair didn't waste much time before turning on Sting, and he announced that the Four Horsemen were back.[53]

Critics were always fast to judge the entertainment value of active feuds and to rate matches, as well as critique the wrestlers' performances. Flair, at nearly 47 years old, was a prime target for this kind of commentary. But pundits couldn't question his dedication to the business. Beginning with his agreement to not only put over Hulk Hogan for the umpteenth time, but to be forcibly retired from competition, Flair was a team player all the way. He did everything asked of him, including losing match after match to Hogan, Sting, and Randy Savage. In September 1995, he needed four weeks off for cataract surgery and recovery. The procedure went well, but instead of Flair getting all of the rest he required, he returned just short of two weeks, and according to the *Wrestling Observer Newsletter*, he was without medical clearance.[54] WCW officials needed him to strengthen ratings, and Flair complied with another maximal effort despite the risk of possible permanent eye damage.

A short time later, Flair suffered a painful shoulder injury, which left him without full function of one arm. It was again thought that he'd step away to recover, perhaps until sometime in late December, but he refused to let up. He participated in the World War III program in Norfolk, putting Sting over by submission on November 26, 1995. Citing Flair's injury, Dave Meltzer wrote, "If there was ever a question of [Flair] being able to have a good match with one arm tied behind his back, it was answered."[55] The truth of the matter was that regardless of the number of pinfalls he took, the slights to his reputation and ego, or the embarrassing scenarios, Flair was bulletproof to his diehard fans. His popularity remained incredibly strong, and while he received criticism, he survived each and every bump in the road with the same loyalty and love for wrestling that he'd displayed since the beginning of his career. His enemies hated it, but Flair was Teflon.

Randy Savage was the winner of the massive three-ring, 60-man battle royal at World War III, and he captured the vacant WCW World Heavyweight title. Headed into Starrcade on December 27 in Nashville, he was slated to wrestle the victor of a special triangle bout between Flair, Lex Luger, and Sting. Flair ultimately won that match when his opponents were counted out. He met Savage shortly thereafter, and with the help of his Horsemen brethren, he pinned the champion and won the WCW championship — his 12th NWA/WCW title and 14th overall.[56] The crowd reaction reaffirmed that Flair was the king of Starrcade, and this show ended the same way it had in 1983 and 1993, with the Nature Boy celebrating as the new world champion. His fans were thrilled, and Flair put all the talk about his best days being behind him to bed. He was, once again, on top of the world.

On the whole, World Championship Wrestling was still a work in progress. The development and success of *Monday Nitro* was remarkable, and the sudden push of Flair back into the top spot was a surprise. In its competition with the WWF, WCW was still missing a few key ingredients, but Eric Bischoff had shown his determination to turn the promotion into a thriving company. With new opportunities in 1996, WCW would turn things up a notch, and certain moves would light the entire industry on fire. Little did anyone know at the time, but professional wrestling was about to enter a new golden age with mainstream acceptance and record profits. The wrestling war between WCW and the WWF would provide endless entertainment and plenty of big business. Although Flair was the reigning champion, his future was uncertain. Who could have predicted that in less than two years Flair would be ostracized from the promotion, embroiled in a million-dollar lawsuit, and facing an unceremonious end to his legendary career? At the end of 1995, the answer was simple: nobody.

CHAPTER 19

THE RATINGS WAR

In the annals of pro wrestling, there are few cities in North America with a more profound history than Philadelphia. The City of Brotherly Love has relished the grappling sport for well over a century, and its competitive nature has steadily drawn audiences to local venues. For instance, on January 4, 1890, the Standard Theatre was "packed to the roof" to see strongman William Muldoon beat the original "Strangler," Evan Lewis. Their "exciting" battle, held under Greco-Roman rules, was spirited from beginning to end, but it resulted in some controversy, as Lewis claimed he wasn't pinned. Lewis was also suffering from illness at the time of the match.[1] The news had fans around the country talking, and the disputed finish was a sticking point for supporters of the Strangler. Flash forward 104 years to a nondescript building two and a half miles southeast of the Standard Theatre, and once again, controversy was stirred up.[2] This time, the wrestling hubbub in Philadelphia was at the ECW Arena. A revolution was beginning, and everyone in the sport was paying attention.

Paul Heyman was the creative administrator of Eastern Championship Wrestling, an independent organization fast approaching its second anniversary. Booking a mix of young talent and recognizable veterans, he had garnered the loyalty of hardcore enthusiasts throughout the northeast, rattling the wrestling establishment with innovation and violence. Tape trading, syndication, and word of mouth sparked national interest in ECW, and Heyman's organization was fast becoming the most popular promotion in the United States.[3] Among the key players in ECW was 29-year-old Shane Douglas, nicknamed the Franchise. Douglas was a solid performer in the ring and distinguished himself in intense promo segments. His articulate interviews were raw and verbalized the essence of ECW's rebellious climate. Not before long, he began to focus his verbal attacks on the booker who had helped oversee his run in World Championship Wrestling five years earlier. That man was Ric Flair.

Douglas was unhappy with the broken promises, politicking, and the lack of upward progress in WCW, and he turned his experiences into shoot-style commentary on ECW TV.[4] The candid segments were groundbreaking in the way they addressed wrestlers and events outside the promotion, which differed greatly from the scripted promos in WCW and the WWF. Douglas targeted his aggression on the Nature Boy, referring to him as "Dick Flair," and issued a challenge to meet in the ring. Notably, Douglas admitted that Flair had been one of his idols growing up as a wrestling fan, saying, "I believe him to be the all-time measuring stick in the business and he was the reason I entered the business."[5] Heyman also had history with Flair stemming from his WCW run as Paul E. Dangerously in 1989, and overall, invoking Flair's name brought a lot of attention to ECW. Later, a small window of opportunity opened for a Douglas-Flair bout in Philadelphia, but despite negotiations, it failed to materialize.[6]

In 1994 and throughout 1995, ECW featured programming on the cutting edge, and the critical response was overwhelmingly positive. WCW, in contrast, was struggling to find a happy medium between pandering to mainstream fans and appeasing the smart crowd.[7] *Monday Nitro* was a beacon of hope, though, as it provided a major showcase for an assortment of unique personalities, and the level of athleticism was raised with the push of talented stars like Chris Benoit, Dean Malenko, and Eddie Guerrero. The possibility of world title changes on the telecast, instead of only during pay-per-views, was an exceptional motivator for fans to tune in. Such an occasion occurred on January 22, 1996, from Las Vegas, when Randy Savage dethroned Flair for the WCW championship. A week later, in Canton, Ohio, Flair beat Hulk Hogan in what was his first ever singles pinfall victory over his longtime rival. He gained the win by using a foreign object — the shoe of Elizabeth, who had accompanied Hogan to the ring.

At that time, Savage and Hogan were aligned with Elizabeth, reminiscent of their days as the Mega Powers in the WWF, as well as with Woman, the former manager of Flair and Doom.[8] But this loose-knit group was on thin ice, and Woman, during the February 5 edition of *Nitro*, turned on Savage in aid of Chris Benoit and the Horsemen. Six nights later at SuperBrawl in St. Petersburg, Elizabeth followed suit by double-crossing Savage, leading to Flair regaining the world title. Acknowledged as "the hottest heel in the United States," Flair was definitely on a roll, and his work was helping WCW reestablish its fledgling house show business. Historically, Baltimore (and Philadelphia for that matter) had been one of Flair's best drawing towns, and his popularity in the northeast dated back to the earliest days of Jim Crockett's expansion. On February 17, 1996, with Flair and Savage in the main event, WCW drew 11,000 spectators to the Baltimore Arena.

Flair's matches were chaotic during this period. He was receiving constant outside assistance from Woman and Elizabeth, as well as Arn Anderson and Kevin Sullivan, and his finishes routinely included some type of referee distraction and illegal interference. The muddled scenarios were riotous, and were a far stretch from the technically driven championship matches of yore. At Uncensored on March 24, Flair joined seven others in a lopsided handicap bout against Hogan and Savage in a three-tiered cage, but the fan favorites got the victory after Savage pinned Flair.[9] The following month, on April 20, Flair uncharacteristically missed a booking in Little Rock due to a missed plane connection from Columbus, Ohio, where his eight-year-old son Reid was participating in a wrestling tournament.[10] In Albany, Georgia, two days later,

Flair was dethroned by the Giant in less than six minutes — pinned after a chokeslam.[11] The match was broadcast on *Nitro* on April 29.

WCW had seemingly turned a corner. With house shows rebounding and *Nitro*'s encouraging growth, Eric Bischoff was more motivated than ever to invest in the future of the company. He hired Scott Hall and Kevin Nash, two recent stars for the WWF, in late May 1996. The Outsiders, as Hall and Nash were branded, threatened to take over, and they issued a challenge to three of WCW's best, indicating that they had an unnamed third member. Meanwhile, Flair entered a feud with Steve McMichael, a former NFL defensive tackle, and Kevin Greene, a current football player for the Carolina Panthers, setting up a tag team bout at the Great American Bash on June 16.[12] Inexperienced as wrestlers, McMichael and Greene received a crash course in fundamentals from Terry Taylor, and they demonstrated their innate athleticism at the Bash against Flair and Arn Anderson. In a shocker, McMichael betrayed Greene, costing them the match, and joined the Four Horsemen.[13]

There were more surprises on the horizon. On July 7 in Daytona Beach at Bash at the Beach, Hulk Hogan turned on the fans and joined the Outsiders, effectively forming the New World Order (NWO) in the process.[14] The bombshell stunned Hulkamaniacs around the globe and rattled the entire industry to its core. Although Hogan's name had been mentioned by experts as a possible third man with Hall and Nash, actually seeing him turn heel was a sight to behold. Fans were both excited and outraged, and that meant TV ratings. *Nitro* took a commanding lead in the "Monday Night Wars" against *Raw*, beginning an unparalleled streak of dominance.[15] Flair's role at the Daytona Bash was a bout against Konnan for the United States title, and with the aid of Woman, he pinned the champion and won the belt. In subsequent days and weeks, Flair continued to feud with Randy Savage on the road, and their box office draw was as reliable and strong as ever. At Hog Wild in Sturgis, South Dakota, on August 10, Flair retained his championship against the always impressive Eddie Guerrero.

As the NWO angle took over as the central storyline for WCW, Flair turned back into a "tweener" in an effort to help the promotion fight off this new aggression. He met Hollywood Hogan on August 15 in Denver at the Clash of the Champions, and he won by DQ after Hall and Nash interfered. During the August 26 edition of *Nitro*, Hogan, Hall, and Nash stopped a bout between the Horsemen and Sting and Lex Luger, attacking the participants.[16] Flair and Arn Anderson ran out but were overwhelmed by their rivals. Hogan spray-painted a black streak on the back of Flair's iconic blond hair, and fans pelted the NWO with cups and crumpled paper as they departed the ring area. The unabashed lawlessness fostered by the New World Order in their gang-style attacks was ground-breaking for its time and place, and WCW was striking all the right chords. Audiences were wholly enthusiastic, and the angle seemed to be getting better and better.

Fall Brawl '96 in Winston-Salem, which was firmly Horsemen country, drew an incredible crowd of 11,000 on September 15, 1996. Flair and Anderson aligned themselves with Sting and Luger in a special War Games battle against the NWO, and they were defeated. Sting, whose loyalty to the WCW had been called into question, walked out on his teammates after briefly engaging their opponents, leaving them a man down. Hogan, Hall, Nash, and an NWO version of Sting took advantage of the four-on-three situation, and officials halted the action after Luger was locked in the Sting's Scorpion Deathlock. Flair traveled overseas a few days later for a tour with New Japan, and in his fourth bout on the trip, he suffered a shoulder injury.[17] Flair had been plagued by shoulder issues in late 1995, but he pushed through the pain. This time was more serious, as his rotator cuff was torn, and he required surgery.[18] He ventured to Birmingham, Alabama, and was treated by renowned orthopedic surgeon Dr. James Andrews.[19]

Initial reports had Flair on the shelf for the rest of the year, but the truth was he would be inactive as a wrestler for much longer than that. But he was needed in other roles because of the tangible effect he had on ratings. To many fans, a memorable Flair interview was far better than most bouts on *Nitro*, and his segments were a must-see.[20] He threw his support behind WCW newcomer Jeff Jarrett in October 1996, and he was in his corner at Halloween Havoc against the Giant. Flair assisted with his trademark low blow, and Jarrett was disqualified. Some weeks later, Flair shared a historic moment in the ring with old friend Roddy Piper, in the city they helped put on the wrestling map — Charlotte — and the audience thoroughly enjoyed their reunion.[21] Piper wrestled Hollywood Hogan at Starrcade on December 29 in Nashville, beating him with a sleeper. The Four Horsemen endured a rough patch during this time, and infighting was at the center of their appearances in early 1997.

Flair's anticipated return occurred on May 18 at Slamboree, also held in Charlotte, and the Nature Boy teamed with Piper and Kevin Greene to beat NWO members Kevin Nash, Scott Hall, and Syxx. In promos, Flair and his rivals traded edgy barbs, magnifying the heat between the two groups. The hugely successful NWO versus WCW rivalry was still the prevailing angle in the promotion, and Flair seamlessly rejoined the warfare right in the thick of the main event scene. Just over 18,000 people packed the Fleet Center in Boston for *Nitro* on June 9, 1997, and were treated to one of the wildest scenes in wrestling history.[22] Flair and Piper tagged against the Outsiders, but their contest was really over before it began, as the fan favorites won by DQ when Syxx interfered. At that point, all hell broke loose, with as many as two dozen wrestlers taking part in a chaotic brawl across the arena. In the ring, Flair was beaten down by the NWO, prior to Sting's surprise arrival, rappelling down from the rafters.

The seemingly uncontrolled environment fostered by the NWO angle only added to the excitement, and crowds were regularly whipped into a frenzy by the bedlam. The relationship between Flair and Piper was destined to fail, and after Flair left the ring area during his tag team bout with Piper against the Outsiders at the Great American Bash, their feud was rekindled in a big way.[23] On July 13 at Bash at the Beach, Piper used his sleeperhold to gain a major triumph over his longtime foe.

Flair was having a busy summer. Aside from his conflict with Piper, Flair kicked Jeff Jarrett out of the Four Horsemen, and he was reunited with his former "advisor" from his WWF run, Curt Hennig. Hennig, and Flair by proxy, spent some time at odds with "Diamond" Dallas Page, and on August 21, they went over Syxx and Konnan at the Clash in Nashville. Hennig refused to formally commit to a role in the Horsemen, but that changed when Arn Anderson, who had been forcibly retired because of a spinal injury, asked him to take his place.[24] During an emotional moment on the August 25 edition of *Nitro*, Hennig accepted.

In what was supposed to be a hilarious skit making fun of the Horsemen, NWO members Kevin Nash, Syxx, Konnan, and Buff Bagwell parodied the August 25 segment the following week on *Nitro*. The over-the-top bit saw the NWO ridicule the Horsemen for their looks and alleged behavior. The scene may have earned some cheap laughs in the moment, but it disrespected Anderson and his forced retirement, causing real-world heat.[25] Without a Horsemen run-in to gain a bit of revenge, it was simply a cruel attack, and it didn't do much to build up the Horsemen as a genuine counter to the NWO. In a return to Winston-Salem for Fall Brawl, the Horsemen attempted to even the score in a War Games matchup, but Hennig turned on the group, and the NWO prevailed. At the end of the contest, Flair was the recipient of a cage door smash to the head, akin to the legendary shot Kerry Von Erich took on Christmas night in 1982.[26]

Commentators sold the seriousness of the incident, and Flair was knocked out of action. He was actually dealing with an ankle injury, so his brief disappearance gave him time to recover.[27] Interestingly, Bret Hart was the latest big name to join WCW, and he was penciled in as Flair's next major opponent. Hart and Flair had had a series of competitive battles in the WWF, and their wrestling history was well-known. But smart fans were also aware of Hart's out-of-the-ring comments about Flair, including the statement that the decorated NWA and WCW champion was "overrated." Hart addressed this topic during a Prodigy chat session in December 1997, affirming that Flair was "one of the best performers this game has ever had." He clarified his opinion about Flair as a wrestler, saying that he wasn't the best grappler he'd ever faced. But he acknowledged the respect Flair had given him and regretted if his previous words had hurt their relationship.[28]

Kevin Eck penned a noteworthy mainstream article about Flair in the *Baltimore Sun* newspaper on December 29, 1997, the same day as *Nitro* at the Baltimore Arena.[29] The two-page piece discussed his history and present role in WCW, and Flair admitted he was more at ease as a heel. "I am, however, comfortable with the level of respect that I get," he said. During the Nitro telecast, Flair actually pulled a copy of the article from his jacket pocket and read a quote by Dave Meltzer of the *Wrestling Observer Newsletter*. Meltzer's statement read, in part, "There's never been a guy, night after night, to put on the performances he has. When you factor that in, he is the greatest in the history of the sport, without question."[30] Despite their differences outside the ropes, Flair and Bret Hart had good chemistry in the squared circle, and their match at Souled Out on January 24, 1998, outshined the main event battle between Lex Luger and Randy Savage.[31] In fact, it was believed they were setting the groundwork for a lengthy feud with a lot of solid potential at the box office.

But the rug was pulled out from underneath them after four matches between January 24 and February 20, 1998. Instead, Flair was booked in a continuation of his feud with Curt Hennig from March into April. It was mentioned during the April 6 edition of *Nitro* that Flair would make an appearance on *WCW Thunder* on Thursday night to make a big announcement. Over the subsequent two days, Flair wrestled at house shows in Fort Myers and Fort Pierce, Florida, and then departed the Sunshine State to support his son Reid at the AAU National grappling tournament in suburban Detroit.[32] WCW officials expected him to be in Tallahassee on April 9 for *Thunder*, and his no-show turned a budding rift between Flair and Eric Bischoff into a full-blown war.[33] Since 1994, observers had watched as WCW focused on Hulk Hogan and his political allies. That pattern had expanded with the arrival of the NWO, and Flair endured a tumultuous ride with plenty of highs and lows.

Overall, though, Flair had certain expectations as to how he should be treated based on his long experience in the business, his success as a multiple titleholder, and everything he had given to WCW through the years. In the months before his contract expired on February 15, 1998, Flair entered into negotiations with the promotion and expressed that he wanted a "substantial income," in addition to "a working environment and relationship with the WCW of fair treatment."[34] According to legal documents, Flair was assured that he'd be treated as the "Babe Ruth of Professional Wrestling,"[35] with all the reverence that came with such recognition. In the December article in the *Baltimore Sun*, Flair said he was "comfortable with the level of respect" he had been getting. But by early 1998, that had changed, and his problems with Eric Bischoff intensified.[36] The dismissal of his promising feud with Bret Hart and an intentional scaling back of his appearances "in order to satisfy demands made by, and commitments to, other wrestlers" essentially devalued his on-air role.[37]

That element, coupled with allegations of "increasingly hostile, rude, threatening, and degrading" treatment by Bischoff created an untenable environment for Flair, and his future in WCW was in doubt.[38] When the Tallahassee situation arose, tensions exploded, and all bets were off.[39] Of course, there were two differing points of view. Flair stated that he had asked for time off to attend Reid's tournament well in advance, while Bischoff considered the no-shows at *Thunder* and three other dates in Minnesota to be a "breach of contract."[40] Bischoff made an impassioned speech to the WCW locker room backstage at *Nitro* on April 13, and, as reported by the *Pro Wrestling Torch* and *Wrestling Observer Newsletter*, he said that he was going to make an example of Flair.[41] The *Observer* account went a step further, claiming that Bischoff "ran Flair down to an amazing degree," saying that Flair's nonappearance had derailed a plan to reunite the Four Horsemen.[42]

Four days later, lawyers for WCW filed a $2 million lawsuit against Flair in Atlanta's Fulton County Superior Court, and surprisingly, its legalese broke kayfabe in its description of wrestling's "story lines."[43] WCW's suit cited his nonappearances and claimed that "Flair's refusal to perform in scheduled events in contravention of his contractual responsibilities significantly disrupted WCW's ability to introduce its planned story line causing significant loss of time, money, and effort by WCW."[44] The court document also referred to Flair's November 1997 "letter agreement" as legal grounds that bound the wrestler to the organization. This letter agreement was not a full and detailed contract, but a precursor to what WCW called an "independent contractor agreement."[45] WCW believed it was legally binding.

Flair and his legal team disagreed. In a countersuit against WCW, they described the November 1997 "proposed agreement" as "an outline of basic economic terms" for a future contract. The full contract, received around January 18, 1998, was "not acceptable" to Flair, and he refused to sign.[46] Flair wanted a judge to affirm that the letter agreement was not a substitute for a valid contract, and that he was free to explore his options, including a possible return to the WWF.[47] There was no question: the loss of Flair as a central personality week to week hurt WCW, and the perceived gamesmanship between the two sides prevented any easy resolution. The lack of respect issue was key to the impasse, and Flair was adamant about his position. "If you don't have to take it, you shouldn't, and I just drew the line," he explained. "I had been vented on one too many times. The furthest thing from my mind was ever wanting to leave WCW."[48]

Fans were perplexed by the turn of events and were more than ready for a Flair return.[49] Rumors about his next move circulated steadily during the summer of 1998, and by September, rumblings indicated a homecoming for Flair sooner rather than later. WCW had lost its consistent ratings lead in the Monday Night Wars, and the WWF was providing stiff competition, strengthened by the incredibly successful "Stone Cold" Steve Austin and Vince McMahon feud. As the no-nonsense, beer-drinking roughneck from Texas, Austin had catapulted to the top of the industry after his 1995 departure from WCW, and his quarrel with the establishment — and his boss, McMahon — had leveled the playing field in the national wrestling war. Eric Bischoff was in a position to capitalize on his genuine heat with Flair and promote a storyline similar to Austin-McMahon, with Flair out to teach his heavy-handed and arrogant boss a lesson.

On September 14, 1998, an excitable sold-out audience at the newly constructed BI-LO Center in Greenville, South Carolina, anxiously awaited the return of the mid-Atlantic's favorite son. *Nitro* was the hottest ticket in professional wrestling that night, and the suspense built and built until a final climax when Flair, dressed in a tuxedo, emerged from behind the curtain.

The Nature Boy received a grand ovation from the crowd, and the prolonged cheers were not only reflective of the local fan base, but also represented the respect from the greater wrestling world as well. Flair, who tended to wear his emotions on his sleeve, was affected by the outpouring of admiration, and this defining moment far and away superseded any storylines, feuds, and personal quarrels. But after Bischoff walked out, and the segment blended the realistic aspects of Flair's return with what was now a full-fledged angle between the two men, and the audience ate up every second of it. "This is real!" Flair shouted at one point. Bischoff told him he was history, and Flair responded, "Fire me? I'm already fired!"[50]

A few weeks later during *Nitro* from Columbia, South Carolina, Arn Anderson and Flair's youngest son, Reid, confronted Bischoff in the ring, and the 10-year-old was clearly unafraid to mix it up.[51] He had words for Bischoff and then tackled him to the mat twice, demonstrating his wrestling prowess. The segment continued with an appearance by Flair and the Horsemen, and altogether, WCW beat the WWF 4.7 to 4.4 in the all-important quarter hour, head to head with a memorable skit of Steve Austin pummeling Vince McMahon in a hospital room.[52] The storyline again blurred the line between reality and kayfabe on December 14, 1998, in Tampa, Florida, but this time the scripted action had viewers legitimately concerned. In the midst of an intense promo about Bischoff, in which Flair was yelling frantically in pure Nature Boy fashion, he grabbed his left arm and sank to the mat in the corner in apparent pain. Officials and medical help ran out, placing him on a stretcher, and he was taken to a local hospital. Bischoff later told the *Nitro* audience that Flair might have suffered a mild heart attack.[53]

Fans and even personal friends were sincerely distressed, and Flair received over 1,000 phone calls of concern.[54] Without an immediate clarification as to the real situation, the wrestling community was on edge, but Flair himself soon confirmed that he wasn't in any real danger. "I'm fine," he told Tom Sorensen in the *Charlotte Observer*. "I didn't have a heart attack, unequivocally." He said that he experienced numbness in his left arm and was discharged from the hospital in Tampa after a battery of tests.[55] Despite Flair's public comments, the heart attack story lingered in WCW telecasts in the run-up to Starrcade. Bischoff garnered even more heat after feigning sadness about Flair's condition and then attacking David Flair during the December 17 episode of *Thunder*. Shockingly, after all the pro-Flair sentiment and the various televised scenarios, Bischoff went over Flair at Starrcade on December 27, using a foreign object to gain the pinfall.

The next night in Baltimore, Flair was energized beyond belief and delivered yet another unforgettable, one-of-a-kind interview. With "Mean" Gene Okerlund holding the microphone, Flair went on a tirade about Bischoff and began undressing in the ring. After getting down to his boxers, he challenged Bischoff to a rematch, and if he won, he'd take control of WCW for 90 days. Flair said he wasn't leaving the ring until he had an answer and handcuffed himself to the top rope.[56] Bischoff agreed, and later in the telecast, Flair forced him to submit to his figure-four. It was a satisfying ending for Flair fans, and with the Nature Boy in a storyline leadership position, his on-camera time expanded. He was all over *Monday Nitro*— making decisions, doing promos, and appearing in matches — and his work was as charismatic and physically vigorous as it had been in recent years. Due to turn 50 on February 25, Flair was overshadowing most of his counterparts as an all-around performer, and the ratings continued to reflect his positive influence on the company.[57]

Notably, David Flair had begun training to become a wrestler, and at the January pay-per-view, the 19-year-old teamed with his father to beat Curt Hennig and Barry Windham.[58] Following the bout, the NWO streamed out to attack the father and son duo, and David was the recipient of a severe whipping with a belt. Flair wanted revenge, and his conflict with the NWO, Bischoff, and Hollywood Hogan was unceasing over the following weeks. On February 21, 1999, at SuperBrawl, Flair challenged Hogan for the WCW title but was defeated when, of all people, David turned on him.[59] It was another twist and turn in the ongoing saga, and although the involvement of his son made it personal, Flair was willing to go along with the promotion's creative direction. At Uncensored on March 14, Flair had a rematch with Hogan, and the WCW belt wasn't the only prize. A victory would permanently secure Flair's spot as company president. Flair triumphed over Hogan that night, with help from referee Charles Robinson and Arn Anderson.[60]

Flair was now a six-time WCW World Heavyweight champion, and it was his first reign as titleholder in three years.[61] But his match with Hogan at Uncensored illustrated a shift in his personality back to a heel, while Hogan modified his act in the other direction, and was seemingly becoming a fan favorite once again. Going forward, Robinson was Flair's ace in the hole, and he aided the champion in matches, typically by either looking the other way when Flair was cheating or by delivering fast counts for pinfalls.[62] Flair still worked his trademark routine, and with the Big Gold back around his waist, it was a throwback to an earlier time for many fans. The champion entered into a four-way contest at Spring Stampede at the Tacoma Dome in Tacoma, Washington, on April 11, 1999, before nearly 18,000 people. Randy Savage made his return as the guest referee, maintaining order as Flair battled Hogan, Sting, and Dallas Page. Savage could only remain impartial for so long. He scaled the top rope and landed his elbow drop on Flair, allowing Page to score a win.

At *Nitro* on April 19 in Gainesville, Florida, Flair was at the center of another off-the-wall segment. After being pinned by Kevin Nash late in the show, he was physically restrained by medical personnel and removed from the venue. Flair's destination was the "Central Florida

Mental Hospital," where he was going to be locked up indefinitely.[63] The following week, footage of him in the insane asylum was featured on *Nitro*, and his interaction with staff and fellow patients was comical. Flair was freed just in time for the May 3 edition of *Nitro* in Charlotte, and he was ready to lash out at his rivals. He wanted to get his hands on Dallas Page, and the two battled in the main event for Page's WCW title. But Randy Savage's interference was costly, and Page pinned Flair to retain the belt.

From a business perspective, and with the knowledge that WCW was losing more and more ground in its ratings war against the WWF, the Charlotte *Nitro*— in Flair's hometown — drew only 6,300 fans and was considered a major disappointment.[64] WCW was making an effort to attract attention with its deep lineup of name superstars, but overall, the promotion was in a downward spiral. Inconsistencies and illogical finishes were eroding the audience, and instead of appealing to the fan base, WCW seemed to be purposely turning off viewers. That included the unceremonious end of Bill Goldberg's popular win streak at the last Starrcade. Flair's recent role had been geared more toward comedy than pushing him as a viable athlete, and that, too, seemed to work against the wishes of loyalists. In April 1999, based on Flair's ratings success, Dave Meltzer acknowledged him as "the biggest star in the promotion," but a few weeks later, following the hospital skits, noted that he had become a "comedic psycho geek."[65] The transition had been quick, and the juxtaposition between those two positions was stark. It exhibited WCW's inability to successfully build up and maintain a roster of must-see personalities. The WWF, with Steve Austin and the Rock, didn't have that problem.

CHAPTER 20
A RETURN TO SANITY

The financial exploits of the "Nature Boy" Ric Flair are legendary. Tales of his extravagant spending have been repeated and repeated again by insiders and during interview segments for years, and always seemed to make for an exaggerated and implausible reality. Flair's appetite for only the finest things in life was genuine and flawlessly translated to his on-screen wrestling character, enhancing the image of his persona. He dressed in expensive clothes, carried the gold title belt, and looked like a million bucks. Inside the ring, he matched that by being the best wrestler in the world. Whether he was cheating his way to victory or matching holds with a contemporary for 60 minutes, he was considered the top all-around grappler in the profession. He earned every dime he made as a hardworking wrestler at the pinnacle of his field, and no one could take that away from him. Most people don't know that Flair had been mindful of his financial well-being from a young age, and he was willing to take advantage of business opportunities to secure his future.

Flair was 24 years old in 1973 when he invested in 7.5 acres of undeveloped land in the Minneapolis area. The cost was $2,700 per acre, and he financed the purchase with the idea of paying for the property over a period of time.[1] The value of the land was expected to grow, and it was a worthwhile venture. At the time, though, he wasn't yet financially established. Prior to entering the wrestling business in late 1972, he had been unemployed for about six months, and his beginnings in the mat world were modest. Working preliminary dates for Verne Gagne on the AWA circuit earned him a small income, but not enough to even afford a middle-class lifestyle. He needed outside help, and the Commercial State Bank in St. Paul kept the Fliehr Family "alive and in groceries" until they left for Charlotte in 1974, according to a 1980 letter written by bank vice president Gerald Fesenmaier.[2] The bank loans, which were so vital at that juncture in their life, totaled more than $1,700.

Not long after his arrival in Charlotte, Flair experienced a steady rise in fame, and his income began to reflect his newfound prominence. The 1975 plane crash temporarily derailed his ascension, but he was determined to overcome what could have been a career-ending tragedy. But during his recovery time, he needed financial assistance, and Jim Crockett Promotions was more than willing to lend a hand. After all, he was the organization's most promising young star. This assistance, as well as other financial advances over a period of years, added up to $36,000 by 1980, and Flair was devoted to paying off every cent.[3] Also, shortly after the plane crash, and before his debt to JCP had increased to that point, Flair had been presented with another investment property opportunity — this time in Florida. For $45,000, he purchased a condo in the newly built Sand Castle I in Indian Rocks Beach. He later sold it for $64,000. He also put money into a limited-liability partnership, investing in the Sand Castle II condominium in that same area, making another $28,400.[4]

Flair carried a quite substantial tax burden prior to winning his first NWA World championship in 1981. As mentioned earlier, he hired a special bookkeeper to assist him in paying down his debt, and Flair even increased his workload to augment his income. Many times, he was on the road seven days a week, and he would typically incur expenses in the neighborhood of $600 for food, travel, lodging, and gym fees.[5] If his next date was more than 250 miles away, he'd usually fly commercial, otherwise, he'd drive. From time to time, Flair chartered a plane for himself to make a booking, which was the much more expensive option.[6] When it came to his public appearance, there was no limit in terms of spending. Flair's "earning power as a wrestler [depended] in part upon his image which he [strived] to maintain," a 1981 court document stated. "This includes maintaining a frequently extravagant lifestyle and high standard of living. Maintenance of his image requires that he be fashionable and well-dressed, not only when making public appearances but whenever seen in public."[7]

Taking into consideration the great sums for his lavish Olivia Walker ring robes, Flair spent thousands of dollars on his wrestling and personal wardrobe. Between 1976 and '78 alone, those expenditures amounted to nearly $20,000.[8] Flair wore custom-made suits, and he was a regular at Franco's of Richmond, Virginia, in the late 1970s. After becoming the NWA champion, he frequented Michael's Fine Clothes for Men in Kansas City, and he made a point of never wearing the same suit on television twice.[9] It was a pricey decision, but Flair was motivated to present himself in the best possible way. On the whole, his hard work and the revenue he brought in seemingly allowed for a lot of leeway in terms of career investment, leisure, and lifestyle. But during his divorce from Leslie, the hard truths of his personal financial welfare were revealed, and the stunning debt amassed by the Fliehr family was front and center.[10]

An impartial third party was called upon to interpret the facts in the case, and on October 29, 1980, a letter was sent from that official, John E. Hodge Jr., to Mecklenburg County judge James E. Lanning. Based on his findings, Hodge informed the judge that he had "some impressions that [were] probably not properly characterized as findings of fact." With regard to their financial troubles, Hodge explained that "the evidence was overwhelming that [Flair] was almost without financial restraint and in his testimony, he admitted as much."[11] He continued: "[Flair] testified that he was proud of the amount he made. My opinion is that he bragged about the amount of money he made, spent as if there was no limit on what they could afford, and isolated Mrs. Fliehr from the truth about both his earnings and the total amount of debt incurred. In short, [Flair] was the primary contributor to the overall financial condition of the parties."[12]

"He has at least two basic problems," Hodge wrote. "He buys what he wants and he wants a lot [and] he has failed to take into account his obligation for the payment of taxes. It is noteworthy to me that even under the extreme circumstances of the past year or so, he has managed to reduce his private debt by, according to his account, approximately $65,000. He has done this largely with the help of financial advice and management by his attorneys and Lillian Scott. Left to his own devices, although he claims to be reformed, it is doubtful to me that he could have done it." In his report, Hodge acknowledged that Flair was "articulate and intelligent," adding, "He is unquestionably a hardworking and dedicated professional, and he is obviously good at what he does. He was essentially candid, forthright, and sincere. In short, I liked him." With respect to Mrs. Fliehr, Hodge was also impressed with her sincerity: "I sensed no vindictiveness or 'I'll-make-him-pay' attitude, rather a quiet conviction to do what [was] necessary, despite its offensiveness to her personally."[13]

The unremitting support of Jim Crockett Promotions through this difficult time, both politically and financially, was crucial for Flair as he rose to the NWA World title in 1981, and it then sustained him throughout subsequent years. But Flair's dedication to the role was what made him a success and a wrestling legend. As time passed, he encountered financial woes of varying degrees, and he later admitted, "I've made millions. I've spent millions."[14] To accommodate his extravagant spending, he'd sometimes receive advances from promoters, called "draws."[15] Out at a bar or restaurant, he wanted Ric Flair, the personality, to be perceived as a big spender. And he was. He'd buy drinks, pick up bar tabs, and he was always heralded as the life of the party. In 1987, he told a Tampa reporter, "For a select few, the money is better than what top football and baseball players make. What people see on television is me — I do live a good life. I have spent a fortune, or a near fortune, on women, and I have a wife and ex-wife to prove it."[16]

Although he had dabbled in business in the past, Flair became a full-fledged entrepreneur with the opening of his first Gold's Gym in Charlotte in 1993. Over the following years, his gym investment expanded to other locations in North Carolina, including Greensboro, Durham, Carrboro, and Hickory. Flair also built a gym on the island of St. Maarten, but the facility was damaged beyond repair by Hurricane Luis in September 1995.[17] In between his active wrestling schedule and his business work, he put in special appearances to meet and greet fans at his various gym locations, signing autographs and taking pictures. Being in the public eye and maintaining the aura of the Nature Boy came naturally to Flair, but he was still a human being and admittedly struggled from time to time. In a 1991 feature article in the *Raleigh News and Observer*, he talked about a self-confidence issue that he had battled two years earlier and disclosed that he had seen a sports psychologist.[18]

"I was having a hard time getting myself up," Flair admitted.[19] His work environment at the time had a lot to do with his burden, and his condition improved after jumping from WCW to the WWF later that year. As a man who had long enjoyed the nightlife and going out to a bar after a wrestling show, Flair said he attempted to scale back the party life not too long thereafter. "I did that for 18 years," he told a newspaper writer in Baltimore. "I tried to quit that around '92. I had to slow down."[20] Displaying the honesty he was known for, Flair said, "Physically, I could still wrestle 300 times a year, but mentally, I'd have a difficult time now. As much as I love wrestling, I'd rather be home with my wife and kids. One of my biggest regrets is that I didn't get to spend time with my older children."[21] In 1999, his oldest son, David, joined him in the wrestling ranks, and he was rapidly improving as an athlete. His daughter Megan graduated from nursing school and was about to get married.[22]

With a schedule that was far less demanding than in his days as the traveling world champion, Flair was able to spend more time with his youngest children, Ashley and Reid, and he appreciated every second of it.[23] But his commitments to WCW still called him to the road, and he was fairly busy through the first half of 1999. On May 9 at Slamboree in

St. Louis, he was disqualified against Roddy Piper and lost his position as company president. Flair regained his spot at the next pay-per-view in Baltimore, winning over Piper on June 13.[24] The promotion's political atmosphere remained unsteady, and Flair was concerned with the direction of his career.[25] A bad back also hampered him at times, but he fulfilled his obligations, and his star-making ability gave a rub to many of WCW's young performers, not only through his in-ring work but behind the scenes with encouragement and advice.[26] The perception that Flair's age was a hindrance to the promotion persisted, and that obstacle never really went away.

The presidency of WCW went to Sting on July 19 during *Nitro* from Rockford, Illinois, when he defeated Flair by submission. Eric Bischoff interjected himself in the finish, calling for the bell when Flair was locked in the Scorpion Deathlock. Later that month, Flair ventured to Japan in support of his son Reid, who was part of an American delegation of amateur grapplers coached by the famed Dick Beyer, better known as the masked Destroyer.[27] Upon his return stateside, Flair missed *Nitro* on August 9, leading to a slew of rumors claiming his tenure in WCW was nearing an end.[28] While there were legitimate questions about his status, Flair focused on his physical health, heeding the advice of his doctor by taking a self-imposed hiatus from active wrestling to rest his back. In the meantime, he turned up at a Four Horsemen reunion in New Jersey and participated in the Jimmy V Celebrity Golf Classic in North Carolina.

Similar to his previous departures, Flair's exodus from television prompted fans to chant "We want Flair" at every turn, and on September 13, he returned on *Nitro*. It was significant because, three days earlier, Flair's longtime rival Eric Bischoff had been moved out of his influential executive position, which seemingly alleviated some of the political pressure on the Nature Boy. But that wasn't exactly the case. Vince Russo, a former writer for the WWF, had been hired in an effort to turn WCW around, and his plan for Flair was unconventional to say the least.[29] At Halloween Havoc on October 24, Flair was defeated by Dallas Page in a strap match and carried out on a stretcher. The Filthy Animals — a group consisting of Konnan, Rey Mysterio Jr., Eddie Guerrero, and Billy Kidman — jumped Flair, dragged him out to the desert, and purportedly buried him. Footage of the scene was shown on *Nitro* the next night, and Kidman proclaimed that "old man Flair" was not coming back.[30]

Russo wanted the spotlight on a crop of younger talent, and it was believed Flair would return to an on-camera role in a few months. Flair continued to wrestle at house shows through the end of the year, and in early January, WCW officials wanted him to return as commissioner. Needless to say, he wasn't thrilled by the proposition and declined.[31] During an appearance on the nationally syndicated *Live with Regis and Kathie Lee* on January 17, 2000, Flair made a surprise announcement, which had the potential to alter the course of his entire life. He revealed that he was strongly considering entering the political arena in an effort to become the next governor of North Carolina. "I'm dead serious," he explained. "I'm putting together a team, and I'm going to take a shot at it."[32] The unlikely fusion of wrestling and politics had been normalized after the stunning 1998 gubernatorial victory of Jesse "The Body" Ventura in Minnesota. Based on Flair's local popularity, his announcement carried real weight. In fact, the story was front-page news in the *Charlotte Observer* the next day.[33]

Admittedly intrigued by the idea, Flair believed there was a real opportunity in front of him. "I love North Carolina," he said. "I'd like to be remembered as more than the best wrestler that ever lived here."[34] Support for the Nature Boy as a candidate swelled, and pundits discussed the effect his entry would have on the race. But the demands on a political aspirant were great, and despite reported attempts to get out of his contract, Flair was still bound to WCW.[35] In February 2000, Flair had a meeting with Governor Ventura in St. Paul, and the conversation helped put things into perspective. "I haven't totally made up my mind, but I can tell you that right now, I'm leaning toward not doing it," he told a reporter. "It's not that I don't want to. I'm flattered so many people have been excited by the idea. The response has been heartwarming. But it would have to be a full-time campaign. I'm not ready for that yet."[36]

After mulling over the endeavor, Flair ultimately decided to forgo a political run.[37]

As expected, Flair rejoined the WCW circus and resumed his feuds with Terry Funk and Hulk Hogan. At SuperBrawl on February 20, 2000, he beat Funk in a violent Texas Death match at the Cow Palace in San Francisco.[38] Hogan was victorious over Flair at the March pay-per-view, Uncensored, in a bloody strap match. A few weeks later, Vince Russo teamed with Eric Bischoff to reset the company, initiating what was supposed to be the foundation for a new and improved WCW.[39] The sudden reorganization vacated all existing championships and set the table for the much hyped New Blood versus Millionaires Club feud. Flair was part of the latter contingent, along with Hogan, the Outsiders, Sting, and Dallas Page, and shoot-style comments were rampant on WCW telecasts. It wasn't altogether shocking when the creative direction for Flair had him butting heads with Shane Douglas — the man who had spent years badmouthing him in what always appeared to be a kayfabe-breaking manner in ECW. Many smart fans were eager to see the Flair-Douglas confrontation, and finally it was going to happen.

But real-world heat didn't necessarily translate to ratings gold, nor did it guarantee in-ring chemistry. The scenario, if not nurtured within the scripted confines of pro wrestling, had the potential of seeming overly forced and unnatural, even though there was a backstory to play off. Unfortunately, this was one of those times, and the interest was just not there. WCW struggled as it tried to gain footing, using gimmick matches, baseball bats, and blood randomly falling from the sky; it lent *Nitro* a high level of unpredictability. As for Flair, he was in a tough spot, once again finding himself in a feud with his son David, in addition to his rivalries with Douglas and Vince Russo. He was physically active, both on TV and at house shows, but he continued to experience pain from his rotator cuff injury, which needed surgery.[40] Since he was unable to properly train, his physique began to suffer, and he often wrestled in street clothes.[41]

The booking style of the promotion was fast, furious, and completely chaotic. On May 15, 2000, Flair pinned Jeff Jarrett to capture his seventh WCW World Heavyweight title, but he was the recipient of a beatdown by Jarrett, Russo, and David Flair afterwards.[42] The next week, Russo stripped him of the belt, and Jarrett regained the title with a victory over Kevin Nash. Nash then proceeded to win the WCW strap in a three-way battle against Jarrett and Scott Steiner at a *Thunder* taping on May 23 in Saginaw, Michigan. From there, Nash handed the belt back to Flair because he never lost it — accounting for Flair's eighth and final WCW title. On that same edition of *Nitro*, on May 29, Flair was defeated by Jarrett with Russo counting the pin, and he lost the championship. It should be noted that in addition to David's involvement, Flair's wife, Beth, and other children were part of the angle.

Flair teamed with his son Reid in a loss to David and Russo on May 30 in Boise, Idaho, during *Thunder*, and then Russo beat Flair in a cage match on June 5 in Atlanta. Flair agreed to put his career on the line against David at the Great American Bash on June 11, and Beth, Megan, Ashley, and Reid were in attendance. With assistance from Ashley and Reid in warding off Russo, Flair beat David by submission to his figure-four in a frenzied affair. The following night, in front of a pro-Flair crowd at the Richmond Coliseum, Ric and Reid were defeated by David and Russo in another unconventional contest. Russo, at one point, called Beth into the ring and told her to hit Ric with a foreign object, but she refused to do so. David locked his father in the figure-four, as security held Reid and Ashley back, and the match was halted when Megan threw in the towel. As a result, Flair was forcibly retired and had some of his famed blond locks shaved off by David and Russo.[43] Faithful Flair supporters in Richmond, who had stood in his corner for more than 25 years, were disgusted by the outcome.

Flair had survived a handful of high-profile hair vs. title matches early in his career, always walking away with his blond mane intact. But this bout on *Nitro*, against his son David and booker Vince Russo, Flair went the extra mile and gave up his hair to the cause. The angle appeared to set up a future payback situation for Flair against Russo, in particular, with the intention of giving Flair back his heat, as well as sending the fans home with a happy ending to the storyline. However, that was never going to happen. As strange as that sounds, this once-in-a-lifetime angle that involved Flair's wife and children, saw him humiliated, and cost him his hair never had a real conclusion favorable to Flair in any way.[44]

Less than two weeks later, on June 25, Flair suffered the loss of his beloved father, Dr. Richard Reid Fliehr, at age 81.[45] Dr. Fliehr had been a respected ob-gyn in the Twin Cities for decades, assisting in the birth of a great number of babies, including future wrestling promoter Gary Juster.[46] When he wasn't tending to the needs of his patients, he was dedicated to the theater and directed 12 main stage shows at the Theatre in the Round in Minneapolis. As an actor, he was known for his tremendous confidence and "booming voice that carried" to all corners of the audience.[47] From his father, Flair learned many important things, including a relentless work ethic that he had carried his entire life. "He was successful in everything he tried, and very unassuming," Flair said. "He was just the greatest, most honest guy I've ever met. I hope I can be half the man my father was. He was such a good person. He shouldn't be remembered as my father — I should be remembered as his son."[48]

Written off TV, Flair went in for surgery on his rotator cuff during the first part of July and needed months to recuperate.[49] On October 30, 2000, he made a subdued return to a beaten promotion on its last legs. Despite all efforts, including a full-on reboot, WCW had failed to make significant progress and was treading water. Rumors of the company being sold circulated, and after the first of the year, it seemed more and more likely. Flair's role as "CEO" put him back in a prime spot on TV, and his fans were grateful the Nature Boy was involved in the week-to-week dealings. He could still be counted on for a memorable interview, but ratings were dismal, and the future appeared bleak at best. In March 2001, AOL-Time Warner decided to cancel its WCW programming on TBS and TNT, effectively ending *Nitro* and *Thunder*.[50] A potential buyer,

Fusient Media Ventures, backed out soon thereafter, leaving the promotion with little chance of survival.

That is, at least in its current form. Before the end of that week, it was announced that World Wrestling Federation Entertainment was going to purchase the WCW brand, tape library, and intellectual property.[51] Vince McMahon had not only won the Monday Night War, but outlasted his only competition, and then bought his rival for pennies on the dollar. It was an unparalleled victory in wrestling history, and it would certainly change the way business was done. For Ric Flair, the sale of WCW was a defining moment, as it closed the door on a major chapter in his personal history. Flair and World Championship Wrestling had been synonymous for years, and the fact that WCW carried the lineage of Jim Crockett Promotions and the NWA strengthened its bonds to Flair. In some respects, Flair was WCW and WCW was Flair, and no one could deny his commitment to the promotion through the years. Even when he could've played a political card, he didn't, and he put fellow wrestlers over time and again. He agreed to wild and unusual stipulations, brought his family into angles, and allowed to have his head shaved. He gave everything he had.

But WCW was finished, and part of Flair was actually happy about it.[52] Notably, he wrestled on the organization's final pay-per-view, Greed, and then faced off with WCW's other franchise player, Sting, on the last edition of Nitro.[53] That event occurred on March 26, 2001, in Panama City, and Sting won with his Scorpion Deathlock. Afterwards, as a tribute to the respect they had for each other, Flair and Sting shook hands and hugged, and the WCW era was officially over.[54] Vince McMahon's 31-year-old son, Shane, appeared on Nitro moments later and announced that he was the new owner of WCW. The scenario pitted Shane against his father in what would be a slow-burning invasion angle, as the WWF brought former WCW workers into the fold.[55] In a way, it was an attempt to re-create the WCW versus NWO intra-promotional war, but when the WWF decided not to buy out the contracts of WCW's heavy hitters — stars like Bill Goldberg, Kevin Nash, Sting, and, of course, Ric Flair — the angle fell flat.

When *Nitro* went off the air, Flair still had more than 22 months on his existing contract with AOL-Time Warner, guaranteeing him $500,000 per year.[56] Since a buyout option was not exercised, he was essentially on paid leave from active wrestling, but it wasn't by choice. In an instant, he lost his connection to the public in an abrupt end to the occupation that had consumed him since he was 23 years old. Having sold out of his gym interests earlier in the year, Flair found other ways to fill the void, but the yearning to be around pro wrestling never diminished.[57] Some months later, he was contacted by the WWF, and arrangements for his return commenced. After the legal particulars were ironed out, he made a surprise return on the November 19, 2001, edition of *Monday Night Raw*.[58] Before a home crowd at the Charlotte Coliseum, he was met by a cascade of cheers, and Flair was affected by the positive response. "I actually got a little emotional," he later said. "I had to get a grip."[59]

Although he was in good condition, he was admittedly not in wrestling shape, but his return didn't demand a physical in-ring comeback.[60] In fact, he was introduced as the co-owner of the WWF, and was a direct rival to Vince McMahon. His on-camera duties included making matches, doing promos, and being at the center of various segments — all of which played to his strengths. Flair was a crowd pleaser, and when surrounded by Hall of Fame talent such as Steve Austin, the Rock, Chris Jericho, and the Undertaker, it made for great TV. The conflict between Flair and McMahon naturally grew to the point of violence and led to Flair's first match in 10 months at the Royal Rumble on January 20, 2002. They battled in a bloody street fight, ending with Flair winning by submission to his figure-four.[61] At WrestleMania on March 17 at the SkyDome in Toronto, Flair challenged the Undertaker's win streak but was defeated in a no-disqualification bout.[62]

A brand split between *Raw* and *Smackdown* occurred shortly thereafter, and Flair drafted a strong lineup of wrestlers for Monday nights, taking the Undertaker, Kevin Nash, Scott Hall, Booker T, Rob Van Dam, and the Big Show. It was during this time that Flair's personal relationship with Hunter Hearst Helmsley grew, and Triple H, as he was more commonly known, considered Flair a mentor. On March 26, 2002, in Philadelphia, after *Smackdown* went off the air, Triple H gave an unscripted promo about Flair and praised him to the high heavens.[63] Flair, who was never good at hiding his emotions, was sincerely moved by his words, and Triple H's advocacy for Flair served to boost his confidence.[64] Steve Austin, who had also joined *Raw*, was the brand's biggest attraction, and Flair's interaction with Stone Cold created some entertaining moments. In a lot of ways, the two men were doing more for the ratings on *Raw* than anyone else on the roster.[65]

The WWF, which became the WWE (World Wrestling Entertainment) in May 2002, was the perfect place for Flair to regain any of his lost dignity, both in and out of the ring. His tenure in WCW and then his time away from the sport had caused undue hardship, and the real Nature Boy was finding himself right before the fans' eyes. "The last two years were just a nightmare for me," he admitted. "[WCW] was a real negative environment."[66] Being in the WWE was a return to sanity in many respects, and Flair was happy to be there. In addition, the level of respect he received finally matched his status as a former multiple world titleholder. He was now an elder statesman in the business, and those in the WWE were giving him the proper acclaim. "Sometimes," he told a reporter, "I'm overwhelmed by how nice everybody is to me."[67]

Wrestlers from the *Raw* brand headed to London, England, for a localized pay-per-view event on May 4, 2002, and the Insurrextion show went according to plan. After all, the promotion typically ran like clockwork. But excess testosterone, down time, and plenty of alcohol could change the atmosphere, and a rather routine trip turned into an embarrassing spectacle. On a Luxury Air 757 flight back to the United States, things got out of hand, and the jaunt across the Atlantic was subsequently dubbed the "Plane Ride from Hell." A civil lawsuit was filed in 2004 by two flight attendants on the plane, and Flair was listed among the defendants, along with Scott Hall, Dustin Rhodes, and the WWE.[68] However, that case was soon settled out of court.[69] Years later, the allegations were brought to the forefront during an episode of the documentary series *Dark Side of the Ring*.[70] Flair issued a statement afterwards, noting, "My issues have been well documented over my 40+ year career." He then denied the allegation that he had forced himself on one of the flight attendants, saying, "It never happened."[71]

CHAPTER 21
TO RETIREMENT AND BACK

The year was 1985, and Ric Flair was at the top of his game. He was hammering it out of the park as both an athlete and a personality, and his Saturday promos on *World Championship Wrestling* continued to cement his legacy as a one-of-a-kind performer. On one glorious morning at the WTBS studios, Flair went on a tirade against Buddy Landel, telling host Tony Schiavone, "You're talking to the Rolex-wearing, diamond-ring-wearing, kiss-stealing, wooooo!, wheeling, dealing, limousine-riding, jet-flying son-of-a-gun, and I'm having a hard time holding these alligators down! Wooooo!" That statement, and the physical manner in which he expressed himself, was a remarkable example of his natural charisma, and for anyone watching, even those catching the program for the first time, it would have been impossible to take their eyes off him. As it was, Flair was always impeccably dressed, adorned in gold jewelry, and then with either the Ten Pounds of Gold or the Big Gold belt, he was the epitome of a world champion professional wrestler.

While it was known at the time that Flair was influential, especially in wrestling circles, it wasn't universally acknowledged or accepted that he was having a wider impact on culture. Traditionally, Hulk Hogan was considered the more marketable wrestler, but the impression Flair made went far beyond the sales of merchandise. His words, style, and mannerisms became a symbol of excellence, to a certain extent, and the fact that he could back up his arrogance in the ring, and was generally considered the best wrestler in the world, elevated Flair to iconic status. Just as Flair had been influenced by the swagger of Joe Namath, athletes, musicians, and Hollywood stars were awestruck by the sly confidence and utter flamboyance of the Nature Boy.[1] Flair transcended the sport of wrestling, and regardless of the crowd, he was the person that fans and other celebrities wanted to meet in person.

People were simply infatuated with Flair. His trademark "Wooooo!" — adopted after listening to rock and roll pioneer Jerry Lee Lewis — had been in his personal repertoire since the 1970s.[2] It was a staple of nearly all of his interviews, punctuating each moment with a panache only he could muster. Fans shouted out "Wooooo" every time Flair delivered his famed chest chop.[3] Going a step further, wrestling enthusiasts began doing the "Wooooo" any time any wrestler would do the chop as well, and that funneled down from the WWF to the independents and then around the world. Soon, the recognizable sound crossed over to other athletic professions and really became a universal way to rouse an audience. In 2002, Charlotte Hornets star Baron Davis did a television commercial with Flair, and from that point forward, local basketball fans shouted "Wooooo" whenever Davis scored a basket. As it was Charlotte, it was apropos.[4]

Flair as a pitchman in commercials wasn't new. His recognizable face and overall likeability made him a good candidate for advertising, and he was hired for various campaigns throughout his life. He appeared in one of his first commercials around 1980 for a local Toyota dealership and earned $500 for the spot.[5] Later in the decade, he did an in-ring commercial promoting the VHS release of the 1986 Great American Bash. He also did a Superstation TBS ad in 1989. During the 2000s, Flair was hired by the North Carolina and Tennessee State Lotteries to promote products, and his promotions were always very successful. His popularity endured, and even when he was a "bad guy" in a wrestling storyline, audiences usually ignored the wishes of promoters and cheered him anyway. It got to the point, in 2003, that he had to purposely insult fans to extract the reaction WWE officials wanted. And even that tactic didn't always work.

As a heel, Flair was an advocate for Triple H, often interfering in his matches. Based on Triple H's idea, a new group known as Evolution was born, and Flair was the cornerstone of the faction. Other members included Dave Batista and Randy Orton, but unfortunately, just as the unit was taking off, both Batista and Orton were injured and the angle was iced. On March 17, 2003, an unusual happening transpired in St. Louis, as Flair was involved in a legitimate backstage physical alteration with his old nemesis Eric Bischoff.[6] For pretty much the duration of his career, Flair was known for being non-confrontational, going out of his way to avoid trouble. He didn't have the personality of an aggressive fighter, and during the tumultuous last years of WCW, he rolled with the punches instead of getting overly heated. But this time was different, and after the years of animosity, he took a more antagonistic tone, and thus the altercation occurred.

He remained in his high-profile role on *Monday Night Raw*, and he did advance promotional work for the company prior to a tour of Australia during the summer. In interviews, Flair relentlessly put over the talent as an ambassador for the WWE. His versatility in and out of the ring made him a valuable asset to the organization, and there was no better position for him to be in, all things considered. Surprisingly, there was one thing that the higher-ups at WWE didn't want Flair doing, and that was his famous "Wooooo." which, according to the *Wrestling Observer Newsletter*, was banned from use on TV.[7] That edict didn't apply on May 19 in Greenville for Flair's World title match on *Raw* against champion Triple H. On that occasion, the Flair of old was in full force, and he gave the animated crowd its money's worth by going through his customary mannerisms and bag of tricks. He strutted, poked Triple H in the eye, delivered a low blow, and used his figure-four, delighting the audience to no end.

There was a sense that Flair was going to upset the champion and win the title, and the crowd could feel it building. Triple H pulled it out, though, landing his Pedigree finisher and scoring a pinfall. After the contest, Steve Austin, the McMahons, Triple H, and the entire WWE locker room entered the ring to pay tribute to Flair. With handshakes and beers, the roster celebrated his 31 years in the industry and respectfully honored his incredible legacy.[8] The next month in Houston, Flair wrestled Shawn Michaels in a singles bout for only the second time, and he beat him on June 15, 2003, at Bad Blood. They had previously battled 12 years earlier during a TV taping in Corpus Christi, and Flair was victorious in that contest as well.[9] But their long-awaited rematch saw Randy Orton, Flair's compadre in Evolution, hit Michaels with a steel chair and place Flair on his opponent for the win. Orton, by this time, had recovered from injury, and Batista would return in October, allowing Evolution to reform at full strength.

Throughout the summer and into the fall of 2003, Flair was quite active on the mat, mostly in tag team bouts, but he also competed with the likes of Bill Goldberg and Chris Jericho. On November 10, 2003, Ric's mother, Kay Fliehr, passed away at the age of 85. She had been in ill health for some time, having suffered two strokes in 1999, and she had developed a type of Parkinson's disease.[10] In 1986, she was asked what it was like to have a son who was a pro wrestler, and she replied, "I imagine it's the same as having a son who's a professional doctor. We put no demands on our children — the only thing we ask is that whatever they decide to do, they do as well as they can. And I certainly think Ric has done as well as anyone could in his sport."[11] Wrestling was not an enjoyable sport to Kay, and she was always concerned for Ric's well-being. "No mother can be totally happy having her son doing something where there's a great possibility that he could be seriously hurt," she said. "For that reason, it's not too much fun to watch him, but I admire his skill very much."[12]

Later in November 2003, the WWE released *The Ultimate Ric Flair Collection* DVD box set, a 10-hour compilation of matches and interviews.[13] Fans were feverish for old-school Flair material, and the collection sold nearly 90,000 copies in its first two months.[14] His 332-page autobiography, *To Be the Man*, was finally released on July 6, 2004. The book, which was several years in the making, was a revealing portrait of the Nature Boy, and Flair didn't shy away from difficult personal stories.[15] Many readers were intrigued by what Flair had to say about a lot of subjects, but his comments about Bret Hart, Mick Foley, and Bruno Sammartino raised some eyebrows.[16] It was compelling discussion from a wrestling legend, and though he created a level of controversy, his statements were highly respected by supporters.

Just before the end of 2003, all four members of Evolution managed to achieve gold at the Armageddon pay-per-view on December 14 in Orlando. Triple H walked away with the World title, Randy Orton beat Rob Van Dam for the Intercontinental belt, and Flair and Batista survived a Tag Team Turmoil match to capture the World Tag straps. It was reminiscent of the Four Horsemen's dominance in the NWA back in the 1980s, and with Flair's involvement, it's hard not to see the parallels. By March 2004, Flair was showing signs of injury, but medical tests were inconclusive as to the source.[17] His neck or back were the suspected problem, but he improved enough to appear at WrestleMania XX in New York City, where he teamed with Orton and Batista to beat Mick Foley and the Rock.[18] Flair and Batista, over the first four months of 2004, traded their tag belts with Booker T and Rob Van Dam, only to drop the championship to Chris Benoit and Edge on April 19. As the year proceeded, Flair had singles matches with Benoit, Edge, William Regal, and Shelton Benjamin.

Orton won the World Heavyweight title and was kicked out of Evolution, adding another dynamic to the *Raw* brand.[19] On September 12 at Unforgiven, Flair assisted Triple H in his title victory over Orton, and then lost a grudge cage match against Orton in the main event of Taboo Tuesday on October 19 in Milwaukee.[20] In early 2005, Flair resumed his feud with Shawn Michaels. Following Batista's victory at the Royal Rumble, he decided he was going after Triple H's World title and would go on to win the World belt at WrestleMania 21 in Los Angeles. As for Flair, he engaged in matches against Batista on the road in one form or fashion through May, often in tag matches and also handicap bouts with

Triple H as his partner. History was made on June 27, 2005, when he had his first singles contest with Olympic gold medalist Kurt Angle, and the two wrestled a classic on *Raw*.[21] Flair was pushed to his physical limit, taking huge bumps, and finally tapped out to Angle's ankle lock.[22]

Using his figure-four to defeat Carlito, Flair added the Intercontinental title to his list of career accomplishments on September 18, 2005, at Unforgiven. Early in October, Triple H turned on him, ending their long association and setting up a series of matches. They fought at Taboo Tuesday on November 1, and Flair took a victory when he escaped the cage first. At the Survivor Series on November 27, the two men went 27 minutes in an exhaustive Last Man Standing battle, and Triple H won the contest with use of his sledgehammer. The intensity of the Flair–Triple H feud was summed up by an impassioned promo the Nature Boy did during the October 17 edition of *Raw*. He talked about his rival wanting to put him out of the business, and as he went along, his intensity increased. By the time he took his jacket off and elbow dropped it, he was completely fired up. But Flair went the full distance, ripping off a bandage from his wounded forehead and smacking it with his hand. Blood gushed down his face in one of the goriest moments in television wrestling history. "Red is green," Flair once declared.[23]

Flair's reign as Intercontinental champion lasted until February 20, 2006. On that night, in Trenton, New Jersey, he was dethroned by Shelton Benjamin.[24] At WrestleMania on April 2 in Chicago, he competed in a Money in the Bank Ladder match, which was a bit out of his element, and the contest was ultimately won by Rob Van Dam. Flair had matches with Umaga and Edge, mended fences with Triple H and Shawn Michaels, and entered a lengthy feud with the animated Spirit Squad. At SummerSlam on August 20, 2006, in Boston, Flair went head to head with Mick Foley, and given their war of words that existed outside the ring, both in interviews and in print, there was definite heat.[25] Their I Quit match included a variety of weaponry, from baseball bats to trash cans, and Flair prevailed when Foley gave up. A few months later, at Cyber Sunday, Flair teamed with old friend Roddy Piper to capture the World Tag Team title from the Spirit Squad. They dropped the belts to Randy Orton and Edge a short time later.[26]

A team of WWE legends, comprised of Flair, Ron Simmons, Sgt. Slaughter, and Dusty Rhodes, faced off with the Spirit Squad at the 2006 Survivor Series in Philadelphia. Of the first four men eliminated, three of them were Flair's teammates. He had an uphill fight against three opponents, but Flair prevailed and was the sole survivor. Going into 2007, Flair continued to wrestle anywhere from a handful to more than 10 matches per month, and he participated in a long feud with Carlito. In April, June, and then in July, he joined the WWE for three different tours overseas, the first two in Europe, and the third in Thailand, Singapore, and Australia. Flair always brought a veteran celebrity presence to the promotion's international programs, and he was well respected by fans worldwide. Following a three-month hiatus, he made a big return to *Raw* on November 26, 2007, in Charlotte. He initially disappointed enthusiasts by talking about retirement, before switching gears and exclaiming, "I will never retire! I will only retire when I'm dead in this ring!"

Fans were ecstatic, and Flair demonstrated his zest for wrestling by taking off his coat and doing his trademark Nature Boy spiel. "I love this business!" he shouted. Smiles soon faded as Vince McMahon's music hit, and the WWE chairman made his way to the ring, strutting as only he could. He told the former champion that he could remain active as long as he kept winning.[27] The first match he lost, he was finished. Randy Orton, the WWE World titleholder and professed "Legend Killer," received the first chance to force Flair into hanging up his boots, but Flair wasn't going down without a fight. With some outside help from Chris Jericho as a distraction, and a low blow, Flair pinned Orton and sustained his career.[28] In subsequent weeks, Flair withstood challenges from Umaga, William Regal, and Triple H, persevering through the early part of 2008. On February 18, during *Raw*, Shawn Michaels, who had not only idolized Flair in his youth but had become good friends with him away from the ring, announced that Flair had been selected for induction into the WWE Hall of Fame.[29]

The honor was well-earned. After 36 years in the industry, Flair had done and seen it all, and his remarkable achievements were going to stand the test of time. The WWE's decision to enshrine him coincided with the ongoing retirement angle on TV, and Michaels was going to play a much bigger role. A week later on *Raw* from Phoenix, Flair said he wanted to face the Heartbreak Kid at WrestleMania 24, and Michaels agreed. Flair had great respect for Michaels. Back in 1995, he told a reporter, "[Michaels is] one of the chosen few that will ever know what it means to be the best at what he does in life. He'll be remembered as one of the all-time greats."[30] The feeling was obviously mutual, and the stage was set for a WrestleMania classic on March 30, 2008, in Orlando. The night before the anticipated event, Triple H inducted Flair into the WWE Hall of Fame, and it was a night full of laughs, memories, and tears. Flair's speech was both reflective and insightful as he talked about his family and his history in the business.[31] At the conclusion, he simply said, "I love you, thank you. Thank you! Wooooo!"

The shared emotions and the standing ovation Flair received during that ceremony carried over to WrestleMania at the Citrus Bowl the next night, when 74,635 fans paid tribute to the Nature Boy. Flair and Michaels went 20 minutes and delivered an intense, visually gripping contest, and the action conveyed the true feeling of the moment. With Flair's future in wrestling on the line, he was fighting with everything he had, and Michaels was the perfect foil.[32] At a critical juncture in their clash, Michaels was setting up his famed Sweet Chin Music, and the audience held its breath. Michaels appeared torn about what he had to do next, and before he unleashed a powerful superkick to his opponent's head, he said, "I'm sorry, I love you." Michaels then pinned the man he had long admired and ended the career of Ric Flair. From bell to bell, the match captivated spectators, and the finish was perfectly executed.[33] The stadium crowd exploded in a spontaneous expression of sentiment and respect as they watched Flair graciously accept his defeat.[34]

Flair was acknowledged and celebrated by his peers and the WWE Universe again the next evening during *Raw*. "The biggest, most devout

Ric Flair fan could not have devised a more appropriate final weekend for the retiring star," wrote Wade Keller in the *Pro Wrestling Torch*. "Flair, the greatest pro wrestler in history by almost any definition, had a weekend that suited his achievements."[35] The fan response and recognition made Flair a proud man, and the sendoff was unparalleled.[36] Expectedly, the people of the mid-Atlantic region were thoroughly appreciative of everything Flair had given them through the years, and the love was reciprocated. Less than a week before WrestleMania, he had been honored in Columbia, South Carolina, the site of so many of his ferocious battles, and given the key to the city. Mayor Bob Coble also declared it "Ric Flair Day."[37] Before a throng of supporters, Flair said, "All the things that I have supposedly accomplished in my career, I'm very proud of, I am most proud of moments like this. It is emotional. It's hard to explain."[38]

Upon receiving the news of Flair's loss at WrestleMania, Tom Sorensen wrote in the *Charlotte Observer*, "The best there ever was finished. And because he is, wrestling will never be the same."[39] A large percentage of the wrestling community agreed. Retirement was not something Flair had looked forward to.[40] But in interviews, he appeared reconciled to the idea of being away from the squared circle, saying that he could see himself retired.[41] He was enthusiastic about his son Reid's entry into the business, as the 20-year-old had recently been signed to a WWE developmental deal.[42] "I want to be very involved and following him very closely each and every day," Flair told a reporter.[43] Still months away from his pro debut, Reid was a highly skilled athlete, having proven himself in amateur wrestling competitions, and his grappling future was bright. Meanwhile, Flair began the transition to the next phase of his life, though wrestling was still very much a part of his existence. In fact, the WWE brought him back for appearances in both June and July 2008.[44]

Over the previous few years, Flair had experienced a lot of change in his personal life. On February 15, 2005, just 10 days before his 56th birthday, Ric separated from his wife, Beth.[45] Three months later, Beth filed a 16-page complaint against her husband with allegations of domestic violence, verbal and emotional abuse, excess use of alcohol, and adultery.[46] The local media picked up on the story and splashed details of their "nasty divorce" across the front page of the *Charlotte Observer*. Personal information relating to Beth's complaint, Flair's indebtedness, and other particulars about their finances became public knowledge.[47] As he had earlier in his life, he was again dealing with a considerable tax debt, and his WWE wages were being garnished by the IRS. Flair denied any abusive behavior, and when asked about the various accusations, his attorney Bill Diehl said, "She accused him of being a bad boy. He accused her of being a bad girl. That's where we stand."[48]

Mecklenburg County Superior Court judge Jane V. Harper, in October 2005, ordered Flair to pay Beth $20,000 a month in post-separation support, while other aspects of the case were deferred to a later date.[49] Flair wanted a quicker resolution and filed for divorce on February 16, 2006. The court declared that their bonds of matrimony were dissolved and granted an "absolute divorce" on May 8, 2006.[50] At the time, Flair was dating Tiffany VanDeMark, a trainer who had previously worked at one of his Gold's Gyms, and he soon moved in with her at 3909 Ayrshire Place in Charlotte.[51] Within weeks of his divorce, Flair was tying the knot again on May 27, 2006, in the Cayman Islands. Among those in attendance were his four children, Triple H, and Dave Batista. VanDeMark's expertise as a trainer helped Flair get into prime shape for his WrestleMania bout with Shawn Michaels, and Flair told a reporter that he hadn't worked out that hard since his legendary 1989 series with Ricky Steamboat.[52]

The extra time in the gym paid off, and Flair had delivered a first-rate performance in the ring. Flair admittedly struggled in the days, weeks, and months following his retirement.[53] Without a rigid wrestling schedule to adhere to, he found himself with a lot of extra time. But opportunities for the Nature Boy were everywhere, both big and small. That was one of the reasons why he asked for his release from his WWE contract during the summer of 2008, as he wanted to explore his options. Once he parted ways from the WWE, effective August 3, he relied on his skilled talent agent, Elaine Gillespie, and the Columbia-based Gillespie Agency received over 1,000 inquiries for Flair within three days. They were fielding offers for reality shows, movies, corporate appearances, and tours of the U.S. and Mexico. "Between now and the end of December, Ric has 17 public appearances scheduled and offers for more come in every day," Gillespie told Flair's longtime friend and reporter Mike Mooneyham.[54]

Heading into the final month of the year, promotions in Charlotte touted the pro debut of Reid Flair on December 6 at Vance High School.[55] Reid was set to team with his brother, David, against the Nasty Boys, and Hulk Hogan would be the special guest referee. Trained in part by George South, and having spent more than two weeks at Harley Race's Eldon, Missouri, camp, Reid was ready to step into the pro ring for the first time. Fittingly, the Flair brothers entered the ring to their father's famous theme song, and Ric was on hand to manage his sons from ringside.[56] Reid and David were both game for their contest with the more experienced Nasty Boys, and they managed to put simulta- neous figure-fours on Brian Knobbs and Jerry Sags. Ric then got in the ring and placed manager Jimmy Hart in the figure-four, and in all, it was a remarkable moment for the Fliehr family. Of course, Reid and David were pronounced the victors by Hogan, and Reid's career was off to a winning start.

By this time, Flair's relationship with Tiffany VanDeMark had come to an end. They had actually separated the June before, and VanDeMark filed a Complaint for Post Separation Support in October. In that legal document, it was alleged that Flair earned "approximately $7,500 to $15,000 per hour for public appearances," and "$750,000 to $1,000,000 gross income per year."[57] A subsequent court filing clarified his income, revealing that he had earned $293,180 between August and December 2008. It was stated that his total debt obligations, including $40,000 owed to the WWE, was over $1.7 million.[58] After various accusations and denials, their marriage officially concluded on August 12, 2009.[59] Flair formed a new relationship with Jacqueline Baines "Jackie" Beems, whom he had met in Chicago, and a whirlwind courtship resulted in matrimony on November 11, 2009. But the turmoil in his personal life continued. A report in the *Charlotte Observer* on February 23, 2010, disclosed a domestic incident that had occurred a few days earlier between the couple.[60]

"Ric and his wife had an unfortunate disagreement late [Sunday] night, which led to his wife being arrested and charged with assault," wrote Flair's representative Melinda Morris Zanoni of Legacy Talent and Entertainment, according to the *Observer* report. "Ric has done nothing wrong. Ric finds this incident unsettling and is committed to correcting any issues in his personal life."[61] Notably, Zanoni had replaced Elaine Gillespie as his agent and was now in charge of his booking schedule. The assault charge was later dismissed after Flair refused to testify against her at trial.[62] They had a second "altercation" in June 2012, also reported by the *Charlotte Observer*, but no one was arrested.[63] It was the final straw, and the couple separated on June 26.[64] Their divorce was finalized on April 6, 2015.[65] Flair's public profile made stories about his challenging personal life front-page news, and websites generated a lot of traffic by posting the lurid details of his rocky relationships.[66]

Flashing back to the months immediately following his WWE release in 2008, Flair was undoubtedly a busy man. He attended the popular NWA Legends Fanfest in Charlotte in August, and then he recorded his first full-length shoot interview with Michael Bochicchio of Highspots in September.[67] Flair had a falling-out with both the promoter of Fanfest, Greg Price, and with Bochicchio.[68] The dispute with Bochicchio related to a $35,000 personal loan he had given Flair. As collateral, the wrestler agreed to give him the prized Ten Pounds of Gold— the legendary NWA belt he wore as world champion.[69] It was later discovered that the belt was already being used as collateral to a different company, and because of that fact, Highspots was unable to recoup its money when Flair failed to pay off his debt.[70] In a 20-page complaint, Bochicchio and Highspots outlined its case against Flair and brought the matter before a judge in Mecklenburg County Superior Court.[71]

The case ultimately went to mediation, and an agreement was reached on Flair's 62nd birthday on February 25, 2011. Soon after, Flair fully complied with the terms and conditions of the case by giving Highspots a check for $35,000, plus 300 autographed photographs. In turn, Highspots returned the NWA belt to Flair, and the case was closed in June 2011.[72] Bochicchio, according to the complaint, had also negotiated a deal in 2009 between Flair and the first-class independent promotion Ring of Honor.[73] The Nature Boy made his ROH debut in Collinsville, Illinois, just outside St. Louis, on March 13. He appeared at a TV Taping on April 9 in Philadelphia and was announced as the new "ambassador" for ROH. In a promo, Flair talked up the company and its wrestlers, and it appeared he had found a new home. But things quickly changed on that front, as the WWE beckoned for his return, and Flair made a surprise appearance at the Judgment Day pay-per-view in Chicago on May 17, 2009.[74]

Flair was juggling two gigs at that point, but because of his allegiance to the WWE, he told ROH that he couldn't do any television work for the promotion. This put the management of Ring of Honor in a bind and forced them to make changes to the May 29 program in Philadelphia.[75] A couple weeks later, on June 13 at the Hammerstein Ballroom in New York City, Flair had a backstage argument with ROH owner Cary Silkin, and after doing a promo, he promptly left the building.[76] Flair fulfilled obligations to ROH on June 26 in Detroit and June 27 in Chicago, and concluded business with the company.[77] Part of his original interest in Ring of Honor had been as a way for his son Reid to gain experience. But Reid's personal struggles, including an arrest for heroin possession, were derailing his promising future.[78] Reid sought treatment for his substance abuse problems, and Flair did everything in his power to support his youngest son.[79]

Late in 2009, Flair joined Hulk Hogan for a four-match series in Australia, and the tour drew successfully in Melbourne and Sydney. Their press conference on November 18 garnered headlines after Flair attacked Hogan on stage, and the scenario was great promotion for their upcoming bouts. Hogan, unsurprisingly, beat Flair in all four of their matches.[80] Flair had been considering a return to the ring for months. His major concern was how both Vince McMahon and Shawn Michaels felt about it, especially after the sendoff he had received for his retirement in 2008.[81] But Flair wasn't ready to call it quits. He still felt like a young man at heart. "I feel like I'm 25," he told a reporter in 2008. "I don't feel any different. Sixty doesn't bother me. Fifty didn't bother me. Forty did because somebody told me I'd have to stop wrestling."[82] The truth was, nobody could tell Flair to stop wrestling, and he would continue until he was absolutely ready to call it a career.

CHAPTER 22

BLOOD, SWEAT, AND TEARS

The love for professional wrestling combined with enormous financial burdens propelled Ric Flair into a more active role in a major American promotion in 2010. He joined Hulk Hogan and Eric Bischoff in TNA, a promising organization with a prime weekly cable outlet on SpikeTV. TNA was looking for a breakthrough moment, and the promotion received a timeslot opposite the WWE's *Raw*, rekindling the Monday Night Wars. Flair's role was initially as an observer, and he soon became a mentor to wrestling prodigy AJ Styles.[1] He expanded his stable, adding Robert Roode, James Storm, and Desmond Wolfe, and later dubbed the group Fourtune. At the Lockdown PPV on April 18, "Team Flair" was defeated by a squad led by Hogan, consisting of Abyss, Rob Van Dam, Jeff Jarrett, and Jeff Hardy. Flair feuded with Jay Lethal, a talented competitor with an uncanny ability to imitate the Nature Boy.[2] During one particular TV segment, Lethal did his whole impression, as Flair got more and more steamed in the ring. The comical scene included a classic back and forth of Flair's famous "Wooooo!"[3]

Contracted to make 65 appearances a year, Flair was a fixture on the weekly telecast, and his enthusiasm was always apparent. His old rival Mick Foley joined him to renew their past feud, and they were never at a loss for words as they delivered memorable promos hyping their Last Man Standing bout on October 7. That match was a stark deviation for Flair, particularly after it descended into a straight hard-core contest with an assortment of weapons. Foley, who was bleeding from a previous wound minutes into the battle, took a baseball bat wrapped in barbed wire to the forehead of his 61-year-old opponent, and Flair was soon gushing as well. At one point, Foley took a big bump off the stage through a table, and another spot saw Flair jump off the top rope onto his rival, sending them both through a table in the ring. At the end, Flair struggled to get up and did his face flop onto thumbtacks that littered the mat, giving Foley the victory.[4] The spectacle had to be seen to be believed.

Flair was affiliated to TNA for the next 18 months. The road was bumpy at times, and both injuries and internal disputes at the promotion over money made things difficult.[5] In the midst of that run, Flair wrestled one of his greatest opponents, Sting, during the September 15, 2011, edition of IMPACT.[6] The two had wrestled their first match 23 years earlier at a house show in Charlotte in December 1987, and only a few months later, Flair had made Sting a national star at the inaugural Clash of the Champions. Even though the match was physically slower than their earlier encounters, the intensity and psychology remained, and their history made it a special occasion. Flair went through his well-known repertoire, using everything from the low blow to his figure-four leglock. He was caught, as he often was, trying to jump off the top rope, and he ably moved when Sting attempted a splash in the corner. But Sting landed a huge superplex, recovered from being hit with brass knuckles, and forced Flair to submit to his Scorpion Deathlock.[7] Flair suffered a defeat and a serious injury to his arm in the process.[8]

Despite the pain and what was believed to be a broken bursa sac in his elbow, Flair was optimistic and upbeat. "I feel great," he told a reporter.[9] The following week, he went up to Boston to surprise Red Sox second baseman Dustin Pedroia in the clubhouse prior to a game against the Baltimore Orioles. Pedroia was a big fan of Flair and was known for hanging an autographed Flair robe above his locker.[10] Flair presented Pedroia with a TNA championship belt, and his visit drew a lot of attention from players and team personnel. "The players were awesome," Flair said afterwards. "They were all so respectful and nice."[11] The admiration for Flair was plentiful among professional athletes, and Flair extended his friendship guys to like Jim Harbaugh, Kevin Greene, Mike Rucker, and Charles Barkley. In January 2014, Harbaugh, who was then the head coach of the San Francisco 49ers, invited Flair to deliver a pep talk to his squad on the eve of their NFC Wild Card game against Green Bay in Wisconsin. The added motivation from Flair helped propel the 49ers to a victory, 23–20.[12]

Interestingly, beginning with the Carolina Panthers and continuing with teams at all levels of sports, a post-game ritual invoking the name, spirit, and flamboyance of Flair became increasing popular in the 2010s.[13] The "Two Claps and a Ric Flair," as it was known, was devised as part of a victory celebration, and teams used the custom — including the famous "Wooooo!" as they rejoiced. Sergio Brown, a safety for the Indianapolis Colts, added a unique spin to the tradition by quoting from Flair's renowned "Rolex-wearing, diamond-ring-wearing" promo, and the entire routine was very entertaining.[14] Flair had received great respect from his professional contemporaries in other sports throughout his career, and in 2012, he received a powerful acknowledgment from the then three-time NBA MVP LeBron James. "When I was a kid, I loved wrestling," James explained. "[Flair] was one of the guys I loved too. I think he's probably one of the creators of what we call swag these days, with the Rolexes and the stretch limos, and all the girls and all that stuff. He's like the creator of swag. Ric Flair definitely kept me watching TV."[15]

While still employed by TNA, Flair got word that the WWE wanted to make him the only individual to be inducted into the Hall of Fame twice.[16] This time around, he would be enshrined as part of the Four Horsemen, and Flair was thrilled. "Being inducted once was one of the greatest accomplishments of my career, so I'm humbled and honored to be recognized again," Flair said in a statement.[17] TNA and the WWE came to a mutually agreeable deal permitting Flair to rejoin his old colleagues on WrestleMania weekend to take part in the ceremony.[18]

Eric Bischoff, whose hot-and-cold relationship with Flair went back more than a decade, was more than supportive of his recognition. "Ric Flair is a very special individual in this business," he told VOC Nation Wrestling radio. "He's done amazing things. He's not flawless, he's not perfect. He's not anything like that. But there is no one in this business that deserves the respect and the honor, quite frankly, of taking center stage on the biggest event in our universe."[19]

On March 31, 2012, at the American Airlines Arena in Miami, Dusty Rhodes — the arch enemy of the legendary Four Horsemen — inducted Flair, Arn Anderson, Tully Blanchard, Barry Windham, and James J. Dillon into the WWE Hall of Fame. It was another landmark occasion, and Flair received his second gold ring. In the weeks that followed, Flair's status within TNA changed, and he was officially released from the organization on May 11.[20] Reports initially circulated that Flair had skipped out on several TNA dates between May 10 and 15, and that he was trying to get out of his contract to jump to the WWE.[21] But that information didn't jibe with the timing of his release, and the WWE indicated that it had made no offer for Flair's return.[22] Nevertheless, Flair was done with TNA, and his schedule was wide open for indie appearances, conventions, and autograph shows.

During the second week of August 2012, Flair ventured to Cave-in-Rock, Illinois, to perform as host at the 13th annual Gathering of the Juggalos festival. He was forced to depart early after the crowd began throwing bottles at the stage.[23] Flair made his long-awaited return to the WWE on December 17 at *Raw* in Philadelphia in a surprise appearance. From the stage, he presented the "Superstar of the Year" Slammy Award to John Cena. Cena graciously accepted the award, but he turned around and gave it to Flair before leaving the stage. With a major bone to pick, CM Punk and Paul Heyman confronted Flair, and Punk criticized both the Nature Boy and Cena, reminding everyone that he had been the WWE champion for 393 days. Flair was unimpressed. He took off his coat and walked to the ring to face the hobbled Punk, who was on crutches, and his manager. But Punk used one of his crutches to knock Flair to the mat, and he had the upper hand. Sly as usual, Flair resorted to his dirty tricks and poked Punk in the eye. He proceeded to put Heyman in the figure-four.[24]

"If I die, I want to die right here or with a woman from Philly," Flair told the crowd a moment later.[25] Flair's participation on *Raw* continued, as he found himself face to face with the members of Shield. He received some timely help from Kane, Daniel Bryan, and Ryback, and he celebrated after fending off the attack.[26]

It's notable that earlier in 2012, shortly after WrestleMania, Flair's daughter Ashley decided to enter the wrestling business, and she traveled to Tampa to begin training under Steve Keirn.[27] With tremendous athletic ability, Ashley made remarkable progress, and she was added to the NXT Divas roster by August. She was also given the ring name Charlotte, as a tribute to her hometown.[28] As for Flair's son Reid, he was still improving as a wrestler and was slated to travel overseas with his father in January 2013 for a tour of All Japan Pro Wrestling. In fact, the elder Flair was scheduled to lace up his boots to participate in a tag team match on January 26 in Ota, Japan. When he was sidelined by a blood clot in his leg, Reid took his place, teaming with Keiji Mutoh in a loss to Tatsumi Fujinami and Seiya Sanada.

While his son Reid remained in Japan for a series of matches to gain further experience and confidence in the squared circle, Flair returned stateside and was very busy with a number of appearances. During the week of February 14, he filmed an episode of *Celebrity Wife Swap* for future broadcast on the ABC Network. His partner on the telecast was Wendy Barlow, known in the wrestling world as Flair's French maid, Fifi, from 20 years earlier during their employment with WCW. In recent months, Flair and Barlow had rekindled their friendship and formed a relationship. Barlow was the mother of four children, including Sophia Kidder, an actress who appeared in six episodes of *The Walking Dead*.[29] *Celebrity Wife Swap* had participants spend the week with a different family, usually presenting a clash of lifestyle and culture. That was certainly the case as Flair traded places with his longtime friend and former ring rival Roddy Piper to spend the week in the Pacific Northwest.[30]

Flair was booked for an appearance on the March 25, 2013, edition of *Raw* from Philadelphia, but he wasn't able to perform due to continued problems with a blood clot in his leg. He went home to Charlotte for treatment, and he was expected to make a few dates the following weekend in Maryland.[31] Having concluded his two-month tour in Japan, Reid Flair had also returned to Charlotte and soon joined his father at his hotel, the Residence Inn off Fairview Road in the SouthPark area of the city.[32] The 25-year-old "had never looked happier," according to a report in the *Charlotte Observer*, and planned to travel with his father to Maryland in just a few days.[33] Tragedy struck instead. On the morning of Friday, March 29, Reid was found unresponsive in his hotel room. Emergency personnel tried to revive him, but their efforts were unsuccessful, and Reid was declared dead.[34] A medical examiner's autopsy later determined that Reid had died of accidental "heroin toxicity."[35]

"We are heartbroken to confirm that Ric's son, Reid Fliehr, has passed away," a statement from Flair's agent, Melinda Morris Zanoni, said. "Reid was 25 and an incredible son, brother, friend, and professional wrestler. No words can describe the grief that Ric and his family are experiencing and they do request privacy during this devastating time."[36] The sadness following his death extended to the far reaches of the wrestling community, and people were gutted by the news. In recent years, Flair has discussed the death of his son on a variety of platforms, including in his second autobiography, *Second Nature: The Legacy of Ric Flair and the Rise of Charlotte*, which was released in 2017, and he candidly shared the harrowing pain of loss with his legion of supporters.[37] He also provided insight into Reid's private struggle, and Flair never held back. His candor spoke to the relationship he shared with the greater public, and his honesty was something he had maintained his entire career.

Taking all of his interviews and books into consideration, it's hard not to acknowledge him as one of the most revealing, outspoken, and expressive athletes of all time. The tears at the Hall of Fame, on *Raw*, in interviews, and at WrestleMania were all real. The blood spilled in the 1970s, '80s, '90s, and 2000s was all real. The hours of wrestling matches, from the parking lots of auto dealerships to the Tokyo Dome, saw Flair give everything he was worth in the ring, and his sweat stained many wrestling mats. Ric Flair had given just about every ounce of himself to the public, and it's difficult to find another athlete in the wrestling world even remotely comparable. Flair never shied away from discussing a subject and was forthright about his divorces, his money problems, and his opinion on all things pro wrestling. Where it became incredibly delicate was when Flair discussed his children and how he feels his own decision-making and just how his conduct has affected them.[38] The emotion was so very real.

Following Reid's passing, Flair endured some hard times, physically and mentally.[39] He reportedly spent a month in the hospital, treating his blood clot, before he relocated to the Tampa area to live with his close friend Joe Gomez. That gave him the opportunity to watch Ashley's training.[40] He traveled to Los Angeles in August to take part in a promotional symposium to discuss the upcoming *WWE 2K14* video game release. Despite Flair's innate ability to be charming and tell stories, WWE officials were not entirely pleased with how the event was handled.[41] As a result, Flair was reportedly removed from a spot at SummerSlam, and contractual talks about a more regular position at the company broke off. Jim Ross, the host of the symposium, was ushered into a hasty retirement as well.[42] However, Flair was back in the good graces of Vince McMahon by the summer of 2014, and he made a big appearance at Madison Square Garden on July 12. He interacted with Triple H and Bray Wyatt, even throwing a few punches the latter's way, before John Cena beat Wyatt to retain his WWE championship.

Cena, who had recently won his 15th World title and was on the brink of tying Flair's record 16, respectfully addressed Flair after his victory.[43] "I don't give a damn how many times I had this," he told the Garden audience. "This would just be leather and gold if there was no 'Nature Boy' Ric Flair." He then called Flair "the greatest of all time."[44] In subsequent months, Flair was active on television and on the road, and he performed as a guest referee for matches featuring Roman Reigns in Australia during August. Several weeks later, he returned to the hospital for a series of surgeries, including an intestinal operation and an appendectomy.[45] In true Flair fashion, he recovered more quickly than expected and was released from the hospital two days early.[46] He was back performing his duties in WWE rings by December. Going into 2015, Flair continued to make sporadic appearances for the promotion, mainly on big occasions, and turned up at a special Hulk Hogan Appreciation Night at Madison Square Garden on February 27.

Along with other Hall of Famers, he participated in a backstage segment at WrestleMania 31 in Santa Clara, California, and celebrated the Intercontinental title victory of Daniel Bryan.[47] On May 6, 2015, the initial episode of *Wooooo! Nation*, a new podcast program hosted by Flair and Conrad Thompson, made its debut on the CBS Radio Play.it network. Kurt Angle, the acclaimed Olympic gold medalist, was the first guest, and over the following weeks, the likes of Mick Foley, Bret Hart, Terry Funk, Steve Austin, and Jim Cornette were interviewed.[48] The conversations were absorbing, and the shrewd perspectives and opinions on historical events made it mandatory listening.[49]

On June 11, 2015, the "American Dream" Dusty Rhodes passed away in Orlando, Florida.[50] He was 69 years old. Rhodes had been an early influence on Flair, dating back to the early 1970s. As Flair rose in prominence, a sharp competitiveness between the two men manifested, leading to challenges in their personal and business relationship.[51] In the ring and behind the microphone, Flair and Rhodes brought out the best in each other, and the ongoing feud between Rhodes and the Four Horsemen was a hot point during the heyday of Jim Crockett Promotions. Despite all their hostilities, there was an equal amount of respect and friendship, and they were close in recent years.[52] Flair always recognized Rhodes's importance, and in 1987, he told a reporter, "Dusty Rhodes has had a great impact on our sport. He was the first cable star, and it opened a lot of doors."[53]

At the end of July, Flair suffered loss again when his friend of over 30 years Roddy Piper passed away in California. The Rowdy Scot was only 61.[54] The bond between Flair and Piper formed when they were both young men at the outset of their careers in the mid-Atlantic region, and it continued in the WWF, WCW, and well into retirement. The light-heartedness in their appearance on *Celebrity Wife Swap* was a testament to their enduring friendship. Flair traveled to Oregon and was a speaker at Piper's funeral.[55]

Ashley Fliehr's growth as a professional wrestler was extraordinary. She was a natural in many respects, much like her father had been, and was destined to be a world-class second-generation star. On September 20, 2015, Charlotte used her figure-four variation submission hold — called the Figure Eight — to force Nikki Bella to concede, and she won her first WWE Divas championship.[56] In interviews, Flair expressed his delight in her success, calling her victory for the Divas belt the proudest moment of his life.[57] The night following her win, on *Raw*, Charlotte and Flair shared a special moment in the ring, and the emotion was palpable.[58] Charlotte's meteoric rise coincided with a women's wrestling revolution in the WWE, and along with Becky Lynch, Sasha Banks, Natalya, and other talented athletes, the entire culture shifted from gimmick matches to incredible main event caliber spectacles.[59] The action was often more enjoyable than matches featuring their male counterparts.

Flair soon joined Charlotte as her second, interfering in matches to ensure she'd keep her title. Charlotte also used tricks from the Nature Boy's villainous playbook, adding another dimension to her already versatile repertoire. At WrestleMania on April 3 in Arlington, Texas, Flair's assistance played a big role in Charlotte's victory over Lynch and Banks, allowing her to become the inaugural WWE Women's champion. Flair was in her corner at Payback on May 1 in Chicago, and he found himself face to face with his old ring nemesis Bret Hart, who was supporting his niece Natalya. After a controversial finish, which saw referee Charles Robinson call for the bell just as Charlotte applied a sharpshooter —in a recreation of the 1997 "Montreal Screwjob" — Hart and Natalya placed that same hold on both Flair and Charlotte to gain a measure of vengeance. Later that month, in an angle on *Raw*, Charlotte publicly berated Flair and announced that she was going forward without him by her side.[60]

All things in pro wrestling eventually cycle back around, and Charlotte and Flair were apparently about to make up in November 2016 when she swerved the viewing audience and slapped her father.[61] It wasn't the reunion many people were hoping to see. Flair was honored by the WWE on March 30, 2017, at the Axxess event prior to WrestleMania 33 in Orlando. The promotion unveiled a bronze statue of Flair in a special ceremony attended by Flair, Wendy Barlow, his children, and other wrestling dignitaries, including Ricky Steamboat and the Rock and Roll Express. Triple H, who revealed the sculpture, told Flair, "Over the years you have gone from being my hero . . . my inspiration to one of my best friends. This is about one thing, and it's about the one thing you are about. And that one word is and always will be for you, respect."[62] For good reason, respect was very important to Flair, and he always appeared to respect the people who respected him.[63]

Those who spent time with Flair understood that alcohol was a big part of his life.[64] Flair liked to work hard and party hard, and he subscribed to the belief that the otherworldly effort he gave to wrestling allowed him to let down his hair and enjoy life.[65] His drinking was discussed in his 2004 autobiography, and allegations of "excess" use were mentioned in court documents.[66] In interviews, Flair never avoided talking about his penchant for the nightlife, and he was attracted to the social culture of high end bars around the world. Admittedly, he had several dark periods in which his drinking was heavier, particularly following the death of Reid.[67] "I drank myself to death for a year," he said. "10:00 in the morning to 2:00 at night. It's the only way I could get away from it."[68] Flair hadn't been acquainted with the word *moderation*, but despite the extreme prevalence of drugs around the business, he never went in that direction.[69]

He didn't need them, and lived the rock and roll lifestyle in his own inimitable fashion. For all the years he was the NWA champion and represented the Alliance on a global scale, he partook in the pleasures of being on the road, and he found a balance between being a party animal and a respectable professional. Across the millions of miles he traveled, the scores of late night establishments he frequented, and the claim that he had had encounters with 10,000 women, Flair never drew negative publicity or embarrassed the business. In fact, there were no stories of improprieties or scandals during his time as champion. Harley Race, who wasn't the kind of man to compliment someone unless they truly deserved it, called Flair a "class act," and the regard for Flair as a person was shared by individuals inside and outside of the business. Even with those he met at autograph signings, airports, or elsewhere in his travels, he attempted to put his best foot forward.

That being said, he was a human being. As a top athlete in a high-profile position, he was aware that eyes were constantly on him, and there was no way to please everyone.[70] All celebrities have to deal with that reality. In professional wrestling, the backstage competitiveness over money and political power made conflict common, and Flair saw his relationships with some wrestlers transform after he became a booker for WCW in 1989. Blame for booking decisions and changes were laid at his feet, regardless if he had made the final call or not. When he made an effort to protect his reputation and stature in the business, there was backlash, and there was a perception that he held younger wrestlers back by constantly being in the main event picture. But the truth was promoters needed him on top because, at times, he was the only wrestler bringing in ratings or selling tickets at the box office.[71] Nevertheless, the slanted opinion that he was purposely maneuvering and working to minimize his contemporaries perpetuated.[72]

As Flair got older, he had to take measures to safeguard his spot. In response, people forged and fostered opinions about his backstage dealings. But how he handled political issues was no different than how Hulk Hogan or Dusty Rhodes did when it came to negotiating for better contracts or creative power. An argument could be made that Flair was much more willing to play ball under adverse conditions, even when a booking wasn't favorable to him. His WCW stint between 1999 and 2001 proved that. With respect to the "10,000" women he'd been with, Flair actually said, "10,000, maybe."[73] The real number is obviously unknown, but his good looks, first-rate style, and fame made him a magnet for the opposite sex. He was hard to miss under any circumstances, and women who were wrestling fans had an idea of what to expect with the Nature Boy.[74]

It was no secret that Flair sought company on the road. As the NWA champion, he mostly traveled alone, and the schedule was often relentless. He told a reporter in 1982 that a regular traveling partner was enormously costly, upward of $8,000 a month for airfare.[75] But he did have companionship from time to time. For instance, around 1982–83, a former beauty contestant from the Pittsburgh area named Janice Mikelonis traveled with Flair to New Zealand.[76] Interestingly enough, an article appeared in the *Pittsburgh Press* on April 16, 1983, announcing the engagement of Mikelonis and Flair, saying a "July 23 wedding [was] planned."[77] However, Flair married Beth on August 27, 1983. Seven years earlier, reporter Robert Hodierne spoke with Flair about the abundance of women around pro wrestlers in the mid-Atlantic area. Over the years, sportswriters with behind-the-scenes access undoubtedly saw more than they revealed, as that side of wrestling culture remained off-limits for public consumption. But it wasn't uncommon for wrestlers to have relations with fans.

Newspaper journalists and writers across many different platforms tended to appreciate Ric Flair, especially those who got to know him. In Charlotte, he was accepted as a "cool" mainstream celebrity, and he was casually mentioned in columns and articles. He'd quickly disarm reporters with his politeness, and his low-key, engaging personality won people over.[78] He was open with interviewers, usually mixing reality with kayfabe to maintain wrestling's secrets. But he always made an effort to be frank about the success and hardships of the industry, going back to very early in his career. In 1978, he appeared on *Sportsline* on WSOC-AM in Charlotte and "talked quietly about the travel, the money, the injuries, and the insecurity" of pro grappling with host Phil Neuman.[79] Flair's stories and the way he presented himself during promos made it all the more real — and intense. The words might have been bunk to promote a storyline, but Flair made it genuine. And he could shift gears when it was necessary to increase the dramatic effect.

He was usually calm and collected off-camera. In 1984, a reporter in small-town North Carolina wanted him to demonstrate his "television talk." Flair hesitated for a moment and then asserted, "Every town and every person deserves a chance to stand face to face with sheer magnificence one time in their lives. It's my pleasure to provide that type of experience for the people of Marion tonight." He gave a wink to the journalist at the end.[80] Naturally, writers enjoyed putting their own spin on things for effect. Bob Wells of the *Greensboro Daily News* said Flair's "sequined cape" appeared to be a "Liberace hand me down."[81] Miami sportswriter Tom Archdeacon stated that Flair looked like a cross between "Liberace and Lonnie Anderson . . . and Broadway Joe [Namath]."[82] Noted columnist Dave Barry referenced Flair's extravagant pre-match robe and said it was "drag-queen style." He also felt Flair used "artificial forehead blood rather than razor blades."[83]

Mike Mooneyham and Tom Sorensen, two talented sportswriters, probably knew Flair the longest and penned articles about the Nature Boy for decades. Pittsburgh journalist and radio host Mark Madden, who acknowledged Flair as his hero growing up, was another well-spoken yet sometimes controversial figure with a longstanding friendship with Flair.[84] Wrestling pundit Bruce Mitchell, a longtime writer for the *Pro Wrestling Torch*, was a Flair expert, and his articles always made for interesting reading. Same went for historians Dick Bourne, David Chappell, and Richard O'Sullivan, each of whom were not only dedicated to studying Flair's life and history but sharing that information with the greater wresting community. With mention of Mark Madden, it's notable that his association with Flair hit the skids in a public manner in March 2022, following a several month stint as cohost of the *Wooooo! Nation Uncensored* podcast.[85] Other relationships over the course of Flair's life seemed to end in a similar manner due to business disagreements or personal reasons, and opinions about those situations, of course, vary.[86]

As mentioned, Flair avoided scandal when he was the perennial world champion in the 1980s and '90s. The darkest cloud, which, in the opinion of some, still casts a shadow over him, comes from the allegations surrounding the 2002 "Plane Ride from Hell." The situation made news at the time, but it didn't garner a wider exposure until *Dark Side of the Ring* featured the story in 2021. One of the flight attendants offered her version of what happened in the episode, and it was a revelation to many viewers. Flair denied that the incident occurred. From all reports, it's obvious that things on that flight were out of control, and there are forever going to be different accounts of what transpired.

There is another unavoidable topic that has to be addressed, and it is the subject of racism. In an interview with Kayfabe Commentaries, former referee, manager, and WWE Hall of Famer Teddy Long revealed that Flair used the N-word when talking to him.[87] Racism has long plagued wrestling, and the sport has had to overcome a lot of prejudice to get where it is today.[88] For decades, wrestling was rife with racial discrimination, and many old-school promoters of earlier generations portrayed characteristically biased and bigoted leaders of industry. It came naturally to them and didn't deter audiences; when promoting wrestlers of color, they used racial stereotypes to sell tickets. That toxicity permeated throughout the sport, and some wrestlers didn't even try to hide their heinous views. Flair admittedly heard racist language early in his career while traveling the circuit, and a few years later, he used words and phrases in mid-Atlantic promos that wouldn't stand up (rightly so) in today's world.[89] Cody Rhodes, in a podcast appearance, mentioned the shameful phraseology being used at the time, and Flair responded by saying, "Back then, you didn't think about it. Nobody was uncomfortable with it."[90] Flair's point proved that racism was deeply imbedded in wrestling culture.

All in all, Ric Flair — the wrestling character — was best known for being a heel. He was celebrated for his innuendo, his racy dialogue, and PG-13 promos. Never did he claim to be wrestling's number one role model or frame his persona as setting an example for youth.[91] His matches were technical and athletic, but he was not the poster child for sportsmanship. He cheated to win. Once the Four Horsemen came around, they relied on a gang mentality to abuse their foes. Outside the ring, Flair chased women and enjoyed the nightlife. His conduct earned an "adults only" rating at times, as he tried to garner laughs from the people around him.[92] It wasn't role model material in any shape or form. Regardless of how appropriate he was, Flair was just being Flair. His conduct wasn't always appreciated, and some of his contemporaries were not impressed by his antics. But Flair has meant different things to different people, and endless opinions of him have been expressed in interviews and print. He is probably the most critiqued and judged individual associated with wrestling today.

For decades, Flair lived the lifestyle he wanted to live, and his extreme conditioning and good health made it possible. But the toll on his body was incredible, and in August 2017, his life came to a crashing halt. A complicated medical emergency put him in intensive care with a 20 percent chance to live. The Nature Boy needed a miracle to survive — and he got it.

CHAPTER 23

THE LEGACY OF
THE NATURE BOY

There is no question about it. Fans, friends, and family members of the "Nature Boy" Ric Flair were scared. After word broke that the 68-year-old Flair was in critical condition in the ICU of an Atlanta-area hospital in August 2017, people took to social media to offer their heartfelt sentiments and prayers.[1] Longtime friend Michael Hayes rushed to the hospital to show his support, while many others in the wrestling world posted words of encouragement and love.[2] The fight of Flair's life began with terrible stomach pains from a blockage in his bowels and developed into the early stages of kidney failure and congestive heart failure. Flair later said, "I crashed in an airplane and broke my back [and] I've been hit by lightning. But this is totally different. Anything I've been through before is nothing like this."[3] His condition was touch and go, and doctors placed him in a medically induced coma to assist in his treatment. Following intestinal surgery and the insertion of a pacemaker, he was sent to a physical rehabilitation center to complete his recovery. The challenge was grueling, and despite all odds, Flair persevered.[4]

"Let it be known worldwide that Nature Boy, Wooooo!, is back up and running, looking as only I can look!" Flair declared a few weeks later. He thanked fans for their support, and his health was steadily improving.[5] Flair recognized how fortunate he was and credited his fiancée, Wendy Barlow, with helping him get through the ordeal. On October 26, 2017, Flair was back in the spotlight, walking the red carpet at the Atlanta screening for the new ESPN Films documentary, *Nature Boy*, about his life. The film, directed by Rory Karpf, premiered on ESPN on November 7, and more than 1.8 million viewers tuned in.[6] To people unfamiliar with Flair's story, the documentary was eye-opening, and Flair was completely honest about all aspects of his past. "Why lie about it?" he asked a radio host when discussing the film. "My life's an open book." Flair also admitted he was happy with the finished product.[7] He acknowledged that people were going to have different opinions on subjects, but that was okay since the footage was truthful.[8]

"I thought the documentary was excellent," Tom Sorensen said afterwards, admitting that some of it was tough to watch.[9] But it was accurate, and Flair's story is indeed a mixed bag of triumph and tragedy. Flair expressed a little disappointment in a few of his friends for their on-screen comments, as the truth was hard to hear.[10] The film was notable for the participation of Flair's first wife, Leslie, and Flair complimented her in his second book, *Second Nature*.[11] Although the documentary brought many sensitive topics to the forefront, and he was still recuperating from his health problems, Flair was getting tremendous media coverage. On October 31, on the studio album *Without Warning*, 21 Savage, Offset, and Metro Boomin released the rap song "Ric Flair Drip." It charted and was later released as a single, complete with a popular video featuring Flair himself.[12] As of 2022, the song had more than one billion streams on Spotify and better than 425 million views on YouTube.

Flair made his WWE homecoming during a Starrcade house show in Greensboro on November 25, 2017. He was honored by the 10,000 fans in attendance and gave an emotional speech to the crowd. He also celebrated with and embraced Charlotte, who defeated Natalya in a cage match.[13] The following January, Flair appeared at the 25th anniversary of *Raw* at the Manhattan Center in New York City alongside other legends, and he received another big ovation.[14] Unsurprisingly, as soon as he was feeling better, he was back to work and on the road.

On February 22, 2018, he walked the red carpet with superstar musician Bad Bunny at the Lo Nuestro Awards in Miami, and in March, he debuted the Ric Flair Collection, his own line of custom-made suits.[15] For a time, he even had an investment in a race horse.[16] That September, Ric and Wendy were united in a special commitment ceremony in Rosemary Beach, Florida, and a number of familiar faces were in attendance, including the Undertaker, Ricky Steamboat, Dolph Ziggler, and Dennis Rodman.[17]

For the 1,000th episode of *Smackdown* on October 16, 2018, Flair reunited with the members of Evolution, and he sang a song with Elias at Starrcade in Cincinnati on November 25. On February 25, 2019, he turned 70, and Barlow planned a surprise birthday party for him a few days earlier at the 1818 Club in suburban Atlanta.[18] The bash was attended by over 150 guests, and many well-known names were present to celebrate with the Nature Boy. NBA legend Charles Barkley and boxing hall of famer Evander Holyfield were two of the most prominent, and Flair was able to reconnect with many of his old friends.[19] On the evening of his actual birthday, he was at the State Farm Arena in Atlanta for *Raw*, where another birthday celebration was to take place. When Flair was supposed head down to the ring, the focus shifted to the backstage area and he was shown on the ground, having been beaten up by his former Evolution mate, Batista. Flair didn't physically work the angle, as the purported assault took place off-camera, but it advanced the storyline feud between Batista and Triple H.[20]

Their conflict ended at WrestleMania 35 in East Rutherford, New Jersey, and Flair helped Triple H score a victory by giving him a sledgehammer, which Triple H used prior to landing his Pedigree for the winning pin. Charlotte, along with Becky Lynch and Ronda Rousey, became the first women to be featured in the main event of WrestleMania later that night, and Lynch took home both the *Raw* and *Smackdown* championships. In May, Flair returned to the hospital and had another procedure on his heart.[21] He was released within a week's time, and he sent his thanks to hospital staff and fans over social media.[22] As a result of this medical issue, Flair had to cancel a scheduled appearance at Starrcast II, a wrestling convention held from May 23 to 26 in Las Vegas. The event was promoted by Flair's former podcast host Conrad Thompson, who by this point had become Flair's son-in-law. Thompson had married Flair's oldest daughter, Megan, on October 13, 2018.

A major *Raw* reunion occurred in Tampa on July 22, 2019, and Flair shared a stage with a Hall of Fame lineup of superstars. He was surrounded by the likes of Steve Austin, Hulk Hogan, Shawn Michaels, Triple H, Booker T, Mick Foley, and Kevin Nash. Stone Cold wrapped things up in the ring with beers and a series of toasts. Late in the summer, Flair began to take exception to the use of "The Man" in association with Becky Lynch, an in-ring rival of his daughter. He owned the trademark of "To Be the Man, You Gotta Beat the Man," and according to reports, he felt he should be compensated by the WWE.[23] Despite the ongoing dispute, Flair continued to appear on *Smackdown* and *Raw*.[24] A new angle was formulated, setting up a 10-man tag team match between "Team Flair" and "Team Hogan" for the Crown Jewel program in Riyadh, Saudi Arabia, on October 31. Flair's squad consisted of Randy Orton, Bobby Lashley, Shinsuke Nakamura, Drew McIntyre, and King Corbin, but they were defeated by Hogan's crew — a team comprised of Roman Reigns, Ali, Rusev, Ricochet, and Shorty G.

In May 2020, Flair signed a new contract with the WWE, and the quarrel over "The Man" was resolved.[25] He participated in a several-months-long storyline with Randy Orton before being "punted" by his former protégé on August 10 during *Raw*.[26] WWE champion Drew McIntyre gained retribution for Flair and the other legends Orton had attacked by downing him in an ambulance match on September 27 at the Clash of Champions event in Orlando. Once Orton was placed into the ambulance and McIntyre won the bout, Flair was shown driving the vehicle. After a few months' hiatus, Flair reemerged in January 2021 in Charlotte's corner, and a developing scenario saw Flair form a bond with Charlotte's ring rival Lacey Evans. The angle wasn't overly popular and, by the end of February, faded away completely.[27] Flair remained busy, performing in commercials and making appearances, and was always eager to offer his thoughts about the business in interviews.[28]

Regardless of his role, Flair was a dutiful employee of the WWE, and he enjoyed being around the youthful talent in the promotion.[29] Flair acknowledged how much the company had helped him, but he also was ready to concede that the two sides had a "different vision" as to his future. With that in mind, Flair requested his release, and on August 3, 2021, the WWE agreed.[30] In a subsequent Twitter post, Flair thanked the WWE, concluding with "Nothing but respect."[31] Several weeks earlier, he moved to Tampa from Atlanta, and he was spending considerable time training with Rob MacIntyre at Hard Nocks South, a private gym. He was also enjoying the weather, boating, and social atmosphere.[32] Unknown to the public at that time, Ric and Wendy were spending some time apart, and in January 2022, an announcement was made that they were going their separate ways.[33]

Wrestling was always on Ric Flair's mind. It was infused into his bones and flowed through his veins. He traveled with Andrade El Idolo, who was then engaged to Charlotte, to Mexico City for Triplemania on August 14, 2021, and he tried to help his future son-in-law in his bout with AAA Mega champion Kenny Omega to no avail. Omega prevailed, retaining his belt. A few weeks later, Flair made a special trip to one of his old haunts, the Chase Hotel in St. Louis, for the NWA's 73rd Anniversary Show, and he was on hand to salute the National Wrestling Alliance.[34] Appreciative of his role in NWA history and what he had given the organization, the fans at the venue honored him with a standing ovation and a number of collective chants, including "Thank you, Ric!" Flair was in his natural environment, speaking from the ring — and his heart — and told a number of stories about his time in St. Louis. One of his more famous tales was how Sam Muchnick would pay him $6,000 to main event at the Kiel, and by the end of the night, after partying at the Landing and in East St. Louis, he'd be lucky to have $1,200 left.

"I'm thanking every one of you fans," Flair told the crowd. "Thanking every wrestler — doesn't matter what company they're in — that remembers me, has treated me fairly, and has given me the respect that the NWA, WWE gave to me. Thank you!"[35] It was a remarkable moment for wrestling history, especially with Flair standing before a gigantic NWA backdrop in the ballroom. Flair exemplified the greatness of the National Wrestling Alliance during his years as champion, and in his global travels, he exceeded all expectations. In his speech to the NWA audience, he made another important comment that needs to be remembered: "Everybody knew how hard I worked." It was true. From his peers to the promoters to fans across the world, the entire wrestling industry and everyone connected to it understood how committed Ric Flair was to being the world champion and to being the best wrestler in the world.

Throughout this book, the fact that Flair lived his gimmick outside the ropes has been discussed. His wrestling image was first shaped in the 1970s, and he made it real by traveling first-class, by limousine or private plane. He purchased extravagant clothing and robes, had his hair perfectly styled, and walked the walk. Behind the microphone, he let his flamboyance explode, and, delivering night after night in the squared circle, he proved his championship caliber. Altogether, it was a remarkable, complete package. Once he left the arena, whether traveling alone as the NWA champion, with the Horsemen, or with a gaggle of other wrestlers, Flair was ready to explore the finer points of whatever city he was in. And his Flair persona came alive at local establishments, to be seen by whoever else was out that night. He'd party well into the night, jump up early the next morning to work out, and repeat the scenario all over again. To other people, even veteran wrestlers, his schedule was unnatural. But Flair thrived on it.

People today understand that the illusion created in professional wrestling wasn't actually an illusion at all when it came to Flair. But he knew when to tone back the outrageousness of his personality to fit the moment, and he was very respectful of people he found himself around in various public settings. It wasn't abnormal for him to call someone "sir," nor was it unusual for someone to be bowled over by his amiable demeanor. "Wrestling is like any sport," Flair explained to a reporter in

1987. "When I'm not competing, I don't carry that hostility I take into the ring. I don't bring my business into my personal life."[36]

He was lighthearted when signing autographs, and he once spent an hour in a three-piece pin-striped suit doing just that for Boy Scouts at the Fairgrounds near Charlotte.[37] Even when the recipient of an autograph wasn't sure who he was or why he was important, and essentially just asked for one because he looked famous, Flair was still easygoing and playful about it.[38]

Turner Broadcasting executive Steve Chamberlain became close friends with Flair following the purchase of Jim Crockett Promotions, and he was taken by his intelligence and talent. From time to time, Flair would pop into his office to chat, and their conversations helped Chamberlain gain a more thorough understanding of the wrestling business. In terms of marketing, Flair was a prize weapon in Turner's arsenal, and one year Chamberlain invited him to sit in the company's booth of at a Video Software Dealers Association convention in Las Vegas. Flair was more than happy to do so, and attendees were wowed by his presence. The line for his autograph grew to immense proportions, and Chamberlain said that he was "a real showstopper!"[39] To this day, Chamberlain cherishes his memories of Flair. Larry Matysik, after resigning from his position in the St. Louis office following difficulties with Bob Geigel in 1983, received an unexpected call at home from Flair, who offered his words of concern during a two-hour conversation. For that reason, "Ric Flair will always have my respect and gratitude," Matysik later wrote.[40]

Flair touched many people on a personal level, and sincerity was a big part of his inborn character. His former attorney Dennis Guthrie spent a lot of time with Flair under both business and personal circumstances, getting to know the entire Fliehr family. With respect to Flair, Guthrie said that, in private, he was "the most gentle, kind individual you'd ever have to meet." As an example of his thoughtfulness, when Guthrie's father was in the hospital, Flair went out of his way to visit him, and Guthrie never forgot his kind effort.[41] Another time, Flair surprised a 19-year-old woman who had been hospitalized after an industrial accident. Barbara

Ann Mullinax was enduring a long road to recovery, and Flair made a special trip to Spartanburg General Hospital to visit her. "Everybody thinks he's so mean and nasty because that's the way he is on television," said Marty Yesberg, Mullinax's cousin. "But I'll tell you, he is a super nice fellow. He did a lot to pick up Barbara's spirits."[42]

In Marion, North Carolina, Flair once received a message from a police officer shortly after arriving to the locker room. He hadn't even had a chance to unpack when he was asked to visit several boys from a home for handicapped children. Flair dropped everything and rushed to see them, giving each of the boys the thrill of a lifetime.[43] "It's a very nice feeling to walk in these places and be so well-received," Flair said. "The fans are really what makes professional wrestling what it is and I feel obligated to do everything I can for them."[44] At conventions and meet-and-greet events, Flair frequently went the extra mile to oblige the people who had come to see him. In 1991, he made a real imprint on many of wrestling's superfans at the Weekend of Champions in New York City.[45] As the headline attraction for a convention featuring Buddy Rogers, Lou Thesz, Bruno Sammartino, and many other greats, Flair couldn't have been more accommodating, and his one-on-one interactions with enthusiasts were tremendous for the sport.

Gary Portz, a talented second-generation wrestler from England, was another individual touched by Flair's kindness. His father, Geoff, had been a mentor to Flair in the AWA, and Flair repaid the favor by helping in Gary's development.[46] Portz was 10 years younger than Flair and just learning the rudiments of the professional landscape after years of amateur grappling. Many times, he worked out in Flair's garage gym in Charlotte, lifting weights, and soon Portz was chauffeuring Flair on the road in his Lincoln Continental. Incredibly generous and caring, Flair was like a big brother, and he eventually became Portz's real-life brother-in-law when Portz married the sister of Flair's then wife, Leslie.[47] They stayed close through the years, and during a television taping in Florida, Flair put over Portz (then wrestling as Scott McGhee) in the middle of the ring. Flair was the world champion at the time, and the victory was a huge boost to Portz's career.[48]

By either making guys look good in the ring or actually dropping a match to them, Flair helped many young wrestlers. Sting and Lex Luger were two notable examples. Others included Butch Reed, Barry Windham, Brad Armstrong, the Road Warriors, and each of the Von Erichs. He assisted wrestlers in other ways too — including by recruiting guys from the territories to Jim Crockett Promotions, usually giving them a nice increase in stature and pay.[49] In other situations, he gave advice to help wrestlers improve. Platinum-blond Buddy Landel was doing his version of the Nature Boy in JCP in 1985, and Flair was onboard with him using the gimmick. One time in Raleigh, Landel entered the building wearing casual beach-style clothing and flip-flops. Flair pulled him to the side and told him, "If you're going to be me, you got to be 'me'" and essentially told him that he'd never be caught dead walking around in public in that kind of attire. Flair was always impeccably dressed, often wearing suits to and from the arena.[50] If Landel was going to be taken seriously in the role, he had to do likewise.

Considering Flair's work ethic and commitment to the business, he earned great respect from his peers. A number of guys have publicly thanked him for his direct influence and help, and with that, he's earned a lot of loyalty.[51] In the ring, Flair was all about doing whatever was necessary to make the match and the moment special, and nine times out of 10, that meant making his opponent appear to be unstoppable, regardless of their talent. He'd control the emotion of the crowd by employing ring psychology, listening to what tactics and styles worked on any given night. Once he hooked the crowd, it was a roller-coaster ride of wrestling entertainment, and Flair ensured that he was the most talked about performer as fans went home. Even when he was defeated, these same statements rang true. In a smaller setting, such as the Chase Hotel in St. Louis or the WTBS studios in Atlanta, Flair's arrogance left its mark on fans. "Now we go to school!" he'd shout from the ring as he prepared for his figure-four, and the audience couldn't help but enjoy the master at work.

At different points in his career, Flair discussed his thoughts on retirement and when he believed he'd hang up his boots for good. In 1986, the 37-year-old told a Minneapolis reporter that he was sure he'd be done by his early 40s and settle into a backstage job with Crockett.[52] Flash forward 36 years, and Flair's love for the game still hadn't diminished. On July 31, 2022, he was set to lace up his boots for one final contest, and his loyal fans were thrilled by the news.[53] He was returning to Nashville, the site of many of his great ring battles, and the 73-year-old was determined to give fans a better match than his last, in 2011 in TNA. For months, he had been working out in the gym, building his strength and stamina. He was also back training in the ring to recondition his body to take light bumps, and brief footage of his sessions with Jay Lethal was posted on social media.[54] Flair brought up the possibility of his pacemaker being unplugged after taking a bump to the mat, but he was seemingly gaining more and more confidence that he was safe.[55]

With great anticipation among the nearly 7,000 fans in attendance, Flair teamed with Andrade El Idolo, his son-in-law, against Lethal and Jeff Jarrett for his last match in Nashville.[56] The 26-minute contest took its toll on Flair, and his exhaustion was clearly evident. He withstood the difficult physical challenge of the moment and prevailed with a pin of Jarrett at the finish.[57] Flair was the first person to admit that he was driven by the thrill of performing before an audience, and that, combined with the constant adulation he received, made it a special and unique historic moment for wrestling.[58] People wanted to honor him, get his autograph, and buy his merchandise. Others hoped for the chance to shake his hand and thank him in person for a lifetime of memories. With videos available on demand on websites like YouTube, footage of Flair's classic matches and promos are now only a few clicks away. The goldmine of off-the-cuff interviews, demonstrating how he went from zero to 60 in a split second and coolly transitioned between a raving wildman and wrestling's greatest playboy, proves that he was in a universe all his own.[59]

Between his two autobiographies and the *30 for 30* documentary, Flair has spoken about his personal life as honest as humanly possible. He has discussed his love for his children, the death of his son Reid, and his four marriages. No writer or pundit can elaborate on these topics any better than he did himself, and his word on these subjects is final. As a sidebar example of Flair's care for his family, during the late 1970s, he wrestled a particularly bloody match in Raleigh, and upon its conclusion, he looked as if he had just stepped off a battlefield. Blood was streaming down his face, and the accompanying sweat undoubtedly stung as it streamed into his forehead wound. Instead of treating his cut or stopping the steady flow, he went to the snack room of the venue to use the phone. Kevin Duffus, a director for WRAL-TV, inadvertently heard the conversation: Flair was talking to his daughter, telling her that he was going to return home soon to see her. It was a touching reminder that Flair was a loving father, and no amount of blood loss was going to stop him from doing what mattered most, and that was calling home to speak to his child.[60]

Before he died in June 1992, Buddy Rogers, the original Nature Boy, offered his opinion about Flair, telling Dr. Mike Lano, "I want everyone to know that Ric Flair is a hell of a worker, and a great guy. I would add Flair to my all-time top worker list of Thesz, Gagne, Valentine, Londos, Ed Lewis, Hodge, Kowalski, and guess who."[61] That was a distinguished list of legends, and Rogers wasn't alone in his admiration for Flair. Harley Race was exceedingly complimentary toward Flair, and Jack Brisco, another former NWA champion, stated, "If there was a man born to the [world heavyweight] title, a man for the times, it was Ric Flair."[62] Terry Funk said that Flair was pleasure to work with and acknowledged him as one of the best performers in the world.[63] Triple H, John Cena, the Rock, Steve Austin, and Hulk Hogan — the greatest names of the modern era — have each praised Flair. Austin, who was pegged as the second coming of Flair during his early WCW stint, called Flair his favorite wrestler of all time.[64]

The man who trained Flair, Verne Gagne watched as his protégé left the AWA and became a global sensation in the NWA. "I think Ric Flair made it bigger than I thought he would," Gagne later admitted. "He's done very, very well. I didn't think he would do that well."[65] Ric Flair's success in professional wrestling is overwhelming. Although the WWE recognizes him as a 16-time world champion, Flair is more accurately a 20-time title-holder. That accounts for nine NWA, eight WCW, two WWF, and one WCW International World titles.[66] He's been enshrined in seven major Halls of Fame, including the WWE twice. He was named "Wrestler of the Decade" for the 1980s by the *Wrestling Observer Newsletter*, and in 1999, he was among the leaders in the online voting for *Time*'s "Person of the Century."[67] To this day, he is honored and celebrated for his wrestling achievements, and it's universally accepted that there will never be anyone quite like the "Nature Boy" Ric Flair ever again.

Flair told a reporter that he had been lucky — that he came along at just the right time.[68] Perhaps that is a little true. But he did the rest of the work himself. With the tools he was given — and Flair credited God with giving him a natural gift — he maximized his success and became a star.[69] His athletic ability and the conditioning he worked so hard to achieve were invaluable assets, and combining his charisma, confidence, and articulation, Flair was the complete package. With his night-to-night consistency, performing great matches in defense of his world championship in cities big and small, he set a new bar for his successors. However, no one ever did succeed him or attempt to live up to his standards. He was the last traveling champion. The territories were eroding right before his eyes, and the next NWA champion had a different set of responsibilities. The maddening schedule for the touring titleholder ended, and the remarkable challenge, which the great champions of the past all endured, ended with the Nature Boy.[70]

In 1981, right around the time of his first World title win, he was asked what he owed the fans. "I owe 'em my homes, my cars, my clothes," he said. "I'm conscious of the fans and I'm conscious of their support. And I'm conscious of what they've made possible for me in my life."[71] He was determined to make people happy. Wrestling supporters who paid their hard-earned money for a ticket would always get a first-class effort when Flair was on the bill, and he never wavered. "I've got a job to do, whether there's 100 people or 20,000 people in the stands," he said.[72] The bond he had with the public was a two-way street, and he got as much out of the connection as the fans did. The hardest thing, though, was saying goodbye.[73] His final match in 2022 was a testament to his heart and wanting to go out on his own terms. No one was telling him how and when to do it.

"I have endured the test of time," Flair once declared.[74] Truer words were never spoken, and there were no goodbyes when it came to the Nature Boy. His legacy would live forever. In the meantime, Flair continued marching to his own beat, and his loyal fans were anxiously waiting to see what he had in store next.

NOTES

CHAPTER 1: A NATURAL CHAMPION

1   This information was estimated by the U.S. Children's Bureau. *Tampa Tribune*, Feb. 23, 1947, 13C.
2   *Vital Statistics of the United States, 1950, Volume I*, 93,cdc.gov.
3   Well-known Los Angeles civic leader Estelle Lawton Lindsey wrote that many of her friends obtained babies from the ill-reputed Tennessee Children's Home Society. *Hollywood Citizen-News*, Feb. 1, 1943, 4.
4   A major article on the "black market" appeared in the *St. Louis Post-Dispatch*, Feb. 4, 1945, G1.
5   *Nashville Banner*, Sep. 12, 1950, 1, *Spokesman Review*, Feb. 24, 1947, 14. Inflation calculator at bls.gov.
6   Tann was from Hickory in Newton County, MS. 1920 U.S. Federal Census. Ancestry.com. She attended Martha Washington College in VA. *Newton Record*, Sep. 12, 1912, 8.
7   *Los Angeles Times*, Dec. 21, 1948, C6.
8   *Nashville Tennessean*, Oct. 26, 1950, 7.
9   A series of six articles written by Nellie Kenyon offered great insight into Tann and her operations. *Nashville Tennessean*, Oct. 22–27, 1950.
10   *Knoxville News-Sentinel*, Dec. 22, 1948, 20.
11   Tann died on Sep. 15, 1950. Her reported age was 59. She had led the Tennessee Children's Home Society in Memphis for 26 years. *Greenwood Commonwealth*, Sep. 16, 1950, 1.
12   The Fliehrs' daughter was named Mary. She was born and died on May 29, 1946, at the U.S. Naval Hospital in Bremerton, WA. The Fliehrs were living in Port Orchard, while Richard was serving in the Navy. Washington State Department of Health Certificate of Death.
13   *To Be the Man* by Ric Flair with Keith Elliot Greenberg, 2004, 4.
14   According to Flair's autobiography, his birth mother was "Olive Phillips, Demaree, or Stewart." His birth father was "listed as Luther Phillips." He also wrote: "Olive Phillips and Luther Phillips did abandon and desert said child" on Mar. 12, 1949. He was "an abandoned, dependent and neglected child," to be placed "under the guardianship of the Tennessee Children's Home Society." *To Be the Man* by Ric Flair with Keith Elliot Greenberg, 2004, 5.
15   On Mar. 18, 1949, the infant was delivered to his adopted parents at 6439 Devereaux in Detroit. Ibid. Flair talked about his adoption in the Ric Flair Shoot Interview by Michael Bochicchio, highspots.com, 2008.

16   Fliehr became a commissioned officer in the U.S. Navy on Oct. 29, 1942, and achieved the rank of LTJG on Jun. 16, 1945. He was stationed in Bremerton, WA, and San Diego, CA, prior to his discharge. He graduated from medical school on Jan. 21, 1946. Correspondence with the Office of the Registrar, University of Minnesota, Apr. 19, 2021.

17   Charles B. Fliehr immigrated to the United States from Saxony around 1845. *Philadelphia Times*, Apr. 21, 1885, 2. He became a preacher in 1863 and served in that capacity until his death. *Allentown Democrat*, Dec. 30, 1915, 7.

18   *Allentown Morning Call*, Apr. 10, 1925, 5.

19   *Allentown Morning Call*, Sept. 17, 1926, p. 17. Solomon's grocery was at 348 Kaighn Ave., less than a mile from the childhood home of "Nature Boy" Buddy Rogers.

20   *Camden Courier-Post*, Jan. 16, 1909, 7.

21   Fliehr was employed by the Virginia and Rainy Lake Company as early as 1909. *Virginia Enterprise*, Dec. 24, 1909, 1.

22   *Duluth Herald*, Oct. 9, 1914, 23.

23   *Duluth Herald*, Jan. 3, 1913, 17.

24   Virginia Senior High School Yearbook, 1927, 69. Harvey Robert Fliehr was born on Oct. 6, 1898, in Camden, while Irma Elizabeth was born on Aug. 6, 1903, in Schenectady, NY.

25   Harvey died after a hunting accident on Nov. 22, 1926. An obit appeared in the Virginia Senior High School Yearbook, 1927, 69.

26   Fliehr and Regan married on Sep. 12, 1925, in St. Louis County, MN. Ancestry.com. Also see *St. Cloud Times*, Aug. 27, 1929, 2.

27   Notably, Alexander Reid Jr. attended Richard Reid Fliehr's wedding in 1941. *Brainerd Daily Dispatch*, Jun. 23, 1941, 5.

28   Richard received acclaim for his portrayal of George Bailey in the "ambitious" presentation of *No More Frontier* in early 1938. *Minneapolis Star*, Feb. 2, 1938, 2.

29   *Brainerd Daily Dispatch*, Jun. 23, 1927, 7.

30   Kinsmiller also served as the superintendent for the foundry. *Brainerd Daily Dispatch*, Jan. 31, 1940, 1.

31   *Brainerd Daily Dispatch*, Jun. 12, 1939, 2.

32   *Brainerd Daily Dispatch*, Mar. 23, 1940, 2.

33   *Brainerd Daily Dispatch*, Jun. 17, 1940, 5.

34   Fliehr graduated on Jun. 14, 1941. Correspondence with the University of Minnesota Office of the Registrar dated Apr. 19, 2021. *Brainerd Daily Dispatch*, Jun. 23, 1941, 5.

35   U.S. Select Military Registers, 1862–1985, Ancestry.com.

36   Correspondence with the University of Minnesota Office of the Registrar dated Apr. 19, 2021.

37   It is unknown when the Fliehrs returned to the Minneapolis area. They were living at 3925 Colorado, according to the 1951 St. Louis Park City Directory. Hennepin County Library Digital Collection, 34.

38   The population grew from 7,737 in 1940 to 22,644 in 1950. "St. Louis Park: A Story of a Village" by Norman Thomas, 1952, slphistory.org/normanthomas.

39   *Minneapolis Star*, Jan. 4, 1956, 4A.

40   *Minneapolis Sunday Tribune*, May 2, 1954, 27.

41   *Minneapolis Sunday Tribune*, Jul. 23, 1961, 9A.

42   *Minneapolis Star*, Jun. 19, 1967, 3A.

43   The Fliehrs moved to a home at 100 Parkview Terrace in Golden Valley.

44   *Minneapolis Star Tribune*, Feb. 16, 1958, 27.

45   According to his autobiography, Flair attended Golden Valley Elementary and Golden Valley Junior High School. *To Be the Man* by Ric Flair with Keith Elliot Greenberg, 2004, 6. Information is unclear. It is believed that his address was in the Meadowbrook Elementary School District.

46   *Raleigh News and Observer*, Jan. 27, 1991, E1, E7.

47   Interview of Ric Flair, *Wrestling Inc.* Podcast, Feb. 24, 2021. *To Be the Man* by Ric Flair with Keith Elliot Greenberg, 2004, 6.

48   He was a member of the Boy Scouts until the ninth grade. *Charlotte Observer*, Nov. 11, 1979, 5D.

49   *To Be the Man* by Ric Flair with Keith Elliot Greenberg, 2004, 9.

50   These incidents were documented in his autobiography. *To Be the Man* by Ric Flair with Keith Elliot Greenberg, 2004, p. 7-8. Flair also talked about these events in the Ric Flair Shoot Interview by Michael Bochicchio, highspots.com, 2008.

51   Fliehr was not pictured in the team photo. *The Viking*, Golden Valley High School Yearbook, 1961–62, pg. 120. Fliehr was also a member of the "Junior Band." Ibid, 43. It's not known what instrument he played.

52   *The Viking*, Golden Valley High School Yearbook, 1962–63, 120.

53   Golden Valley shared the championship with Orono High School, which also went 7–1. Golden Valley outscored opponents 136 to 41 during the season. *Golden Valley Press*, Nov. 12, 1964, 12. For a team photo with Fliehr included, see *Minneapolis Star*, Sep. 4, 1964, 11B.

54   *Golden Valley Press*, Apr. 29, 1965, 3.

55   Flair later said that his parents were considering sending him to "Glen Lake," which may have been the Glen Lake Home School for Boys in Minnetonka, a school for troubled youths. *Wooooo! Nation* Podcast Episode #4. Based on all known information, it appears that Fliehr transferred to Wayland sometime between Nov. 1964 and Mar. 1965. Fliehr was not listed in the 1964–65 yearbook. However, a student named "Flair," wearing number 31, appears in a J.V. basketball team photo. *Pillars*, Wayland Academy Yearbook, 1964–65, 97. He played basketball for Wayland as a sophomore, as confirmed by his senior yearbook.. *Pillars*, Wayland Academy Yearbook, 1967–68, 27. It's likely that he enrolled after most yearbook photos were taken.

56   *Greensboro Daily News*, May 18, 1980, F1.

57   In his autobiography, he admitted: "It took me five years to graduate from high school." *To Be the Man* by Ric Flair with Keith Elliot Greenberg, 2004, 10. He said that he was on the "13-year plan" in high school. *Wooooo! Nation* Podcast Episode #5.

58   Fliehr was listed as a junior in 1965–66, making him part of the Class of 1967. *Pillars*, Wayland Academy Yearbook, 1965–66, 34. Fliehr was listed as a junior in 1966–67 as well, making him now part of the Class of 1968. *Pillars*, Wayland Academy Yearbook, 1966–67, 175.

59   *Greensboro Daily News*, May 18, 1980, F3.

60   Correspondence with Peter Radford, Oct. 7, 2020.

61   *Pillars*, Wayland Academy Yearbook, 1966–67, 76.

62   *Milwaukee Journal*, Nov. 5, 1966, 17.

63   Fliehr won the championship at 183 pounds. *Beaver Dam Daily Citizen*, Feb. 20, 1967, 4. Also *Pillars*, Wayland Academy Yearbook, 1966–67, 92–93.

64   *Beaver Dam Daily Citizen*, Jan. 9, 1967, 4.

65   *Pillars*, Wayland Academy Yearbook, 1967–68, 90.

66   *Fond du Lac Commonwealth Reporter*, May 15, 1968, 19.

67   Flair called MacArthur his "roommate" at Wayland. *Ric Flair WCW Satellite Footage from 1993 vs. Rick Rude*, youtube.com. In both of his books, as well as in interviews, Flair has discussed hitchhiking to Florida to enjoy spring break with MacArthur. *To Be the Man* by Ric Flair with Keith Elliot Greenberg, 2004, 9, *Second Nature: The Legacy of Ric Flair and the Rise of Charlotte* by Ric Flair & Charlotte with Brian Shields, 2017, 70–71.

68   MacArthur was named as having "Most School Spirit." in the *Pillars*, Wayland Academy Yearbook, 1965–66, 111.

69   *Pillars*, Wayland Academy Yearbook, 1967–68, 27, 77–78.

70   *Beaver Dam Daily Citizen*, Jan. 20, 2000, 4.

71 Ibid.

72 *Greensboro Daily News*, May 18, 1980, F3.

73 In his book, Flair called him, "Jim Fierke." *To Be the Man* by Ric Flair with Keith Elliot Greenberg, 2004, 10.

74 Flair talked about this entire situation in his University of Michigan, Signing of the Stars appearance on Feb. 3, 2016.

75 *Whitewater Register*, Jun. 13, 1968, 8.

76 Correspondence with Jack Dean, Oct. 1, 2020.

77 The Fliehrs moved to 6409 Colony Way in Edina around 1965.

78 The review was written by Whitney Bolton. *Fort Myers News-Press*, Jul. 19, 1968, 4.

79 A group photo of Minnesota Theater Company personnel appeared in the *Minneapolis Tribune*, May 5, 1963, 3.

80 For example, Fliehr appeared on KTCA-TV in Mar. 1960. *Minneapolis Morning Tribune*, Mar. 16, 1960, 35. He also appeared on WLOL (1330) in Oct. 1968. *Minneapolis Star*, Oct. 15, 1968, 21B.

81 *Minneapolis Star*, May 17, 1968, 18A.

82 Fliehr was granted his master's degree in theater arts on Mar. 18, 1972. Correspondence with Office of the Registrar, University of Minnesota, Apr. 19, 2021.

83 Flair claimed that he was "good enough to get a football scholarship at the University of Minnesota." *Greensboro Daily News*, Nov. 2, 1976, B4.

84 The Big Ten rule was established in Dec. 1961. *Minneapolis Star*, Dec. 8, 1961, 2D. Fliehr was designated a "non-predictor." Interview of Ric Flair, *Steve Austin Podcast*, 2013.

85 A photo of Fliehr in a football uniform, presumably taken while at Minnesota, appeared in his *30 for 30* ESPN documentary. He wore number 32. It should also be noted that he wore number 44 at Wayland Academy. *Pillars*, Wayland Academy Yearbook, 1967–68, 90. Flair was a physical education major. *Leslie Goodman Fliehr v. Richard Morgan Fliehr, alias Ric Flair*, Mecklenburg County General Court of Justice, District Court Division, Case No. 79-CVD-5549.

86 Correspondence with Doug Kingsriter, May 2021.

87 *University of Minnesota Sports News*, Oct. 22, 1968, 4.

88 *Wooooo! Nation* Podcast Episode #28.

89 Flair said he went to summer school for "two days." *30 for 30* Documentary, ESPN Films, 2017.

90 *Charlotte Observer*, Apr. 24, 1987, 4B. *To Be the Man* by Ric Flair with Keith Elliot Greenberg, 2004, 66.

91 Fliehr's address was confirmed in the *University of Minnesota Student Directory*, 1968–69, 74.

92 Correspondence with Don Ewers, Apr. 15, 2021.

93 Correspondence with Office of the Registrar, University of Minnesota, May 13, 2021.

94 *Miami News*, Mar. 13, 1986, 6B.

95 *Minneapolis Star*, Jan. 13, 1971, 19D.

96 The Guardian Life Insurance Company was at 4900 Viking Drive in Edina, MN. Flair received six months' training. *Leslie Goodman Fliehr v. Richard Morgan Fliehr, alias Ric Flair*, Mecklenburg County General Court of Justice, District Court Division, Case No. 79-CVD-5549.

97 Flair made $500 a month. Ibid. Flair said he made $30,000 in his first year. *To Be the Man* by Ric Flair with Keith Elliot Greenberg, 2004, 13.

98 He remained in that job for 18 months. *Leslie Goodman Fliehr v. Richard Morgan Fliehr, alias Ric Flair*, Mecklenburg County General Court of Justice, District Court Division, Case No. 79-CVD-5549. Flair talked about his time selling insurance during the Ric Flair Shoot Interview by Michael Bochicchio, highspots.com, 2008.

99 *Charlotte Observer*, Apr. 24, 1987, 4B.

100 Interview with Ric Flair, *Valuetainment Podcast with Patrick Bet-David*, Apr. 5, 2018.

101 Flair wrote that his father was a deacon at this particular church. *To Be the Man* by Ric Flair with Keith Elliot Greenberg, 2004, 22.

102 A picture of the couple appeared in the newspaper as well. *Minneapolis Tribune*, Sep. 12, 1971, 19E. Light was a lifelong friend. Following Light's passing in 2016, Flair offered his condolences in a social media post, stating that he appreciated "all the years of fun together," and that they were some of his "most cherished memories." Ric Flair, the Nature Boy, Facebook Post, Apr. 29, 2016.

103 Correspondence with Office of the Registrar, University of Minnesota, Apr. 19, 2021. Flair later said he considered becoming a dentist. *30 for 30* Documentary, ESPN Films, 2017.

104 *Minneapolis Star*, Apr. 4, 1968, 61.

CHAPTER 2: FROM FLIEHR TO FLAIR

1 University of Minnesota Athletics website, gophersports.com.

2 Ordemann was a two-time claimant to the American heavyweight championship.

3 "Scissors" Joe Stecher was a three-time world heavyweight champion between 1915 and 1928.

4 *Minneapolis Tribune*, Jul. 2, 1937, 26.

5 Gagne was born in the vicinity of Hamel and Corcoran, two small villages northwest of Minneapolis. Various documents and databases list his birth as having taken place in one of these two locations.

6 Mrs. Elsie Gagne passed away on Jan. 29, 1938. *Minneapolis Tribune*, Jan. 30, 1938, M8.

7 *Minneapolis Tribune*, Feb. 20, 1944, S2.

8 He won Big Nine championships in 1947–49, NCAA titles in 1948–49, and an AAU title in 1949. The Big Nine was formerly known as the Big Ten, but changed its name after the University of Chicago left the conference in 1946.

9 *Minneapolis Morning Tribune*, May 4, 1949, 25.

10 Problems between Fred Kohler of Chicago, who was Gagne's primary promotional supporter, NWA President Sam Muchnick, and Lou Thesz were responsible for the political chaos.

11 Tony Stecher died on Oct. 10, 1954, at age 65. *Minneapolis Star*, Oct. 11, 1954, 28.

12 The states included MN, ND, SD, NE, and WI, plus sections of IL, IA, and CO. Gagne also promoted in Winnipeg, MB.

13 Flair talked about his early interest in wrestling. *Down Home with the Carolina Camera* with C.J. Underwood, WBTV-3, 1981. *Second Nature: The Legacy of Ric Flair and the Rise of Charlotte* by Ric Flair & Charlotte with Brian Shields, 2017, 4.

14 *To Be the Man* by Ric Flair with Keith Elliot Greenberg, 2004, 6.

15 Interview of Ric Flair, *Wrestling Observer*, 1999.

16 *To Be the Man* by Ric Flair with Keith Elliot Greenberg, 2004, 9.

17 The play was entitled *As You Like It*, and it was directed by Edward Payson Call. *Minneapolis Star*, Apr. 14, 1966, 1.

18 *In Search of an Audience: How an Audience was Found for the Tyrone Guthrie Theatre* by Bradley G. Morison and Kay Fliehr, 1968, 76.

19 *Greeley Tribune*, Jun. 14, 1969, 13.

20 *Minneapolis Star*, Aug. 9, 1971, 26.

21 Patera's older brother, Jack, was an assistant coach for the Minnesota Vikings. *Minneapolis Star*, Aug. 11, 1971, 2D.

22 Patera set a record of 505 pounds for the clean and press. *Oakland Tribune*, Jul. 24, 1972, 48.

23 *To Be the Man* by Ric Flair with Keith Elliot Greenberg, 2004, 13–14. Flair also talked about meeting Patera. *Wooooo! Nation* Podcast Episode #5. The restaurant was at 4700 Excelsior Blvd. It was known for its "Swinging Private Rooms" and George's famous filet mignon. Musical performers at the establishment included Joey Strobel and the Runaways.

24 Patera attended Rick's wedding to Leslie. *Minneapolis Tribune*, Sep. 12, 1971, 19E.

25 They also had two other roommates. Interview of Ken Patera, *Hannibal TV* Podcast, Oct. 18, 2020.

26 *To Be the Man* by Ric Flair with Keith Elliot Greenberg, 2004, 15.

27 A fan of weightlifting, Fliehr began to take the sport more seriously and hoped to be as strong as Patera. He bought all the weightlifting magazines. Ric Flair Shoot Interview by Michael Bochicchio, highspots.com, 2008.

28 Interview of Ric Flair, *Wrestling Inc.* Podcast, Feb. 24, 2021.

29 *Wooooo! Nation* Podcast Episode #28.

30 *Minneapolis Star*, Sep. 7, 1972, 2D.

31 *Chicago Daily News*, Sep. 2–3, 1972, 23.

32 *Daily Oklahoman*, Jun. 14, 1971, 23. Also see *Minneapolis Star*, May 20, 1972, 15A.

33 Interview of Ken Patera by Alex Marvez. Scripps Howard News Service, Dec. 23, 2010.

34 Gagne interviewed him for about an hour. Ric Flair Shoot Interview by Michael Bochicchio, highspots.com, 2008. Also see *To Be the Man* by Ric Flair with Keith Elliot Greenberg, 2004, 16. Flair later said that Gagne's "admission standards" were harder than the University of Minnesota and that he had to "wait to get in." *Charlotte Observer*, Apr. 24, 1987, 4B.

35 Ibid., *To Be the Man* by Ric Flair with Keith Elliot Greenberg, 2004, 22.

36 *Raleigh News and Observer*, Jan. 27, 1991, 7E.

37 Ric Flair Shoot Interview by Michael Bochicchio, highspots.com, 2008. Also *To Be the Man* by Ric Flair with Keith Elliot Greenberg, 2004, 17.

38 Interview of Ric Flair, *Wrestling Inc.* Podcast, Feb. 24, 2021.

39 Fliehr said he wanted to quit three additional times. *30 for 30* Documentary, ESPN Films, 2017. In a separate interview, Fliehr said he quit three times. *Wooooo! Nation* Podcast Episode #1. There are different variations of the stories about Rick quitting Gagne's camp. See Interview of Greg Gagne with Judd Zulgad, 1500 ESPN, 2017.

40 Photos from the training camp appeared in the *Minneapolis Tribune*, Picture Section, Mar. 25, 1973, 14–19.

41 Jim Brunzell described the training under Robinson. Interview of Jim Brunzell, *Two Man Power Trip of Wrestling* Podcast, Aug. 7. Robinson talked about the training. Interview of Billy Robinson by Mike Johnson, *PWInsider*, Mar. 4, 2014. Additional sources about the camp include *Minneapolis Tribune*, Nov. 12, 1972, 1C, 5C. *Mpls. St. Paul Magazine*, Oct. 26, 2018.

42 Greg Gagne discussed this topic at length. Interview of Greg Gagne by James Guttman, *World Wrestling Insanity*, Feb. 15, 2010.

43 Weather conditions were checked in the *Minneapolis Star*, Oct. 11 to Nov. 28, 1972.

44 Interview of Billy Robinson by Mike Johnson, PWInsider.com, 2009.

45 *To Be the Man* by Ric Flair with Keith Elliot Greenberg, 2004, 15–16.

46 Greg Gagne estimated that Fliehr dropped 40 pounds, going from 298 to 258. Interview of Greg Gagne by James Guttman, *World Wrestling Insanity*.

47 *To Be the Man* by Ric Flair with Keith Elliot Greenberg, 2004, 19–20.

48 It was said that Patera trained for "10 weeks," and that he had "30 practice matches." *Minneapolis Tribune*, Dec. 10, 1972, 3C. If this report is accurate, it's likely that Flair engaged in a similar number of practice bouts before his actual debut.

49 *Sioux Falls Argus-Leader*, Dec. 6, 1972, 18.

50 An attempt to locate an article about the Patera-Gadaski match in Willmar, MN, was unsuccessful. Correspondence with Willmar Public Library, Mar. 19, 2021.

51 Interview of Ken Patera, *Two Man Power Trip of Wrestling* Podcast, Nov. 2, 2018.

52 *Minneapolis Tribune*, Dec. 10, 1972, 3C. Patera, "in his debut" beat Goulet in 7:09. *Minneapolis Tribune*, Dec. 11, 1972, 7C.

53 *To Be the Man* by Ric Flair with Keith Elliot Greenberg, 2004, 22.

54 Scott pinned Gadaski in 12:22. *Minneapolis Tribune*, Dec. 11, 1972, 7C.

55   *Rice Lake Chronotype*, Dec. 13, 1972, 9–10.

56   The photo caption read, "Patera tosses foe in pro mat debut." *Rice Lake Chronotype*, Dec. 13, 1972, 9–10.

57   There is a remote possibility that a show was actually held in the vicinity of Rice Lake, Minnesota, which was north of Duluth. A search of the Duluth newspaper came up empty. Correspondence with Duluth Public Library, Sep. 3, 2021.

58   *The Ring's Wrestling*, Aug. 1982, 17.

59   *Ric Flair Fan Club Newsletter*, #11, 15.

60   Goulet recalled Flair when he broke into the business, and confirmed he wrestled him in one of his first pro matches. *Rene Goulet Shoot Interview*, RF Video.

61   *Fargo Forum*, Dec. 10, 1972, D8.

62   It should be noted that Californian Ric Drasin worked the AWA territory for a few months early in 1972 and reportedly influenced the way Gagne spelled Flair's first name.

63   *Minneapolis Tribune*, Jan. 1, 1973, 3C.

64   *The Ring's Wrestling*, Aug. 1982, 17. Since it's not known if Flair wrestled Gadaski prior to Dec. 30, this may have been the match often remembered as his pro debut — despite at least a half dozen matches earlier in the month. It's believed that his parents were in attendance for this show.

65   *Dusty Rhodes Shoot Interview*, RF Video, circa 2000.

66   *Minneapolis Star*, Apr. 5, 1973, 1C.

67   Flair discussed the tricks Rhodes and Murdoch would play. *Wooooo! Nation* Podcast Episode #4. Also *To Be the Man* by Ric Flair with Keith Elliot Greenberg, 2004, p. 24-25.

68   Flair reportedly lost to Johnny Fargo on Jun. 13 in San Antonio. He then teamed with Rick Hunter against Rhodes and Murdoch on Jun. 14 in Corpus Christi. *Corpus Christi Times*, Jun. 14, 1973, 8G. Rhodes and Mulligan were co-owners of the Head-Lock Ranch and specialized in registered Red Angus cattle. A famous photo of Flair, Rhodes, Murdoch, Ray Stevens, and a young Dustin Rhodes was taken on this trip and published in Blackjack Mulligan's autobiography.

69   *To Be the Man* by Ric Flair with Keith Elliot Greenberg, 2004, 25–26.

70   Flair discussed his thoughts on Rhodes. *Wooooo! Nation* Podcast Episodes #7, #8.

71   Interview of Blackjack Mulligan by Mike Johnson, PWInsider.com.

72   In his autobiography, Flair stated that he asked Gagne if he could be "Ricky Rhodes" prior to his pro debut. *To Be the Man* by Ric Flair with Keith Elliot Greenberg, 2004, 20. Rhodes was told about the name idea on a trip to Bismarck, SD. *Dusty Rhodes Shoot Interview*, RF Video, circa 2000.

73   Ibid.

CHAPTER 3: ON THE RISE

1   The median household income in the U.S. in 1970 was $9,870. Emmett F. Spiers, John F. Coder, and Robert W. Cleveland, *Income in 1970 of Families and Persons in the United States*, Oct. 4, 1971, census.gov/library/publications/1971/demo/p60-80.html.

2   The "Golden Greek" Jim Londos is believed to be one of the first wrestlers to become a millionaire.

3   *New York Daily News*, Dec. 6, 1932, 46.

4   *David Crockett Shoot Interview*, RF Video.

5   *Minneapolis Tribune*, Jan. 8, 1973, 2C. Since records are incomplete, it's unknown if this was Flair's first ever wrestling win.

6   Correspondence with George Schire, Apr. 5, 2021.

7   These matches occurred between Apr. 14, 1973, and Jun. 9, 1973.

8   André was often advertised as standing 7-foot-4. *Minneapolis Star*, Jan. 12, 1972, 4D.

9   Interview of Ric Flair, *Wrestling Inc.* Podcast, Feb. 24, 2021.

10   Also on the tour were Buddy Wolff and Skandor Akbar. Interview of Skandor Akbar by Mike Johnson, PWInsider.com, Aug. 2009. Flair talked about carrying Rhodes's and Murdoch's bags on this trip. *The Ric Flair Show* Podcast Episode #1.

11   *Wooooo! Nation* Podcast Episode #3 and *To Be the Man* by Ric Flair with Keith Elliot Greenberg, 2004, 25.

12   *Green Bay Press-Gazette*, Oct. 15, 1973, B2. Tony Rocca was a journeyman wrestler whose career lasted from at least 1963 to 1988, and he shouldn't be confused with "Argentina" Antonino Rocca.

13   That night, Flair was defeated by Sonny King. *Fort Worth Star-Telegram*, Oct. 16, 1973, 2C. Also on the card was Ali Vaziri (Khosrow Vaziri), a fellow graduate from Verne Gagne's training camp. Vaziri had been in the Dallas territory since early Sep. 1973.

14   Flair lost to Dale Lewis in both Dallas and San Antonio. *Dallas Morning News*, Oct. 17, 1973, 3B, *San Antonio Light*, Oct. 18, 1973, 2G. The Corpus Christi newspaper listed Flair as "Rick Flare" for a bout with Blackjack Mulligan. *Corpus Christi Times*, Oct. 18, 1973, 4E. No results were located for Flair's bout with Mulligan. Mulligan talked about traveling with Flair and McDaniel to Houston. Interview of Blackjack Mulligan by Mike Johnson, PWInsider.

15   *Des Moines Register*, Sep. 1, 1972, 1.

16   It was reported that the contract was worth more than $400,000. *Minneapolis Star*, Nov. 8, 1973, 1D.

17   Among the others in Gagne's Class of 1973 training camp were Buddy Rose and Sgt. Slaughter.

18   Tom Tomashek wrote an article about the Flair-Taylor bout. He said that one of Flair's tactics drew blood from Taylor's nose. Their match lasted 7:10. *Chicago Tribune*, Dec. 18, 1973, C3.

19   The Flair-Taylor match was televised in Chicago on Jan. 25, 1974, on channel 44. *Chicago Daily News*, Jan. 19–20, 1974, TV Section, 21.

20   *Superstar Billy Graham: Tangled Ropes* by Billy Graham with Keith Elliot Greenberg, 2006, 151–154.

21   Ed Garea, in *Wrestling Eye* magazine, wrote: "[Flair] also seemed destined for the preliminary ranks as long as he stayed in the AWA." *Wrestling Eye*, Aug. 1987, 18.

22   Ancestry.com.

23   *Minneapolis Star*, Jan. 16, 1974, 9D. They lived in the complex of Colonial Village, which was reportedly built in 1972. *Minneapolis Star-Tribune*, Jun. 24, 2016, D6.

24   Flair said he was making approximately $120 a week. *To Be the Man* by Ric Flair with Keith Elliot Greenberg, 2004, 33.

25   Bruggers ventured to the Charlotte territory in early Nov. 1973.

26   *Wooo! The Ric Flair Record Book* by Steve Helwagen, 1996, 118.

27   *Charlotte Observer*, Apr. 2, 1973, C1.

28   David Crockett talked about the diversity and success of his father's business. *David Crockett Shoot Interview*, RF Video.

29   Ringley married Frances Crockett in 1959. *Charlotte News*, Aug. 25, 1959, 3B. It's notable that Ringley attended the same high school (Virginia High School in Bristol, VA) as Crockett Sr. Also *Jim Crockett Promotions: The Good Old Days* Documentary, 2013.

30   *David Crockett Shoot Interview*, RF Video, *Jim Crockett Promotions: The Good Old Days* Documentary, 2013. It's not exactly clear when Ringley was ushered aside. He was still president of the company as of Aug. 1974. *Charlotte Observer*, Aug. 7, 1974, B1. His divorce from Frances Crockett was final as of Nov. 10, 1975. Ancestry.com.

31   Scott was from Dalmeny, Scotland, near Edinburgh.

32 Scott had gained experience as a booker for Stu Hart in Calgary. *The Psychology of Scott: Shoot Interview with George Scott*, 2010.

33 Scott worked in mid-card and preliminary matches for the AWA between Sep. 1972 and Jul. 1973. An unconfirmed report claimed that Scott actually wrestled Flair on Jun. 9, 1973, in Chicago.

34 Gagne expected to be paid a 10 percent commission on all of Flair's bookings when he wrestled for non-AWA offices for at least five years. *Wooooo! Nation* Podcast Episode #7, .This was also talked about during the *Gene Okerlund Shoot Interview*, RF Video. Also see *To Be the Man* by Ric Flair with Keith Elliot Greenberg, 2004, 33–34. Later, Flair and Gagne agreed that Flair would give him a flat amount of $2,500 as opposed to 10 percent of his bookings. *To Be the Man* by Ric Flair with Keith Elliot Greenberg, 2004, 33-34.

35 *Greensboro Daily News*, Nov. 2, 1976, B4.

36 Ric Flair Shoot Interview by Michael Bochicchio, highspots.com, 2008. Additional sources include: *Wooooo! Nation* Podcast Episode #7, Interview of Ric Flair, *Wrestling Inc.* Podcast, Feb. 24, 2021, and *To Be the Man* by Ric Flair with Keith Elliot Greenberg, 2004, 34.

37 *Down Home with the Carolina Camera* with C.J. Underwood, WBTV-3, 1981. *Superstar Billy Graham: Tangled Ropes* by Billy Graham with Keith Elliot Greenberg, 2006, 131.

38 Flair had wanted to use the Dusty elbow as early as the end of training camp with Gagne. *To Be the Man* by Ric Flair with Keith Elliot Greenberg, 2004, 19–20.

39 In total, they won the championship five times. "American Wrestling Association World Tag Team Title," last updated Sep. 1, 2020, wrestling-titles.com/awa/awa-t.html.

40 David Crockett recalled meeting Flair on Apr. 4, 1974. *Wooooo! Nation* Podcast Episode #7. That was over a month before Flair's local wrestling debut. It's possible that Flair went to Charlotte for an initial meeting, and then returned to the Twin Cities prior to relocating to North Carolina permanently.

41 Ibid.

42 It was $9 a night to stay at the motel. Ric Flair Shoot Interview by Michael Bochicchio, highspots.com, 2008. The Orvin Court (also called the Orvin Inn) was at 307 N. Graham St. in Charlotte.

43 *Charlotte Observer*, May 14, 1974, 6B.

44 *Greensboro Daily News*, May 17, 1974, B7. An advertisement for this show listed Flair as "Ricky Flair." *Greensboro Daily News*, May 12, 1974, B4.

45 Flair was listed as "Rick Flare." *Richmond Times-Dispatch*, May 18, 1974, B5. Thatcher later recollected his match against Flair. *Wrestler's Eye Radio* with Les Thatcher and Mike Johnson, PWInsider Elite, Jul. 29, 2017.

46 *Charlotte Observer*, Jul. 15, 1973, H1.

47 Hawk made his Charlotte debut for "Big" Jim Crockett on May 7, 1951. *Charlotte Observer*, May 8, 1951, 20. Hawk was a four-time Eastern States Heavyweight champion and a four-time Atlantic Coast Tag titleholder with Swede Hanson.

48 *Greenville News*, May 28, 1974, 14. Flair was initially billed as Hawk's nephew. midatlanticgateway.com. Also see "Hawk and Hanson: The Blond Bombers" by Mike Mooneyham, mikemooneyham.com. Notably, Flair had been listed as a "relative" of the Anderson Brothers in some publications as early as May 1974. *Burlington Times-News*, May 22, 1974, 3C.

49 *Greensboro Record*, Jul. 5, 1974, B8.

50 An example of Hawk-Flair promos from 1974 is available on YouTube. "Ric Flair & Rip Hawk Promo on Swede Hansen (sic) & Tiger Conway Jr. (Mid-Atlantic, 1974)." Joe Dombrowski's Pro Wrestling Library, May 18, 2020.

51 *To Be the Man* by Ric Flair with Keith Elliot Greenberg, 2004, 44.

52 Ibid, 41. Ric and Leslie briefly lived in an apartment before renting a home on Farm Pond Lane on the east side of Charlotte. *Leslie Goodman Fliehr v. Richard Morgan Fliehr, alias Ric Flair*, Mecklenburg County General Court of Justice, District Court Division, Case No. 79-cvd-5549.

53   The gate was over $50,000. *Greensboro Record*, Nov. 29, 1974, B6.
54   Jones pinned Flair at the finish. *Charleston News and Courier*, Dec. 7, 1974, 3B.
55   *Greensboro Daily News*, Jan. 17, 1975, D6.
56   *To Be the Man* by Ric Flair with Keith Elliot Greenberg, 2004, 31.
57   *Spartanburg Herald-Journal*, Aug. 18, 1974, B2.

CHAPTER 4: A NEW DESTINY

1   *Des Moines Register*, Feb. 18, 1940, J2.
2   Among the other wrestlers on Pfefer's circuit were the Zebra Kid, the Demon, "Gorgeous" George Winchell, and the Super Swedish Angel.
3   Flair later said that "a promoter" felt he "resembled and wrestled very similar" to Rogers and gave him the "Nature Boy" handle. *Ric Flair WCW Satellite Footage from 1993 vs. Rick Rude*, youtube.com. *To Be the Man* by Ric Flair with Keith Elliot Greenberg, 2004, 45,*Charleston Post and Courier*, Nov. 1, 1992, 15C.
4   Audio file from Apr.–May 1975, David Chappell, Mid-Atlantic Gateway, midatlanticgateway .com.
5   Ibid.
6   The radio host was Fred Nabors. Audio file from around Jul. 1977, Ibid.
7   *New York World-Telegram and Sun*, Mar. 15, 1950.
8   Audio file from Apr.–May 1975, David Chappell, Mid-Atlantic Gateway, midatlanticgateway .com. Also see *Staunton Leader*, Aug. 19, 1975, 9.
9   "Ric Flair Becomes the 'Nature Boy'" by Dick Bourne, midatlanticgateway.com/2018/05/ ric-flair-becomes-nature-boy.html, May 16, 2018.
10   Audio file from Apr.–May 1975, David Chappell, Mid-Atlantic Gateway, midatlanticgateway .com.
11   *Greensboro Daily News*, Feb. 21, 1975, B10.
12   *Charlotte Observer*, Mar. 10, 1975, 3B.
13   Interview of Ric Flair, *Steve Austin Podcast*, 2013.
14   *Wooooo! Nation* Podcast Episode #31.
15   *Jim Crockett Promotions: The Good Old Days* Documentary, 2013. Greg Valentine said something similar to this about McDaniel. NWA Legends Fanfest Q&A DVD, highspots.com.
16   *Jim Crockett Promotions: The Good Old Days* Documentary, 2013.
17   *To Be the Man* by Ric Flair with Keith Elliot Greenberg, 2004, 36–40.
18   Flair and Valentine battled McDaniel and André on Jun. 26 in Anderson, SC, and on Jul. 1 in Columbia, SC, and lost both matches. They also participated in at least two six-man tag bouts on the opposite side of André and Wahoo.
19   *Richmond Times-Dispatch*, Aug. 9, 1975, B6.
20   *Newport News Daily Press*, Sep. 21, 1975, D6.
21   National Transportation Safety Board (NTSB) Report Identification IAD76Al021, File Number 3-3277. Farkas served in the U.S. Army as a crew chief and air traffic controller during the war. *55+ Unite!: Welcome All Wise Working Women* by Georgian Lussier, 2011. His dates of service were Aug. 4, 1969, to Mar. 13, 1971. Ancestry.com.
22   *Charlotte Observer*, Mar. 8, 1988, 22. For several years, Farkas was affiliated with Union Airmotive, Inc., based out of Goose Creek Airport. *Charlotte News*, Dec. 15, 1972, 16B.
23   He relied on the "lay of the land, compasses and flying on sight." *Charlotte Observer*, Oct. 6, 1975, C1. According to the NTSB report, Farkas was "Not Instrument Rated." NTSB Report Identification IAD76Al021, File Number 3-3277.

24 Flair said it was a "beautiful day." Ric Flair Shoot Interview by Michael Bochicchio, highspots.com, 2008.

25 *Jim Crockett Promotions: The Good Old Days* Documentary, 2013. Crockett reportedly said he had the flu. *Wooooo! Nation* Podcast Episode #7. There had been a party at Wahoo McDaniel's place the night before the accident. Crockett and Flair had attended. Ric Flair Shoot Interview by Michael Bochicchio, highspots.com, 2008.

26 *Charlotte Obesrver*, Sep. 30, 1975, 14B.

27 Flair was scheduled to wrestle Wahoo McDaniel that night. *Charlotte News*, Oct. 15, 1975, B1.

28 Payload information found at planephd.com.

29 Ric Flair Shoot Interview by Michael Bochicchio, highspots.com, 2008.

30 *Jim Crockett Promotions: The Good Old Days* Documentary, 2013. Flair later said they were having a "normal flight." *Charlotte News*, Oct. 15, 1975, B1.

31 The crash was near the intersection of Gordon Rd. and N. 23rd St. *Wilmington Star-News*, Oct. 5, 1975, 1, *Charlotte Observer*, Oct. 5, 1975, 1.

32 Valentine described the crash a little differently than other reports did. He also talked about his injuries. *Tampa Tribune*, Dec. 15, 1977, C1. Flair said Valentine was not wearing a seatbelt. *Wooooo! Nation* Podcast Episode #28.

33 *David Crockett Shoot Interview*, RF Video.

34 Flair said he had compression fractures of his T10, T11, and T12 vertebrae. *30 for 30* Documentary, ESPN Films, 2017, *Charlotte News*, Oct. 15, 1975, B1,Interview with Ric Flair,*Valuetainment Podcast with Patrick Bet-David*, Apr. 5, 2018.

35 Ibid.

36 *Charlotte News*, Oct. 14, 1975, 7A.

37 *Charlotte News*, Oct. 15, 1975, B1.

38 NTSB Report Identification IAD76Al021, File Number 3-3277.

39 Correspondence with Georgian Lussier, Aug. 10, 2021.

40 Flair wrote that Farkas died "a year later." *Second Nature: The Legacy of Ric Flair and the Rise of Charlotte* by Ric Flair & Charlotte with Brian Shields, 2017, 108.

41 *Charlotte Observer*, Mar. 8, 1988, 22.

42 *Tampa Tribune*, Dec. 15, 1977, C1.

43 *Charlotte Observer*, Oct. 5, 1975, 1.

44 *Greensboro Daily News*, Oct. 12, 1975, C3.

45 *Jim Crockett Promotions: The Good Old Days* Documentary, 2013. Also *Wooooo! Nation* Podcast Episode #7.

46 *Asheville Citizen*, Oct. 4, 1975, 14. Flair had also been booked to meet Ken Patera in Charlotte on Oct. 6. He was replaced by Gene Anderson. *Charlotte Observer*, Oct. 7, 1975, 4B.

47 Graham replaced Flair in several matches against Wahoo McDaniel beginning on Oct. 13, 1975, in Greenville. *Greenville News*, Oct. 14, 1975, 11. Graham had been wrestling in the Dallas territory through early Oct. 1975. Mulligan departed the WWWF to join JCP in early Nov. 1975. Interview of Blackjack Mulligan by Mike Johnson, PWInsider.com. Angelo Mosca also joined the promotion in Nov. 1975.

48 *Charlotte News*, Oct. 15, 1975, B1.

49 Interview with Ric Flair, *Valuetainment Podcast with Patrick Bet-David*, Apr. 5, 2018.

50 Johnston was an orthopedic surgeon. *Charlotte Observer*, Sep. 7, 1975, D1. The Miller Clinic was at 1822 Brunswick Ave. in Charlotte.

51 *The Psychology of Scott: Shoot Interview with George Scott*, 2010, Ric Flair Shoot Interview by Michael Bochicchio, highspots.com, 2008.

52 Flair talked about the injury and making his return. Interview with Ric Flair, *Valuetainment Podcast with Patrick Bet-David*, Apr. 5, 2018.

53 Woods and Jones beat Graham and Mulligan in the tag bout. *Columbia State*, Dec. 31, 1975, 12A.

54 *Columbia State*, Dec. 30, 1975, 4A.

55   Flair scored the winning pinfall. Research provided by historian Mark Eastridge.

56   The main event was Paul Jones vs. Angelo Mosca. *Greensboro Daily News*, Feb. 1, 1976, C11. It was reported that Flair did a TV angle, where he ripped up sympathy cards sent in by fans.

57   It affected him mentally and physically. Flair was quoted as saying, "Following the plane crash a year ago, I guess I became a little more reserved. Maybe I wasn't quite myself for a while." *Greensboro Daily News*, Nov. 2, 1976, B4.

58   Flair talked about Mulligan teaching him on the road. *Wooooo! Nation* Podcast Episode #31.

59   Flair and Mulligan both lived on Pineborough Rd. Flair resided at 1042 and Blackjack at 1030. They used the same realty company and attorney, and each paid $36,000 for their home. Robert D. Windham, Deed of Trust, Mecklenburg County Property Records, Mar. 5, 1976; Richard M. Fliehr, Deed of Trust, Mecklenburg County Property Records, Mar. 18, 1976.

60   *Charlotte News*, Oct. 15, 1975, B1.

61   Flair said he was back in the air in Feb. 1976. Interview of Ric Flair by Dave Meltzer, 1999.

62   *New York Daily News*, Mar. 2, 1976, 55.

63   *New York Daily News*, Apr. 27, 1976, 65.

64   Eight thousand fans were in attendance. *Tampa Tribune*, Apr. 19, 1976, 8C.

65   *Wrestling 1975 Annual #14*, Victory Sports Series, 20–21.

66   *Charlotte Observer*, May 30, 1976, 2F.

67   The card drew 5,090. Ibid. Also see *Charlotte Observer*, May 4, 1976, 4B.

68   *Charlotte News*, May 25, 1976, 3C.

69   A full description of this match was provided in the *Charlotte Observer*, May 30, 1976, 2F. Flair discussed the table incident. *Wooooo! Nation* Podcast Episode #15.

70   Flair still wore the glasses and headbands at times in 1977, in conjunction with the robes.

71   Walker was also known as Mr. Wrestling II. Olivia and Johnny Walker were married in 1963. California Marriage Index, Ancestry.com. Early in Flair's career, he imported the robes from HI, where Olivia lived. She later moved to College Park, GA, near Atlanta.

72   *Atlanta Constitution*, Mar. 29, 1988, F1.

73   Ibid.

74   *Charlotte Observer*, May 30, 1976, 2F.

75   *Greenville News*, May 7, 1975, 27.

76   *Greenville News*, Jan. 5, 1976, B1.

CHAPTER 5: GREENBACKS, GOLD, AND GROUPIES

1   The Fliehr home, at 1042 Pineborough Rd., was built in 1975. The pool was added in 1976. Mecklenburg County (NC) Property Records. *Charlotte Observer*, May 30, 1976, 1F.

2   *To Be the Man* by Ric Flair with Keith Elliot Greenberg, 2004, 13, *Greenville News*, May 7, 1975, 27.

3   *Charlotte Observer*, May 30, 1976, 1F.

4   *Daily Tar Heel*, Sep. 13, 1979, 4–5.

5   Ibid.

6   Rufus R. Jones and Angelo Mosca were the others. *Charlotte Observer*, May 30, 1976, 1F.

7   Ibid.

8   *Greensboro Daily News*, Sep. 6, 1976, B6.

9   *Greenville News*, Sep. 12, 1976, 5C.

10   *Greensboro Daily News*, Sep. 27, 1976, B7.

11   Bolo Mongol and the Masked Superstar were portrayed by Bill Eadie. "The Death of Bolo Mongol and the Birth of a Superstar" by Dick Bourne, midatlanticgateway.com.

12   Wisniski was born on Aug. 2, 1951, in San Francisco. California Birth Index, Ancestry.com.
      His name was later legally changed to Gregory Lee. Texas Department of Labor and
      Standards Wrestling Contract, Apr. 6, 1979, and Mecklenburg County (NC) Property Records,
      Dec. 17, 1985.

13   According to records, Flair and Valentine teamed for the first time on Sep. 24, 1976, in
      Lynchburg, VA, against Tiger Conway Jr. and Wahoo McDaniel.

14   *Greensboro Daily News*, Oct. 17, 1976, B8.

15   Denver was victorious in the basketball game. *Greensboro Daily News*, Oct. 15, 1976, D1.

16   The newspaper erroneously stated that Flair and "Johnny" Valentine had won the belts.
      Greensboro Daily News, Dec. 28, 1976, B6.

17   *Richmond Times-Dispatch*, Dec. 28, 1976, B9.

18   *Charlotte Observer*, May 30, 1976, 1F. Flair said he made $100,000 for the first time ever in
      1976. *To Be the Man* by Ric Flair with Keith Elliot Greenberg, 2004, 63. According to court
      records, Flair made $123,075 in 1976. *Leslie Goodman Fliehr v. Richard Morgan Fliehr, alias
      Ric Flair*, Mecklenburg County General Court of Justice, District Court Division, Case No.
      79-CVD-5549.

19   He was married to Paula Sprotte. Correspondence with Robert Hodierne, Feb. 27, 2021.
      Pillars, Wayland Academy Yearbook, 1965–66.

20   This show was held on Apr. 1, 1976. Research provided by historian Mark Eastridge.

21   *Charlotte Observer*, May 30, 1976, 1F.

22   Correspondence with Robert Hodierne, Feb. 27, 2021.

23   *Charlotte Observer*, May 30, 1976, 1F.

24   An article about "ring rats" appeared in the *Cedar Rapids Gazette*, Jun. 4, 1978, 4E.

25   *Greensboro Daily News*, Nov. 2, 1976, B4.

26   Ibid.

27   *Greenville News*, May 25–26, 1976.

28   *Greensboro Record*, Mar. 29, 1976, B1.

29   *Charlotte Observer*, May 30, 1976, 2F.

30   It was said that Flair suffered a gallbladder injury in a bout against Ricky Steamboat in
      Winston-Salem. *Miami News*, Mar. 13, 1986, 6B. However, Flair didn't wrestle Steamboat
      for the first time until around Apr. 1977. The gallbladder operation is mentioned in *Leslie
      Goodman Fliehr v. Richard Morgan Fliehr, alias Ric Flair*, Mecklenburg County General
      Court of Justice, District Court Division, Case No. 79-CVD-5549.

31   A report stated that Flair was "fully recovered after a recent operation that sidelined him for
      several weeks." *Columbia State*, Mar. 6, 1977, 7B.

32   *Richmond Times-Dispatch*, Apr. 2, 1977, B8.

33   Steamboat joined JCP in late Feb. 1977. Flair discussed Steamboat's entry to JCP in *To Be the
      Man* by Ric Flair with Keith Elliot Greenberg, 2004, 66–69, *Wooooo! Nation* Podcast Episode
      #6.

34   After the match, Flair and Valentine battered Steamboat until Wahoo McDaniel ran out to
      make the save.

35   The title change occurred in a cage match on May 8, 1977, at the Charlotte Coliseum. Wahoo
      McDaniel served as the guest referee. *Charlotte Observer*, May 9, 1977, 12A.

36   *Richmond Times-Dispatch*, Jul. 30, 1977, C3.

37   At a birthday party in Nov. 2007, Johnny Weaver told Dick Bourne the story about
      how honored Flair was to win the United States championship from Bobo Brazil.
      Correspondence with Dick Bourne, Apr. 26–27, 2021.

38   Jerry Kozak was the "front" for the Amarillo Wrestling Club from the late 1960s into the '70s.

39   Research provided by historian Mark Eastridge.

40   The Funk brothers and Rip Hawk were also on the card. *Amarillo Globe-Times*, Aug. 19,
      1977, 35. Flair also appeared in Lubbock, TX, on Aug. 19 and lost to Ricky Romero by DQ.

Lubbock Avalanche-Journal, Aug. 21, 1977, B5. Lubbock was promoted by Nick Roberts, the father of Nickla Ann Roberts, who would later become Baby Doll. Baby Doll spoke about meeting Flair when she was young. *Baby Doll Shoot Interview*, RF Video, 2000.

41   It is believed this match was taped at KFDA-TV studios on either Wednesday, Aug. 17, or Saturday, Aug. 20. Additional information provided in the article, "Crockett TV in Texas (1977–1978)" by Dick Bourne, midatlanticgateway.com, Nov. 14, 2017. Another report stated that Flair wrestled Ervin Smith.

42   Audio of Flair talking himself up is available at midatlanticgateway.com.

43   "Crockett TV in Texas (1977–1978)" by Dick Bourne, midatlanticgateway.com, Nov. 14, 2017. Also *Atlanta Constitution*, Aug. 26, 1977, 13D.

44   One of Flair's gimmicks was using a foreign object in his kneepad.

45   *Charleston News and Courier*, Oct. 22, 1977, 7A.

46   *Charlotte Observer*, Aug. 23, 1977, 4B, *Greensboro Daily News*, Oct. 31, 1977, B8.

47   *Charlotte Observer*, Nov. 28, 1977, 5C.

48   *Corpus Christi Caller*, Dec. 16, 1977, 2C.

49   *Miami Herald*, Dec. 22, 1977, 2D.

50   Sam Muchnick's tenure as NWA president ended at the Aug. 1975 convention in New Orleans. He was succeeded by Jack Adkisson (Fritz Von Erich) of Dallas.

51   *St. Louis Post-Dispatch*, Jan. 6, 1978, 5B. Kernodle had been wrestling in West Texas at the time.

52   As a result of Kernodle's no-show, Omar Atlas wrestled two matches that night. He also battled Bob Brown to a draw. *St. Louis Post-Dispatch*, Jan. 7, 1978, 6A.

53   Flair had wrestled main events in Amarillo on Sep. 15, 1977, and in Atlanta on Dec. 9, 1977.

54   "Dream Team: Flair and Valentine (Part 5)" by David Chappell, midatlanticgateway.com, Aug. 14, 2016.

55   *Charlotte Observer*, Apr. 10, 1978, 6B.

56   The show was taped on Apr. 12, 1978, and broadcast the following week.

57   Audio file from Apr. 1978, David Chappell, midatlanticgateway.com. The robe was made by Olivia Walker. She was upset that it was destroyed. *Atlanta Constitution*, Mar. 29, 1988, 6F.

58   Among those to wrestle Mulligan in subsequent bounty matches were Greg Valentine, Masked Superstar, and Ken Patera.

59   *Greensboro Daily News*, Jul. 3, 1978, B5.

60   The match was Flair and Kim Duk vs. Baba and Jumbo Tsuruta. Flair pinned Baba for the first fall.

61   *St. Louis Post-Dispatch*, Mar. 4, 1978, 6A.

62   Flair had already wrestled Race two previous times. The first occurred on Apr. 12, 1977, in Columbia, SC, and they went to a double DQ. *Columbia State*, Apr. 13, 1977, 2C. This may have been Flair's first NWA World title match. In their second bout, on May 15, 1977, in Greensboro, they battled to a double countout. *Greensboro Daily News*, May 16, 1977, B7.

63   Race won the first fall by pinfall, but Flair took the second with his figure-four. Flair was counted out in the third by referee Charles Venator. *St. Louis Post-Dispatch*, Oct. 7, 1978, 6A.

CHAPTER 6: THE RACE TO THE TOP

1   Gerald Martin wrote in 1976 that Flair's "white locks" brought back "memories of the constantly-primping Gorgeous George." *Raleigh News and Observer*, Jun. 20, 1976, B3.

2   *Charlotte News*, Oct. 15, 1975, 3B.

3   *Greensboro Daily News*, Nov. 2, 1976, B4.

4   Ibid.

5   *Spartanburg Herald-Journal*, Jul. 27, 1980, B3.

6   Ibid.

7   *Greensboro Daily News*, May 30, 1976, D5.

8   *Daily Tar Heel*, Sept. 13, 1979, Weekender, 4–5.

9   *Raleigh News and Observer*, Jun. 20, 1976, B3.

10 Interview of Ric Flair by Jeff Glor, *CBS Evening News*, Feb. 21, 2009.

11 Scott was known as a "slow burn" booker. Interview of Blackjack Mulligan by Mike Johnson,
    PWInsider.

12 Several hundred fans were turned away. *Charlotte Observer*, Dec. 27, 1978, 3C. Flair and
    Mulligan also drew 13,447 in Greensboro on Thanksgiving night (Nov. 23, 1978). *Greensboro
    Daily News*, Nov. 24, 1978, E3.

13 *Greensboro Daily News*, Nov. 6, 1978, B5. Flair and Studd had captured the title on Oct. 30.
    Greenville News, Oct. 31, 1978, 3B.

14 This situation was explained in *United States Championship: A Close Look at Mid-Atlantic
    Wrestling's Greatest Championship* by Dick Bourne, 2015, 89.

15 *Greensboro Daily News*, Dec. 31, 1978, E5.

16 NWA World champion Harley Race assisted in creating the "beat up" look Steamboat
    sported on TV following the Flair incident. *Wooooo! Nation* Podcast Episode #6.

17 The operation, it is believed, took place in Aug. 1978. It was mentioned in a Bob Quincy
    column in the *Charlotte Observer*, Sep. 5, 1978, 3B.

18 *Charlotte Observer*, Nov. 11, 1981, B1.

19 Flair later said, "It almost ended my career." *Hays Daily News*, Jul. 25, 1982, 13.

20 *Charlotte Observer*, Nov. 11, 1981, B1.

21 It appears that Flair was using the figure-four as early as Jan. 1978, perhaps earlier.

22 It's notable that the Destroyer (Dick Beyer) also used a spin and crossed his opponent's left
    leg over right, pre-dating Flair's version of the hold. Another masked wrestler, Mr. Wrestling
    (Tim Woods), used the spinning element when applying the hold, but he crossed the right
    leg over left. Woods was a regular in the mid-Atlantic area, and he may have influenced Flair
    to some degree. Jumbo Tsuruta and Ted DiBiase used the spinning technique as well, but it
    is unclear when they started utilizing that particular version.

23 *Georgia Championship Wrestling*, Apr. 25, 1981.

24 It is believed that Crockett and Tunney discussed this arrangement at the Aug. 1978 NWA
    convention in Las Vegas. The deal was mentioned in the *Charlotte Observer*, Sep. 22, 1978,
    4B. George Scott's connections to Ontario also played a role in brokering this deal. JCP
    talent debuted in Toronto on Oct. 22, 1978. Flair beat Steamboat by DQ on that card. Years
    later, Flair said, "The first time I ever came to Toronto, I didn't know what to expect. I knew
    nothing about Toronto, and nothing about Canada." "A Great Flair for Toronto" by Greg
    Oliver, Jul. 27, 2006, slamwrestling.net.

25 Tunney became a member of the NWA in Nov. 1949. He served as president of the NWA in
    1960–61.

26 *Wooooo! Nation* Podcast Episode #15.

27 *Belleville News-Democrat*, Sunday magazine, May 17, 1981, 8.

28 Jim Cornette, *Mid-Atlantic Films Vol. 10*, DVD.

29 The service station was at 6151 Albemarle Rd.

30 Correspondence with Terry Brown, Mar. 21, 2021. Flair later bought a 1974 Lincoln
    Presidential limo.

31 Ibid.

32 Ibid.

33 *To Be the Man* by Ric Flair with Keith Elliot Greenberg, 2004, 77. The time-frame in which
    these tickets were received is unknown.

34 The address was 4910 McAlpine Farm Rd. Deed of Trust, Mecklenburg County Property Records, Oct. 31, 1977. The home was built in 1975, and, according to 2021 records, it had 3,941 square feet. Mecklenburg County Property Record Card, property.spatialest.com/nc /mecklenburg#. Additional information was found in the *Charlotte Observer*, Aug. 21, 1977, 19B, *Charlotte Observer*, Sep. 13, 1981, 12G. A more detailed description of the home was provided in *Leslie Goodman Fliehr v. Richard Morgan Fliehr, alias Ric Flair*, Mecklenburg County General Court of Justice, District Court Division, Case No. 79-CVD-5549.

35 Snuka went to JCP directly from Don Owen's Pacific Northwest territory in late Oct. 1978.

36 Orndorff was also a JCP newcomer, having arrived in early Nov. 1978. Snuka and Orndorff won the NWA World Tag Team title on Dec. 26, 1978, in Richmond. *Richmond Times-Dispatch*, Dec. 27, 1978, D6.

37 Terry Justice, *All-Star Grappler*, Vol. 1, No. 10.

38 *Greensboro Daily News*, Apr. 2, 1979, B7.

39 Flair lost to Snuka by DQ on Apr. 12 in Norfolk, but no-showed the next night in Richmond. He was replaced by John Studd against Dino Bravo. *Richmond Times-Dispatch*, Apr. 14, 1979, C2.

40 *Wrestling '79*, Apr.–May 1979, Vol. 4, Issue #9. Also *Greensboro Daily News*, Apr. 23, 1979, B6 and "Trial Run: The Origins of Ric Flair's First Babyface Turn (1979)" by Dick Bourne, Oct. 16, 2020, midatlanticgateway.com/2020/10/ric-flair-early-turn-1979.html.

41 *Greensboro Daily News*, May 6, 1979, C12.

42 It's unclear if Rhodes demanded a future U.S. title shot from Flair in exchange for teaming with him on Jun. 3.

43 *Greensboro Daily News*, Jun. 4, 1979, B7.

44 The newspaper report stated that Rhodes beat Flair "with a suplex." *Greensboro Daily News*, Jun. 18, 1979, B7.

45 The influence of Ray Stevens was discussed in chapter 3.

46 For Flair's six shows prior to Jul. 8, he earned $6,880, which was his largest one week total between Mar. 1979 and Jan. 1980. Of that, $688 went to the Briarbend Investment Company. *Leslie Goodman Fliehr v. Richard Morgan Fliehr, alias Ric Flair*, Mecklenburg County General Court of Justice, District Court Division, Case No. 79-CVD-5549.

47 Attendance was 6,517. *Greensboro Record*, Jul. 9, 1979, B7. The duration of the match is likely incorrect. It is believed the match was much shorter.

48 *Spartanburg Herald-Journal*, Jul. 22, 1979, B3.

49 George Scott was the special referee. *Greensboro Record*, Aug. 13, 1979, B8.

50 *Charlotte Observer*, Sep. 2, 1979, 6C.

51 Rogers departed the promotion before the end of 1979, and Gene Anderson assumed the managerial role.

52 *Richmond Times-Dispatch*, Dec. 31, 1979, C3.

53 Flair was announced as the new champion. *Greensboro Daily News*, Apr. 7, 1980, B4.

54 The show was held on Apr. 20, 1980, with 7,320 in attendance. *Greensboro Daily News*, Apr. 21, 1980, B5.

55 Flair and Valentine momentarily paused their feud and teamed up against the Iron Sheik and Jimmy Snuka on Jun. 8, 1980, in Greensboro. Valentine ended up smashing Flair with Gene Anderson's cane. The move legitimately broke Flair's nose and caused other injuries to his face. Read "The Cane that Wouldn't Break: Greg Valentine Shatters Ric Flair's Face" by Dick Bourne, Jan. 20, 2022, midatlanticgateway.com.

56 *Charlotte News*, Jul. 28, 1980, 9C.

57 *St. Louis Post-Dispatch*, Mar. 9, 1980, 7D. Pat O'Connor was the guest referee. Flair earned $1,875.77 for this program. St. Louis Wrestling Club, Inc. Payoff Information, *Leslie Goodman Fliehr v. Richard Morgan Fliehr, alias Ric Flair*, Mecklenburg County General Court of Justice, District Court Division, Case No. 79-CVD-5549.

58   The referee was Joe Tangaro. Attendance was 10,781. *Belleville News-Democrat*, Mar. 30, 1980, B7.

59   St. Louis Wrestling Club General Ledger, Posted by Steve Yohe, wrestlingclassics.com message board, Feb. 24, 2014. When adjusted for inflation, his earnings equated to $12,631.62 in 2022. bls.gov.

60   *Belleville News-Democrat*, Apr. 28, 1980, B6. Attendance was 10,196 and Flair earned $2,631.34. Race earned the same amount. St. Louis Wrestling Club General Ledger, Posted by Steve Yohe, wrestlingclassics.com message board, Feb. 26, 2014.

61   *Greensboro Daily News*, May 18, 1980, F1.

62   *Charlotte Observer*, Feb. 14, 1979, B1.

63   *Charlotte Observer*, Nov. 11, 1979, 5D.

64   *Daily Tar Heel*, Sept. 13, 1979, 4–5.

65   Ibid.

66   *Wooooo! Nation* Podcast Episode #7. *To Be the Man* by Ric Flair with Keith Elliot Greenberg, 2004, p. 77–80. An article in the *Greensboro Daily News* reported that he was split from his wife. It also stated that he had "two daughters," which was inaccurate at the time. *Greensboro Daily News*, May 18, 1980, F1, F3.

67   *Leslie Goodman Fliehr v. Richard Morgan Fliehr, alias Ric Flair*, Mecklenburg County General Court of Justice, District Court Division, Case No. 79-CVD-5549.

68   Ibid.

69   Minnesota Birth Index, Ancestry.com.

70   *Leslie Goodman Fliehr v. Richard Morgan Fliehr, alias Ric Flair*, Mecklenburg County General Court of Justice, District Court Division, Case No. 79-CVD-5549.

71   Flair moved into the Essex apartments at 4948-A Sardis Rd. in Aug. 1979. Ibid.

72   Consent Order, Ibid, Sep. 19, 1979.

73   *To Be the Man* by Ric Flair with Keith Elliot Greenberg, 2004, 17.

CHAPTER 7: TEN POUNDS OF GOLD

1   *Daily Tar Heel*, Sept. 13, 1979, 4–5.

2   Mid-Atlantic TV wrestling was shown in the Tampa and Buffalo areas. *Greensboro Daily News*, May 18, 1980, F1. The name of *Wide World Wrestling* was changed to *World Wide Wrestling* in 1978. Wrestling historian Richard Sullivan post at WrestlingClassics.com Message Board, Mar. 9, 2017.

3   *Raleigh News and Observer*, Jul. 8, 1979, E1.

4   Blackjack Mulligan said they did 150 interviews. Interview of Blackjack Mulligan by Mike Johnson, PWInsider.com.

5   *Virginian Pilot and the Ledger Star*, Jan. 7, 1979.

6   Ibid.

7   *Charlotte News*, Jul. 11, 1979, D1.

8   *Winston-Salem Journal*, Feb. 25, 1979.

9   *Charlotte Observer*, May 30, 1976, F1, *Greensboro Daily News*, May 18, 1980, F1.

10   *Miami Herald*, Jul. 6, 1978, E2.

11   Ibid.

12   *Greensboro Daily News*, May 18, 1980, F3. Contrary to the report in the press, Flair made $154,285 in his best year, 1978. *Leslie Goodman Fliehr v. Richard Morgan Fliehr, alias Ric Flair*, Mecklenburg County General Court of Justice, District Court Division, Case No. 79-CVD-5549.

13   *Orangeburg Times and Democrat*, Jul. 10, 1978, 7A.

14   Current version of the Ric Flair Record Book and wrestlingdata.com.

15   The dates were Jan. 3, Jan. 10, and Jan. 31.

16   *Charlotte Observer*, Aug. 25, 1980, 5B.

17   The match lasted one hour. *Raleigh News and Observer*, Aug. 27, 1980, 21.

18   Race lost the NWA belt to Dusty Rhodes on Aug. 21, 1979, but regained it five days later in Orlando. He then dropped the title to Giant Baba on Oct. 31 in Nagoya, Japan, and won a rematch on Nov. 7 in Amagasaki.

19   The convention was held Sep. 22–23, 1980.

20   Lou Thesz was initially acknowledged as National Wrestling Alliance World champion at the 1949 annual convention in St. Louis.

21   Geigel was affiliated with Gust Karras, Pat O'Connor, and George Simpson in the formation of Heart of America Sports Attractions, Inc., in 1963. This group booked wrestlers throughout KS, IA, and parts of MO.

22   Barnett sold out of Australia and purchased a stake in the Atlanta promotion in 1973.

23   *Charlotte Observer*, Nov. 29, 1977, 4B.

24   *Palm Beach Post-Times*, Dec. 29, 1974, E1.

25   *Charlotte Observer*, Nov. 29, 1977, 4B.

26   Crockett Sr. served as the NWA's first vice president in 1964, 1965, and 1970. He was second vice president in 1963 and 1968, and he was a member of the board of directors for at least three consecutive years (1969–71) but likely much longer. Crockett Jr. also served as a second vice president in 1976–77.

27   Crockett discussed the political challenges of the NWA World title in *David Crockett Shoot Interview*, RF Video. There was also some talk about Flair's size. Pat O'Connor reportedly said he was too small to be champion. *Wooooo! Nation* Podcast Episode #7.

28   *Kansas City Times*, Nov. 21, 1980, F6.

29   Both the *Greensboro Daily News* and *Greensboro Record* stated that Flair won the U.S. championship in this bout. *Greensboro Daily News*, Nov. 28, 1980, C6, *Greensboro Record*, Nov. 28, 1980, C4.

30   *Charlotte Observer*, Dec. 26, 1980, 13A.

31   Between 1976 and '80, Piper held the Americas championship on five occasions and the Pacific Northwest Heavyweight title twice.

32   *Richmond Times-Dispatch*, Nov. 2, 1980, B16.

33   These AWA matches were reportedly held on Oct. 3, 1973 (TV) and Nov. 17, 1973, in Davenport, IA. Another TV bout was said to have been held on Nov. 10, but this may be erroneous.

34   Unknown *Mid-Atlantic* television show, Late Jan. 1981.

35   *Raleigh News and Observer*, Jan. 28, 1981, 16.

36   Flair discussed his friendship with Piper. *To Be the Man* by Ric Flair with Keith Elliot Greenberg, 2004, 83–88. Piper talked about Flair in his autobiography as well. *In the Pit with Piper: Roddy Gets Rowdy* by Roddy Piper with Robert Picarello, 2002, 91, 115–116, 119.

37   *Greenville News*, Jan. 27, 1981, 4B. Scott was also a participant in two six-man tag team matches in Columbia on Feb. 3 and in Norfolk on Feb. 5.

38   Flair lost matches to Roddy Piper, Ted DiBiase, Bob Sweetan, Ivan Koloff, Rufus R. Jones, Dusty Rhodes, Jack Brisco, and Mike Graham.

39   Jack Brisco talked about this tradition. *Brisco: The Life and Times of National Collegiate and World Heavyweight Wrestling Champion Jack Brisco* by Jack Brisco, as told to William Murdock, 2003, 133. A good example of another future champion suffering defeats in the same way was Terry Funk in 1975. In the month prior to his NWA title victory, he suffered at least nine losses in FL, TX, Kansas City, Los Angeles, and the mid-Atlantic region.

40   Although the vote for Flair happened at the 1980 convention, the decision of specifically when the title switch would occur may not have been made until later. Flair said he didn't

know about the match with Rhodes until "two weeks" before it took place in Kansas City. Ric Flair Shoot Interview by Michael Bochicchio, highspots.com, 2008.

41   Before losing the belt to Rhodes, Race had traded the NWA belt with Tommy Rich, losing it on Apr. 27, 1981, and then regaining the strap on May 1, 1981. When he regained the belt, Race became a six-time champion.

42   The time of the match was 23:54. Flair later said that it wasn't a good match. *To Be the Man* by Ric Flair with Keith Elliot Greenberg, 2004, 93. Flair's parents and Jim Crockett were in attendance.

43   *Kansas City Times*, Sep. 18, 1981, D6. Video of the match circulated around the NWA and was played on local television broadcasts. The graphic on the tape misspelled Flair's name as "Rick Flair." Flair talked about the title change with Michael Hayes. *Wooooo! Nation* Podcast Episode #22.

44   As a formality, the incoming titleholder had to post a $25,000 belt deposit, or "performance bond," with the NWA to ensure they'd adhere to the schedule and best interests of the organization. Flair posted the money and it was held by Jim Barnett, the NWA secretary-treasurer.

CHAPTER 8: "DIAMONDS ARE FOREVER"

1   Flair was not the 15th overall reign but the 15th individual to hold the championship. This does not include the reigns of Leo Nomellini or Édouard Carpentier.

2   Flair was scheduled to team with Wahoo McDaniel against Roddy Piper and Abdullah the Butcher. *Richmond Times-Dispatch*, Sep. 18, 1981, D5. He was replaced by Jay Youngblood. *Richmond Times-Dispatch*, Sep. 19, 1981, C5. In Des Moines, Rhodes was advertised to defend against Race. *Des Moines Register*, Sep. 18, 1981, 3B.

3   In addition to Richmond, he had other matches scheduled for Charlotte, Rocky Mount, and Norfolk.

4   WTBS was on Channel H in Des Moines in 1981.

5   *Georgia Championship Wrestling*, Sep. 19, 1981.

6   Ibid.

7   *Mid-Atlantic Championship Wrestling*, circa late Sep. 1981.

8   *Georgia Championship Wrestling*, Sep. 26, 1981.

9   In newspaper advertising, Brown was billed as a challenger against Rhodes. *Junction City Daily Union*, Sep. 16, 1981, 11. The result of this match is unknown.

10   Fans in Junction City watched WTBS on cable channel 12.

11   Their match occurred in Miyagi, Japan. Flair had beaten Tenryu in a TV match in Raleigh on Oct. 22, 1980. Tenryu worked for JCP in 1980–81.

12   *Wooooo! Nation* Podcast Episode #8. This would have been when Funk was the traveling NWA champion.

13   Flair was defeated by Tsuruta on Apr. 27, 1978, in Noheji, Japan. Harley Race was in Flair's corner for the 1981 bout. Race, in 2004, confirmed that he went to Japan with Flair to guard against what was perceived to be a double-cross threat by Tsuruta and the head of All Japan, Shohei "Giant" Baba. Race didn't believe Flair had anything to worry about. Race and Jack Brisco agreed that Tsuruta was an honorable guy. Interview of Harley Race and Jack Brisco, *Ringside Live*, wrestlingclassics.com, 2004.

14   The NWA convention was held Oct. 10–12, 1981. Shohei Baba, Hisashi Shinma, and Dory Funk Jr. were also in attendance. *Monthly Pro Wrestling*, Dec. 1981.

15   Flair said in 1979, "Usually the people who criticize [pro wrestling] don't know anything about it." *Daily Tar Heel*, Sept. 13, 1979, 4–5.

16   This was according to Flair's testimony. *Charlotte Observer*, Oct. 15, 1981, D1. The man, Bill
     Newton, denied that he was drunk. He also said that he hadn't gone over to Flair to instigate
     a fight. *Charlotte News*, Aug. 17, 1981, 1.

17   *Charlotte Observer*, Oct. 15, 1981, D1.

18   Flair was arrested on Aug. 15 or 16, 1981, and was released on bond. *Charlotte Observer*,
     Aug. 18, 1981, B1. He had matches both days.

19   *Charlotte News*, Aug. 17, 1981, 1.

20   *Charlotte Observer*, Oct. 15, 1981, D1, *Charlotte News*, Oct. 15, 1981, B4.

21   *Charlotte Observer*, Mar. 9, 1982, B2.

22   On Oct. 19, 1981, Flair beat Al Madril in Fort Worth. *Fort Worth Star-Telegram*, Oct. 20, 1981,
     D4. It is believed that Madril was the reigning Texas Heavyweight champion.

23   *Palm Beach Post*, Oct. 27, 1981, D4.

24   Flair pinned Race in Tampa on Oct. 27 and beat Rhodes by DQ in St. Petersburg on Oct. 31,
     1981. *Tampa Tribune-Times*, Nov. 1, 1981, D9.

25   The second tour ran from Nov. 16 to 19, 1981.

26   *To Be the Man* by Ric Flair with Keith Elliot Greenberg, 2004, 95. Flair and Mulligan incor-
     porated Southern Championship Wrestling, Inc., on Apr. 3, 1981, in NC.

27   *NWA Championship Wrestling* aired locally on WBIR-TV, channel 10, in Knoxville on
     Saturdays at 2:30 p.m. The show debuted around May 1981 and was taped in the WBIR
     Studios.

28   Interview by Anne See. *Ric Flair Fan Club Newsletter #7*, Apr. 1982.

29   The first bout happened on Nov. 6. The results of both matches are unknown.

30   *Greensboro Record*, Nov. 27, 1981, C2.

31   Muchnick began his career as an assistant for wrestling promoter Tom Packs in the 1930s.
     He became an independent promoter during the 1940s and ran steady opposition to Packs
     beginning in 1945.

32   The Checkerdome was previously known as the St. Louis Arena. Larry Matysik cited the
     attendance number as 19,819 and said it was sold out "days in advance." *Wrestling at the Chase:
     The Inside Story of Sam Muchnick and the Legends of Professional Wrestling* by Larry Matysik,
     2005, 226.

33   *St. Louis Post-Dispatch*, Jan. 3, 1982, F5.

34   In addition to Geigel, St. Louis was owned by Pat O'Connor, Verne Gagne, and Harley
     Race.

35   While on the road as NWA champion, Flair wasn't always the heel. For instance, in Portland
     on Apr. 13, 1982, he faced off against Buddy Rose, who was hated in the Pacific Northwest.
     Rose was the "bad guy" in their match. Flair was cheered because, as the stipulation stated,
     Rose would be forced to leave the territory if he lost. So it wasn't that Flair was a fan
     favorite; he was just more popular than the man he was wrestling. Flair did beat Rose, and
     the latter left the territory after his Apr. 15 contest, headed for a tour of Japan.

36   *Ric Flair Fan Club Newsletter #7*, Apr. 1982. The match occurred on Feb. 3, 1982, at WPCQ
     Studios in Charlotte. In Jul. 1981, the promotion ended its weekly television operations in
     Raleigh and shifted them to WPCQ.

37   Youngblood was the son of longtime wrestler Ricky Romero.

38   *Mid-Atlantic Championship Wrestling*, Feb. 3, 1982.

39   Ibid.

40   *Greensboro Daily News*, Feb. 22, 1982, B7.

41   Footage was shown during *Mid-Atlantic Championship Wrestling*, Mar. 6, 1982.

42   *Charlotte Observer*, Apr. 5, 1982, A9.

43   *Greensboro Daily News and Record*, Aug. 8, 1982, E8.

44   See a detailed article about this situation written by David Chappell at midatlanticgateway.com.

45   *Mid-Atlantic Championship Wrestling*, Aug. 21, 1982.

46　Flair beat Reed in that match. *Miami Herald*, Apr. 9, 1982, F12.

47　*Mid-Atlantic Championship Wrestling*, Aug. 21, 1982.

48　*St. Louis Post-Dispatch*, Nov. 21, 1981, A7.

49　*Dallas Morning News*, Jan. 27, 1982, B8.

50　The tours extended from Apr. 10 to Apr. 16, 1982 and Sep. 26 to Oct. 2, 1982.

51　*The Ring's Wrestling*, Aug., 1982, 16–19, Correspondence with Kate Mast, Jan. 7, 2021.

52　Ibid.

53　*Down Home with the Carolina Camera* with C.J. Underwood, WBTV-3, 1981.

54　The Harrell family lived in Havana, FL. Additional information from North Carolina Certificate of Marriage, License Number 1975, Aug. 24, 1983.

55　*Second Nature: The Legacy of Ric Flair and the Rise of Charlotte* by Ric Flair & Charlotte with Brian Shields, 2017, 108, *Tallahassee Democrat*, Feb. 22, 1976, E6.

56　*Leslie Goodman Fliehr v. Richard Morgan Fliehr, alias Ric Flair*, Mecklenburg County General Court of Justice, District Court Division, Case No. 79-CVD-5549. Flair and Harrell were introduced to each other by one of the Embers, a popular North Carolina–based musical group. *Raleigh News and Observer*, Jan. 27, 1991, E1, E7, Flair talked about meeting Beth. *To Be the Man* by Ric Flair with Keith Elliot Greenberg, 2004, 105–107.

57　Flair later said he owed the IRS $130,000. *To Be the Man* by Ric Flair with Keith Elliot Greenberg, 2004, 111–112.

58　State of North Carolina, Power of Attorney Legal Document, Nov. 3, 1982, Mecklenburg County (NC) Property Records.

59　State of North Carolina, Power of Attorney Legal Document, Sep. 8, 1982, Mecklenburg County (NC) Property Records, Revocation of Power of Attorney, Sep. 8, 1982, Mecklenburg County (NC) Property Records.

60　*Charlotte News*, Sep. 13, 1978, 23. Guthrie served as a captain in the U.S. Army and received two bronze stars in Vietnam. mhc-law.com.

61　Myers Park High School Yearbook, 1958. Guthrie worked as a Mecklenburg County assistant district attorney from 1971 to 1974. mhc-law.com.

62　Interview with Dennis L. Guthrie, Oct. 2, 2020.

63　*Leslie Goodman Fliehr v. Richard Morgan Fliehr, alias Ric Flair*, Mecklenburg County General Court of Justice, District Court Division, Case No. 79-CVD-5549.

64　Ibid.

65　The agreement was made on Mar. 1, 1978, and was to last for six years, ending on Feb. 28, 1984. According to the documentation, Flair wanted "to obtain the assistance of the partnership in furthering his career." Memorandum of Agreement, Ibid. Flair discussed this on *Wooooo! Nation* Podcast Episode #7 and in *To Be the Man* by Ric Flair with Keith Elliot Greenberg, 2004, 111–112.

CHAPTER 9: THE MAGNIFICENT ONE

1　Barnett had a good relationship with Flair. In addition to booking the champion, Barnett handled his payoffs. *Wooooo! Nation* Podcast Episode #41.

2　*Ric Flair Fan Club Newsletter* #9, Oct. 1982.

3　Flair wrestled in a tuxedo. Attendance was 5,674. *Miami Herald*, Jun. 24, 1982, D9.

4　GCW debuted in Columbus, OH, on Sep. 28, 1980.

5　Between Oct. and Dec. 1981, Flair made three appearances in Columbus, OH.

6　Backlund was born on Aug. 14, 1949, in Princeton, MN, northwest of the Twin Cities. He won the WWWF championship on Feb. 20, 1978.

7   Backlund's matches with Race occurred in 1978 and 1980, and his bout with Bockwinkel happened in 1979.

8   In a 1982 kayfabe article, Flair called Backlund and Bockwinkel "regional champions." He said, "I am THE world champion." It was also noted that the NWA covered more territory worldwide than the WWF and AWA together. *The Ring's Wrestling*, Aug. 1982, 16–19.

9   During the segment, brief video clips of Flair and Backlund in action were shown. *Georgia Championship Wrestling*, Jul. 3, 1982.

10 Flair discussed the match with Backlund. *Wooooo! Nation* Podcast Episode #28. *To Be the Man* by Ric Flair with Keith Elliot Greenberg, 2004, 98. This match was tied for number one as "Match of the Year" with Dynamite Kid and Tiger Mask's bout on Aug. 5, 1982, in Tokyo. *Wrestling Observer Newsletter 1982 Yearbook*, 5.

11 Flair won two of three falls. *St. Louis Post-Dispatch*, Mar. 27, 1982, A7. Bruiser had Flair pinned during the bout, but the referee had been knocked down and rendered unable to score the victory.

12 *Ric Flair Fan Club Newsletter* #8, Jul. 1982, 27.

13 Flair and Bruiser wrestled on opposite sides of a tag team match in St. Louis on Dec. 3, 1982.

14 *Wichita Eagle-Beacon*, Aug. 15, 1982, D2.

15 The restaurant was at 430 E. Douglas Ave. and the Century II was at 225 W. Douglas Ave.

16 Flair wrestled Rufus R. Jones in Hannibal on Aug. 13, 1982. The result is unknown. The WMC-TV studio was at 1960 Union Ave., just east of downtown Memphis.

17 *Championship Wrestling*, Aug. 14, 1982.

18 Ibid.

19 Ibid.

20 *Memphis Commercial Appeal*, Dec. 28, 1982, B3.

21 *Memphis Commercial Appeal*, Jan. 11, 1983, B3. Jim Cornette discussed this on his *Cornette's Drive-Thru* Podcast, Episode #124.

22 *Hutchinson News*, Aug. 15, 1982, 1.

23 The dealership was at 1200 East 30th Ave. in Hutchinson.

24 Correspondence with Michael O'Mara, Feb. 16, 2021.

25 Ibid. *Hutchinson News*, May 30, 1980, 1.

26 *Hutchinson News*, Aug. 14, 1982, 20.

27 Correspondence with Michael O'Mara, Feb. 16, 2021.

28 The July before, Flair appeared in another small town in KS, and again did his job to the best of his ability. That town was Hays, which had a population slightly better than 16,000. Flair was quoted as saying: "This is the smallest crowd and smallest town I've ever wrestled for. But I have a contract with the promoters and I have to go where they want me to." *Hays Daily News*, Jul. 21, 1982, 13.

29 *Ric Flair Fan Club Newsletter* #10, Jan. 1983, 27.

30 1982 National Wrestling Alliance Meeting Minutes.

31 Letter from Jim Barnett to the NWA membership, dated Sep. 13, 1982. Jim Crockett also didn't attend the convention. David Crockett attended instead.

32 1982 National Wrestling Alliance Meeting Minutes.

33 Ibid. During this tour, Flair had additional matches in Port of Spain, Trinidad, Waterford, Barbados, and Santo Domingo, Dominican Republic.

34 Flair was also supposed to defend his championship in Mexico City on Sep. 17, 1982, against El Halcón (José Ortiz). Plans changed after Flair had problems with his work visa.

35 *Ric Flair Fan Club Newsletter* 12, Jul. 1983, 17. Flair had defeated Jovica on Sep. 1, 1982, at the Jean Pierre Sports Complex in Port of Spain.

36 *Port of Spain Gazette*, Dec. 14, 1982.

37 *Ric Flair Fan Club Newsletter* #12, Jul. 1983, 17.

38 Information and photos from the match appeared in *Listin Diario*, Dec. 21, 1982, A6.

39 Flair discussed his match with Veneno. *Wooooo! Nation* Podcast Episode #15.
40 Their match ended in a double DQ. The newspaper called it a "draw." *Dallas Morning News*, Aug. 16, 1982, 44.
41 The show was broadcast on channel 39 in Dallas. *World Class Championship Wrestling*, Dec. 11, 1982.
42 This Dallas show drew a $102,000 gate. *"Playboy" Gary Hart: My Life in Wrestling* by Gary Hart with Philip Varriale, 2009. This was the first $100,000 gate in Texas wrestling history. *Wrestling Observer Newsletter*, Jan. 3, 1994.
43 *Dallas Morning News*, Dec. 26, 1982, B22. Flair was declared the winner in 24:02.
44 The attendance was 15,498. *Greensboro Daily News*, Nov. 26, 1982, D4.
45 This incident was taped at the WPCQ-TV studios on Nov. 24, 1982.
46 Their match was part of the annual Three Kings wrestling event.
47 *Tampa Tribune*, Dec. 29, 1982, C6.
48 *Ric Flair Fan Club Newsletter* #11, Apr. 1983, 14. Also *Orlando Sentinel*, Jan. 15, 1983, B6.
49 The suspension was for a year. *Wrestling Observer Newsletter*, Apr. 1983, 13.
50 *Miami Herald*, Feb. 10, 1983, D8. The gate was in excess of $75,000. *Wrestling Observer Newsletter*, Apr. 1983, 13.
51 *Wrestling Observer Newsletter*, Apr. 1983, 13.
52 This near title change is asterisked in most NWA World title histories.
53 The attendance ranged from 16,765 to 19,000. *Wrestling Observer Newsletter*, Apr. 1983, 11–12, *Wrestling Observer Newsletter*, Nov. 24, 2003. The gate was a new record in St. Louis at the time. Both Flair and Brody earned $5,958.81. *Wrestling Observer Newsletter*, Nov. 10, 2014, f4wonline .com. Brody used the name "King Kong Brody" in the Central States area in deference to Dick the Bruiser.
54 *Wrestling Observer Newsletter 1982 Yearbook*, 10.
55 *Wooooo! Nation* Podcast Episode #22. Flair was named the 1982 Wrestler of the Year by the *Wrestling Observer Newsletter*. In the "Hardest Worker in the Ring" category, Flair was tied for number one with Tiger Mask. *Wrestling Observer Newsletter 1982 Yearbook*, 5.

CHAPTER 10: A FLARE FOR THE GOLD

1 Undated article written by Paul Haskins, *Winston-Salem Sentinel*, *Ric Flair Fan Club Newsletter* #9, Oct. 1982, 13.
2 Photos of Flair and Crawford appeared in *Ric Flair Fan Club Newsletter* #8, Jul. 1982, 7, and *Ric Flair Fan Club Newsletter* #11, Apr. 1983, 4.
3 By Apr. 1982, the fan club had over 150 members in the U.S. and Canada, with one member from England. *Ric Flair Fan Club Newsletter* #7, Apr. 1982, 1.
4 Photos of Flair and his new watch appeared in *Ric Flair Fan Club Newsletter* #10, Jan. 1983, 3.
5 *Ric Flair Fan Club Newsletter* #13, Oct. 1983, 11.
6 *Ric Flair Fan Club Newsletter* #11, Apr. 1983, 15.
7 Flair was originally slated to appear in Steve Rickard's New Zealand territory, including Singapore and Kuala Lumpur, between Feb. 27 and Mar. 5, 1983. NWA World Champion Booking Schedule, Jan. 10, 1983. These dates may have later changed.
8 It's also possible the Flair-Brown match was previously taped.
9 NWA World Champion Booking Schedule, Jan. 10, 1983.
10 *Greensboro Record*, Mar. 14, 1983, B5.
11 In a promotional advertisement, the tag team bout was listed above the Flair-Valentine match.
12 Bryson stated that capacity attendance was 15,078. *Greensboro Daily News*, Unknown Date.

Another report had the attendance at 15,547 with between 3,000 and 5,000 turned away. *Greensboro Record*, Mar. 14, 1983, B5.

13 Piper was disqualified for throwing Flair over the top rope. Flair also faced off with Piper on May 10 in Portland and May 11 in Seattle. Both shows drew more than 4,000 spectators.

14 Flair called Tunney "one of the greatest and most involved men in the history of professional wrestling" in a TV promo for Tunney's 50th anniversary show on Nov. 13, 1981.

15 Following Sam Muchnick's retirement, the owners of the St. Louis Wrestling Club were Bob Geigel, Pat O'Connor, Verne Gagne, and Harley Race.

16 Matysik quit his general manager position for the St. Louis Wrestling Club following the Feb. 25, 1983, show. *Wrestling at the Chase: The Inside Story of Sam Muchnick and the Legends of Professional Wrestling* by Larry Matysik, 2005, 180. He reportedly remained on as a TV commentator through part of March.

17 Race explained that the title was moved back to him from Flair in the midst of the war between the NWA and WWF in St. Louis. *To Be the Man* by Ric Flair with Keith Elliot Greenberg, 2004, 112. However, it should be noted that the WWF didn't invade St. Louis until Dec. 1983.

18 The main event was originally slated to be King Kong Brody against Blackjack Mulligan. *St. Louis Post-Dispatch*, May 18, 1983, 4B. Mulligan no-showed the event.

19 *Ric Flair Fan Club Newsletter* #12, Jul. 1983, 8–9. It is believed that Matthews had replaced Matysik as lead interviewer on the St. Louis TV program.

20 Tsuruta won 1–0, taking the only fall in 29:39. *Wrestling Observer Newsletter*, Jul. 1983, 10. Since the bout didn't see two falls won by either competitor, Flair retained his belt. Flair talked about traveling back to the U.S. with Roddy Piper and Dick Slater. Interview with Ric Flair, *Valuetainment Podcast with Patrick Bet-David*, Apr. 5, 2018.

21 A match description was provided by Nancye Deem. *Ric Flair Fan Club Newsletter* #12, Jul. 1983, 8–9.

22 The program was shown on Jun. 18, 1983. A show summary was provided by David Taub, midatlanticgateway.com.

23 Race assumed the champion's schedule, including a big show in Dallas on Jun. 17, 1983, versus Kevin Von Erich. Fans were surprised when Race appeared as the titleholder instead of Flair. Some angry patrons chanted, "We want Flair." *Wrestling Observer Newsletter*, Aug. 1983, 4.

24 Flair also defeated Bob Brown, George Wells, and Butch Reed. The tournament matches were described by Nancye Deem. *Ric Flair Fan Club Newsletter* #13, Oct. 1983, 4.

25 Ibid, 10.

26 *Wrestling Observer Newsletter*, Aug. 1983, 16.

27 Articles and Letters to the Editor, *Wrestling Observer Newsletter*, Aug.–Nov. 1983.

28 *Wrestling Observer Newsletter*, Sep. 1983, 19. It is arguable that Race's tenure as champion had any effect on the war in St. Louis. Matysik discussed the problems that plagued his promotion and his eventual final show on Oct. 29, 1983, in his book, *Wrestling at the Chase: The Inside Story of Sam Muchnick and the Legends of Professional Wrestling* by Larry Matysik, 2005, 187.

29 Race revealed that he was burned out as champion, his marriage was failing, and he was losing money in the Kansas City promotion. He was ready to step away as titleholder. *King of the Ring: The Harley Race Story* by Harley Race with Gerry Tritz, 2004, 114–115.

30 *Mid-Atlantic Championship Wrestling*, Jul. 30, 1983. *The Ultimate Ric Flair Collection* DVD Set, World Wrestling Entertainment, 2003.

31 In a previous interview segment on *World Wide Wrestling*, Flair introduced his children, Megan and David. Orton, after declaring his allegiance to Flair, held young David.

32 Orton and Slater landed a double piledriver on Flair. Orton also used a neckbreaker. *The Ultimate Ric Flair Collection*.

33 The church was at 6800 Sardis Rd. in Charlotte.

34 Flair and Harrell obtained their marriage license on Aug. 24, 1983. Jim Crockett signed the document as a witness. Mecklenburg County Certificate of Marriage, License Number 1975, Aug. 31, 1983. Also see *Charlotte News*, Sep. 6, 1983, 9D.

35 Bob Caudle mentioned that Flair might never wrestle again. *Mid-Atlantic Championship Wrestling*, Sep. 24, 1983.

36 The article stated that Flair's father, "Dr. Paul Fleir," was his personal physician. *Charlotte Observer*, Sep. 16, 1983, 4C.

37 The program was taped on Sep. 21, 1983, in Shelby, NC.

38 Slater and Orton wrestled Scott McGhee and Steve Muslin.

39 *The Ultimate Ric Flair Collection* DVD Set, World Wrestling Entertainment, 2003.

40 The show was aired at CCTV locations in NC, SC, and VA. There were additional outlets in Puerto Rico, the Virgin Islands, and Venezuela. *Greensboro Record*, Nov. 25, 1983, D4.

41 Flair gave it this name during *Mid-Atlantic Championship Wrestling*, Oct. 22, 1983, which had been taped on Oct. 12. *The Ultimate Ric Flair Collection* DVD Set, World Wrestling Entertainment, 2003. The spelling "Flare" was interchangeable with "Flair" in advertising and articles.

42 Attendance was 15,457. *Greensboro Record*, Nov. 25, 1983, D4. On the day of Starrcade, the Greensboro skies were overcast and rain was persistent. A cold front was hammering cities to the north, and there was precipitation from the Carolinas up through NY with snow at the greater altitudes to the west. *Greensboro Record*, Nov. 24, 1983, A37, *Greensboro Record*, Nov. 25, 1983, 1, A7. Flair mentioned a snowstorm affecting the region. *To Be the Man* by Ric Flair with Keith Elliot Greenberg, 2004, 116.

43 The music was composed by Richard Strauss in 1896. The portion that was played was the initial fanfare, entitled, "Sunrise." It was popularized in Stanley Kubrick's 1968 film, *2001: A Space Odyssey*. Notably, *Also sprach Zarathustra* was the opening theme used in concerts by Elvis Presley. Elvis used it at the Greensboro Coliseum in Apr. 1972. *Greensboro Daily News*, May 11, 1972, 6. Gary Hart claimed that the Spoiler used the music in the Dallas territory prior to Flair. *"Playboy" Gary Hart: My Life in Wrestling* by Gary Hart with Philip Varriale, 2009. Flair said Dusty Rhodes picked the song for him. *Wooooo! Nation* Podcast Episode #41.

44 The robe was featured on the A&E broadcast of *WWE's Most Wanted Treasures* on Jun. 20, 2021, and was valued at $50,000. The owner was a longtime wrestling collector, West Potter.

45 Former NWA World champion Gene Kiniski was the special guest referee.

46 During the bout, commentator Gordon Solie mistakenly stated that Flair was already a two-time NWA champion.

47 *The Ultimate Ric Flair Collection* DVD Set, World Wrestling Entertainment, 2003. This match was second place in "Match of the Year" honors, *Wrestling Observer Newsletter*, Jan. 1984, 18.

48 *Ric Flair Fan Club Newsletter* #15, Apr. 1984, 6.

49 *King of the Ring: The Harley Race Story* by Harley Race with Gerry Tritz, 2004, 117.

50 *Starrcade: The Essential Collection (1983–2000)* DVD Set, World Wrestling Entertainment, 2012.

51 *World Championship Wrestling*, Nov. 26, 1983.

52 Ibid. Flair had a lot of respect for Gordon Solie, and they traveled together often. Flair called Solie shortly before his death in Jul. 2000, and Solie told him he loved him. *Wrestling Observer Newsletter*, Aug. 7, 2000, f4wonline.com.

53 *Dallas Morning News*, Dec. 26, 1983, 12B. The attendance was listed as 19,675. *Wrestling Observer Newsletter*, Jan. 1984, 27–28.

54 The *Wrestling Observer Newsletter* honored him as its "Wrestler of the Year" for 1983, while also acknowledging him as "Most Charismatic." Ibid, 12, 16.

55 Dave Meltzer wrote that Von Erich "was most likely going to be Ric Flair's successor on the NWA throne." *Wrestling Observer Newsletter*, Apr. 1984, 2. Flair discussed Von Erich being a future NWA champion. *Wooooo! Nation* Podcast Episode #24.

56 Von Erich passed away on Feb. 10, 1984. *Dallas Morning News*, Feb. 11, 1984, A33.

57 The funeral was held at 10:00 a.m. in Denton, TX.

58 *Dallas Morning News*, Feb. 16, 1984, 32A.

59 Flair beat Windham by DQ before 4,937 fans. *Miami Herald*, Feb. 16, 1984, 8D.

60 Flair discussed what happened in *Gong Magazine*, May 1984, 14–15.

61 Unidentified Christchurch newspaper, circa Mar. 20, 1984, Vern Ross Wrestling Collection, Hocken Library Archives & Manuscripts, University of Otago, Dunedin, New Zealand.

62 Ibid. Race wrestled Gerry Morrow instead.

63 Flair said it was the idea of Race and Steve Rickard. *To Be the Man* by Ric Flair with Keith Elliot Greenberg, 2004, 124.

64 Flair talked about this situation on his podcast. *Wooooo! Nation* Podcast Episode #31.

65 Results and information provided by historians Haruo Yamaguchi and Steve Ogilvie. Photos of this match appeared in *Gong Magazine*, May 1984.

66 Race said that nobody knew that Boesch was in Wellington at that time. *To Be the Man* by Ric Flair with Keith Elliot Greenberg, 2004, 124.

67 Race wore the NWA belt for a match with Flair on Mar. 21 in Auckland.

68 *Gong Magazine*, May 1984, 14–15.

69 See articles in *Singapore Monitor* and *Berita Harian*, Mar. 1984. Reportedly, Flair also participated in a battle royal and beat Ed Moretti on the other two nights in Singapore.

CHAPTER 11: THE WRESTLING WAR

1 Details of the sale were outlined in an agreement signed by Vincent McMahon Sr., Robert Marella, Phil Zacko, Arnold Skaaland, and Vincent K. McMahon, dated Jun. 5, 1982. The latter's company, Titan Sports, became the official organization behind the WWF, replacing the Capitol Wrestling Corporation, which was later dissolved.

2 *Michael LeBell v. Vincent Kennedy McMahon, Titan Sports, Inc., Capital Wrestling Corporation, and Does 1 to 20, inclusive*, Superior Court of California for the County of Los Angeles, Case No. C 568 506. Also correspondence with Jeff Walton, Jun. 2016.

3 Barnett likely became the NWA's treasurer around 1976.

4 McMahon was at war with Ole Anderson over cities in OH. Anderson was a partner with Barnett in Georgia Championship Wrestling.

5 McMahon, for a period of time in 1983, featured clips of NWA and AWA stars on his USA Cable Network program *All-American Wrestling*.

6 Piper left JCP in Jan. 1984, whereas Valentine finished in Mar., and Orton in early Apr.

7 Hogan was voted "Best Baby Face." *Wrestling Observer Newsletter 1983 Yearbook*, 12.

8 *Minneapolis Star and Tribune*, Apr. 25, 1983, 6D. Hogan had thrown Bockwinkel over the top rope before the pinfall and was disqualified, thus allowing Bockwinkel to retain his belt.

9 *Wrestling Observer Newsletter 1983 Yearbook*, 12.

10 Ibid.

11 Steamboat had actually retired to focus on his gym business.

12 This number includes St. Louis and the Central States territories as separate entities, which was the historical norm, despite being owned by the same outfit in the 1980s.

13 The episodes were on Oct. 2 and Nov. 6, 1983. The "Update" segment appeared on Apr. 7, 1984.

14 The article was entitled "The Von Erichs: A Dominant Family of Wrestling."

15 *Wrestling at the Chase: The Inside Story of Sam Muchnick and the Legends of Professional Wrestling* by Larry Matysik, 2005, 182–183.

16 The stadium was in Irving, TX, a suburb of Dallas.

17 The gate was $402,000. *Wrestling Observer Newsletter*, Jun. 28, 1999.
18 *Dallas Morning News*, May 7, 1984, B8. Flair talked about his match with Von Erich. *Wooooo! Nation* Podcast Episode #22.
19 *Newark Star-Ledger*, May 6, 1984, E13.
20 There was talk of having Flair challenge Steamboat for the U.S. championship instead.
21 The night Kerry Von Erich won the belt, Gary Hart asked Jack Adkisson how long he was going to hold it and was told "18 days." *"Playboy" Gary Hart: My Life in Wrestling* by Gary Hart with Philip Varriale, 2009. The title change to Von Erich was not mentioned on WTBS, as it was believed that news that Flair had lost his belt would negatively affect ticket sales for the Meadowlands card. However, Flair did mention the loss on WTBS during a June telecast, claiming he won it back from Von Erich "10 days" after losing it. *Eastern Wrestling News*, Jun. 1984, 4.
22 Details of Von Erich's reign and the title change in Japan were featured in *Wrestling All Stars*, Oct. 1984, 14–19. Von Erich's reign was called an "18-day loan." *Miami News*, Mar. 13, 1986, B6.
23 Correspondence with Charles Warburton, May 26, 2021.
24 Photographs from his appearance in Staten Island appeared in *Wrestling's Main Event*, Sep. 1984, 26–27.
25 Ibid. The NWA also relied heavily on promotion from WTBS. JCP also had TV in New York City on WXTV, channel 41, a Spanish-language station. A promotional advertisement with a photo of Flair ran in the *New York Daily News*, Apr. 28, 1984, 37. On the same page was a picture of Hulk Hogan, advertising the WWF on WOR-TV.
26 *A Night of Champions*, Official NWA Program, May 29, 1984. It should be noted that quotes attributed to wrestlers in wrestling publications were often crafted by writers, instead of taken verbatim from actual interviews. It is unknown if this was a genuine Flair interview.
27 Attendance was "almost 14,000." *Jersey Journal*, May 30, 1984, 38. Attendance was "14,500." *Newark Star-Ledger*, May 30, 1984, 66. 15,000 people were present. *Wrestling's Main Event*, Sep. 1984, 35. Earlier in this same article, it was said that "25,000 fans turned out to witness this big 'Night of Champions.'" Ibid, 28. A typical sellout for wrestling at the Meadowlands was in the 20,000 range.
28 It was reported to be the NWA's first card in the New York City area "in nearly 20 years." *A Night of Champions*, Official NWA Program, May 29, 1984. The NWA was also promoting in Baltimore, having run shows on Feb. 16 and Apr. 7, 1984. Flair headlined the second show, defeating Jack Brisco.
29 Undated episode of *World Championship Wrestling*, circa early Feb. 1984.
30 McMahon officially took over the WTBS slot on "Black Saturday," Jul. 14, 1984.
31 Dick Bourne wrote a detailed article about Wahoo's heel turn, entitled "The Betrayal of Chief Wahoo McDaniel (Part Three)," dated Jul. 22, 2018, midatlanticgateway.com.
32 *Greensboro News and Record*, Aug. 19, 1984, E4. In television promos, "Silver Star" was spelled "Silver Starr" or "SilverStarr." Article by Dick Bourne entitled "Highs and Lows: Silver Starr '85 and the Crockett Ballpark Fire," dated May 6, 2016, midatlanticgateway.com.
33 *Greensboro News and Record*, Mar. 17, 1985, B8.
34 The attendance was reported to be 11,969. *Charlotte News*, Feb. 26, 1985, 2C.
35 *Dusty Rhodes Shoot Interview*, RF Video, circa 2000.
36 *Miami Herald*, Jul. 2, 1984, 7D, *Miami News*, Jun. 30, 1984, 3B.
37 Flair talked about Crockett hiring Rhodes in his book. *To Be the Man* by Ric Flair with Keith Elliot Greenberg, 2004, 112.
38 Donna Crawford, head of the Ric Flair Fan Club, and her husband, Steve, attended the Starrcade Rally in Greensboro. At that event, they met and spoke with Flair's wife, Beth. *Ric Flair Fan Club Newsletter* #17, Nov. 1984, 1.
39 Frazier was the world heavyweight boxing champion from 1970 to 1973.
40 Footage of this event was shown on *World Wide Wrestling*, Oct. 13, 1984.

41   *Greensboro News and Record*, Nov. 23, 1984, C2.

42   *Philadelphia Inquirer*, Feb. 5, 1985, 4E.

43   *Philadelphia Inquirer*, Feb. 6, 1985, 2E.

44   *Wrestling Observer Newsletter*, Mar. 25, 1985, 13.

45   Steamboat made his WWF debut at a television taping at WTBS Studios in Atlanta on Mar. 2, 1985.

46   *World Championship Wrestling*, Apr. 6, 1985.

47   *Eastern Wrestling News*, Apr. 1985, 7.

48   Ibid, 12.

49   Rumors spread about a possible Flair jump to the WWF in 1983. *Eastern Wrestling News*, Nov. 1983, 4, 9.

50   On Oct. 28, 1985, in Fort Worth, Flair did wrestle Lance Von Erich, who was not a genuine member of the Von Erich clan. They went to a double DQ.

51   Flair's minimum annual salary of $170,000 in May 1985 equates to $469,458, as of Jun. 2022. bls.gov.

52   Memorandum of Agreement between Jim Crockett Promotions and Richard M. Fliehr, dated May 1, 1985. Notably, the press reported that Crockett had signed Flair "to an exclusive 3 year personal services contract." *International Wrestling News*, May 1985, 6.

CHAPTER 12: A CUSTOM-MADE CHAMPION

1   It was estimated that WrestleMania drew "close to $4 million." *Wrestling Observer Newsletter*, Apr. 15, 1985, 17. Another report stated that it "grossed about $12 million," which included the live gate, CCTV, and limited PPV reach. *Los Angeles Times*, Jun. 7, 1985, E7.

2   Hogan being from Venice Beach was part of his gimmick. He was really from the Tampa, FL, area.

3   *Sports Illustrated*, Apr. 29, 1985. Hogan was a guest veejay on MTV with Cyndi Lauper on Apr. 30, 1985. *Sun-Sentinel*, Apr. 30, 1985, E5. Hogan appeared on *The Tonight Show* with host Joan Rivers on Jul. 11, 1985. *New York Daily News*, Jul. 11, 1985, 95.

4   *Hulk Hogan's Rock 'n' Wrestling* premiered on CBS on Sep. 14, 1985.

5   *World Championship Wrestling*, Jun. 8, 1985. The match referenced was probably the 60-minute draw between Flair and Magnum in Greensboro on May 26, 1985.

6   *World Championship Wrestling*, Jun. 15, 1985.

7   *Spartanburg Herald-Journal*, Jul. 27, 1980, B3.

8   *Greensboro News and Record*, May 27, 1985, B5. Over the following three weeks, Flair and Magnum wrestled at least five additional times, including matches in Atlanta, Pittsburgh, and Philadelphia.

9   *World Championship Wrestling*, Jun. 15, 1985.

10   Ibid.

11   During commentary for an Arn Anderson match on WTBS, Ole Anderson mentioned that he was "brothers" with Arn. Tony Schiavone then stated that Ole's father and Arn's father were indeed brothers, which would have made them cousins. Ole proceeded to change the subject. *World Championship Wrestling*, Apr. 6, 1985. The confusion of how Ole and Arn were related continued, with sources calling them cousins or uncle and nephew.

12   Flair, during the Jun. 15 episode of *World Championship Wrestling*, mentioned Koloff's attack on his "close friend" David Crockett and said that Nikita had his attention now. *World Championship Wrestling*, Jun. 15, 1985. Koloff gave Crockett a Russian Sickle clothesline on *World Wide Wrestling*, Jun. 15, 1985. The Flair-Koloff match was billed as "The Freedom Challenge."

13   The booking pattern was pretty obvious: On the WTBS show, Flair tended to perform more as a heel, whereas on the syndicated program, with local reach in the mid-Atlantic area, he was a fan favorite. For instance, prior to a match with Mike Davis on *World Wide Wrestling*, Flair reached out to shake opponent Mike Davis's hand, which was a classic babyface move. *World Wide Wrestling*, Jul. 6, 1985. This was less than a month after the Magnum T.A. incident.

14   Flair rode in the WSOC-TV, channel 9, "Chopper."

15   *Charlotte Observer*, Jul. 8, 1985, 10A.

16   A portion of the Bash show was released on VHS as part of the *Ringmasters* VHS tape from *Pro Wrestling Illustrated* and Vestron Video. The tape was 60 minutes in length. The show was also featured in the Dec. 1985 issue of *Pro Wrestling Illustrated*.

17   Flair made six appearances in Houston during that time frame. For his Jun. 28, 1985, bout with Magnum, Flair earned $900 and was paid $654 for transportation fees. Paul Boesch Wrestling Collection.

18   *Wrestling Program*, Houston, TX, Jun. 28, 1985.

19   *World Wide Wrestling*, Jul. 6, 1985.

20   The gate was $18,000. *Wrestling Observer Newsletter* #5, Jul. 1, 1985.

21   The Lexington show drew 8,000 to Rupp Arena for the "Bluegrass Spectacular." *Wrestling Observer Newsletter*, Sep. 19, 1985, 2–3, *Lexington Herald-Leader*, Sep. 5, 1985, C7. The Memphis card at the Mid-South Coliseum drew 9,496. *Memphis Commercial Appeal*, Oct. 2, 1985, D5.

22   Flair defeated McDaniel in two of three falls at the Battle of the Belts in Tampa on Sep. 2, 1985. *Tampa Tribune*, Sep. 4, 1985, 8C. This show was syndicated in more than a dozen markets. *Wrestling Observer Newsletter*, Sep. 19, 1985, 2.

23   An interview with Dr. Joseph Estwanik, who was attending to Rhodes, was shown on *World Championship Wrestling* and *World Wide Wrestling*, Oct. 12, 1985, thehistoryofwwe.com /jcp85.htm. Estwanik was a physician at the Metrolina Orthopedic Sports Medicine Clinic in Charlotte. Instead of his ankle, Rhodes's "left foot" was said to have been injured. *Mid-Atlantic Championship Wrestling*, circa Oct. 1985, *The Ultimate Ric Flair Collection* DVD Set, World Wrestling Entertainment, 2003. In some reports, it was claimed that Flair and the Andersons had broken Rhodes's leg.

24   *Mid-Atlantic Championship Wrestling*, circa Oct. 1985, *The Ultimate Ric Flair Collection* DVD Set, World Wrestling Entertainment, 2003.

25   It appears that the "hard times" promo was featured on *Mid-Atlantic Championship Wrestling* and *World Wide Wrestling*, with Rhodes delivering a different version on *World Championship Wrestling*. All three were likely broadcast on Nov. 9, 1985.

26   While it is unknown, it is likely Flair traveled back to his home in Charlotte after the Lansing date on Oct. 15, 1985, prior to venturing to Japan. If so, it would have pushed his total mileage over 10,000 for this period.

27   Flair said that Tsuruta was his stiffest opponent. *Wooooo! Nation* Podcast Episode #41.

28   Tsuruta won the AWA title from Bockwinkel on Feb. 23, 1984, in Tokyo, Japan.

29   The time of match has been listed as 34:03 and as 34:31.

30   The match was held in Shizuoka. They also wrestled Genichiro Tenryu and Jumbo Tsuruta in Kyoto on Oct. 22 (a loss by countout) and Riki Choshu and Yoshiaki Yatsu (double DQ) on Oct. 23 in Mito.

31   Following this angle, both DiBiase and Murdoch went to Japan, where the former participated in the AJPW Real World Tag League and the latter wrestled in the NJPW IWGP Tag Team League series in Nov. and Dec. 1985.

32   *Mid-Atlantic Championship Wrestling*, circa Oct. 1985, *The Ultimate Ric Flair Collection* DVD Set, World Wrestling Entertainment, 2003.

33   It is believed this was during a localized television promo. The date is unknown. *Four Horsemen: A Timeline History* by Dick Bourne, 2017, 17. Anderson, by the end of Oct. 1985, had physical possession of the World TV belt after Dusty Rhodes had been stripped of the

honor because of his injury. He was not officially recognized until he won a tournament in Jan. 1986.

34 *The Ultimate Ric Flair Collection* DVD Set, World Wrestling Entertainment, 2003.

35 *Wrestling Flyer Interview Collection* #1 by John Clark, 34. Landel was fired in Dec. 1985.

36 *Winnipeg Free Press*, Jan. 17, 1986, 48. Flair and Bockwinkel were on opposite sides of a six-man tag team match on Sep. 4, 1979, in Raleigh, NC.

37 *Jersey Journal*, Feb. 25, 1986, 20. Also see *Newark Star-Ledger*, Feb. 25, 1986, 73 and *Wrestling Observer Newsletter*, Mar. 17, 1986, 2.

38 Flair talked about this occasion. *Ricky Morton Podcast* #10, Dec. 7, 2017, *New York Daily News*, Feb. 23, 1986, 16.

39 *Charlotte Observer*, May 30, 1976, F1.

40 Flair and his wife moved into the home around Mar. 1984. He mentioned it during an interview in *Gong Magazine*, May 1984, 14–15. Crockett's office was at 6300 Carmel Rd. When the Fliehrs were wed, they listed Crockett's office as their place of residence on their marriage certificate. Mecklenburg County Certificate of Marriage, License Number 1975, Aug. 31, 1983.

41 The address was 9527 Hunting Court, and it reportedly cost $138,000. Deed of Trust, Mecklenburg County Property Records, Sep. 12, 1985.

42 *New Zealand Wrestling Special*, 1, Sep. 1984.

43 Ibid.

44 Bob Heller wrote: "The Ric Flair people see in the wrestling ring and the Ric Flair fans see in TV interviews is, the man insists, the real Ric Flair." *Greensboro Daily News*, Nov. 2, 1976, B4. Flair said: "I got where I am because I knew that you can't be in the public eye and not be real." *Nashville Tennessean*, Sep. 3, 1989, F1.

CHAPTER 13: THE HORSEMEN RIDE

1 The WWF had a cable presence on the USA Network, whereas Jim Crockett had WTBS, and the AWA had ESPN.

2 This content includes the WWF's cartoon telecast on Saturday mornings on CBS.

3 The title was declared vacant after a controversial match between Wahoo McDaniel and Ricky Steamboat on Jun. 24, 1984, in Greensboro. On that evening, McDaniel won the belt after Tully Blanchard hit Steamboat with a chair.

4 Windham and Rotundo were known as the "U.S. Express."

5 Flair and Windham had last wrestled in a singles match on Jun. 26, 1984, in Tampa. They battled to a draw. They were also on the opposite sides of two tag team matches on Jul. 13 in St. Louis and Jul. 29, 1984 in Ocala, FL.

6 Flair actually introduced the belt during his pre-match interview with Buddy Colt.

7 For more details, read *Big Gold: A Close Look at Pro Wrestling's Most Celebrated Championship Belt* by Dick Bourne with Dave Millican, 2014.

8 The initial name plate on the new belt misspelled Flair's first name as "Rick."

9 Many times in 1986, Flair would shake hands with his opponent before the match to cheers, then deliberately cheat. In Flair's match against NWA World Junior champion Denny Brown during *NWA Pro* on Jul. 12, 1986, he shook hands with Brown at the outset and then won via his figure-four. He grabbed the ropes and held the move after the bell, as if trying to injure Brown.

10 Before the match, Flair confirmed that the greatness in another wrestler brings out the best in him.

11 Flair and Windham did the same finish that Flair and Rick Martel had done in Japan. Flair attempted a cross body off the ropes, Windham caught it, and the momentum carried both

over the top rope. The main difference was once they were on the floor in Orlando, they prevented each other from getting back into the ring.

12   *Wrestling Observer Newsletter*, Mar. 3, 1986, 3. The bout was also named "Match of the Year." *Wrestling Observer Newsletter 1986 Yearbook*, 48–49.

13   *Wrestling Observer Newsletter 1985 Yearbook*, 4.

14   Flair won that award in 1981, 1984, and 1985. *Pro Wrestling Illustrated*, Mar. 1986, 44.

15   Lou Thesz and Ole Anderson went a step further and stated that all of Flair's matches were repetitious. "He's wrestling the same match he was wrestling 10 years ago," Thesz said in 1991. "He should change his style a little bit." *Pro Wrestling Torch Annual IV*, Summer 1991, 26. Anderson commented on Flair's routine in his book. *Inside Out: How Corporate America Destroyed Professional Wrestling* by Ole Anderson with Scott Teal, 2003.

16   Flair was quoted as saying that his job was "different" than Hogan's. *Miami News*, Mar. 13, 1986, B1.

17   Some parents were concerned about JCP programming with these types of interview segments. See letters to the editor, *Wrestling Forum*, Jul. 30, 1987, 8.

18   *Wrestling Observer Newsletter*, Feb. 3, 1986, 7. Also see *Wrestling Observer Newsletter*, Feb. 17, 1986, 4.

19   Garvin was billed as living in Atlanta, GA.

20   Flair threw the referee out of the way prior to Rhodes entering the ring. It appears, though, that Garvin lost the match by DQ because of Rhodes's outside interference. *World Championship Wrestling*, Dec. 28, 1985.

21   In the telecast, Flair and Garvin sparred verbally and physically. In one promo, Garvin said, "I am your master when it comes to that ring. I know that." It should be noted that Garvin's knockout punch was missed by the TV camera and happened just out of frame. Even on replay, the punch was not shown. After Flair was knocked out, J.J. Dillon called it a "cheap shot." *World Championship Wrestling*, Jan. 18, 1986.

22   The card was taped on Feb. 2, 1986, before an estimated 10,000 fans.

23   Referee Tommy Young did not see Garvin's foot on the bottom rope during the pin. *Superstars on the Superstation*, Feb. 7, 1986.

24   The Philadelphia bout was said to be a Texas Death match. *Philadelphia Inquirer*, Mar. 23, 1986, D2. *Greensboro News and Record*, Mar. 30, 1986, B10.

25   It was billed as Rhodes's final shot at the world heavyweight title, but, of course, it wasn't.

26   The Road Warriors beat Ron Garvin and Magnum T.A. in the finals.

27   Only 3,000 fans turned out for the matinee, and another 13,000 at night.

28   Flair had pulled off Rhodes's boot and used it on his opponent first, while the referee, Tommy Young, was knocked down. After the match, Rhodes also hit Young with the boot. Near the end of the bout, Flair ran over and grabbed Rhodes's valet, Baby Doll, on the ring apron.

29   Flair was being interviewed by Tony Schiavone and David Crockett, only to be cut off by the music of the Rock and Roll Express, who were going to the ring for a match in the WTBS Studio. *World Championship Wrestling*, Mar. 29, 1986.

30   Ibid.

31   The match was Dusty Rhodes and the Rock and Roll Express against Flair, Arn Anderson, and Tully Blanchard. The attendance was 6,219. *Greensboro News and Record*, Apr. 21, 1986, B6. Footage of this situation was shown on *World Championship Wrestling*, Apr. 26, 1986.

32   The incident occurred on May 26, 1986, in Greenville after a six-man tag team match. *Greenville News*, May 27, 1986, C4. Footage was shown on *World Championship Wrestling*, May 31, 1986. Ole Anderson returned in mid-Jun.

33   NWA president Bob Geigel discussed the "14" city Great American Bash tour and congratulated Jim Crockett on behalf of Alliance members. Ibid.

34   Other performers included George Jones, Joe Ely, and Delbert McClinton.

35   David Crockett explained the problems at the Bash. *David Crockett Shoot Interview*, RF Video.

36   Memphis on Jul. 4 drew 1,900, and Cincinnati on Jul. 9 drew around 3,900.

37 Tom Sorensen, of the *Charlotte Observer*, estimated the attendance at 20,000. *Charlotte Observer*, Jul. 6, 1986, B4. Other estimates had the crowd size as high as 23,000. The helicopter was again from WSOC, channel 9, in Charlotte. WSOC sports director Harold Johnson arrived with Flair and acted as a ring announcer for the main event.

38 The Crockett family was equally important on the promotional end of things.

39 These title defenses occurred between Jul. 1 and 26, 1986.

40 This was the 13th night of the Great American Bash tour.

41 *Greensboro News and Record*, Jul. 27, 1986, B6. Flair's reign was the longest for an NWA World champion since Harley Race between 1977 and 1979 (926 days).

42 *World Championship Wrestling*, Aug. 2, 1986.

43 *Wrestling Observer Newsletter*, Aug. 10, 1986, 10.

44 Footage of the Kansas City and St. Louis matches was shown during *World Championship Wrestling*, Aug. 16, 1986.

45 The famed group added one more on Aug. 17, 1986 when Baby Doll turned on Dusty Rhodes in Charlotte and joined the clique. This surprising turn occurred during a Flair-Rhodes match, broadcast on *NWA Pro Wrestling* on Aug. 23, 1986.

46 Flair talked about Magnum and the car accident. *Wooooo! Nation* Podcast Episodes #6, #9, #28.

47 Flair visited Magnum in the hospital. Interview of Ric Flair, *Steve Austin Podcast*, 2013. Flair laid the world title belt on Magnum's chest in the ICU and told him that when he got out of the hospital, he'd take it from him in the ring. *Jim Crockett Promotions: The Good Old Days* Documentary (2013).

48 Footage of the attack and the formation of the "Superpowers" in Philadelphia was shown on *World Championship Wrestling*, Oct. 25, 1986.

49 The original plan for Starrcade '86 was likely going to be Flair vs. Magnum T.A. Ric Flair Shoot Interview by Michael Bochicchio, highspots.com, 2008.

50 Koloff talked about his match with Flair. Interview of Nikita Koloff by John Poz, *Two Man Power Trip of WrestlingPodcast*, 2021.

51 Notably, the other members of the Four Horsemen wrestled in Greensboro that night, as Starrcade was once again held in two different locations.

52 Flair was said to have won. *Greensboro News and Record*, Nov. 28, 1986, C4.

53 Windham arrived on Dec. 1, 1986, in Fayetteville, NC.

54 The program was held on Sep. 19, 1986, in Bloomington, and Flair beat Dusty Rhodes by DQ.

55 According to existing records, Flair's last match in the Twin Cities was May 4, 1974, in Minneapolis and he was defeated by Baron von Raschke. It was claimed that Flair wrestled Bruiser Brody in St. Paul on May 28, 1984, but no evidence has ever been found.

56 *Minneapolis Star and Tribune*, Sep. 20, 1986, 1A.

57 Ibid, 8A.

58 *Raleigh News and Observer*, Jan. 27, 1991, 7E.

59 *Minneapolis Star and Tribune*, Sep. 20, 1986, 8A.

60 She was born at 1:08 p.m. Certificate of Live Birth, North Carolina Department of Human Resources.

61 It is believed that Megan and David lived with their mother, Leslie, in New Hope, MN.

62 Flair's children, Megan and David, spoke about his absence when they were children. *30 for 30* Documentary, ESPN Films, 2017.

63 The closest he would've come on any regular basis was Des Moines, which was booked out of the Kansas City office. Des Moines was less than four hours from Minneapolis by car.

64 *30 for 30* Documentary, ESPN Films, 2017.

65 For example, JCP earned approximately $311,000 in Dec. 1984, and then made $1,208,677 in Dec. 1985. The company grossed $6.5 million in 1984–85. Jim Crockett Promotions, Inc. Wrestling Revenues, 1981–88.

66 Ibid.

CHAPTER 14: FIVE-TIME CHAMPION

1   *To Be the Man* by Ric Flair with Keith Elliot Greenberg, 2004, 95.

2   *Nashville Tennessean*, Sep. 3, 1989, F1.

3   *Knoxville News-Sentinel*, Oct. 17, 1986, Detours Section, 9.

4   *Nashville Tennessean*, Sep. 3, 1989, F1.

5   *Miami News*, Mar. 13, 1986, B1.

6   *Knoxville News-Sentinel*, Oct. 17, 1986, Detours Section, 9.

7   Undated article written by Paul Haskins, *Winston-Salem Sentinel*, *Ric Flair Fan Club Newsletter* #9, Oct. 1982, 13.

8   *Nashville Tennessean*, Sep. 3, 1989, F1. A report earlier in his career stated that Flair bleached his hair "every third week." *Greensboro Daily News*, May 18, 1980, F1.

9   Flair stated that he bled every night of the Bash tour and ultimately for 42 straight nights. *To Be the Man* by Ric Flair with Keith Elliot Greenberg, 2004, 152.

10 *Greensboro Daily News*, May 18, 1980, F1.

11 *Miami News*, Mar. 13, 1986, B1.

12 Ibid.

13 *Gong Magazine*, May 1984, 14–15.

14 He wrestled twice on Apr. 6 and 14, 1985.

15 Flair recited this story on a series of podcast interviews, including *Valuetainment Podcast with Patrick Bet-David*, Apr. 5, 2018, *Don't Tell Me the Score*, Feb. 6, 2020, and *Talk is Jericho*, Unknown Date, plus an interview on PWInsider with Mike Johnson, Jul. 30, 2020.

16 He reportedly missed a few tag team matches. *Eastern Wrestling News*, Apr. 1985, 13.

17 Ibid.

18 Crockett accompanied him on the journey back to Japan as well.

19 Letter from Lou Thesz to Sam Muchnick dated Nov. 13, 1956, reprinted in NWA Bulletin #3, Nov. 16, 1956.

20 *Knoxville News-Sentinel*, Oct. 17, 1986, Detours Section, 8–9. Flair wrestled in Los Angeles on Aug. 28 and then Knoxville on Aug. 29, 1986.

21 Wrestler Tracy Smothers said he didn't think Flair slept more than four hours a night. *Tracy Smothers Shoot Video*, RF Video. Flair talked about his lack of sleep and being in the gym early in the morning. *Wooooo! Nation* Podcast Episode #2.

22 At his fittest, Flair said he could do 500 squats in 14-minutes. *Wooooo! Nation* Podcast Episode #15.

23 *To Be the Man* by Ric Flair with Keith Elliot Greenberg, 2004, 65. Information about the StairMaster from *Wichita Eagle-Beacon*, Jan. 17, 1984, Advertising Section, 3.

24 Flair also said: "When you wrestle against the caliber of people I do four or five nights a week, you stay in shape." *Hays Daily News*, Jul. 21, 1982, 13.

25 *Miami News*, Mar. 13, 1986, B1.

26 *Knoxville News-Sentinel*, Oct. 17, 1986, Detours Section, 9.

27 *Woodstock Northwest Herald*, Jul. 21, 1987, 5.

28 *Miami News*, Mar. 13, 1986, B1.

29 *Knoxville News-Sentinel*, Oct. 17, 1986, Detours Section, 9.

30 *Wrestling Observer Newsletter 1986 Yearbook*, 56.

31 *Orangeburg Times and Democrat*, Aug. 26, 1987, 13A.

32 The Horsemen, as well as Dusty Rhodes and the Rock and Roll Express, who were there backing up Windham, surrounded the ring. This program was taped on Jan. 13, 1987, in Columbia, SC.

33 The card was taped on Jan. 20. *World Wide Wrestling*, Jan. 24, 1987.

34 The Los Angeles show was at the Great Western Forum in Inglewood, CA.

35   The deal was finalized on May 1, 1987. *Charlotte Observer*, May 6, 1987, E1, E14. Crockett purchased the UWF for $4 million to be paid over a 10-year period. *Best of the Wrestling Observer 1983–1987*, 42.

36   Flair's chase for Precious began as early as Feb. 1987. Notably, she was the real-world wife of Jimmy Garvin.

37   *World Championship Wrestling*, Apr. 4, 1987.

38   This show, part of the Great American Bash, drew 10,532. *Greensboro News and Record*, Jul. 12, 1987, B10.

39   *World Championship Wrestling*, Jul. 18, 1987.

40   *World Championship Wrestling*, Jul. 25, 1987.

41   In Miami, the masked "War Machine," also known as Big Bubba (Ray Traylor), was a substitute for an injured J.J. Dillon. This show drew 17,251 fans. *Miami Herald*, Aug. 1, 1987, 5C.

42   Flair and Luger headlined "Battle of the Belts III" on Sep. 1, 1986, at the Ocean Center in Daytona Beach. They wrestled to a 1–1 draw in a two-of-three-falls match.

43   Rhodes came up with the idea to put Luger in the Horsemen. *Wooooo! Nation* Podcast Episode #9.

44   Revenue for the month was over $3.1 million. Jim Crockett Promotions, Inc. Wrestling Revenues, 1981–88.

45   Flair wrestled Road Warrior Hawk on that program. Attendance was reportedly 23,500. *Charlotte Observer*, Jul. 19, 1987, 7C. Flair won by DQ. *Wrestling Observer Newsletter*, Jul. 27, 1987, 1.

46   *Wrestling Observer Newsletter*, Aug. 3, 1987, 7. A different report stated that Flair was bothered by his sciatic nerve. *Wrestling Forum*, Jul. 30, 1987, 14. It was later said that Flair suffered a "broken neck" in 1987, although the timing is unclear. *Wrestling Observer Newsletter*, Mar. 17, 2003, f4wonline.com.

47   In Chicago, Flair and Arn Anderson attacked Animal before the latter's scheduled bout with the champion. Flair was, in turn, disqualified, but no official match took place. Ibid.

48   Flair was a team player. He had no problem dropping the NWA belt to Garvin. *Wooooo! Nation* Podcast Episode #28.

49   *Wrestling Forum*, Jul. 30, 1987, 7.

50   *Wrestlers Are Like Seagulls: From McMahon to McMahon* by James J. Dillon with Scott Teal and Philip Varriale, 2005, 144–145.

51   *Wrestling Forum*, Nov. 30, 1987, 6. JCP lost 25 percent of its viewership after Garvin had captured the championship. *Best of the Wrestling Observer 1983–1987*, 42.

52   The WWF ran its inaugural Survivor Series on Thanksgiving night in opposition.

53   Five local live matches, in addition to the Starrcade show from Chicago via CCTV, were presented to fans Thanksgiving night in Greensboro. A similar program was staged in New Orleans.

54   *World Championship Wrestling*, circa Nov. 1987.

55   Starrcade grossed an estimated $1.3 million. *Best of the Wrestling Observer 1983–1987*, 45.

56   The UWF was finished as an individual entity by Dec. 1987.

57   *Multichannel News*, Feb. 8, 1988, 5.

CHAPTER 15: A RETURN TO GLORY

1   The Bunkhouse Stampede initially debuted in Dec. 1985.

2   *New York Daily News*, Jan. 25, 1988, 59. In direct opposition, the WWF ran its first Royal Rumble show live on the USA cable network.

3   A description of Luger's turn appeared in the *Orangeburg Times and Democrat*, Dec. 16, 1987, 11A.

4   Both the Clash and WrestleMania had a 4:00 p.m. EST start time. This was considered payback by JCP for the WWF's efforts to sabotage Starrcade '87 and the Bunkhouse Stampede PPVs.

5   It was claimed that they had wrestled a 45-minute draw.

6   Flair vs. Sting was named "Match of the Year." *Wrestling Observer Newsletter 1988 Yearbook*, 40.

7   *Wrestling Observer Newsletter 1988 Yearbook*, 41.

8   *Wrestling Observer Newsletter 1988 Yearbook*, 6.

9   The negotiations reportedly began in July 1988. *Wrestling Observer Newsletter 1988 Yearbook*, 4. A different source stated that negotiations began as early as Feb. 1988. *Charlotte Observer*, Sep. 27, 1988, 20B.

10 *Charlotte Observer*, Mar. 16, 1988, 6D.

11 *Second Nature: The Legacy of Ric Flair and the Rise of Charlotte* by Ric Flair & Charlotte with Brian Shields, 2017, 152–154.

12 Deed of Trust, Mecklenburg County Property Records, May 20, 1988. The home was built in 1987.

13 Blanchard's contract expired as of May 1 and Anderson's contract ended Jun. 18, 1988. *Proposal for the TBS Purchase of Jim Crockett Promotions, Inc.* by Blair Schmidt-Fellner, 1988, 11–13.

14 *The Arn Show* Podcast #67, Dec. 23, 2020.

15 Anderson and Blanchard debuted at a TV taping in Fort Wayne, IN. They took Bobby Heenan as their manager and became known as the "Brain Busters."

16 *Wrestling Observer Newsletter 1988 Yearbook*, 8.

17 Ric Flair Shoot Interview by Michael Bochicchio, 2008.

18 *Second Nature: The Legacy of Ric Flair and the Rise of Charlotte* by Ric Flair & Charlotte with Brian Shields, 2017, 111–112.

19 Ric Flair Shoot Interview by Michael Bochicchio, 2008.

20 *Proposal for the TBS Purchase of Jim Crockett Promotions, Inc.* by Blair Schmidt-Fellner, 1988, 8.

21 Correspondence with Blair Schmidt-Fellner, Feb. 3, 2021.

22 Ibid. Flair talked about Ted Turner, and said they had similarities. *The Nashville Tennessean*, Sep. 3, 1989, F1. Flair and Turner were photographed together for the cover of *Wrestling 89*, fall 1989.

23 Ibid.

24 Schmidt-Fellner told Flair at a Ramada Inn gathering in Norfolk on the evening of Starrcade 1988. Ibid.

25 Ric Flair Shoot Interview by Michael Bochicchio, 2008.

26 Flair discussed this situation and his falling out with Crockett. *Wooooo! Nation* Podcast Episode #7.

27 According to Wrestlingdata.com, as of Mar. 8, 2022.

28 Flair missed matches in Nashville, Chattanooga, Atlanta, and Rock Hill between Apr. 25 and Apr. 28, 1988.

29 *Wrestling Observer Newsletter 1988 Yearbook*, 45.

30 The show was the first PPV effort between Crockett and Turner Home Entertainment.

31 *Atlanta Journal and Constitution*, Nov. 3, 1988, D2.

32 Flair reportedly was on the verge of quitting in late Oct. *Wrestling Observer Newsletter*, Nov. 7, 1988, 5.

33 *Wrestling at the Chase: The Inside Story of Sam Muchnick and the Legends of Professional Wrestling* by Larry Matysik, 2005, 189.

34 *Wrestling Observer Newsletter*, Nov. 28, 1988, 4. Strangely, Flair was booked for only nine matches in Dec. 1988. He had but two matches in the first 24 days of the month.

35 Ibid, 6.
36 There was another factor in Rhodes being urged to resign (effectively pushed out). In late Nov. 1988, Rhodes did a TV angle with the Road Warriors, which saw a spike "injure" his eye. The scene included blood and went against a no-blood rule TBS had instituted and drew complaints from viewers. Rhodes was gone from the NWA by mid-February, 1989.
37 Gilbert's partner was initially billed as "Mr. X." *World Championship Wrestling*, Jan. 21, 1989.
38 *Pro Wrestling Torch*, Apr. 6, 1989, 8.
39 Ibid, 4. Jim Herd discussed this event during the *Conversations with Conrad* interview with Conrad Thompson, Nov. 8, 2020.
40 The other judges were Lou Thesz and Pat O'Connor.
41 Dr. Joseph Estwanik discussed Flair's condition. *World Championship Wrestling*, May 27, 1989.
42 Jim Herd said that Flair wanted to quit. *Conversations with Conrad* interview with Conrad Thompson, Nov. 8, 2020.
43 *Kayfabe Commentaries Timeline Series* with Jim Cornette.
44 *Pro Wrestling Torch*, Aug. 24, 1989, 4. Flair discussed his time as booker. *Wooooo! Nation* Podcast Episode #12.

CHAPTER 16: THE ROAD TO TITAN

1   The Ding Dongs were voted number one for "Worst Gimmick." *Wrestling Observer Newsletter 1989 Yearbook*, 54.
2   *New York Times*, Nov. 26, 1989, F1.
3   This edict was mentioned in wrestling "dirt sheets" in 1988 and 1989.
4   Jim Herd Interview, *Wrestling Observer Live*, Feb. 16, 2001. The angle was discussed on *Wooooo! Nation* Podcast Episode #8.
5   *Pro Wrestling Torch*, Sep. 21, 1989, 3.
6   *Wrestling Observer Newsletter 1989 Yearbook*, 42.
7   Ibid, 28. *Pro Wrestling Illustrated*, Mar. 1990.
8   *Pro Wrestling Torch*, Dec. 14, 1989, 2.
9   *Wrestling Observer Newsletter 1989 Yearbook*, 9.
10 *Philadelphia Daily News*, Apr. 3, 1989, 6. "Rasslin' Radio" was on WIP 610 AM on Saturday mornings.
11 An NWA show was held at the Civic Center in Philadelphia that night, but Flair was not on the card. The banquet was $75 a seat. *Philadelphia Daily News*, Apr. 3, 1989, 6.
12 Ric Flair "Wrestler of the Decade" Banquet VHS, presented by the Squared Circle Fan Club and *Rasslin' Radio*, Directed by Randy Salaman, 1989.
13 *Pittsburgh Post-Gazette*, Nov. 11, 1988, 14.
14 Ibid.
15 *Matwatch*, Vol. 1, No. 21, Nov. 14–20, 1988.
16 The book was tentatively entitled, "How to Really Turn Today's Women On!" Correspondence with Steve Chamberlain, Mar. 2, 2022.
17 *Conversations with Conrad* interview with Conrad Thompson, Nov. 8, 2020. The "negative viewer perception of Flair" was discovered through "TBS research" in Oct. 1989. *Matwatch*, Vol. 5, No. 2, Jan. 13–19, 1992, 2.
18 *Pro Wrestling Torch*, Oct. 5, 1989, 4.
19 A full description of their argument was featured in *Chokehold*, Oct. 17, 1989, 1–4. Correspondence with Lance LeVine, Apr. 1 and Apr. 3, 2021.
20 *Matwatch*, Vol. 2, No. 19, Oct. 30–Nov. 5, 1989.

21 *Matwatch*, Vol. 2, Nos. 27–28, Dec. 25, 1989–Jan. 7, 1990, 4.

22 Ibid, 3. Notably, Flair said he was not booking the promotion in Nov. 1989, around the time of his "I Quit" match against Terry Funk. He said that Kevin Sullivan was doing it. *Wooooo! Nation* Podcast Episode #10.

23 Flair finished with 25, Lex Luger 35, and the Great Muta 0.

24 Arn Anderson returned to the promotion following his WWF run on Nov. 28, 1989. There had also been talk of Tully Blanchard returning as well, but contractual talks between the wrestler and WCW fell through.

25 Ric Flair Interview, *Wrestling Observer Live*, 1999. Sting had earned the title shot based on his Starrcade 1989 victory.

26 Flair had teamed with the Andersons to beat the Great Muta, Buzz Sawyer, and Dragon Master in a cage match in the show's main event. Sting was injured trying to get into the cage.

27 Ric Flair Shoot Interview by Michael Bochicchio, highspots.com, 2008.

28 A copy of Flair's letter was featured in *The Midnight Express and Jim Cornette — 25th Anniversary Scrapbook* by Jim Cornette with Tim Ash, 2009, 164.

29 *Matwatch*, Vol. 2, No. 35, Feb. 26–Mar. 4, 1990, 4.

30 Ibid.

31 The Dec. 3 showing had a 3.3 rating with 1.68 million homes. *Matwatch*, Vol. 2, No. 25, Dec. 11–17, 1989, 5. The Jan. 7 program had a 3.2 rating with 1.63 million homes, which was the number one wrestling show on cable that week. *Matwatch*, Vol. 2, No. 30, Jan. 15–21, 1990, 6.

32 Flair wrestled TV bouts against Zenk on Feb. 2 and Pillman on Feb. 17, 1990.

33 *Wrestling Observer Newsletter*, Apr. 16, 1990, 10. It was said that Flair's contract gave him three-days' notice prior to a scheduled title change and that he didn't receive that advance notification. If true, it differed greatly from the perception of Flair's "creative control" at the time. It was presumed Flair could authorize or veto any title change, which would have given him the power to decline any title loss to Luger regardless of three days' notice.

34 Jim Herd Interview, *Wrestling Observer Live*, Feb. 16, 2001. Flair received a two-year contract extension through the end of 1993. *Matwatch*, Vol. 2, No. 41, Apr. 9–15, 1990, 1–2. The contract extended through 1994, according to *Wrestling Observer Newsletter*, Apr. 23, 1990, 3. *Matwatch* later stated that Flair's contract extension wasn't signed in March and was still an ongoing issue in May 1990. *Matwatch*, Vol. 2, No. 45, May 21–27, 1990, 5. A further update was provided in July, stating that his "contract renewal" was "through 1994 but [contained] some kind of escape clause at the end of 1992." It was said that the "extension years" were for "an average in the $400,000–500,000 range." *Matwatch*, Vol. 3, No. 3, Jul. 16–22, 1990, 5.

35 Lex Luger and El Gigante, a 7-foot-6 former basketball player, were also members of the group.

36 *Miami Herald*, Aug. 19, 1990, 10D. According to current records, it appears Flair wrestled on Jul. 8 in Roanoke and then on Jul. 9 in Gainesville, GA.

37 Harley Race subbed for Flair on the road. *Matwatch*, Vol. 3, No. 5, Jul. 30–Aug. 5, 1990, 1. It was reported elsewhere that Flair had suffered a serious knee injury on Jul. 13 in Dallas.

38 *Matwatch*, Vol. 3, No. 11, Sep. 10–16, 1990, 8.

39 *To Be the Man* by Ric Flair with Keith Elliot Greenberg, 2004, 194–195. Also discussed on *Wooooo! Nation* Podcast Episode #5. The concept of borrowing names from iconic Hollywood films for wrestlers was toyed with by Jim Herd throughout 1990. An Associated Press article about the idea was printed in the *Arkansas Gazette*, Mar. 1, 1990, A2.

40 It was said Herd ordered Flair to cut his hair as a "show of loyalty." *Matwatch*, Vol. 5, No. 2, Jan. 13–19, 1992, 2.

41 *Matwatch*, Vol. 2, No. 5, Jul. 24–30, 1989, 3.

42 Flair discussed these self-confidence problems in Interview of Ric Flair, *Wrestling Inc.* Podcast, Feb. 24, 2021, Interview of Ric Flair, Ariel Helwani Podcast, May 12, 2021.

43 An estimated 5,000 people braved a snowstorm to see the important card live.

44 Beth Fliehr reportedly sat ringside. *Wrestling Then & Now*, Issue #14, Mar. 1991, 1.

45 *Raleigh News and Observer*, Jan. 27, 1991, E1, E7.

46 *Matwatch*, Vol. 4, No. 5, Feb. 4–10, 1991, 1.

47 Notably, the NWA Board of Directors instructed WCW to no longer use the "NWA" name in Oct. 1990. *Pro Wrestling Torch*, Sep. 26, 1991, 1.

48 thehistoryofwwe.com/wcw91.htm. Baltimore was reported to be "804 paid." *Matwatch*, Vol. 4, No. 23, Jun. 10–16, 1991, 5. Flair wrestled Brian Pillman in Norfolk and then faced El Gigante in Baltimore and Philadelphia.

49 Flair was quoted in a Jul. 3 article, saying: "I just talked to Herd two weeks ago and he said I'd be [with WCW] the rest of my life. They had always called me their flagship wrestler." *Miami Herald*, Jul. 3, 1991, 3C.

50 Overall, Clash XV received a 3.9 rating. Flair and Eaton, at the tail end of the show, received a 4.3 rating, "the lowest-rated topliner for any Clash." *Matwatch*, Vol. 4, No. 24, Jun. 17–23, 1991, 1.

51 *Matwatch*, Vol. 4, No. 26–27, Jul. 1–14, 1991, 5.

52 *Miami Herald*, Jul. 3, 1991, 3C. Another report claimed Flair was making between $700,000 and $750,000 a year. *Pro Wrestling Torch*, Jul. 4, 1991, 1.

53 A piece in the *Pro Wrestling Torch* mentioned Dusty Rhodes's possible appetite for revenge stemming from what happened between himself and Flair in late 1988. In addition, Herd and Rhodes were making Flair the "scapegoat" for WCW's inability to draw better numbers. Ibid, 8.

54 *Miami Herald*, Jul. 3, 1991, 3C.

55 *To Be the Man* by Ric Flair with Keith Elliot Greenberg, 2004, 203–204.

56 Flair was fired on the morning of Monday, Jul. 1, 1991, only hours before the Macon show. *Pro Wrestling Torch*, Jul. 4, 1991, 1. WCW had the ability to terminate Flair with 30 days' notice, according to his contract. *Miami Herald*, Jul. 3, 1991, 3C. Also see Jim Herd Interview, *Wrestling Observer Live*, Feb. 16, 2001 and *Wooooo! Nation*. An official termination document was reportedly faxed to Flair's attorney, Dennis Guthrie, likely occurring on Jul. 1.

57 *Pro Wrestling Torch*, Jul. 11, 1991, 1. Flair was acknowledged as the world champion by the NWA until the week of Sep. 8, when Jim Herd was voted president and he stripped Flair of recognition. *Pro Wrestling Torch*, Sep. 26, 1991, 1.

58 It is unclear if this meeting occurred on Jul. 8 or Jul. 31, 1991.

59 *Conversations with Conrad* interview with Conrad Thompson, Nov. 8, 2020.

60 *Matwatch*, Vol. 4, No. 29, Jul. 22–28, 1991, 1.

61 *Matwatch*, Vol. 4, No. 32, Aug. 12–18, 1991, 1.

62 *Matwatch*, Vol. 4, No. 34, Aug. 27–Sep. 2, 1991, 3. Herd believed Guthrie was going to sue them over the quote. *Conversations with Conrad* interview with Conrad Thompson, Nov. 8, 2020.

CHAPTER 17: FROM WRESTLEMANIA TO STARRCADE

1 *Scranton Times*, Feb. 6, 1991, 15.

2 *Philadelphia Daily News*, Jun. 20, 1991, 5.

3 Dr. Zahorian was found guilty on 12 counts. *Pro Wrestling Torch*, Jul. 4, 1991, 1.

4 *New York Daily News*, Jul. 17, 1991, 48.

5 The Undertaker's incredible WrestleMania streak began on Mar. 24, 1991, at WrestleMania VII.

6 Dillon took a backstage role for the WWF after leaving the NWA in 1989.

7 Interestingly, WCW officials instructed ring announcer Gary Michael Cappetta to tell the live audience at the Great American Bash that the promotion had tried to re-sign Flair, but he turned them down. *Pro Wrestling Torch*, Jul. 18, 1991, 1.

8   A report in the *Torch* newsletter stated that Flair was "happier now than any time in the last couple years," about joining the WWF. *Pro Wrestling Torch*, Aug. 15, 1991, 1. Flair later said one of the reasons he went to the WWF was so he could say he had wrestled against everyone. *Ric Flair WCW Satellite Footage from 1993 vs. Rick Rude*, youtube.com.

9   Ric Flair Shoot Interview by Michael Bochicchio, highspots.com, 2008, *To Be the Man* by Ric Flair with Keith Elliot Greenberg, 2004, 206. Interview with Dennis L. Guthrie, Oct. 2, 2020.

10 *Superstars* emanated from Edmonton on Aug. 10 and *Wrestling Challenge* from Calgary on Aug. 11. Both shows were taped weeks in advance.

11 *Pro Wrestling Torch*, Sep. 12, 1991, 1. Flair stated that his salary increased to $800,000 per year. *To Be the Man* by Ric Flair with Keith Elliot Greenberg, 2004, 206.

12 Upon his arrival in the WWF, Flair used his customary theme song, the "Sunrise" section of the tone poem *Also Sprach Zarathustra*. This was later changed to the "Dawn" section of that same song — a different variation that Flair used for most of his WWF run.

13 *Prime Time Wrestling*, Sep. 9, 1991.

14 *Superstars of Wrestling*, Sep. 28, 1991. The NWA requested return of the "Big Gold" belt "on or about" Oct. 1, 1991. Flair in turn asked for his $25,000 belt deposit back, which was first posted in 1981, plus accrued interest. It was claimed that his belt deposit had already been repaid "in approximately 1984." *National Wrestling Alliance, Inc. v. Richard M. Fleihr [sic] a/k/a Ric Flair*, Mecklenburg County General Court of Justice, Superior Court Division, Case No. 91-CVS-14583. Flair disagreed with that assertion. The WWF was prevented from showing the "Big Gold" belt on TV, and used a pixilated image in attempt to keep the on-camera theatrics going. Flair was sent a check for the belt deposit and the "Big Gold" was returned to the NWA. Flair talked about this during *The Ric Flair Show* Podcast Episode #2.

15 Their last match was on Jun. 21, 1985, in St. Louis, and Kerry won by DQ.

16 It should be noted that Flair and Hogan actually wrestled three days earlier, on Oct. 22 at the Hara Arena in Dayton, OH. Hogan substituted for Piper and lost by countout. This was technically the first ever Flair-Hogan bout.

17 *Pro Wrestling Torch*, Nov. 7, 1991, 5–6.

18 Hogan beat Flair by disqualification at the Garden on Nov. 30 and Dec. 29, 1991. Flair's win over Roddy Piper at the Garden on Oct. 28 was his first "MSG" appearance since Apr. 26, 1976.

19 Martel lasted 52:17 in the 1991 Royal Rumble.

20 Flair later said that he found out an hour before the match that he was going to win. *Wooooo! Nation* Podcast Episode #28.

21 This is based on current records.

22 *Superstars of Wrestling*, Mar. 7, 1992, and Mar. 14, 1992. The photos were also seen in *WWF Magazine*, Apr. 1992, 40–41. The photos were doctored by Flair.

23 Flair later explained that his match with Savage was not improvised, but precisely scripted in advance. They practiced the match beforehand. Flair was also instructed not to bleed during the bout. *Wooooo! Nation* Podcast Episode #3.

24 Flair and Savage was not the main event of WrestleMania. Their bout was around the midway point of the show. Hogan and Justice went on last. WrestleMania VIII, Peacock Network Streaming Service.

25 A detailed look at the WWF's problems was featured in the *Pro Wrestling Torch*, Mar. 19, 1992, 1–12.

26 *Prime Time Wrestling*, Sep. 14, 1992.

27 Flair talked about his matches against Hart in Europe. Ric Flair Interview, *Wrestling Observer Live*, 1999.

28 *Montreal Gazette*, Dec. 4, 1992, D3. The bout with the Warrior was declared a no contest.

29 Hart landed a superplex and then gained a submission with his sharpshooter finisher.

30   Ibid. Flair discussed this in his book, *To Be the Man* by Ric Flair with Keith Elliot Greenberg, 2004, 222. It was initially reported that Flair had injured his neck against Bret Hart. *Pro Wrestling Torch*, Oct. 19, 1992, 2.

31   A full explanation of the cause of this condition was found at Mayoclinic.org.

32   *Montreal Gazette*, Dec. 4, 1992, D3. Two physicians believed his injury threatened his career. *Pro Wrestling Torch*, Oct. 26, 1992, 3.

33   *To Be the Man* by Ric Flair with Keith Elliot Greenberg, 2004, 222. During his time off, Flair campaigned for U.S. President George H.W. Bush in his reelection bid. He traveled on a train with President Bush from Atlanta into the Carolinas. *Montreal Gazette*, Dec. 4, 1992, D3. In scheduled matches against the Ultimate Warrior and Bret Hart, Flair was replaced by Ted DiBiase, Kamala, Nailz, and Papa Shango.

34   *Pro Wrestling Torch*, Jan. 11, 1993, 5.

35   The salary amount was unconfirmed. *Pro Wrestling Torch*, Jan. 11, 1993, 1, Feb. 15, 1993, 3. Flair's contract was dated Feb. 16, 1993, and was 21 pages long with 11 sections and 51 subsections. *Richard M. Fliehr a/k/a Ric Flair v. World Championship Wrestling, Inc.*, Case No. 98-CVS-8351, Mecklenburg County Superior Court, Jun. 11, 1998.

36   The bout between Flair and Mr. Perfect was taped on Jan. 18 and broadcast on Jan. 25, 1993.

37   Flair was also named "Readers Favorite Wrestler" for the ninth year in a row. *Wrestling Observer Newsletter*, Jan. 20, 1993, f4wonline.com.

38   Herd resigned from WCW in Jan. 1992. *Matwatch*, Vol. 5, No. 2, Jan. 13–19, 1992, 1. It should be noted that after Flair left WCW in 1991, fans at live events often chanted, "We want Flair!"

39   *Wrestling Observer Newsletter*, Feb. 22, 1993, f4wonline.com.

40   After Flair was stripped of world title status by the NWA in Sep. 1991, a tournament was held to determine a new champion. Masa Chono beat Rick Rude in the finals to capture the NWA belt on Aug. 12, 1992. The Great Muta ended Chono's reign on Jan. 4, 1993, before losing the championship to Windham at SuperBrawl.

41   Dusty Rhodes came up with this idea. *83 Weeks with Eric Bischoff* Podcast Episode #7, Jun. 13, 2018.

42   *WCW Worldwide*, May 1, 1993.

43   Flair and Anderson won the two-of-three-falls bout in two-straight. The Clash was held on Jun. 17, 1993, in Norfolk, VA.

44   *Pro Wrestling Torch*, Jun. 21, 1993, 3.

45   Rude was shown wearing the NWA belt during the Jul. 8, 1993, taping at MGM Studios in Orlando. It was later broadcast on WCW Worldwide on Oct. 9.

46   *WCW Saturday Night*, Aug. 28, 1993.

47   The NWA tried to obtain the "Big Gold" belt through legal means, but WCW proved ownership. *Big Gold: A Close Look at Pro Wrestling's Most Celebrated Championship Belt* by Dick Bourne with Dave Millican, 2014, 185–188.

48   Rude beat Flair by DQ.

49   Flair discussed this tour of Europe. *Wooooo! Nation* Podcast Episode #6.

CHAPTER 18: THE HEART AND SOUL OF WCW

1   *Charlotte Observer*, Apr. 24, 1987, 4B.

2   *Charlotte Observer*, Dec. 27, 1993, B1.

3   Ibid.

4   Ibid.

5   Flair said the purple robe had been "lucky" and was "probably the best one" he had. *New York Daily News*, Dec. 22, 1993, C25.

6   *Pro Wrestling Torch*, Jan. 1, 1994, 8.

7   Meltzer also stated that it was "easily the most memorable of all his title wins." *Wrestling Observer Newsletter*, Jan. 3, 1994, f4wonline.com. The original plan for the main event of Starrcade '93 was Vader defending, and ultimately losing his championship, to Sid Vicious. In Oct. 1993, Vicious and Arn Anderson had a serious real world altercation in England, and as a result, Vicious was removed from the Starrcade show. Flair was called upon to replace Vicious, and once everything was said and done, far exceeded expectations.

8   It was said that his four kids would be in the audience for the first time. *New York Daily News*, Dec. 22, 1993, C25.

9   The promotional advertisement was initially featured in *Multichannel News*, in its Dec. 20, 1993 issue. *New York Daily News*, Dec. 23, 1993, 82.

10 The new gym was at 6010 Fairview Road in Charlotte. Flair discussed his new gym during a "Wrestling Insiders" interview on Apr. 17, 1993. *Pro Wrestling Torch*, Apr. 26, 1993, 9. On Saturday, May 1, during a special grand opening celebration, Flair and Arn Anderson were on hand to sign autographs. Randy Savage, who was still with the WWF, was billed as appearing at the gym on May 5. *Charlotte Observer*, Apr. 30, 1993, 12A.

11 The gym featured Cybex aerobic and fitness equipment. *Macrolease International Corporation d/b/a Cybex Leasing Services v. Ric Flair's Gold's Gym Aerobic & Fitness, Inc., and Richard Fliehr*, Case No. 96-CVS-823, Mecklenburg County Superior Court, Charlotte, NC.

12 *Pro Wrestling Torch*, Apr. 26, 1993, 9.

13 *Kansas City Star*, Jan. 10, 1994, C6. The Gators won 41–7 on Jan. 1, 1994, at the Louisiana Superdome. Wearing a Florida hat, Flair was also on the sidelines for the Nov. 10, 1990, game between the Gators and GeorgiaBulldogs, which the Gators won 38–7. TBS broadcast the game and Jim Ross later talked about the missed opportunity to have the commentators mention Flair and promote WCW. *Grilling JR* Podcast Episode #81. It is not known if this was the game Ross was referencing or how many games Flair attended on the sidelines. Nevertheless, it's pretty well-known that TBS failed to take advantage of promotional opportunities and to enlarge the WCW fan base. Kirk Kirkpatrick, a player on the Gators in 1990, was good friends with Joe Gomez, who was also close with Flair. *Florida Today*, Nov. 11, 1990, 7C. Gomez wrestled in WCW during the 1990s. Kirkpatrick founded the Riverside Recovery of Tampa.

14 Ibid.

15 A photo of Flair appeared in the newspaper the next day, as he prepared to sign an autograph for Jim Paek of the Pittsburgh Penguins. *Pittsburgh Post-Gazette*, Feb. 12, 1994, C6. Flair received the second loudest ovation of the evening, behind Mario Lemieux. *Pro Wrestling Torch*, Mar. 5, 1994, 3.

16 *Pittsburgh Post-Gazette*, Feb. 9, 1994, C3.

17 *Wrestling Observer Newsletter*, Feb. 28, 1994, f4wonline.com. Flair appeared on the Feb. 16, 1994, edition of King's radio program.

18 The press conference, held on Jan. 27, 1993, was to promote WrestleMania in Las Vegas. *Pro Wrestling Torch*, Feb. 8, 1993, 2.

19 *Pro Wrestling Torch*, Mar. 19, 1994, 3 and *Wrestling Observer Newsletter*, Feb. 28, 1994, f4wonline .com.

20 The match was featured during *WCW Saturday Night* and had been taped several weeks prior on Feb. 28, 1994.

21 Hogan's name was actually mentioned during the Dec. 18, 1993, edition of *WCW Saturday Night* and also during a TV taping on Jan. 31, 1994, for programs to be aired in March.

22 *Miami Herald*, Jan. 30, 1994, 15D. Flair and Hogan also appeared together on the cover of *Pro Wrestling Illustrated*, Apr. 1994.

23   Bischoff discussed hiring Flair as booker. *Controversy Creates Cash* by Eric Bischoff with Jeremy Roberts, 2006, 108.

24   Eric Bischoff Shoot Interview, RF Video, *Controversy Creates Cash* by Eric Bischoff with Jeremy Roberts, 2006, 116-118, *To Be the Man* by Ric Flair with Keith Elliot Greenberg, 2004, 232-233.

25   *Wrestling Observer Newsletter*, Apr. 25, 1994, f4wonline.com.

26   The match aired on *WCW Saturday Night* on May 14, 1994.

27   Flair was a baby face versus Windham.

28   *Orlando Sentinel*, Jul. 16, 1994, E1, E4.

29   Bash at the Beach scored an estimated 248,000 buys on pay-per-view worth $6.45 million. *Matwatch '95*, Vol. 3, No. 1, Jan. 1995, 1.

30   *Orlando Sentinel*, Jul. 18, 1994, 1.

31   Ibid, A4.

32   There was talk, even some expectations for Hogan to lose the title back to Flair in 1994, setting up a third bout.

33   *Matwatch '95*, Vol. 3, No. 1, Jan. 1995, 2.

34   *Wrestling Observer Newsletter*, Oct. 24, 1994, f4wonline.com.

35   *South Bend Tribune*, Starwatch Section, Oct. 16, 1994, 3M.

36   *Pro Wrestling Torch*, Oct. 29, 1994, 5.

37   With the contract extension, it was reported that Flair would earn almost $1.2 million dollars from WCW. *Matwatch '95*, Vol. 3, No. 1., Jan. 1995, 2. Taking into consideration Flair's initial contract for three years, plus this two-year extension, he was locked in with WCW until Feb. 15, 1998. *Richard M. Fliehr a/k/a Ric Flair v. World Championship Wrestling, Inc.*, Case No. 98-CVS-8351, Mecklenburg County Superior Court, Jun. 11, 1998.

38   The numbers for Halloween Havoc did not live up to the expectations of WCW officials. *Wrestling Observer Newsletter*, Jan. 9, 1995, f4wonline.com.

39   The retirement of Flair was named "Most Disgusting Promotional Tactic" for 1994, *Wrestling Observer Newsletter*, Jan. 16, 1995, f4wonline.com.

40   *Charlotte Observer*, Oct. 29, 1994, 2B.

41   *Pro Wrestling Torch*, Oct. 29, 1994, 6.

42   Ibid, 3.

43   *WCW Saturday Night*, Mar. 18, 1995.

44   *WCW Saturday Night*, Apr. 1, 1995.

45   *WCW Saturday Night*, Apr. 15, 1995.

46   Inoki's first choice for an opponent was Hulk Hogan, but he didn't want to make the trip. "Oral History of Pro Wrestling's 1995 Historic Excursion into North Korea," by Dan Greene, si.com, Apr. 27, 2015.

47   Ibid. Flair and Inoki wrestled in the main event of night two, on Apr. 29, 1995. It was later broadcast on pay-per-view in the United States on Aug. 4, 1995. The crowd estimate was also reported as anywhere between 170,000 and 190,000 fans.

48   It appears that Flair may have won only one of those bouts, on Jul. 28, 1995 in Charlotte.

49   *Wrestling Observer Newsletter*, Jul. 17, 1995, f4wonline.com. This was also mentioned in *Controversy Creates Cash* by Eric Bischoff with Jeremy Roberts, 2006, 203.

50   Flair discussed his feud against Anderson. *Wooooo! Nation* Podcast Episode #5.

51   Flair and Anderson argued after a handicap match loss to Vader at Clash of the Champions XXXI on Aug. 6, 1995, in Daytona Beach.

52   Flair won the first contest on Oct. 2 in Denver, and Anderson took the second in a cage match on Oct. 9 in Chicago.

53   Technically, Flair and Sting won by DQ over Anderson and Pillman once Flair attacked Sting, and a triple-team ensued. He had claimed he was jumped by their opponents prior to the show, but later revealed that to be not true. Chris Benoit became the fourth member of the Horsemen in Nov. 1995. *Four Horsemen: A Timeline History* by Dick Bourne, 2017, 109.

54 *Wrestling Observer Newsletter*, Oct. 9, 1995, f4wonline.com. Flair returned for *Nitro* on Oct. 2 in Denver. Flair discussed this surgery in *To Be the Man* by Ric Flair with Keith Elliot Greenberg, 2004, 251–252.

55 *Wrestling Observer Newsletter*, Dec. 11, 1995, f4wonline.com.

56 It was reported that Flair didn't find out that he was winning the belt until the night of the event. *Pro Wrestling Torch*, Dec. 30, 1995.

CHAPTER 19: THE RATINGS WAR

1 *Philadelphia Times*, Jan. 5, 1890, 6.

2 The Standard Theatre was at 1124 South Street, while the ECW Arena was at 2300 South Swanson Street.

3 ECW was voted the number two "Best Promotion" in the annual *Wrestling Observer* awards. Number one was New Japan Pro Wrestling. *Wrestling Observer Newsletter*, Jan. 22, 1996, f4wonline.com.

4 Douglas said that his comments were a shoot and that he stood behind his words. *Shane Douglas Shoot Interview*, The Hannibal TV, 2018. He also affirmed this on his website. Franchisefansite.com/march30.html.

5 Ibid.

6 This would have been prior to their feud in WCW. *Shane Douglas Shoot Interview*, The Hannibal TV, 2018. In around Mar. 1999, Flair spoke about Douglas during an appearance on *WCW Live*.

7 It was reported that WCW achieved its first profitable year in 1995, after $30 million in losses over the previous six years. *Baltimore Sun*, Feb. 15, 1996, Live Section, 3.

8 Woman (Nancy Toffoloni) managed Doom in 1989 and then Flair in early 1990.

9 Flair teamed with Arn Anderson, Lex Luger, Kevin Sullivan, the Barbarian, Meng, Z-Gangsta, and the Ultimate Solution. Aside from Flair and Anderson, the other members of this team were part of the Dungeon of Doom.

10 This was the "Tournament of Champions," held on the Ohio State Fairgrounds. Over 2,000 wrestlers participated in the event from 26 states. *Columbus Dispatch*, Apr. 21, 1996, 7F. Also see *Wrestling Observer Newsletter*, Apr. 29, 1996, f4wonline.com.

11 Flair stated that as a result of the missed booking, WCW punished him, and thus, he lost the WCW Title to the Giant on *Nitro*. *To Be the Man* by Ric Flair with Keith Elliot Greenberg, 2004, 254. Kevin Sullivan explained that they put the belt on The Giant because they needed a heel champion for Hulk Hogan to wrestle when he returned. *Kevin Sullivan Kayfabe Commentaries Shoot Interview*.

12 McMichael was known for his lengthy tenure as a member of the Chicago Bears (1981–1993), and retired in 1994 following a year with Green Bay. Greene signed with the Carolina Panthers in May 1996 after several years with the Pittsburgh Steelers. This angle got some mainstream attention, as Greene appeared on *The Tonight Show* on May 28 and talked about the situation.

13 McMichael hit Greene with a briefcase, and Flair pinned Greene.

14 Gene Okerlund, on WCW's 1-900 Phone Line, mentioned rumors that Flair or Hogan could've been the third man with Hall and Nash at the Bash. *Pro Wrestling Torch*, Jul. 6, 1996, 12.

15 *Nitro* beat *Raw* for "84 consecutive weeks." wwe.com/classics/wcw/history-of-wcw.

16 The Chris Benoit and Steve McMichael versus Sting and Lex Luger bout was a no contest.

17 The injury came during a match with Kensuke Sasaki in Tokyo on Sep. 21.

18 After returning from Japan, Flair appeared for two tag team matches against Hall and Nash

in Ohio, on Sep. 28 in Columbus and Sep. 29 in Steubenville. The promotion portrayed an attack by the Outsiders on Flair, knocking him out of the bout, and Benoit wrestled by himself. The Outsiders won both matches.

19 Footage of Flair in rehabilitation in Birmingham was shown during *Nitro* on Nov. 11, 1996.

20 On Mar. 10, 1997, Flair "got the biggest reaction of anyone on" *Nitro*. *Wrestling Observer Newsletter*, Mar. 17, 1997, f4wonline.com.

21 *Monday Nitro*, Dec. 9, 1996.

22 Announced attendance was 22,000. The gate was $243,946. *Wrestling Observer Newsletter*, Jun. 16, 1997, f4wonline.com.

23 Flair was fighting Syxx at the time. The event was held on Jun. 15, 1997, in Moline, IL.

24 Anderson's last match was in late Jan. 1997.

25 Kevin Nash later apologized for the skit. *To Be the Man* by Ric Flair with Keith Elliot Greenberg, 2004, 254–256. Eric Bischoff discussed this skit in his book, *Controversy Creates Cash* by Eric Bischoff with Jeremy Roberts, 2006, 250–251. The NWO did a second Horsemen parody on Feb. 22, 1999.

26 A Horsemen defeat in the War Games matchup in Winston-Salem was heavily criticized by pundits.

27 Flair injured his ankle after landing on a camera cable upon exiting the ring. *Baltimore Sun*, Dec. 29, 1997, D4.

28 Prodigy Chat, Dec. 7, 1997. Also see *Wrestling Observer Newsletter*, Dec. 15, 1997, f4wonline.com.

29 Flair told Gary Juster it was one of his favorite articles and wanted a copy to frame. *Old School in Session with Gary Juster Podcast*, Ring of Honor Wrestling, 2021.

30 *Baltimore Sun*, Dec. 29, 1997, D4. Following Flair's last match in Jul. 2022, Meltzer wrote: "Was [Flair] the best ever? I used to think so, but wrestling evolves and changes. In time you learn you can never make that call, because every era is different. What I will say is that in his prime he was the best of his era." *Wrestling Observer Newsletter*, Aug. 8, 2022, f4wonline.com.

31 Hart defeated Flair by submission in 18:02, utilizing his Sharpshooter. The match was considered the best on the entire card. It was Hart's first match in WCW.

32 The tournament was held at the Pontiac Silverdome. Reid placed first in his weight class.

33 Additionally, Flair reportedly missed bookings in Minneapolis for *Nitro* on Apr. 13, in Mankato on Apr. 14 and in Duluth on Apr. 15. *Atlanta Journal-Constitution*, Apr. 21, 1998, B1.

34 *Richard M. Fliehr a/k/a Ric Flair v. World Championship Wrestling, Inc.*, Case No. 98-CVS-8351, Mecklenburg County Superior Court, Jun. 11, 1998.

35 Ibid.

36 Flair talked about his problems with Bischoff. *To Be the Man* by Ric Flair with Keith Elliot Greenberg, 2004, 250–252. During his contract negotiations with WCW, "the parties' relationship deteriorated drastically." *Richard M. Fliehr a/k/a Ric Flair v. World Championship Wrestling, Inc.*, Case No. 98-CVS-8351, Mecklenburg County Superior Court, Jun. 11, 1998.

37 Ibid.

38 Ibid.

39 Flair stated that he was fired by Bischoff. *To Be The Man* by Ric Flair with Keith Elliot Greenberg, 2004, 265.

40 Flair reportedly gave "notice months in advance." *Atlanta Journal-Constitution*, Jul. 5, 1998, B5. *Controversy Creates Cash* by Eric Bischoff with Jeremy Roberts, 2006, 275. Also see *Atlanta Journal-Constitution*, Apr. 21, 1998, B1, and Eric Bischoff Shoot Interview, RF Video. WCW's full complaint was outlined in *World Championship Wrestling, Inc. v. Richard M. Fliehr a/k/a Ric Flair*, Superior Court of Fulton County, State of Georgia, Apr. 17, 1998.

41 *Pro Wrestling Torch*, Apr. 18, 1998, 1, *Wrestling Observer Newsletter*, Apr. 20, 1998, f4wonline.com.

42 *Wrestling Observer Newsletter*, Apr. 27, 1998, f4wonline.com. The latter was also confirmed in the Amended Complaint, *World Championship Wrestling, Inc. v. Richard M. Fliehr a/k/a Ric Flair*, Superior Court of Fulton County, State of Georgia, May 14, 1998.

43 Ibid. This point was picked up on by newspapers in Atlanta and Charlotte.

44 Ibid.

45 Ibid. *Richard M. Fliehr a/k/a Ric Flair v. World Championship Wrestling, Inc.*, Case No. 98-CVS-8351, Mecklenburg County Superior Court, Jun. 11, 1998.

46 The reasons were outlined in his legal complaint. Ibid.

47 Flair's attorney, Bill Diehl, told a reporter, "We don't have a contract." *Charlotte Observer*, Jun. 12, 1998, C1. Flair's suit against WCW mentioned that Flair "had discussions with the WWF after it became clear that plaintiff and defendant would not finalize an agreement." *Richard M. Fliehr a/k/a Ric Flair v. World Championship Wrestling, Inc.*, Case No. 98-CVS-8351, Mecklenburg County Superior Court, Jun. 11, 1998. Flair considered showing up at the WWF's Unforgiven event on Apr. 26, 1998, at the Greensboro Coliseum. He was advised by lawyers not to do it. *Wooooo! Nation* Podcast Episode #12.

48 *Atlanta Journal-Constitution*, Jul. 5, 1998, B1.

49 Flair hadn't wrestled since Apr. 8, 1998.

50 *Monday Nitro*, Sep. 14, 1998. This episode of *Nitro* beat *Monday Night Raw* in the ratings, 4.54 to 3.99. *Wrestling Observer Newsletter*, Sep. 21, 1998, f4wonline.com. Flair's segment drew a 5.4 and was the highest quarter hour of the night. *Pro Wrestling Torch*, Sep. 19, 1998, 1.

51 This occurred on Oct. 5, 1998.

52 *Wrestling Observer Newsletter*, Oct. 12, 1998, f4wonline.com.

53 *Monday Nitro*, Dec. 14, 1998.

54 He received 200 calls at his home. *Charlotte Observer*, Dec. 16, 1998, 2B. Flair talked about the secrecy of the angle. *Wooooo! Nation* Podcast Episode #4.

55 *Charlotte Observer*, Dec. 16, 1998, 2B.

56 Flair said this Baltimore promo was one of his favorites. *Wooooo! Nation* Podcast Episode #15.

57 *Wrestling Observer Newsletter*, Jan. 25, 1999, f4wonline.com. Flair enjoyed a surprise party for his 50th birthday at the Piper Glen Country Club. *Charlotte Observer*, May 9, 1999, 1.

58 The Souled Out program was held on Jan. 17, 1999, in Charleston, WV. David Flair was reportedly training at the WCW Power Plant.

59 David Flair, who was initially masked, used a taser on his father, helping Hogan get the victory.

60 The bout at Uncensored was a first-blood cage match.

61 That was the longest stretch of his career without being world champion since he first won the NWA crown in 1981.

62 Robinson would be nicknamed Little Naitch.

63 According to the storyline, David Flair had signed the papers putting his father in the hospital.

64 Paid attendance was 6,379. *Wrestling Observer Newsletter*, May 10, 1999, f4wonline.com.

65 *Wrestling Observer Newsletter*, Apr. 26, 1999, *Wrestling Observer Newsletter*, May 17, 1999, f4wonline.com.

CHAPTER 20: A RETURN TO SANITY

1 *Leslie Goodman Fliehr v. Richard Morgan Fliehr, alias Ric Flair*, Mecklenburg County General Court of Justice, District Court Division, Case No. 79-CVD-5549.

2 Letter from Gerald Fesenmaier to James Crockett, dated Apr. 8, 1980, Ibid.

3 Letter from David E. Johnson, JCP Treasurer, "To Whom It May Concern," dated Oct. 2, 1980, Ibid.

4 Flair invested $10,400 for 5 percent interest. Ibid.

5 $600 in 1981 equals over $2,000 in 2022, according to the inflation calculator. bls.gov.

6   *Leslie Goodman Fliehr v. Richard Morgan Fliehr, alias Ric Flair,* Mecklenburg County General Court of Justice, District Court Division, Case No. 79-CVD-5549.

7   Ibid.

8   This included $13,675 for his "wrestling clothes" in 1976. Ibid.

9   Michael's, at 1830 Main Street in Kansas City, MO, was sometimes mentioned by Flair during interviews. Flair later shopped at Taylor Richards & Conger in Charlotte. *Wooooo! Nation* Podcast Episode #28.

10   *Leslie Goodman Fliehr v. Richard Morgan Fliehr, alias Ric Flair,* Mecklenburg County General Court of Justice, District Court Division, Case No. 79-CVD-5549.

11   "Mr. Fliehr" was substituted for "Flair" in the letter itself. Letter from John E. Hodge Jr. to Judge James E. Lanning, dated Oct. 29, 1980, Ibid.

12   Ibid.

13   Ibid.

14   *Atlanta Journal-Constitution,* Jul. 5, 1998, B1.

15   Flair talked about a big draw he got from Gary Juster at the Meadowlands. Ric Flair Shoot Interview by Michael Bochicchio, highspots.com, 2008.

16   *Tampa Tribune,* May 8, 1987, 10EH.

17   Flair discussed his gym business and the hurricane that hit St. Maarten. Ric Flair Shoot Interview by Michael Bochicchio, highspots.com, 2008.

18   *Raleigh News and Observer,* Jan. 27, 1991, E7.

19   Ibid.

20   *Baltimore Sun,* Dec. 29, 1997, D4.

21   Ibid.

22   *Charlotte Observer,* May 9, 1999, 13A. Megan Fliehr married Mark W. Ketzner. Minnesota, U.S. Marriage Index, Ancestry.com. She was married on Sep. 25 in Minneapolis. *Wrestling Observer Newsletter,* Oct. 4, 1999, f4wonline.com.

23   Both children attended Providence Day School in Charlotte. *Charlotte Observer,* May 9, 1999, 13A.

24   Flair won by DQ after Buff Bagwell interfered at the Great American Bash show.

25   *Pro Wrestling Torch,* Jul. 3, 1999, 3.

26   Flair reportedly earned respect from younger wrestlers by giving a pinfall to Buff Bagwell in an eight-man tag team match during the Jun. 14 edition of *Nitro* in Washington, D.C. *Wrestling Observer Newsletter,* Jun. 21, 1999, f4wonline.com. Flair's back problems were attributed to arthritis stemming from the injuries he suffered in the 1975 plane crash. *Charleston Post and Courier,* Aug. 22, 1999, D12.

27   Beyer was a well-known amateur grappler out of Syracuse University who then wrestled professionally from 1954 to 1993. Flair reportedly met Beyer early in his career while working in the AWA.

28   It was reported that an angle between Flair and Shane Douglas was scheduled for the Aug. 9 edition of *Nitro. Charleston Post and Courier,* Aug. 22, 1999, D12. "Ric Flair's WCW days are numbered," one article exclaimed. *Ottawa Sun,* Aug. 14, 1999, 48.

29   *Wrestling Observer Newsletter,* Oct. 11, 1999, f4wonline.com.

30   *Monday Nitro,* Oct. 25, 1999.

31   *Wrestling Observer Newsletter,* Jan. 10, 2000, f4wonline.com.

32   *Charlotte Observer,* Jan. 18, 2000, 1.

33   Ibid. The Associated Press ran a story about it as well.

34   *Charlotte Observer,* Jan. 18, 2000, 1.

35   *Wrestling Observer Newsletter,* Dec. 12, 1999, f4wonline.com.

36   Flair met with Governor Ventura on Feb. 16, 2000. *Charlotte Observer,* Feb. 17, 2000, B1, B4.

37   The initial filing deadline to run for public office was Feb. 7, 2000. Flair had the option of running as an independent candidate and needed to submit approximately 96,000 signatures

to get on the ballot by June. *Charlotte Observer*, Jun. 4, 2000, 4C. Flair had been politically active in the past, throwing his support behind President George H.W. Bush, South Carolina Governor Carroll Campbell, and other Republican figures, both on the national and local stages. Flair said he was asked to run for governor "five times." He admitted that he had "too many skeletons in the closet." *Arizona Republic*, USA weekend, Mar. 12–14, 2004, 16.

38   Indicative of WCW's diminished popularity, SuperBrawl had a low buy rate. *Wrestling Observer Newsletter*, Mar. 13, 2000, f4wonline.com. Also see *Pro Wrestling Torch*, Feb. 26, 2000, 8.

39   This occurred on Apr. 10, 2000 in Denver, CO, during *Nitro*.

40   It was Flair's right shoulder.

41   Flair discussed his physical condition after coming back from rotator cuff surgery. *To Be the Man* by Ric Flair with Keith Elliot Greenberg, 2004, 297.

42   *Monday Nitro*, May 15, 2000.

43   Reid also had some of his hair shaved off. *Monday Nitro*, Jun. 12, 2000.

44   Outside the ring, Russo helped him with a financial issue in WCW. *To Be the Man* by Ric Flair with Keith Elliot Greenberg, 2004, 293–295.

45   Dr. Fliehr passed away at 10:10 a.m. at Carolinas Medical Center in Charlotte. North Carolina Department of Health and Human Services, Certificate of Death. He had resided at the Carriage Club with his wife, Kay, which was located at 5800 Old Providence Rd. in Charlotte. *Charlotte Observer*, Jun. 27, 2000, 6B.

46   *Old School in Session with Gary Juster Podcast*, Ring of Honor Wrestling, 2021.

47   Obituary written by Lucy Y. Her. *Minneapolis Star Tribune*, Jun. 30, 2000, B6.

48   *Charlotte Observer*, Jun. 27, 2000, 4B.

49   Surgery was performed by Dr. James Andrews in Birmingham on Jul. 7, 2000. *Wrestling Observer Newsletter*, Jul. 17 and Jul. 24, 2000, f4wonline.com.

50   *Sun-Sentinel*, Mar. 20, 2001, 3E.

51   *Los Angeles Times*, Mar. 24, 2001, C2.

52   Interview with Ric Flair by Nick Hausman, *Wrestling Inc.* Podcast, Feb. 24, 2021. Also see *Second Nature: The Legacy of Ric Flair and the Rise of Charlotte* by Ric Flair & Charlotte with Brian Shields, 2017, 200.

53   At Greed on Mar. 18 in Jacksonville, FL, Flair teamed with Jeff Jarrett in a loss to Dusty and Dustin Rhodes.

54   Flair also did a memorable promo from the ring during the final *Nitro*, putting over some of the great wrestlers who worked for the company, as well as mentioning that Vince McMahon "Senior" voted for him to be world champion in 1981. *Monday Nitro*, Mar. 26, 2001.

55   The WWF did bring in talented stars from WCW, including Lance Storm, Billy Kidman, Shane Helms, Chavo Guerrero Jr., Mike Awesome, Booker T, and Dallas Page.

56   Flair's three-year contract started Feb. 16, 2000, and was going to end on Feb. 15, 2003. Research by Chris Harrington and David Bixenspan, WCW Payroll Records and Talent Contract Database, sites.google.com/site/chrisharrington. He had a total of 22 months and 10 days left on his contract when *Nitro* signed off for the last time.

57   *Charlotte Observer*, Jan. 4, 2001, 2B.

58   Flair's legal team was able to get him out of his AOL-Time Warner contract, and he then signed a three-year deal with the WWF. *Charlotte Observer*, Nov. 21, 2001, C1.

59   Flair said it was "one of the top three or four moments" in his career. Ibid.

60   With regard to his condition, he said he needed to lose some weight. *Daily Oklahoman*, Dec. 28, 2001, 17.

61   Flair talked about not being ready for the bout with McMahon. *Wooooo! Nation* Podcast Episode #5.

62   The Undertaker, after the win, was 10-0 at WrestleMania.

63   In the main event, McMahon and Kurt Angle beat Flair and Triple H.

64   Triple H helped Flair work through his confidence problems. Interview with Ric Flair by Chris Jericho, *Talk is Jericho*, Jericho Cruise, Feb. 14, 2020.

65   *Wrestling Observer Newsletter*, May 6, 2002, f4wonline.com.

66   *Daily Oklahoman*, Dec. 28, 2001, 17.

67   *Orlando Sentinel*, TV Time Plus, Dec. 30, 2001–Jan. 5, 2002, 12.

68   *Taralyn Cappellano, a single person; Heidi Doyle, a married person v. World Wrestling Entertainment, Inc., et al*, Superior Court of the State of Arizona in and for the County of Maricopa, Case No. CV2004-005976, Mar. 29, 2004.

69   See Notice of Settlement, Ibid, May 14, 2004 and Notice of Dismissal, Ibid, May 28, 2004. The case was moved from Superior Court to the U.S. District Court for the District of Arizona.

70   *Dark Side of the Ring*, Vice TV, Sep. 16, 2021.

71   Statement by Ric Flair on Twitter, @RicFlairNatrBoy, Sep. 20, 2021.

CHAPTER 21: TO RETIREMENT AND BACK

1   Rap superstar Snoop Dogg talked about Flair's influence on the hip-hop community. *30 for 30* Documentary, ESPN Films, 2017. Flair is mentioned in the lyrics of dozens of songs, including by Killer Mike, Cam'Ron, Kanye West, and Soulja Boy. See "11 Best Ric Flair Lyrics," by Adelle Platon, Oct. 3, 2016, billboard.com.

2   Interview with Ric Flair by Jeff Glor, *CBS Evening News*, Feb. 21, 2009.

3   Flair inherited the chest chop from the likes of Johnny Valentine, Wahoo McDaniel and Terry Funk, and it became one of his most used offensive weapons.

4   *Charlotte Observer*, Jan. 19, 2002, C1.

5   *Leslie Goodman Fliehr v. Richard Morgan Fliehr, alias Ric Flair*, Mecklenburg County General Court of Justice, District Court Division, Case No. 79-CVD-5549.

6   *Wrestling Observer Newsletter*, Mar. 24, 2003, f4wonline.com.

7   *Wrestling Observer Newsletter*, May 5, 2003, f4wonline.com.

8   Flair said that the Greenville moment helped get him back on his feet and made him comfortable in the WWE. *Daily Oklahoman*, Mar. 12, 2004, 20D.

9   The first Flair-Michaels bout happened on Dec. 2, 1991, and was broadcast on *Prime Time Wrestling* on Dec. 16. It was also featured on the *Invasion 92* VHS release.

10   She passed away at 8:50 a.m. at the Laurels at Carolina Place assisted living facility in Pineville, NC. North Carolina Department of Health and Human Services, Certificate of Death. Also *Charlotte Observer*, May 9, 1999, 1A, and *To Be the Man* by Ric Flair with Keith Elliot Greenberg, 2004, 276.

11   In a photo for the newspaper, Mrs. Fliehr is shown holding a wrestling picture of her son and standing next to a framed photograph of Flair when he was young. *Atlanta Journal-Constitution*, May 11, 1986, B8.

12   Ibid.

13   The set was released on Nov. 18, 2003 and included three discs.

14   *Wrestling Observer Newsletter*, Feb. 23, 2004, f4wonline.com. The "first run" of the DVD reportedly sold out in three days. *Arizona Republic*, USA Weekend, Mar. 12–14, 2004, 16.

15   Flair had talked about doing a book in 1999. Ric Flair Interview, *Wrestling Observer Live*, 1999. Updates about the progress of Flair's book appeared in various issues of the *Wrestling Observer Newsletter* in 2003 and 2004. Flair and Mark Madden talked about the production of the book. *Wooooo! Nation* Podcast Episode #13.

16   Bret Hart wrote a lengthy response to Flair's comments, which were featured on his website on Jul. 12, 2004. It should be noted that Foley had initially discussed Flair in his popular 1999

autobiography, *Have A Nice Day: A Tale of Blood and Sweatsocks*. Sammartino didn't believe Flair was the greatest performer ever. He liked Flair, but as a complete performer, he felt Nick Bockwinkel was better. *Pro Wrestling Torch Annual IV*, Summer 1991, 41.

17   *Daily Oklahoman*, Mar. 12, 2004, 20D.

18   Flair and Foley discussed this match. *Wooooo! Nation* Podcast Episode #5.

19   Orton had captured the World Title from Benoit at SummerSlam on Aug. 15, 2004.

20   This was Flair's first pay-per-view main event since WCW's Greed in Mar. 2000.

21   Flair and Angle were on opposite sides of a tag team match on Mar. 26, 2002 in Philadelphia.

22   *Monday Night Raw*, Jun. 27, 2005.

23   Interview with Ric Flair by Jeff Glor, *CBS Evening News*, Feb. 21, 2009.

24   Notably, Benjamin grew up in South Carolina and got hooked on wrestling watching Jim Crockett Promotions.

25   Flair and Foley had a backstage incident at *Raw* in Huntsville on Dec. 13, 2004. This was discussed on *Wooooo! Nation* Podcast Episode #5.

26   Flair and Piper won the championship on Nov. 5, 2006 and lost the belts on Nov. 13, 2006.

27   Behind-the-scenes, Flair said that McMahon told him that he was retiring, even though Flair didn't necessarily want to. *Wooooo! Nation* Podcast Episode #15.

28   *Monday Night Raw*, Nov. 26, 2007.

29   *Monday Night Raw*, Feb. 18, 2008. Michaels talked about Flair's influence. *Orlando Sentinel*, Mar. 29, 2008, D2. Michaels also talked about idolizing Flair during a radio show with Jim Ross in Mar. 1993. *Pro Wrestling Torch*, Mar. 29, 1993, 2.

30   *Pittsburgh Post-Gazette*, Weekend, Aug. 25, 1995, 6.

31   The speech reportedly lasted more than an hour.

32   Flair said that Michaels carried him in the bout. *Wooooo! Nation* Podcast Episode #4.

33   The contest earned five stars. Wade Keller wrote that Flair, with "considerable help" from Michaels, "delivered one of absolutely the best matches of his career." *Pro Wrestling Torch*, Apr. 5, 2008, 1. It was voted number two in the "Worked Match of the Year" category. *Wrestling Observer Newsletter*, Jan. 26, 2009, f4wonline.com.

34   Flair's WrestleMania robe, boots, and trunks were sent to the National Museum of American History at the Smithsonian. americanhistory.si.edu.

35   *Pro Wrestling Torch*, Apr. 5, 2008, 1.

36   Flair had high praise for his retirement weekend. *Wooooo! Nation* Podcast Episode #15, Interview with Ric Flair by Nick Hausman, *Wrestling Inc.* Podcast, Feb. 25, 2021, *Second Nature: The Legacy of Ric Flair and the Rise of Charlotte* by Ric Flair & Charlotte with Brian Shields, 2017, 4.

37   *Charlotte Observer*, Mar. 25, 2008, 2B. In 1989, South Carolina Governor Carroll Campbell declared Sep. 12, "Ric Flair Day" in the state. *Columbia State*, Sep. 17, 1989, 4D. Throughout his life, Flair received similar honors in Minneapolis, Norfolk, and Charleston, while also receiving the keys to Greensboro and Myrtle Beach.

38   *Charlotte Observer*, Mar. 25, 2008, 2B. A few weeks after Flair's retirement, U.S. Representative Sue Myrick honored Flair with a short speech on the floor of the House of Representatives. "Often imitated but never duplicated, his legacy will forever be synonymous with the world of professional wrestling," she said, also referring to him as "Charlotte's favorite son." *Charlotte Observer*, Apr. 21, 2008, 2B.

39   *Charlotte Observer*, Mar. 31, 2008, 13C.

40   *Charlotte Observer*, Jan. 4, 2008, C1.

41   Ibid.

42   Reid signed a deal with the WWE in Dec. 2007. 411mania.com, Dec. 12, 2007.

43   Bostonnow.com, quotes reprinted in *Pro Wrestling Torch*, Apr. 5, 2008, 3.

44   The Jun. 16 appearance in Salt Lake City was on camera and Flair did an angle with Chris Jericho during *Raw*. On Jul. 15 in Charlotte, Flair was featured off-camera during the *Smackdown* program and did an in-ring promo about his hometown.

45 The Fliehr family had lived at 7205 Piper Point Lane since Aug. 1998. The five-bedroom, six-bathroom property was over 10,000 square feet. Mecklenburg County (NC) Property Records. The home was on the Piper Glen Country Club Golf Course.

46 *Elizabeth Ann Fliehr v. Richard Morgan Fliehr*, Mecklenburg County General Court of Justice, District Court Division, Case No. 05-CVD-9647, Complaint dated May 24, 2005.

47 *Charlotte Observer*, Dec. 2, 2005, 1A, 11A.

48 Ibid.

49 *Elizabeth Ann Fliehr v. Richard Morgan Fliehr*, Mecklenburg County General Court of Justice, District Court Division, Case No. 05-CVD-9647, Order dated Oct. 5, 2005.

50 Richard M. Fliehr v. Elizabeth Ann Fliehr, Mecklenburg County General Court of Justice, District Court Division, Case No. 06-CVD-3550, Judgment of Divorce, dated May 8, 2006. They had been married 22 years. A 32-page "separation, property settlement and alimony/spousal support agreement" was signed by Flair and Beth Fliehr on Aug. 7, 2007. On May 14, 2013, Mrs. Fliehr filed a Complaint for Breach of Contract, Specific Performance, Attorney's Fees, and Motion for Preliminary Injunction. Elizabeth Ann Fliehr v. Richard Morgan Fliehr, Mecklenburg County General Court of Justice, District Court Division, Case No. 13-CVD-8813, dated May 14, 2013. A default judgment was awarded to Mrs. Fliehr. Flair was ordered to pay $628,916.56, plus interest. Ibid, Sep. 23, 2013.

51 Flair and VanDeMark's personal history is highlighted in the book, *Inside the Ring: From Tap Out to Champion — A Memoir by Tiffany VanDeMark* by Tiffany L. VanDeMark, 2018.

52 *Peoria Journal-Star*, Mar. 27, 2008, cited in the *Pro Wrestling Torch*, Apr. 5, 2008, 3.

53 *Second Nature: The Legacy of Ric Flair and the Rise of Charlotte* by Ric Flair & Charlotte with Brian Shields, 2017, 4, 68–69.

54 *Charleston Post and Courier*, Sep. 28, 2008, postandcourier.com.

55 Articles appeared in the *Charlotte Observer* on Nov. 23 and Nov. 29, 2008.

56 Flair had given a speech to the crowd earlier in the show. Beth, Ashley, and Megan Fliehr were ringside.

57 *Tiffany L. Fliehr v. Richard M. Fliehr*, Mecklenburg County General Court of Justice, District Court Division, Case No. 08-CVD-24267, Complaint for Post Separation Support, dated Oct. 30, 2008.

58 This amount included alimony to Beth Fliehr, lawyer fees, and a mortgage. *Tiffany L. Fliehr v. Richard M. Fliehr*, Mecklenburg County General Court of Justice, District Court Division, Case No. 08-CVD-24267, Order for Post Separation Support and Attorney's Fees, dated Feb. 10, 2009. With regard to his ongoing debt problems through the years, Flair was the defendant in over a dozen civil cases about money between the 1990s and 2010s.

59 *Tiffany L. Fliehr v. Richard M. Fliehr*, Mecklenburg County General Court of Justice, District Court Division, Case No. 09-CVD-14045, Judgment of Divorce, dated Aug. 12, 2009. To read more about their relationship, see *Second Nature: The Legacy of Ric Flair and the Rise of Charlotte* by Ric Flair & Charlotte with Brian Shields, 2017 and *Inside the Ring: From Tap Out to Champion — A Memoir by Tiffany VanDeMark* by Tiffany L. VanDeMark, 2018. Also see Interview with Ric Flair by Nick Hausman, *Wrestling Inc.* Podcast, Feb. 25, 2021.

60 *Charlotte Observer*, Feb. 23, 2010, 2B.

61 Ibid.

62 *Charlotte Observer*, Jul. 15, 2010, 2B.

63 *Charlotte Observer*, Jun. 28, 2012, B1.

64 Following their separation, Flair was ordered to pay spousal support. In Jul. 2013, a Mecklenburg County Judge ordered him to pay $4,000 a month. According to a report, he failed to submit payment, and an order for his arrest was issued on Jul. 3. At the time, Flair owed $32,352.51. *Charlotte Observer*, Jul. 17, 2013, 6B. The warrant was rescinded in Feb. 2016. PWInsider.com, Feb. 29, 2016.

65   *Jacqueline Fliehr v. Richard Fliehr*, Mecklenburg County General Court of Justice, District Court Division, Case No. 13-CVD-19968, Judgment of Absolute Divorce, dated Apr. 6, 2015. Flair later said that he paid alimony to three women at the same time. Interview with Ric Flair by Nick Hausman, *Wrestling Inc.* Podcast, Feb. 25, 2021. Flair also admitted that he paid $1.5 million in alimony. *Wooooo! Nation* Podcast Episode #11.

66   A lengthy article, discussing both his relationships and financial problems, was featured on Grantland.com in Aug. 2011. "The Wrestler in Real Life: Ric Flair's Long, Steady Decline," by Shane Ryan, grantland.com. Flair disagreed with a claim in that article, specifically that he suffered from "alcoholic cardiomyopathy," and there was talk of him suing the website. "Ric Flair Is Threatening To Sue Grantland Over 'Falsehoods' In Their Story, Even Though The 'Falsehoods' Came from Flair's Book," by Jack Dickey, Aug. 28, 2011, deadspin.com. Also see the original claim in *To Be the Man* by Ric Flair with Keith Elliot Greenberg, 2004, 304. Flair pointed out that he was misdiagnosed and he never had the medical condition. *Charleston Post and Courier*, Sep. 4, 2011, C2.

67   The 2008 NWA Legends Fanfest was a major success. Wrestling historian Steve Johnson wrote: "The big draw of the four-day Fanfest was unquestionably Ric Flair." "Legends Abound at Charlotte Fanfest," by Steven Johnson, Aug. 18, 2008,slamwrestling.net. *The Ric Flair Interview* was billed as "the shoot interview of a lifetime," and was over 10-hours in length. The 3-disc set is available at highspots.com. The Flair shoot was voted #2 for "Best Pro Wrestling DVD," behind the *Ric Flair Definitive Collection* DVD set. *Wrestling Observer Newsletter*, Jan. 26, 2009, f4wonline.com.

68   The situation with Price pertained to the 2009 edition of the Legends Fanfest between Aug. 6 and Aug. 9 at the Hilton University Place Hotel in Charlotte. A detailed statement by Price was featured by Mike Johnson on PWInsider.com on May 25, 2010. It was notable that Flair had attended that convention and reunited with the original members of the Four Horsemen, while also inducting Blackjack Mulligan into the Hall of Heroes.

69   Physical possession of the belt was turned over to Highspots.

70   Highspots was in the process of auctioning off the NWA belt in Oct. 2009 when it was forced to halt because of this development. The bidding was up to $75,000. See *Wrestling Observer Newsletter*, Oct. 19, Oct. 26, and Nov. 16, 2009, f4wonline.com.

71   Highspots, Inc., and Michael Bochicchio v. Richard Fliehr, a/k/a Ric Flair, Mecklenburg County General Court of Justice, Superior Court Division, Case No. 10-CVS-8620, Complaint, dated Apr. 20, 2010.

72   *Ibid*, Joint Voluntary Dismissal with Prejudice, dated Jun. 24, 2011 and Release and Consent Order, dated Jun. 27, 2011.

73   The complaint stated that Highspots was to receive a 10 percent commission for Flair's Ring of Honor appearances. Ibid, Complaint, dated Apr. 20, 2010.

74   Flair returned to the WWE to help Batista against Randy Orton, Cody Rhodes and Ted DiBiase.

75   ROH had promoted Flair's appearances for its HDNet program.

76   Cary Silkin explained what occurred during an episode of *Last Stop Penn Station Podcast* with Cary Silkin and Ian Riccaboni, Sep. 3, 2021. Also see *Wrestling Observer Newsletter*, Jun. 8, 2009, f4wonline.com. Flair had originally been scheduled to perform as a guest referee that evening.

77   According to court records, Flair was advanced $50,000 for five appearances and then another $35,000 for seven television appearances. He made four of the live appearances — missing one in Montreal on Jul. 24, 2009. He made one TV appearance, but missed the six others. For that reason, ROH was owed $41,420. Ring of Honor Wrestling, Inc. v. Richard Fliehr a/k/a Ric Flair, Bucks County Court of Common Pleas, Case No. 2010-00866; Silkin discussed this situation at length. *Last Stop Penn Station Podcast* with Cary Silkin and Ian Riccaboni, Sep. 3, 2021.

78   *Charlotte Observer*, Apr. 28, 2009, 2B.

79   Flair talked about the substance abuse problem being a "disease" in an interview with Alex Marvez in May 2009. A summary was featured on tpww.net, May 14, 2009.

80 Their matches included Nov. 21 in Melbourne, Nov. 24 in Perth, Nov. 26 in Brisbane, and Nov. 28 in Sydney. The latter was the most successful, drawing 11,000 to the Acer Arena.

81 McMahon reportedly gave his "blessing" to Flair to work the "Hulkamania" tour in Australia. *Wrestling Observer Newsletter*, Oct. 26, 2009, f4wonline.com. Flair was thankful to McMahon for his help through the years, and the latter had loaned Flair money on several occasions, including a 1992 loan to help pay Flair's IRS debt. *Valuetainment Podcast with Patrick Bet-David*, Apr. 5, 2018.

82 *Charlotte Observer*, Feb. 25, 2009, C1.

CHAPTER 22: BLOOD, SWEAT, AND TEARS

1 Flair watched the Kurt Angle-A.J. Styles match during the Jan. 4, 2010 broadcast. Styles would adopt Flair's fashion sense by wearing a suit in interviews and a colorful robe to the ring.

2 An article about Lethal, mentioning his impressions of Flair and Randy Savage, appeared in the *Charlotte Observer*, Aug. 1, 2010, 4K. Flair was referred to as Lethal's "boyhood hero." In an angle leading up to this feud, Flair "lost" his WWE Hall of Fame ring to Hulk Hogan following an in-ring defeat to Abyss on Apr. 26. Hogan gave the ring to Lethal, who, in turn, returned it to Flair.

3 This occurred during the Jun. 17, 2010, edition of *IMPACT*, live from Orlando, FL.

4 *TNA IMPACT*, Oct. 7, 2010.

5 Flair suffered a torn rotator cuff during a match with Doug Williams in Jan. 2011. *Charleston Post and Courier*, Sep. 18, 2011, C8. Details about Flair's outside-the-ring struggles within TNA were provided by Mike Johnson in a report on PWInsider.com, May 21, 2012.

6 Their match included several unique stipulations. If Sting was victorious, he would receive a match with Hulk Hogan at Bound for Glory on Oct. 16, 2011. If Flair won, Sting would be forced to retire. The match was taped on Sep. 12.

7 Flair had hit Sting with brass knuckles given to him by Hulk Hogan.

8 Flair said he landed on his arm wrong. "That just comes from not working enough," he explained. *Charleston Post and Courier*, Sep. 22, 2011, C2.

9 *Charleston Post and Courier*, Sep. 18, 2011, C8. Flair's injury was later determined to be a torn left triceps, and it was reported that surgery would be needed. However, he recovered without needing the procedure. Flair was quoted as saying, "[My doctor] told me it was a miracle. He said, 'Ric, you're one in a million.'" *Charleston Post and Courier*, Oct. 9, 2011, C9.

10 *Boston Herald*, Aug. 3, 2011, 51.

11 *Boston Herald*, Sep. 21, 2011, 56. Flair also threw out the first pitch and read the starting line-up. The Orioles won the game, 7–5. Flair returned to Fenway Park on Jun. 25, 2021 to take part in Dustin Pedroia's retirement ceremony, and presented him with another championship belt. Associated Press, Jun. 26, 2021. Josh Reddick, Pedroia's teammate, was also a fan of Flair's. In 2019, while playing for the Houston Astros, he appeared on the field wearing a Flair robe. Flair was on hand to meet Reddick and other fans, and he delivered the ceremonial first pitch. *Houston Chronicle*, Aug. 22, 2019, C5.

12 Flair was quoted as saying that his heart was "with the 49ers all the way to the end," and his endorsement of San Francisco upset fans of the Charlotte-based Carolina Panthers. Carolina had won the NFC South Division and played the 49ers on Jan. 12, 2014. Steve Smith, a wide receiver for Carolina who owned a Flair robe, was said to be "real disappointed" by Flair's comments. Later, Flair said, "My heart will always be with the Panthers." *Charlotte Observer*, Jan. 7, 2014, 1A, 9A. He also stated: "What can I say? I've always been a very good heel." *Charlotte Observer*, Jan. 10, 2014, 6C. Harbaugh defended Flair by saying, "What's the matter

with having two favorite teams? I think Ric Flair is a fantastic guy. He spoke very highly of Carolina." *Charlotte Observer*, Jan. 9, 2014, 2C. Panthers head coach Ron Rivera called Flair "a good man," and was surprised by the attention the story received. *Charlotte Observer*, Jan. 10, 2014, 6C. Flair reportedly received death threats as a result of this situation. *New York Daily News*, Jan. 10, 2014, 87. The 49ers beat Carolina, 23–10.

13 Teams at the professional, college, and high school levels enjoyed this ritual. Among the more well-known teams were the Carolina Panthers, Indianapolis Colts, and the Chicago Cubs. *Chicago Tribune*, Jul. 31, 2015, S2.

14 On Jan. 7, 2015, Flair surprised Brown during an interview on Sirius XM's *The Opening Drive* program and spoke about his rendition of Flair's famous promo.

15 *Sun-Sentinel*, Dec. 28, 2012, 3C.

16 Since that time, seven other wrestlers have been inducted more than once as well, including Hulk Hogan, Shawn Michaels, and Bret Hart.

17 *Pro Wrestling Torch*, Mar. 31, 2012, 15.

18 As part of the deal, Christian, a WWE contracted wrestler, made a TNA appearance at Slammiversary 10 on Jun. 10, 2012, in Arlington, TX.

19 VOC Wrestling Nation Radio, Mar. 7, 2012, cited in the *Pro Wrestling Torch*, Mar. 17, 2012, 15. TNA President Dixie Carter was also very supportive, saying: "It was the easiest decision in the world. Why would I ever consider keeping a man who is so deserving of that second award from being recognized? I would never have stopped Ric from receiving an award that is so deserved." *Busted Open Radio Show*, Apr. 2012, cited in the Pro *Wrestling Torch*, May 15, 2012, 14. Flair said that there was an issue with TNA letting him go, and he was ready to quit over it. Interview with Ric Flair by Nick Hausman, *Wrestling Inc.* Podcast, Feb. 25, 2021.

20 Twelve days later, TNA filed a lawsuit against the WWE, reportedly for interference with existing contracts and breach of contract, among other things. *TNA Entertainment, LLC. v. Brian S. Wittenstein, World Wrestling Entertainment, Inc.*, Davidson County Chancery Court, Case No. 12-0746-III, May 23, 2012. Also see *Nashville City Paper*, May 24, 2012.

21 This included the Sacrifice PPV on May 13, 2012.

22 PWInsider.com, Jun. 12, 2012.

23 Flair was reportedly hit in the head with a water bottle. PWInsider.com, Aug. 14, 2012. Also see *Charlotte Examiner*, Aug. 16, 2012. Flair discussed this event. *Wooooo! Nation* Podcast Episode #31.

24 *Monday Night Raw*, Dec. 17, 2012.

25 *Charleston Post and Courier*, Dec. 23, 2012, 8.

26 The Flair-Punk segment earned a 3.20 quarter hour, and the overall rating for *Raw* was the highest it had been in several months. *Wrestling Observer Newsletter*, Dec. 24, 2012, f4wonline.com.

27 Flair discussed her entry into the wrestling business. Interview with Ric Flair by Nick Hausman, *Wrestling Inc.* Podcast, Feb. 25, 2021. This is also discussed at length in *Second Nature: The Legacy of Ric Flair and the Rise of Charlotte* by Ric Flair & Charlotte with Brian Shields, 2017, 133–134, 136–137.

28 *Charlotte Observer*, Dec. 6, 2015, 6A.

29 Kidder did an incredibly detailed Oral History Interview with her mother, Wendy, which provides insight and facts about their family and background. "It's the Polish in you . . . it's them. It's their spirit carrying you through," by Sophia Kidder, medium.com, Nov. 25, 2018.

30 Piper joined Wendy and her four kids in GA, while Flair ventured to Oregon to spend the week with Roddy's wife, Kitty, and their two children. The program aired on Jun. 30, 2013.

31 *Charlotte Observer*, Mar. 28, 2013, B1.

32 Flair was temporarily living at the hotel in a two-bedroom suite. *Charlotte Observer*, Apr. 7, 2013, 11A. The address of the hotel was 6030 Piedmont Row Dr., and the room was 617. North

Carolina Department of Health and Human Services, Medical Examiner's Certificate of Death, filed Apr. 3, 2013.

33 Ibid.

34 Ibid.

35 North Carolina Department of Health and Human Services, Medical Examiner's Certificate of Death, Supplemental Report of Cause of Death signed by Thomas D. Owens, MD, and dated Jun. 14, 2013.

36 "Reid Fliehr Found Dead in Charlotte Hotel," by Greg Oliver, slamwrestling.net, Mar. 29, 2013.

37 *Second Nature: The Legacy of Ric Flair and the Rise of Charlotte* by Ric Flair & Charlotte with Brian Shields, 2017, 291–293. Reid's passing was discussed at length in Flair's *30 for 30* Documentary, ESPN Films, 2017. Also see Interview with Ric Flair, *Valuetainment Podcast with Patrick Bet-David*, Apr. 5, 2018, and Interview with Ric Flair by Nick Hausman, *Wrestling Inc.* Podcast, Feb. 25, 2021.

38 *Second Nature: The Legacy of Ric Flair and the Rise of Charlotte* by Ric Flair & Charlotte with Brian Shields, 2017, 6–7, Interview with Ric Flair by Nick Hausman, *Wrestling Inc.* Podcast, Feb. 25, 2021.

39 Flair was quoted as saying, "[Reid] died on my watch." *Atlanta Journal-Constitution*, Nov. 6, 2017, D2.

40 *Charlotte Observer*, Jul. 17, 2013, 6B. PWInsider.com, Oct. 28, 2013. Flair talked about the importance of Gomez's friendship. "Ric Flair Remembers Wrestlers Bruiser Brody and Joe Gomez," Pro Wrestling Stories, youtube.com, Dec. 6, 2020.

41 Flair talked about the event. Interview of Ric Flair, *Steve Austin Podcast*, 2013.

42 *Wrestling Observer Newsletter*, Sep. 23, 2013, f4wonline.com.

43 At the time, Cena was a three-time World Heavyweight champion and a 12-time WWE World champion, giving him 15 reigns in total. He had won his 12th championship on Jun. 29, 2014, at Money in the Bank in Boston. WWE acknowledged 16 World titles for Flair, but the real number was higher. Cena ultimately tied Flair's record on Jan. 29, 2017, when he beat A.J. Styles for his 16th World title at the Royal Rumble. Flair said he had no problem with Cena tying his record and complimented him during a 2017 Wrestlecon Q&A event. PWInsider.com, Mar. 30, 2017.

44 "WWE MSG John Cena w/ Ric Flair vs. Bray Wyatt w/ Triple H — July 12th, 2014," New Scott, youtube.com, Feb. 21, 2021.

45 Flair had three surgeries within 11 days. He discussed these operations. *Busted Open Radio Show*, Jun. 10, 2019.

46 *Wrestling Observer Newsletter*, Sep. 29, 2014, Oct. 20, 2014, f4wonline.com.

47 Among the other hall of famers were Ron Simmons, Roddy Piper, and Bret Hart. Flair also inducted Tatsumi Fujinami into the WWE Hall of Fame the night before.

48 The podcast ran until Apr. 2016 and had 46 episodes. A second podcast, *The Ric Flair Show*, was launched during the summer of 2016 on MLW Radio. It had 24 episodes and ended around Jan. 2017.

49 In the world of wrestling, where kayfabe has been such an ingrained part of the business, stories have often taken on a life of their own and the wrestlers themselves have become storytellers. There has also been the occasional misremembered historical fact. For instance, Flair told Steve Austin in 2013 that he was in Puerto Rico the night Bruiser Brody was killed. Interview of Ric Flair, *Steve Austin Podcast*, 2013. Flair clarified that he wasn't there in another interview. "Ric Flair Remembers Wrestlers Bruiser Brody and Joe Gomez," Pro Wrestling Stories, youtube.com, Dec. 6, 2020.

50 *Orlando Sentinel*, Jun. 12, 2015, C3.

51 Rhodes offered a strong opinion about Flair during his RF Video shoot interview. He referred to him as a "flim-flam man." He added, "I beat his ass three times." *Dusty Rhodes Shoot Interview*, RF Video, circa 2000.

52 Flair talked about Rhodes at length with David Crockett during the Dusty Rhodes Tribute Show, *Wooooo! Nation* Podcast Episode #7.

53 *Tampa Tribune*, May 8, 1987, 10EH.

54 Piper passed away on Jul. 31, 2015. *Chicago Tribune*, Aug. 2, 2015, 28.

55 *Wrestling Observer Newsletter*, Aug. 17, 2015, f4wonline.com, Flair spoke about Piper at length during the "Rowdy Roddy Piper Tribute Show, *Wooooo! Nation* Podcast Episode #14.

56 Charlotte won the title at Night of Champions in Houston, TX.

57 Flair talked about Charlotte in *Wooooo! Nation* Podcast Episode #5, 9, 12. In the latter episode, he said that she was better than he was. Also see Interview with Ric Flair by Chris Jericho, *Talk is Jericho*, Jericho Cruise, Feb. 14, 2020.

58 *Monday Night Raw*, Sep. 21, 2015.

59 During Charlotte's feud with Paige in late 2015, Reid's name was used, and the angle drew criticism.

60 *Monday Night Raw*, May 23, 2016.

61 *Monday Night Raw*, Dec. 5, 2016.

62 "WWE Unveils Amazing Ric Flair Statue in Emotional Ceremony," by Josh Barnett, usatoday.com, Mar. 30, 2017.

63 Flair talked about respect. *Busted Open Radio Show*, Jun. 10, 2019.

64 Kamikazes were his drink of choice at one point.

65 As Shreveport writer Kathryn Usher stated it, "If you work as hard as this man does, you are entitled to let off steam the way he does." *Shreveport Journal*, Nov. 14, 1985, 2C.

66 *To Be the Man* by Ric Flair with Keith Elliot Greenberg, 2004, 110, *Elizabeth Ann Fliehr v. Richard Morgan Fliehr*, Mecklenburg County General Court of Justice, District Court Division, Case No. 05-CVD-9647, Complaint dated May 24, 2005. In a 2017 article, Flair said, "I drank 20 vodkas a day, easy. I spent almost $1.2 million on drinking last year alone." *Atlanta Journal-Constitution*, Nov. 6, 2017, D1.

67 Flair stated that he drank a lot during his tenure in TNA. Interview with Ric Flair by Nick Hausman, *Wrestling Inc.* Podcast, Feb. 25, 2021.

68 *30 for 30* Documentary, ESPN Films, 2017.

69 Flair talked about moderation. *Wooooo! Nation* Podcast Episode #15.

70 Flair once said: "You can be just another wrestler and have a private life. To be a champion, you have to be dedicated." Undated article written by Paul Haskins, *Winston-Salem Sentinel*, *Ric Flair Fan Club Newsletter* #9, Oct. 1982, 13.

71 Flair routinely had the best quarter hour ratings for *Nitro* and often on *Raw* as well.

72 For an array of opinions about Flair, both positive and negative, see the clip compilation video, "Pro Wrestlers on How Ric Flair is in Real Life — Outside WWE," Title Match Wrestling, youtube.com, Jun. 30, 2020. For other opinions of Flair, see the article by Richard Steinberg, the former WCW director of marketing services, on prowrestlingstories.com, and listen to Konnan's comments. "Konnan On: The Real Reason Why Ric Flair Falls Out with Everyone," Keepin' It 100 Official, youtube.com, Jun. 29, 2022.

73 *30 for 30* Documentary, ESPN Films, 2017. Flair said, "I said 10,000 women, but that's rough math. It could've been 8,500." *Atlanta Journal-Constitution*, Nov. 6, 2017, D1.

74 Women often attempted to interact with Flair at arenas. For instance, in 1986, a "Miss Jones" sent a message back to Flair at the Miami Beach Convention Center, and he went to the arena door to talk to her. A writer noted that they had an "animated conversation." Later, after fans insulted and threw cups at Flair, the woman smiled and said, "Why do you think they call him 'Slick Ric'?" *Miami News*, Mar. 13, 1986, B1, B6.

75 Undated article written by Paul Haskins, *Winston-Salem Sentinel*, *Ric Flair Fan Club Newsletter* #9, Oct. 1982, 13.

76 Mikelonis participated in a local Miss U.S. Teen pageant in 1975. *North Hills News Record*, Jun. 18, 1975, 27. A photo of Mikelonis with Lia Maivia in New Zealand, identified as "Ric

Flair's traveling companion," was located in the files of the Arcadian Vanguard Wrestling News Archive, posted on Twitter on Oct. 15, 2020. She was mentioned during *Wooooo! Nation* Podcast Episode #25.

77   *Pittsburgh Press*, Apr. 16, 1983, B4.

78   A reporter in Newport News noted Flair's politeness and watched as Flair thanked his police escort from the ring. *Newport News Daily Press*, Jun. 26, 1988, 64.

79   *Charlotte Observer*, Nov. 3, 1978, 4C.

80   *McDowell News*, circa Feb. 1984, *Ric Flair Fan Club Newsletter* #15, 8.

81   *Greensboro Daily News*, Jul. 3, 1978, B5.

82   *Miami News*, Mar. 13, 1986, B6.

83   *Miami Herald Tropic Magazine*, Aug. 18, 1985, 20, 23.

84   *Pittsburgh Post-Gazette*, Weekend Magazine, Oct. 21, 1994, 19.

85   Madden and Flair exchanged posts on Twitter.

86   One of the most notable was Flair's non-association with his former best friend, Arn Anderson. Jim Crockett Jr. was another.

87   Kayfabe Commentaries, interview of Teddy Long, 2014.

88   Accusations of racist language were made against Ole Anderson, Dusty Rhodes, and Dick Murdoch. See *Tony Atlas Shoot Interview*, "Kamala on Dusty Rhodes Racist Rumors," The Hannibal TV, youtube.com, Jun. 19, 2020, and *Superstar Billy Graham: Tangled Ropes* by Billy Graham with Keith Elliot Greenberg, 2006, 134. There was also a racial tone to comments made during a 1990 angle between the Four Horsemen and Junkyard Dog, also involving Rocky King. *Matwatch*, Vol. 5, No. 2, Jan. 13–19, 1992, 2.

89   Flair used controversial language in feuds with Bobo Brazil and Rufus R. Jones. Audio file from around Jul. 1977, David Chappell, midatlanticgateway.com. Also see *To Be the Man* by Ric Flair with Keith Elliot Greenberg, 2004, 40, 120.

90   *The Ric Flair Show* Podcast Episode #2.

91   In 1989, Flair said, "I haven't exactly been a role model for children." *The Nashville Tennessean*, Sep. 3, 1989, F1.

92   Flair was known for showing his penis to women. He'd also walk around in one of his famous robes, but naked underneath. *Wooooo! Nation* Podcast Episodes #4, 10, 31. In her shoot interview, Baby Doll said that Flair showed up naked at her hotel door. *Baby Doll Shoot Interview*, RF Video, 2000. Missy Hyatt talked about this behavior in her autobiography. *Missy Hyatt: First Lady of Wrestling* by Missy Hyatt with Charles Salzberg and Mark Goldblatt, 2001, 107, 109. This subject was discussed in the *30 for 30* Documentary, ESPN Films, 2017.

CHAPTER 23: THE LEGACY OF THE NATURE BOY

1   Flair was reportedly admitted on Friday, Aug. 11, 2017, and the news broke two days later. "Wrestling Legend Ric Flair Fighting for His Life after Decades of Alcohol Abuse: Health Scare Tamed 'Nature Boy,'" by Elissa Rosen and Lindsay Kimble, Sep. 20, 2017, People.com. "Ric Flair Hospitalized," by Paul Jordan, pwinsider.com, Aug. 13, 2017. Some sources stated that he was admitted on Saturday, Aug. 12. It should be noted that Flair was living in Lawrenceville, GA, outside of Atlanta by this time. He said he moved there because of Wendy Barlow. *Wooooo! Nation* Podcast Episode #9. Another reason was provided in a 2017 article, which stated that Flair moved away from Charlotte because of the *Charlotte Observer*'s coverage of Reid's death. *Atlanta Journal-Constitution*, Nov. 6, 2017, D2.

2   Among those to offer their thoughts publicly were Harley Race, John Cena, Hulk Hogan, Jerry Lawler, Triple H, Gene Okerlund, Jim Ross, and Kurt Angle.

3 "Wrestling Legend Ric Flair Fighting for His Life after Decades of Alcohol Abuse: Health Scare Tamed 'Nature Boy,'" by Elissa Rosen and Lindsay Kimble, Sep. 20, 2017, People.com.

4 Flair spoke about his medical challenges with *People* magazine, ESPN's *Dan LeBatard Show*, *Busted Open Radio Show*, Mike Johnson of *PWInsider*.com, Ariel Helwani, and others. Also see *Atlanta Journal-Constitution*, Nov. 6, 2017, D2. Flair had to regain his strength and the ability to walk, and he dealt with memory loss for several months.

5 Flair also wore a shirt that read, "I ain't dead yet, motherf---ers." *Charlotte Observer*, Sep. 11, 2017, 6A.

6 PWInsider.com, Nov. 8, 2017.

7 *Shan and RJ Radio Show*, Date Unknown.

8 Ibid.

9 Tom Sorensen radio appearance, circa Nov. 2017.

10 Jim Ross was one of them. Flair spoke about Ross. Interview with Ric Flair by Nick Hausman, *Wrestling Inc.* Podcast, Feb. 25, 2021. Flair talked about Shawn Michaels as well. *Busted Open Radio Show*, Jun. 10, 2019. Flair apologized to Ross. *Grilling JR* Podcast, Aug. 29, 2018.

11 *Second Nature: The Legacy of Ric Flair and the Rise of Charlotte* by Ric Flair & Charlotte with Brian Shields, 2017, 48.

12 The video was reportedly filmed around Feb. 2018 and released on Mar. 1, 2018.

13 *Wrestling Observer Newsletter*, Dec. 4, 2017, f4wonline.com.

14 Raw 25 Years was held on Jan. 22, 2018.

15 A video promoting the Ric Flair Collection, a clothing line made by Mr. Custom Made, was featured on Flair's YouTube channel on Mar. 21, 2018.

16 Flair was gifted a percentage of the racehorse Lost in Time in 2018 by owner Scott Robinson. Ric Flair Stables, LLC was incorporated in FL on Mar. 2, 2018. The company dissolved in Sep. 2020.

17 Also in attendance were Shane Helms, Joe Gomez, Dave Finlay, and Michael Hayes. PWInsider.com, Sep. 13, 2018. Reports often claimed that Flair and Barlow were married. "It was just a ceremony. We were never married," Flair later said. "WWE Superstar Ric Flair and Wendy Barlow Split, Say They Were Never Actually Married," by Tristan Balagtas and Elissa Rosen, People.com, Jan. 31, 2022.

18 The party was held on Feb. 22, 2019, in Duluth, GA.

19 Among the others in attendance were Ricky Steamboat, Dennis Rodman, Triple H, Chris Jericho, and Shane McMahon.

20 *Monday Night Raw*, Feb. 25, 2019.

21 Flair was admitted to the Gwinnett Medical Center on May 16. A report ran on TMZ and also in the *Charlotte Observer*, stating that Flair was suffering from a "very serious" medical issue, although it was denied by family. *Charlotte Observer*, May 17, 2019, 13A. Flair discussed his health. *Busted Open Radio Show*, Jun. 10, 2019.

22 *Charlotte Observer*, May 23, 2019, 4A.

23 The serial number for that trademark is 77789943, and it was filed in 2009. Uspto.gov. Flair attempted to trademark "The Man" around that same time. *Wrestling Observer Newsletter*, Sep. 9, 2019, f4wonline.com.

24 Flair made an appearance during the Sep. 17, 2019, edition of *Smackdown* from Atlanta. Rapper Offset also appeared wearing a Ric Flair robe.

25 *Wrestling Observer Newsletter*, May 25, 2020, f4wonline.com. "Becky Lynch and Ric Flair's Legal Battle over 'The Man' Nickname, Explained," by Martin James Dickinson, Sportster.com, Apr. 10, 2022. It's notable that Flair and Lynch exchanged words on social media and in interviews in 2021 and 2022.

26 The "punt" wasn't actually shown. The lights in the arena went out. *Monday Night Raw*, Aug. 10, 2020.

27 Evans had announced her real-life pregnancy, and as part of the storyline, it was insinuated that Flair was the father. During a memorable backstage promo with Charlotte on *Raw*, Flair said, "I never said the baby was mine." Charlotte said she loved her father but told him to "Go home." *Monday Night Raw*, Feb. 22, 2021. Flair talked about the angle. Interview of Ric Flair, Ariel Helwani Podcast, May 12, 2021. As for Charlotte's success, between 2015 and 2023, she has captured a combined 13 World titles.

28 Flair appeared in commercials for Car Shield in 2021.

29 Flair called them "kids." Interview with Ric Flair by Nick Hausman, *Wrestling Inc.* Podcast, Feb. 25, 2021.

30 "Ric Flair Released," wwe.com, Aug. 3, 2021.

31 Statement by Ric Flair, on Twitter, @RicFlairNatrBoy, Aug. 3, 2021. Also see *Pro Wrestling Torch*, Aug. 4, 2021, 11. Following the "Plane Ride from Hell" episode of *Dark Side of the Ring* in Sep. 2021, Flair was removed from the opening montage of WWE programming, and his merchandise was taken off the WWE website. *Wrestling Observer Newsletter*, Sep. 27, 2021, f4wonline.com. Flair returned to the WWE television "open" in Jul. 2022.

32 "From Tampa, Ric Flair Is Training for One Last Match at 73," by Paul Guzzo, *Tampa Bay Times*, May 24, 2022.

33 It was reported that they had been living apart for six months. "WWE Superstar Ric Flair and Wendy Barlow Split, say they were never actually married," by Tristan Balagtas and Elissa Rosen, People.com, Jan. 31, 2022.

34 The program was held on Aug. 29, 2021.

35 "Ric Flair at the NWA 73rd Anniversary Show (8/29/21)," Lou Gregory, youtube.com, Aug. 30, 2021.

36 *Charlotte Observer*, Apr. 24, 1987, 4B.

37 *Charlotte Observer*, Nov. 11, 1979, 5D.

38 *Shreveport Journal*, Nov. 14, 1985, 2C.

39 Interview with Steve Chamberlain, Feb. 10, 2021.

40 *Wrestling at the Chase: The Inside Story of Sam Muchnick and the Legends of Professional Wrestling* by Larry Matysik, 2005, 181.

41 Interview with Dennis L. Guthrie, Oct. 2, 2020.

42 *Gaffney Ledger*, Apr. 4, 1986, 1.

43 *McDowell News*, circa Feb. 1984, *Ric Flair Fan Club Newsletter* #15, 8.

44 Ibid.

45 The convention was held Aug. 24–25, 1991, and was promoted by John Arezzi.

46 In addition to Portz, Flair trained Stan Lane and assisted in the training of Otis Sistrunk and Barry Windham.

47 He married Toni Yetta Goodman on Dec. 19, 1980, in Hillsborough County, FL.

48 Portz said he had three heroes in his life: his dad, Dynamite Kid, and Ric Flair. Interview with Gary Portz, Oct. 14, 2020.

49 For example, Flair pushed to bring in Arn Anderson, Jim Cornette and the Midnight Express, and the Rock and Roll Express.

50 Interview with Tommy Young, Oct. 8, 2020.

51 Some insiders call Flair "Champ."

52 *Minneapolis Star and Tribune*, Sep. 20, 1986, 8A.

53 Flair wrestled more than 5,600 matches in his career. wrestlingdata.com, Jul. 2022.

54 Flair and Lethal were training at the latter's "Lethal Academy wrestling school in Tampa.

55 "From Tampa, Ric Flair is training for one last match at 73," by Paul Guzzo, *Tampa Bay Times*, May 24, 2022.

56 Andrade married Charlotte Flair on May 27, 2022.

57 Flair's retirement show drew the second largest independent gate in North American wrestling history. *Wrestling Observer Newsletter*, Aug. 8, 2022, f4wonline.com.

58   *Second Nature: The Legacy of Ric Flair and the Rise of Charlotte* by Ric Flair & Charlotte with Brian Shields, 2017, 4.

59   Flair's promos were all improvised. He once said: "I don't rehearse anything. I don't write anything down. I just go out on television and rant." *Greensboro Daily News*, Nov. 2, 1976, B4.

60   Interview of Kevin Duffus, Oct. 2, 2020.

61   *Wrestling Then & Now*, Feb. 1992, 5. Rogers passed away in June 1992.

62   *25 Years after Starrcade with Ric Flair and Harley Race*, Highspots Home Video, 2009, *Brisco: The Life and Times of National Collegiate and World Heavyweight Wrestling Champion Jack Brisco* by Jack Brisco, as told to William Murdock, 2003, 260–262. Notably, Brisco explained that he normally didn't lend money to fellow wrestlers, but he trusted Flair enough to loan him $1,000, and Flair promptly paid him back in full. Brisco also called Flair "a great guy" and wrote that he was "over like no one [he] had ever seen."

63   *Terry Funk: More than Just Hardcore* by Terry Funk with Scott E. Williams, 2006, 148.

64   Interview of Ric Flair, *Steve Austin Podcast*, 2013.

65   *Torch Talk Collection*, Volume One, 64.

66   This doesn't count the NWA title situations involving Jack Veneno, the Midnight Rider, or Harley Race, the latter being the occurrence in New Zealand in 1984. Flair was world champion for over 3,400 days.

67   Flair was later removed from the vote. "A Flair for the Absurd," by Dave McKenna, washingtoncitypaper.com, Apr. 2, 1999.

68   *New Zealand Wrestling Special*, Issue #1, Sep. 1984.

69   *25 Years after Starrcade with Ric Flair and Harley Race*, Highspots Home Video, 2009.

70   The NWA belt meant a lot to him, and he enjoyed the role of champion. *New Zealand Wrestling Special*, Issue #1, Sep. 1984, *Wooooo! Nation* Podcast Episode #5. Flair was asked how he survived so long with the NWA belt, and he answered, "I survived because I loved the business." Interview of Ric Flair, *Steve Austin Podcast*, 2013.

71   *Down Home with the Carolina Camera* with C.J. Underwood, WBTV-3, 1981.

72   Undated article written by Paul Haskins, *Winston-Salem Sentinel*, *Ric Flair Fan Club Newsletter* #9, Oct. 1982, 13.

73   Interview with Ric Flair by Jeff Glor, *CBS Evening News*, Feb. 21, 2009.

74   *Atlanta Journal-Constitution*, Jul. 5, 1998, B1.

ACKNOWLEDGMENTS

T
o one degree or another, I've been invested in researching professional wrestling for the past 30 years, and it will be a commitment that will continue well into the future. I've always strived to be comprehensive and meticulous in my work, and instead of capitalizing on the extreme sensationalistic stories that have thrived within the industry, I've taken a purely historical approach. I want the facts to speak for themselves. My intention has never been to present a bias or favoritism, but to allow the truth to rise to the surface, utilizing a range of contemporaneous, primary sources. With a book such as this, I understood the overall importance of being thorough and going the extra mile to present the facts for readers in effort to reveal the complete story.

Going into this project, I recognized that there were going to be challenges. After all, Ric Flair has been one of the most talked about figures in pro wrestling history. He has appeared in innumerable interviews, has written two autobiographies, and has been the central figure of several mainstream documentaries. In shoot interviews, nearly every wrestler between the 1970s and present day have been asked about Flair, and each have provided not only their opinion, but endless road stories. With all of this information already available, what else could possibly be said about the "Nature Boy?" From my point of view, there was a lot. In fact, I was not interested in allowing the narrative and general themes of other projects to influence this biographical effort. I was more focused on providing a sincere chronological study of Flair's life and career without any of the skewed or judgmental perspectives that have spawned in recent years, triggered more by developments in his personal life than his Hall of Fame accomplishments.

There is a fundamental right for fans to have an opinion of Ric Flair. These views could be wholly positive stemming from his glory days as the traveling world champion or direct criticism about his last match in Nashville. There are other critics who are heavily influenced by the controversy surrounding the infamous "Plane Ride from Hell." Regardless of the viewpoint, I knew that Flair remained a hugely polarizing figure, and I wanted to tell his story with the right amount of respect and honor that he was due. *The Last Real World Champion* is my effort to do just that, offering a straightforward and essential historical volume to wrestling literature.

No book of this magnitude can be written in a vacuum. I was fortunate enough to interact and correspond with many knowledgeable insiders, journalists, and historians to garner a wider background and understanding of not only Flair's tenure in the business, but of the territorial era. It should be noted that I began researching this project shortly after finishing my biography on the original "Nature Boy," Buddy Rogers, which culminated in a book entitled *Master of the Ring*. Unfortunately, I launched my research efforts during the summer of 2020, right in the midst of the COVID-19 pandemic. Due to the high stress environment, and the restrictions at libraries and archives across the nation, I met a lot of resistance. For months and months, certain documentation was unattainable, and people who might have normally been open to conversing about a well-known wrestling figure were suddenly unavailable.

Nevertheless, these roadblocks didn't stall progress for long, and I later made up for it by communicating with some of the best and brightest researchers and historians associated with the industry. I lucked out early on by getting in touch with the multitalented Ohio State sportswriter Steve Helwagen, who during the 1990s created a valuable Flair resource, *Wooo! The Ric Flair Record Book*. Steve was also the editor for the *Eastern Wrestling News* newsletter in the 1980s, and both publications were incredibly important to my work. Blair Schmidt-Fellner, Steve Chamberlain, Dennis L. Guthrie, Tommy Young, Gary Portz, Jim Herd, Kevin P. Duffus, Jack Dean, Peter Radford, Terry Brown, Jeff Carr, Lou Charlip, Don Ewers, Doug Kingsriter, Kate Mast, Michael O'Mara, and Robert Hodierne were all helpful and gracious in their responses to my inquiries. I can't thank them enough for their time and assistance.

Kara Crawford — the daughter of Donna Kay Crawford, president of the Ric Flair Fan Club during the 1980s — was also very supportive of this project and provided some great photos of Flair from her mother's collection.

Don Luce was the greatest wrestling historian of our time and his passing, on April 24, 2023, was a major loss for the wrestling world. His constant efforts to document and record the history of the business was inspiring. Don was always ready to help whenever needed.

While doing the complicated research for this project, I was able to correspond with many knowledgeable individuals, and assistance came from a host of different directions. I'd like to acknowledge the direct aid and support I received, and the overall work of the following people: Steve Yohe, Steve Ogilvie, George Schire, Koji Miyamoto, Haruo Yamaguchi, Matt Farmer, Mike Johnson, Jim Cornette, Rich Schwantz, Daniel Chernau, Dave Davis, Mark Eastridge, Van Nowlin, Lance Peterson, Gary Juster, Alex Marvez, Greg Price, Mike Korcek, Dave Clay, Charles Warburton, Bob Bryla, John Pantozzi, Scott Dickinson, Andrew Calvert, George Napolitano, Pete Lederberg, Eric Krol, Lance LeVine, Richard O'Sullivan, Bruce Mitchell, Dave Meltzer, Jim Nasella, George Klima, Tommy Fooshee, Tom Burke, Joe Carolei, Jon Langmead, Peggy Lathan, Coveh Solaimani, Bertrand Hebert, Roy Lucier, Jeff Bowdren, Paul J. MacArthur, Mike Rodgers, Greg Oliver, Steve Johnson, Scott Teal, Mark Hewitt, Dr. Mike Lano, Jason Campbell, Bob Barnett, John Arezzi, Georgian Lussier, Sue Forshee Cooper, Larry Quinn, Ray Klosowski, Dirk Lindenbeck, Steve Bartell, Jon Boucher, Bobbie Scott,

Kathryn Usher, and Paul D. Buckley. The research of the late J Michael Kenyon and Jim Zordani was also invaluable.

In addition to his longtime support and friendship, Brian Last of the Arcadian Vanguard Podcast Network has been a primary source for information on all things professional wrestling. His various podcasts and other resources, including *The Wrestling News* and the Kayfabe Memories website, are vital for all wrestling fans.

A big thank you goes out to Dick Bourne and David Chappell of the Mid-Atlantic Gateway website (midatlanticgateway.com) for their incredible work through the years. Their website is a treasure trove of nostalgia and rare information, and I laud both men for their insightful research and for the attention to detail they bring to the history of wrestling. For decades, Mike Mooneyham has entertained and enlightened wrestling fans through his historical columns in the *Charleston Post & Courier*. Few people can equal his body of work, and even less can match his knowledge of professional wrestling. The impressive library of podcasts under the watchful eye of Conrad Thompson is essential listening for anyone interested in the history of wrestling. The History of WWE website (thehistoryofwwe.com), run by Richard Land, is another fundamental resource for quick facts and results.

In terms of assistance from various libraries and institutions, I must first acknowledge the incredible work of Amy Miller of the Broward County Library System. For over 20 years, she has helped me obtain rare publications on microfilm from around the world. My appreciation goes out to Amy and the entire Interlibrary Loan team at the Broward County Main Library in Fort Lauderdale, Florida, for their help and support. I received additional assistance from libraries throughout the world, from Japan and New Zealand to Kansas and North Carolina. Some important research was received from the Heritage Library Division in Trinidad and Tobago. The University of Minnesota also provided key dates and clarification.

Joy Curtiss, a professional genealogist from Family Tree Traditions, was a huge help during the research for this project, and I want to acknowledge and express my gratitude for her tireless efforts.

I'd like to thank and give a major shout out to my patrons, who have joined me on Patreon (patreon.com/timhornbaker). We are building an incredible primary source archive of wrestling history, and I look forward to what the future holds.

Outside of my family, there is no one who understands my research and writing style, and the quirkiness that comes along with it, than my editor at ECW Press, Michael Holmes. Michael has been with me on my writing journey for nearly 20 years, and we've created three books that I'm really proud of. This is our fourth project together, and I think it properly demonstrates the evolution of my career as a wrestling historian and writer. I thank Michael for giving me the freedom and support to do what I love doing.

The late, great Bobby Davis was an inspiration through and through, and his words were a constant source of encouragement and strength. I miss him. Jodi and I send our best wishes to Sylvia.

Through thick and thin, my wife, Jodi, has been the best partner anyone could've asked for. Her positive attitude, encouragement and extraordinary strength have carried our family when times got tough, and when I needed a boost, she was right there to provide it. Without her, due to a sudden health problem I endured, I probably wouldn't have survived 2022. I also want to thank and share my love with Timothy and Barbara Hornbaker, Melissa Hornbaker, Virginia Hall, Sheila Babaganov, Frances Miller, Debbie and Paul Kelley, and John and Christine Hopkins.

Jodi and I send our love to L.W. Hornbaker for being our entire world.

This book is also available as a Global Certified Accessible™ (GCA) ebook. ECW Press's ebooks are screen reader friendly and are built to meet the needs of those who are unable to read standard print due to blindness, low vision, dyslexia, or a physical disability.

At ECW Press, we want you to enjoy our books in whatever format you like. If you've bought a print copy just send an email to ebook@ecwpress.com and include:

- the book title
- the name of the store where you purchased it
- a screenshot or picture of your order/receipt number and your name
- your preference of file type: PDF (for desktop reading), ePub (for a phone/tablet, Kobo, or Nook), mobi (for Kindle)

A real person will respond to your email with your ebook attached. Please note this offer is only for copies bought for personal use and does not apply to school or library copies.

Thank you for supporting an independently owned Canadian publisher with your purchase!